THE BRITISH
COUNTRY HOUSE IN THE
EIGHTEENTH CENTURY

MANCHESTER
UNIVERSITY PRESS

general editor:
CHRISTOPHER BREWARD

THE BRITISH COUNTRY HOUSE
IN THE EIGHTEENTH CENTURY

CHRISTOPHER CHRISTIE

MANCHESTER UNIVERSITY PRESS
Manchester and New York

distributed exclusively in the USA by St Martin's Press

Published by Manchester University Press
Oxford Road, Manchester M13 9NR, UK
and Room 400, 175 Fifth Avenue, New York, NY 10010, USA
http://www.man.ac.uk/mup

Distributed exclusively in the USA by
St Martin's Press, Inc., 175 Fifth Avenue, New York,
NY 10010, USA

Distributed exclusively in Canada by
UBC Press, University of British Columbia, 6344 Memorial Road,
Vancouver, BC, Canada V6T 1Z2

British Library Cataloguing-in-Publication Data
A catalogue record for this book is available from the British Library

Library of Congress Cataloging-in-Publication Data applied for

ISBN   0 7190 4724 2   *hardback*
        0 7190 4725 0   *paperback*

First published 2000

06   05   04   03   02   01   00   10   9   8   7   6   5   4   3   2   1

Designed in Caslon with Chisel display
by Max Nettleton FCSD
Typeset by
Graphicraft Limited, Hong Kong
Printed in Great Britain
by Bell & Bain Ltd, Glasgow

Contents

List of illustrations

PLATES

Acknowledgements

First of all I should like to thank Professor Diana Donald for her great help, encouragement and friendship during the time that I have spent with this book. The staff of various institutions have also been extremely helpful, especially at the Central Reference Library in Manchester.

I also wish to thank Camilla Costello and Olive Waller of *Country Life* Picture Library, and Edward Gibbons of the National Trust. Jane Bedford has undertaken the huge task of typing this work, and I am very grateful to her for all her patience with my handwriting, and to Pauline Crosby for typing preliminary work. I am also very much in debt to Peter Ferriday, a great friend of many years standing, for his advice and encouragement.

Patricia Gardner who has acted as my research assistant and written a chapter of this book deserves my very special thanks for all her trouble, particularly over illustrations and correspondence with galleries and private owners of works of art. I also wish to record my thanks to Stephen Yates who has helped with photography.

I should also like to thank Hilary Howard for her help and efforts on my behalf. Finally I must record my gratitude to Marjorie Christie for her great patience and good humour.

Introduction

The British country house in the eighteenth century was of major importance architecturally, artistically, socially and economically. The purpose of
this book is to discuss these matters in the period *c*. 1700 to 1830 in a way
which will introduce the subject to undergraduate and postgraduate students
as well as to the general reader. There is here an overview of the different
kinds of scholarship which have been concerned with the country house, and
of some of the wider cultural issues of Georgian history which affected them.

Country houses have become popular subjects for scholars and indeed
places of pilgrimage, and in the last two decades especially,[1] concepts of heritage
and the conservation of the countryside are matters of national and even international debate. Country houses have come to be regarded as a very significant feature of British heritage. In 1974 the exhibition 'The Destruction of
the Country House' at the Victoria and Albert Museum in London was
already warning of how this heritage was crumbling, if not disappearing
completely in places.[2] More recently Peter Mandler has traced the beginnings
of our awareness of 'heritage' in this country as far back as the taste for
older country houses and the popularisation of the Middle Ages in the novels
of Sir Walter Scott such as *Ivanhoe* (1819) and *Kenilworth* (1821), both of
which reached a wide public.[3]

In addition to our awareness that country houses are either disappearing or changing beyond recognition, we are beginning to notice the diminish-
ing amount of countryside which was once part of their estates. The need to
develop 'brown-field sites' as opposed to 'green-field sites' – which may well
include parkland and meadows – sacrificed to motorways and airport run-
ways, is an important issue for consideration today. Our concern is at least
in part due to the beauty of the surviving parks and landscaping, and also
the British taste for the Picturesque which we 'inherit from our ancestors'
taste for travel.

This book examines the country houses in Great Britain at a time –
the Georgian period – when a sense of British identity began to emerge.

'Great Britain' came into being with the Act of Union in 1707 which linked England and Wales – themselves united in 1536 – to Scotland.[4] In 1800 the Act of Union with Ireland was passed,[5] and during the Hanoverian period dynastic links, the common cultural experiences, such as the Grand Tour, even perhaps the advantages of a place at Westminster, connected the country house owners of Great Britain. The spoils of a new empire also contributed a magnificence and elegance to their properties.

Some proprietors owned country houses in more than one of the different kingdoms of the United Kingdom. The Earls of Bute, also Barons of Cardiff, owned Mount Stuart in Scotland, Luton House in England and Cardiff Castle in Wales. The second Duke of Argyll was Duke of Greenwich and owned Inveraray Castle in Scotland and Sudbrook House, by James Gibbs, in Surrey. Owners patronised the same architects, artists and furniture makers: Scots portrait painter Allan Ramsay painted Welsh landowner Lord Mansel of Margan. Sir Joshua Reynolds painted Lord Dalkeith, son of the third Duke of Buccleuch, who himself inherited two vast Baroque houses, Drumlanrig Castle in Dumfriesshire and Boughton House in Northamptonshire. Scots architect Robert Adam found patronage in England, Scotland, Wales and Ireland. Yorkshire furniture maker Thomas Chippendale was favoured particularly, with the custom of English landowners such as Lord Harewood, and Scots such as Lord Dumfries and the Homes of Paxton in Berwickshire.

However, the countryside was not only regarded as an important retreat for leisure, it was believed to be the place from which the nation's leaders must spring and the untainted paradise which must sustain them. The country house might also provide a 'court' which could shelter artists, writers, musicians, and even actors. Music, drama and reading were important aspects of life there.

If the countryside was considered a place of purity, sublimity even, for eighteenth-century writers, the city was thought to be the source of luxury and profligate consumption. It was here that much, although by no means all, the furniture of country houses was bought. The country house was made fashionable by regular visits to London and other cities by the nobility and gentry, and the 'middling sort' was also tempted to be extravagant. The innovations in furniture design, the changing use of rooms and the development of different social habits play a part in the evolution of what has become a significant and highly valued part of British history.

NOTES

1 Our knowledge of the way of life in country houses and the intricacy of their fabric has been explored in the most scholarly fashion by Mark Girouard, especially in *Life in the English Country House*, Yale University Press, London, 1978. John Cornforth has also written numerous articles in *Country Life* magazine and works including *The Inspiration*

of the Past: Country House Taste in the Twentieth Century, Viking, Harmondsworth, 1985, and *The Search for a Style*, André Deutsch, London, 1988.

2 Roy Strong, Marcus Binney and John Harris, *The Destruction of the Country House 1875–1975*, Thames and Hudson, London, 1974. See also John Harris, *No Voice From The Hall*, John Murray, London, 1998. The author discusses visits made to 200 country houses between 1946 and 1961 and describes houses and their estates in their death throes.

3 Peter Mandler, *The Fall and Rise of the Stately Home*, Yale University Press, London, 1997, p. 4. Mandler considers the early nineteenth-century houses which were regarded as foreign and distant from the populace at large at a time when older houses suggested a golden era of national unity.

4 Linda Colley, *Britons: Forging the Nation 1707–1837*, Vintage, London, 1994, p. 11.

5 *Ibid.*, p. 154.

The country house and money

The building of country houses in the eighteenth and early nineteenth centuries in Great Britain was of national significance. They were a major expression of artistic, political and economic endeavour. About 150 houses were built in England alone in the first half of the eighteenth century, a country with a population of perhaps 5,250,000 in 1700. The population of Scotland might have been about one million at this time, Ireland's two million, and that of Wales, 350,000. In lands which were essentially rural, with fields and animals visible from the centre of most towns, the country house and its estate must, at the beginning of this period especially, have seemed extensive and powerful. With a large family and perhaps forty servants, a country house might well have seemed an enormous and complex organisation to a population, four-fifths of which lived in villages and hamlets of 700 inhabitants.[1]

The builders of eighteenth-century country houses were clearly very rich. A rich aristocrat might have an income of £40,000 a year. The Duke of Bedford had £30,000 in 1700,[2] whereas a male labourer earned perhaps ten to twenty pounds a year, and professional men such as lawyers and surgeons had £500 per annum. The aristocracy in Georgian Britain formed a small highly successful group, defined by membership of the House of Lords and confined during the eighteenth century to 1,003 persons. Within the ranks of country house builders and owners there were, of course, wide variations between the great aristocrats, the *nouveau riches*, and the gentry. William Beckford was able to spend £400,000 on Fonthill in Wiltshire[3] whereas Sir Mark Pleydell Bart., maintained his inherited house Coleshill in Berkshire on £2,700 in the late 1730s.[4] Where did the money come from?

The principal support of a country house was the way in which its land and estates were exploited. The Physiocratic idea of land and agricultural produce being the sources of real wealth was challenged by Adam Smith in *The Wealth of Nations* (1776).[5] Nevertheless he recognised the part played in Britain's economy by aristocratic consumption.[6] In the main, aristocrats

1] Thirlestane Castle, Berwickshire. The entrance front, 1590s, 1670, with additions in the 1840s

were great spenders who constantly needed wealth to build, to collect, to commission portraits and furniture, but also to display a magnificent local presence on their estates for social and political reasons. The Duke of Newcastle's steward invited Thomas Turner to join the celebrations at his estate at Halland in Sussex to mark the taking of Cape Breton. There was a bonfire of 600 faggots, two barrels of beer given to the populace, 'a very good supper' for the principal tradesmen of the neighbourhood and a dinner for the gentlemen of Lewes and parishes in the vicinity.[7] The estate was at the centre of national, rural entertainment of the rich, some, men who could afford to, travelled from one seat to another to enjoy it.[8]

The ownership of land was really the preserve of a privileged minority. The law of entailment limited the number of estates on the market and agrarian improvements produced substantial income from land by the 1770s, which discouraged further the sale of agricultural land.[9] In Scotland many of the great estates were in the eastern fertile coastal plane. This area contained the splendid houses of the Earl of Haddington at Mellerstain, the Earl of Lauderdale at Thirlestane Castle [1], the Marquess of Tweeddale at Yester, and particularly the Duke of Buccleuch who was the greatest landowner in the Lowlands at Dalkeith Palace,[10] perhaps the grandest of all classical houses in Scotland designed by James Smith in 1702–11.[11] The lesser Scots landowners occupied the western hilly areas of the country. However, only 400 landowners had an annual rent of £2,000, and another 1,000 owned land worth £500 a year.[12] In Ireland most Catholics were excluded from landowning and whilst 75 per cent of the population was Catholic it only owned 14 per cent of the land.[13]

5

The enclosure of land certainly helped landowners to enrich themselves. Enclosure involved exchanging traditional strips of land and dividing up the commons, and the aim was to provide each landowner larger areas of property. Rotation of crops and communal growing were abolished. During the eighteenth century a parliamentary act established the individual enclosure. In each case the major landowners of a particular area or village would petition parliament for a bill to enclose the village. Frequently smaller landowners opposed such bills but usually only 75 per cent to 80 per cent of the landowners had to be in favour for the bill to go forward. Eventually commissions valued every holding and redistributed the land so that each owner was given a parcel of land in proportion to the acres held previously in the open fields. In the eighteenth century the great landowners bought out the small freeholders. Copyholds for lives and beneficial leases were no longer renewed by manorial lords and the aristocracy and gentry were able to acquire acres that had formerly belonged to yeomen and the great estates were consolidated.[14]

Less controversial, perhaps, was engrossing, which at the most straightforward level involved agricultural tenancies being reorganised to produce bigger farms. An industrial landowner could organise this process within his own estate and enclosure was not essential.[15] Both Arthur Young and the French Physiocrat Quesnay believed that the creation of large farms was necessary before agricultural improvement and modernisation could begin.[16] Improvement could take many forms. The Earls of Scarborough owned Lumley Castle in County Durham [2], Sandbeck House in Yorkshire and Glentworth Hall in Lincolnshire. The third Earl's income in 1747 was £16,950.[17] He was able to employ James Paine at both Glentworth and Sandbeck and at the latter built new offices, kitchens, new farm buildings, stables, new greenhouses and a magnificent new east front was added to the house.[18] Thomas Coke, Earl of Leicester, succeeded to his estates in 1707 (and when he came of age in 1718, they lay in Norfolk, Suffolk, Kent, Buckinghamshire, Oxfordshire, Staffordshire, Somerset, Dorset and London). The estates were gradually improved by more intensive farming, new crops were introduced and capital expended upon his lands. By 1749 he had an income of about £15,000 per annum.[19] Holkham Hall, William Kent's grand design in Norfolk for Leicester cost a total of £92,000 between 1732 and 1765.[20]

Thomas Coke, the great-nephew of the first Lord Leicester who succeeded to the estates in 1776 was, of course, a great agricultural pioneer. Although he did not introduce many of the innovations attributed to him, he encouraged enterprise in his tenantry and especially the intensification of arable cultivation in Norfolk.[21] His income by 1806 was about £29,500 per annum,[22] which despite debts allowed him to maintain Holkham, and at the sheep shearings there he provided convivial dinners for two hundred combined with a display of agricultural equipment and new techniques.[23]

The third Earl Spencer, the most typical Whig landed magnate of his age, was a man not unlike Coke of Norfolk.[24] The heartland of his estates lay in Warwickshire and Northamptonshire with his large Elizabethan country house, Althrop, remodelled by Henry Holland at a cost of more than £16,500 by about 1790.[25] In this decade gross rental was about £3,500 a year, but estate expenses amounted to £15,000 per annum which led the Spencers into debt.[26] The second earl had been an extravagant builder, and the third was a prominent figure in politics, as well as in agriculture, heading the Smithfield Club and the Royal Agricultural Society.[27] By 1832 debts had risen to £60,000 although much was invested in progressive agriculture.[28]

Landlords were eager to make money, especially as the wars with France (1793–1802 and 1813–15) caused immense inflation. They were inclined to press their tenants to be less conservative in their methods, and then hope to raise their rents. Letting by the year grew far more frequent. This was true in Wales, especially of the progressive Faenol estate where almost all the tenants held their land by annual lease by 1800.[29] In Scotland exploitation was attempted earlier. In Dumfries and Galloway the black cattle trade had expanded with England in 1720 which led to the creation of huge stone enclosures with drystone dykes. There was considerable resistance to this particular form of enclosure and the Galloway Levellers, in 1724, went out at night in bands and used sharp poles to push over the stone walls.[30] A further resistance to the extension of property rights of landowners in Scotland was the despoiling of plantations of trees, hacked down to provide for the small cottage hearth.[31] If Scottish black cattle supplied London's

2] Lumley Castle, Co. Durham. Drawn and engraved by Edward Blore, 1823

demand for meat, the Dublin Society, founded in 1733, attempted, less successfully perhaps, to stimulate agrarian reform. Irish export cattle were much smaller than English breeds and in general agriculture was, as Adam Young was to note even in the 1770s, backward.[32]

Landowners were considerable investors in mining, stimulated by the demands of a growing industrial need and of an increased population.[33] Lord Scarborough exploited the Lumley Colliery on his Durham estates in the 1770s. Lumley Castle was a country house in the centre of industrialisation. A turnpike road was made from the castle to a nearby farm, itself close to the colliery, and from there to the village, and the agent dealing with the colliery occupied rooms in the castle.[34] Under the terms of their lease, Lord Scarborough's tenants had to provide horses to move coal to the river, and it is clear that agrarian and industrial activities coexisted. Eventually the colliery was leased to the Lambton family in the 1780s.[35] They became Earls of Durham and embellished and extended Lambton Castle.[36]

In Wales the 1780s were important years for the slate industry. The Earl of Uxbridge had been a major exploiter of minerals under his land, receiving £2,000 per annum in royalties for ore under his estates.[37] The Pennant family for whom Thomas Hopper built massive Norman Penrhyn Castle in Caernarvonshire [3], used a fortune acquired through their Jamaican slave plantation to consolidate the quarries dispersed over their estate. In 1790 Richard Pennant built a road to connect his quarries to the coast and

3] Penrhyn Castle, Caernarvonshire. Architect Thomas Hopper, *c.* 1827–47

there, near Bangor, he established Port Penrhyn to serve the slate industry. The local landowners, rather than industrialists from elsewhere, followed his example.[38]

The Leveson-Gower family who built Trentham Hall in Staffordshire and eventually acquired through marriage Dunrobin Castle in Sutherland, were also industrial entrepreneurs. The second Earl Gower was created Marquess of Stafford in 1786 and the Dukedom of Sutherland followed in 1833, but it was the first Earl Gower who exploited the mineral resources of his Shropshire estates, and invested £4,000 in the Trent and Mersey Canal. Trentham Hall, rather like Lumley Castle, became an 'industrial head-quarters'.[39] Lord Gower was able through membership of the House of Lords, and his parliamentary influence, to get through the passage of the Trent and Mersey Canal Act.[40]

Landed gentlemen frequently complained about the way in which they were taxed by the government to finance the national debt – a debt held by the new city men and merchants. In 1733 a critic wrote scornfully of 'A set of brocaded tradesmen cloaked in purple and fine linen . . . raising to themselves immense wealth, so as to marry their daughters to the first rank, and leave their sons such estates as to enable them to live on in the same degree'.[41]

However, landed society was shot through with money from trade and commerce, and many old and new county and aristocratic families who occupied magnificent houses acquired wealth from non-agrarian sources throughout the eighteenth century. Great trading companies such as the East India Company, the South Seas Company and the Royal Africa Company as well as participation in banking supported gentry and aristocracy. Both noblemen and 'new gentlemen' served as members of the Court of the Directors of the South Sea Company before the bubble burst. John, second Duke of Argyll and his brother the Earl of Islay were directors and had links with banking through their friendship with John Law. Christopher Desbouverie was a director from 1711 to 1715; his elder brother inherited a baronetcy, but he became a Turkey merchant, a director of the Levant Company and the ancestor of the Pleydell-Bouveries, Viscounts Folkestone of Longford Castle. Edward Harley was a wool dealer, prominent in the Levant Company and the brother of Robert Harley, Earl of Oxford, who was the founder of the South Sea Company and Queen Anne's Chief Minister.[42] Lord Oxford's son established the magnificent collections at Wimpole Hall, Cambridgeshire. Robert Benson, also a member of the dir-ectors of the court, succeeded Harley as Chancellor of the Exchequer in 1711, and was raised to the peerage as Lord Bingley and built Palladian Bramham Park in Yorkshire.[43]

Sometimes former gentry reacquired land and house. The most infam-ous was the Cashier of the South Sea Company, Robert Knight, of Barrells, Henley-in-Arden, Warwickshire.[44] He built Luxborough House near Chigwell in Essex, absconded to France, when others were ruined, and then returned in 1742. His son was created an Irish peer as Lord Luxborough and Earl of Catherlough and married Lord Bolingroke's daughter who became a patron of Shenstone.[45]

Although men like Lord Catherlough were referred to as '... Riff Raff with Titles ...'[46] they were by no means held in contempt by all. A Huguenot knight, Theodore Janssen, a South Seas director, acquired Wimbledon, a splendid house eventually bought by the Duchess of Marlborough, who herself made £100,000 out of the South Sea Company.[47] He wrote *A Discourse of Trade* and *General Maxims of Trade*, assembled a large library and was made a baronet in 1715 'at Special request of Prince of Wales'. Such men were active in several spheres. South Seas director Harcourt Master was a money lender and Receiver General of Land Tax for London and Middlesex; he married the Earl of Leicester's sister and before the South Sea bubble burst his assets were thought to be £70,760. Another director, Thomas Reynolds, a Lancashire landowner, acquired the sinecure of Provost Marshall of Barbados.[48]

Service in the East India Company was another way of making a huge fortune. Both Robert Clive and Warren Hastings, although not the richest nabobs, acquired spectacular houses. The Annual Register claimed that Clive's fortune was £1,200,000, his jagir was worth £27,000 a year,[49] and he possessed a lucrative salt monopoly. Claremont, his house in Surrey, cost about £30,000, but he had other properties including Lord Montfort's estate on the Herefordshire/Worcestershire borders which he bought for £70,000 where there was no house on the 7,500 acres.[50]

Warren Hastings, who was Governor of Bengal, bought back family land and embellished Daylesford in Gloucestershire at a cost of £54,000. Hastings came back from India with a fortune of £80,000, and had an annuity of £4,000 for a period of twenty-eight and a half years.[51] However, other officials in India were sometimes richer and often more highly honoured. Clive had only received an Irish baronetcy, Hastings no honours, Cornwallis, who succeeded Hastings as Governor of Bengal, was made a Marquess and was remunerated more generously.[52] Some officials were honoured at home as well as being enriched by native princes. Lord Macartney, Governor of Madras from 1781–85 was offered the Governorship of India, made an earl and also seems to have declined the 'usual' offer of £30,000 made by the Nawab of Arcot.[53]

The rich nabob was drawn to the public's attention by such satires as Samuel Foote's *The Nabob*.[54] Immense fortunes were certainly made: Henry Davenport lived in splendour at Davenport House, Shropshire, in the 1720s.[55] Sir Thomas Rumbold returned from India in 1770 aged thirty-four with a fortune of £87,000, was made a baronet for capturing Pondicherry, and commissioned Thomas Leverton to design a saloon at Woodhall Park, Hertfordshire [4] in an Adam-Wyatt style.[56] Rumbold had been Clive's ADC,

4] Watton Wood Hall (now Woodhall House), Hertfordshire, architect Thomas Leverton, 1772–82

and Paul Benfield, another nabob who had obtained his fortune in Madras, eventually bought the house from Rumbold's widow in 1794 for £125,000. He added three large rooms, but despite his great wealth became bankrupt in 1801 and Woodhall was sold for £180,000 to Samuel Abel Smith, a banker. It was clearly a house for men of great, if on occasion, brief fortune.[57] In the third quarter of the eighteenth century Scottish landowners who had been useful at Westminster as MPs often succeeded in finding places for sons in government service in the colonies.[58] John Johnstone returned to Scotland from India in 1760 worth £300,000, established a parliamentary interest and bought three estates.[59] He was able to employ Robert Adam at Alva House, Clackmannanshire, and to have his portrait painted by Henry Raeburn [5].[60]

Fortunes were certainly to be made in the West Indies through sugar and slavery. Until the end of the eighteenth century, most English people accepted slavery as part of overseas trade and as supplying essential labour.[61] The sugar business represented about £50,000,000 of capital invested in estates, and more than half these investments were held by absentees from the West Indies who were resident in England. The absentee owners had great wealth and social prestige in England which allowed them to mould colonial legislation. They were members of the Commons or they lobbied it successfully.[62]

The Lascelles family were able to employ John Carr of York, Robert Adam and Thomas Chippendale to create Harewood House near Leeds,[63] in part, through having connections with Barbados, one member of the family marrying a Barbadian heiress and another being the Collector of Customs on the island. The Beckford family was not untypical as West Indian planters in regarding England as their homeland,[64] and from their fortunes arose Palladian Fonthill Splendens to be followed fairly swiftly by Gothic Fonthill Abbey. When such families came home to England they brought with them

5] Sir Henry Raeburn, *John Johnstone of Alva, Betty Johnstone and Miss Wedderburn, c. 1795*

as servants black slaves, and as many as ten thousand lived here in the eighteenth century.[65]

Some landowners were forced to leave England for the West Indies. William Coker, born on the island of Nevis, lived for many years on his estate Woodcotes in east Devon.[66] He was a small landowner and a JP. His debts, however, forced him to mortgage his estate to John Pinney, a more substantial proprietor in Nevis, who also owned an estate at Somerton Endleigh in Somerset for £3,300.[67] Finally Coker offered to go out to Nevis and take charge of the Pinney estate as manager.

As well as commerce, banking could also produce a fortune to sustain a country house and estate, and eventually to produce a gentry or aristocratic family. The most important bankers who built a major house were the Hoares whose Palladian Stourhead in Wiltshire was embellished by a magnificent landscape garden with grotto and Pantheon [6]. The Smith family bankers of Nottingham were first found in London as the firm of Smith, Payne and Co. in 1759.[68] They owned two country houses, Wycombe Abbey in Buckinghamshire and Gydyr Castle in North Wales. The barony of Carrington was given to Robert Smith (1752–1838) and his son, who was a Buckinghamshire MP and Lord Lieutenant for the county changed his surname to Carrington to give the appearance of a descent from the seventeenth-century Viscount Carrington.

Joseph Banks of Sheffield, a moneylender and attorney, spent £40,000 between 1705 and 1727 in building up his estate and country house at Revesby Abbey in Lincolnshire.[69] Further down the social scale, John Beckett, a Barnsley grocer and land jobber, with his son a Leeds banker, bought Somerby near Gainsborough in 1786.[70] Country bankers were at an advantage since they were holders of mortgages and lent money, and knew of imminent sales. Other middle-class professional men were keen to join country society and physicians such as Samuel Gordon of Newark was created a baronet and bought Haverholme Priory near Sleaford.[71]

Offices, sinecures and the legal profession provided an income and position for many country house owners in the eighteenth century. The Duke of Newcastle amassed a large fortune from his office of Secretary of State, possibly as much as £10,500 per annum by 1728,[72] and enough to maintain Vanburgh's Claremont in Surrey, one of Newcastle's many country houses, which became one of the most sumptuous of retreats from London. The first and second Marquesses of Rockingham were able to pay for Henry Flitcroft's Wentworth Woodhouse, with its Palladian front nearly one hundred yards long, out of income,[73] and leave a larger estate, despite the house costing £80,000.[74] The Duke of Chandos was able to amass a huge income from a variety of sources, and one of these was his office as Paymaster General to the Forces from which he probably made £600,000 between about 1705 and 1713.[75] This most certainly would have contributed to the cost of Cannons, his palatial house designed by James Gibbs in Middlesex.

6] Hoare's Bank (C. Hoare and Co.), Fleet Street, London, 1829. The present building designed by Charles Parker

The union of the English and Scottish parliaments in 1707 meant that great Scottish aristocrats looked to London for wealth and advancement, despite retaining pride in their country.[76] They did well out of the union, better than their Irish counterparts, but the number of political places was seriously reduced for the Scottish gentry.[77] They managed to retain their power in their local areas of Scotland as heritors and justices.[78] The great aristocrats such as the Duke of Buccleuch at Dalkeith Palace or the Marquess of Tweeddale at Yester in East Lothian formed a *noblesse de l'épée* and used their rank and fortune to ensure positions for their sons.[79] The second Duke of Argyll became Commander-in-Chief of the British Army in 1747.[80] The third Duke spent hours a week furthering Scottish affairs to the advantage of his supporters through government bodies in London and could be expected to be 'waited upon' when he stayed overnight in Edinburgh or Glasgow on his way to Inveraray Castle by the Lord Provost of Glasgow or Edinburgh.[81]

There was also a distinct *noblesse de robe* in Scotland. During the eighteenth century about 90 per cent of those entering the Faculty of Advocates were from landed families. Senators of the College of Justice, who were the most successful advocates, had the title of Lord of Session.[82] Henry Dundas, Viscount Melville, was appointed Solicitor General at the age of twenty-four. He was the son of Robert Dundas of Arniston House, Midlothian, and he became a powerful figure in Scotland, especially in the Lowlands, being appointed Lord Advocate and Treasurer to the Navy.[83] The fifth Viscount Stormont, educated at Westminster and Christ Church, had an impressive legal career, becoming Lord Chief Justice in 1756, and being created an English earl, of Mansfield, in 1776.[84] He remodelled Scone Palace, Perthshire, and decorated it with French furniture [plate 1] and acquired Kenwood, the Robert Adam house, as his southern seat.[85] The fifth Earl of Lauderdale of Thirlestane Castle, was a member of the Faculty of Advocates and had a post at the Royal Mint, with a salary of £600 a year.[86]

Offices and sinecures were especially useful. The second Earl of Stair was a subscriber to *Vitruvius Britannicus*, a steadfast supporter of the Hanoverian dynasty in Scotland and ambassador to the French court between 1715 and 1720. After his recall, his zeal focused, with the help of William Adam, upon the layout of his estates at Castle Kennedy in Ayrshire and Newliston in Midlothian.[87]

In the eighteenth century the Celtic ruling classes were drawn to the centre of political power as never before. The Scots were the most successful in becoming politicians at Westminster,[88] acquiring sinecures, and grand country houses in both England and Scotland – the Earls of Bute and Mansfield being amongst the most prominent. The Protestant ascendancy, despite being no more than one-tenth of the population of Ireland, was successful enough to gain government places.[89] Some men were successful 'throughout the British Empire'. The Irish Earl of Moira, became Commander-in-Chief in Scotland in 1803, married Flora, Countess of Loudoun, a Scots heiress, and was made Governor-General of India and Marquess of Hastings by his friend the Prince Regent.[90] He commissioned Archibald Elliot to remodel Loudoun Castle in Ayrshire [7].[91] The Prince Regent also made Lord Conyngham a marquess in 1816 and appointed him Lord Steward of the Household and Constable of Windsor Castle. Far more remunerative was Lady Conyngham's position as royal mistress, since she received £80,000 worth of jewels from George IV and left £200,000 when she died. The interior of Slane Castle was magnificently restored for the King's visit by Francis Johnston.[92]

Both *arriviste* and old Anglo-Norman Irish families did well after the union of the English and Irish parliaments in 1801. Castles like Dunsany and Malahide were enlarged.[93] However, there were Welsh gentry families which remained essentially local. They were less dependent for their social position upon wealth and impressive seats and more concerned with ancestry. The Salusbury's of Denbighshire's ancestry went back to medieval Welsh princes, and the Mansels of Margam in Glamorgan found a fake Norman ancestor.[94] The Wynns of Denbighshire did, however, celebrate family pride with designs for Wynnstay by Robert Adam, and a London house executed by him at 20 St James's Square.[95]

War clearly made money for the ambitious as we have noted with the career of the Duke of Chandos. The great military hero of the early eighteenth century, the Duke of Marlborough, was able to spend £260,000 on

7] Loudoun Castle, Ayrshire. Architect Archibald Elliott, 1804

his palace at Blenheim by 1716.[96] Younger sons found lucrative places in the army and navy. The navy, after the Jacobite scare died down, attracted a few members of the Scots nobility: Lord Colville of Culross became a Rear-Admiral in 1762. In 1778 the Earl of Northesk became an Admiral of the White,[97] Lord Nelson, a great naval hero, could not be rewarded as Marlborough was, but his family were honoured and enriched. £5,000 a year was settled by the King upon Nelson's brother who was made an earl and Trafalgar House in Wiltshire and its estate were bought for him at a cost of £120,000.[98]

The church also provided a place for younger sons. In Wales all the bishops were sons of English noble families, staunchly Hanoverian and cosmopolitan in their tastes. Elegant rectories of well-to-do Anglo-Welsh clergy adorned the countryside. By the early nineteenth century elegant Gothic and Tudor style houses of the gentry and clergy adorned the countryside, which itself stimulated an interest in the Picturesque.[99]

The landowner also increased his wealth by developing towns and villages and indeed whole areas of cities. The Duke of Bedford, and the Grosvenor family developed the London area of Bloomsbury and Belgravia respectively.[100] By 1739 the fourth Lord Berkeley of Stratton had laid out Bruton Street and Berkeley Street and his mother had even developed an earlier scheme for Berkeley Square.[101] Some aristocrats had acquired land in order to increase their political hold on particular towns. The development of Nottingham was advanced through the passing of several enclosure acts which permitted the urban development of land around the town. In the 1780s and 1790s the Dukes of Rutland and Newcastle accelerated this process by selling their property in and around the borough of Nottingham.[102]

Other aristocratic and gentry families enriched themselves similarly. The Pulteneys and Grays played such a role in the development of Bath, for example.[103] In Ireland landlord villages went hand-in-hand with the centralising of the landed estates of the Ascendancy.[104] In Scotland there were many examples, some notorious, of the development of villages being linked to new forms of industry and employment. The third Duke of Argyll began to plan the new town of Inveraray [8] near his castle which Roger Morris had designed as a feudal 'toy fort'. By the 1760s, an inn, court-house and gaol were in use, although most of the attempts to establish new industries occurred in the old town. A spinning school was opened, and various Argyll lairds were behind the establishment of a coarse linen factory in Dunoon.[105]

Sir John Sinclair of Ulbster devoted himself to improving the livestock and fisheries of his estates, founded the British Wool Society and rebuilt the town of Thurso.[106] The Honourable Society of Improvers promoted the early model village and as many as 130 were probably built in Scotland. Elie, St Monance, Anstruther and Pittenweem were established by Sir John Anstruther of Leuchars. In place of 'a village of smugglers' was a village of manufacturing, spinning and weaving. However, a ruthless group of landowners forced Highlanders from their settlements to go and live in new townships on the coast to live by crofting and kelping.[107]

The first and second Marquesses of Donegal were absentee landlords in Ireland, and they owned a quarter of a million acres of land including Belfast.[108] The first Marquess erected buildings such as the Old Exchange and the Assembly Rooms there from the late 1750s onward, and by the early nineteenth century the harbour was improved and iron foundry established.[109] However, it was essentially in England that the Donegals lived, the second Marquess being educated at Eton and Oxford and the family rebuilding Fisherwick Park, Staffordshire, a vast Palladian house with a landscape by Capability Brown.[110] The first Marquess probably had an income of £31,000 a year from his Irish rents alone.[111]

Another somewhat urban money-making activity was the creation of canals. The third Duke of Bridgewater initiated the Bridgewater canal from his coal mines at Worsley in Lancashire to Manchester between 1759 and 1761 in order to carry coal cheaply.[112] Eventually the Duke provided himself with an income from coal of £110,000 a year.[113] One of his heirs, the seventh Earl of Bridgewater, who was far more interested in splendid country seats than the Duke, inherited two million pounds from him. With James Wyatt's help he remodelled Ashridge in Hertfordshire in 1813 at a cost of £300,000.[114]

8] Inveraray, Argyll. View from Dun na Cuaiche. Work by John Adam initially (1751) followed by Cruciform plan produced by Robert Mylne, 1774

Mundane commercial activity certainly produced large fortunes and huge houses. In Ireland magnificent Russborough in County Wicklow was designed by Richard Castle in 1841 for Joseph Leeson, first Earl of Milltown, whose father had made a fortune as a brewer.[115] In 1789 Nicholas Lawless, a woollen manufacturer, shocked Dublin society by accepting a barony. Haughty members of the ascendancy were critical: 'His person has more of the stiffness of a French dancing master than of the easy disengaged air of a well bred gentleman, and his voice is peculiarly unpleasing, it having a sharp and querulous tone, grating ... to the ear ... The great object on which his heart is fixed, next to the accumulation of money is the attainment of a peerage'.[116]

Lawless, the new Lord Cloncurry, braved jokes about blankets and commissioned Oliver Grace to build Lyons in County Kildare in 1797 at a time when his Irish estates were considered to be worth £12,000 a year. In 1802, the second baron, who considered himself something of an amateur architect, employed Richard Morrison to alter and enlarge Lyons, and incorporate statuary and chimneypieces he sent home from the Grand Tour.[117] Textiles were more important to Mary Countess of Lauderdale, wife of the seventh Earl who had a fortune of £60,000 with which to support Thirlestane Castle in Berwickshire. This derived from the method of silk manufacture discovered by Sir Thomas Lombe, Lady Lauderdale's father, in 1719.[118] Money, then, might come from a variety of sources, and the feudal and the *parvenu* often shared a common source of wealth.

Because country houses were places of expense and taste, they were frequently introduced into the important debate on luxury which continued throughout the eighteenth century. Luxury was especially connected with building and furnishing in the mind of Nicholas Barbon, for example, when in the 1690s he wrote *A Discourse of Trade*. Building, furnishing and adorning houses was a way of expressing 'the Pomp of Life'. To build magnificently was to create something which few could afford to imitate and grand architecture therefore made 'the most proper and visible Distinction of Riches and Greatness'.[119]

Bernard de Mandeville in *The Fable of the Bees: or Private Vices, Public Benefits* (1714) was critical, however, that 'bees' were burdened with an obligation to force them to be deferential, by a display of aristocratic magnificence. The populace, he argued, had no opportunity to see the intimate private luxury of many of the interiors of the nobility. Mandeville approved of luxury because it led to the spread of wealth throughout a nation, whereas abstemiousness and frugality did not produce a rich country.[120]

John Dennis who did, unlike Mandeville, believe that luxury was necessary for the distinction of rank and to subordinate the lower orders, was anxious about the affects of the spending throughout society. Opposing Mandeville's views in *Vice and Luxury Public Mischief or Remarks on the Fable of the Bees* (1724), he expressed the view that the pursuit of luxury had caused the fall of Sparta and Rome, and had contributed to the National

Debt in England.[121] There was in fact growing concern that luxury was becoming an attribute of the middling sort and many aristocrats were enabled to live a more luxurious existence through fortunes derived from, as we have seen, coal and canals.

Ancient Greek and Roman laws had banned the middle classes from a leading role in government. Socrates, Cato, Cicero and St Augustine had agreed.[122] In England in the 1730s and 1740s writers as such Lord Bolingbroke and other Tories disapproved of the newly rich Whigs who were without birth or breeding, and whose families had not previously taken a part in government.[123] The Glorious Revolution of 1688 was seen as a moral revolution and it resulted in a desire for the reform of manners, initiated by the great landed magnates who had begun the political revolution. It was the country gentlemen that Bolingbroke and other heads of great traditional families believed in as national leaders. Bolingbroke wrote: 'the landed men are the true owners of our political vessel'. Politics, it was believed, should be conducted by men of good birth, classical education and social grace.[124]

Since the seventeenth century the church had emphasised the value of country life as something untainted, and the idea of the rural retreat as a gateway to paradise.[125] However, the natural leaders, springing from the countryside, turned out not to be so pure. Sir Robert Walpole, who should, as a middle-ranking squire, have had all the unadorned virtues hoped for in the nation's governors, was unexpectedly flawed, according to current theories about men of his class. To the general theatre-going public he was a symbol of acquisitiveness, recognisable as 'Bob Booty' in Gay's *The Beggars' Opera*.[126] Walpole's administration, it was held, was steeped in financial corruption, which, Bolingbroke felt, echoed the corruption of society as a whole, jittering with financial instability and greed at the time of the South Sea Bubble in 1722. Walpole's own self-indulgence was criticised in *The Craftsman*, the principal opposition paper which claimed, in 1730, that the housekeeping expenses at Houghton amounted to £1,500 a week.[127] The house itself expressed a new taste for sumptuousness with variegated, plumbed-in marble buffets with silver taps, solid mahogany fittings and a village swept arrogantly away to create a setting for the new dwelling.[128]

Daniel Defoe believed that the luxury of the nobility and gentry, old and new, would destroy them. He supported the production of luxurious objects in general, because like Mandeville he believed that it permitted the spread of wealth through the nation. He hoped that the newly well-to-do tradesmen might buy up the estates of ruined aristocrats, and, providing they themselves did not succumb to greed and luxury, they might gain political power.[129]

This general spread of luxury was something of which the philosopher David Hume approved. He supported the idea of widespread pleasure derived from the object. A refined and artistic society grew up in a spirit of luxury which Hume defined as 'great refinement in the qualification of the senses'. The public-spirited acts which were a feature of the era of the Enlightenment in which Hume lived were to be applauded, he believed, but they could be more easily ensured if supported by the wealth derived from the supply of luxury goods.[130]

This spread of luxury through the middling orders was clearly observable everywhere by the 1770s, when Tobias Smollett wrote *Humphry Clinker* (1771). In the novel Bramble observes: 'When I see a number of well-dressed people of both sexes, sitting on the crowded benches, exposed to the eyes of the mob . . . I despair of their want of taste and decorum'. He seems to be expressing a fear that their stylishness is an affront to the poor, and might incite social disturbance.[131] The great economist Adam Smith in *The Theory of Moral Sentiments* (1759) expressed the idea, common by the middle of the eighteenth century, that the luxuries of great families helped to redistribute wealth throughout the nation.[132] Later in *The Wealth of Nations* (1776) he observed that 'Noble palaces, magnificent villas, great collections of books, statues, pictures, . . . are frequently both an ornament and an honour, not only to the neighbourhood, but to the whole country to which they belong. Versailles is an ornament and an honour to France, Stowe and Wilton to England'.[133]

Whilst Smith does not seem to have considered the flaunting of luxury as showing a 'want of decorum' (like Bramble), he did emphasise that the puritans with their frugality were not undermining the economy, and that saving and investment were more important than endless consumption.[134] Indeed he considered that the great landowners who craved endless luxurious trappings, sold their political birthright: they unseated tenants who brought them no profit and replaced them with provident improving ones from whom they could demand very high rents, which might pay for their aristocratic indulgence on luxury items. Such new tenants demanded in return longer leases, and greater security of tenure, so that they gained greater independence. This destroyed the power of the traditional nobility especially in the countryside itself, Smith believed.[135]

Even at the beginning of the nineteenth century not all writers were in favour of the declining position of the landed nobility and gentry. William Cobbett defended their natural leadership and wrote that: 'The ancient nobility and gentry of the kingdom . . . have been thrust out of all public employment' and that 'a race of merchants and manufacturers and bankers and loan-jobbers have usurped their place'.[136] Smith himself had no faith in the economic benefits to the nation of the country gentleman who spent his revenue in a profane and sumptuous table, and in maintaining a great number of menial servants, and a mixture of dogs and horses. However, he considered that the interests of the merchants and manufacturers who were replacing the older aristocracy in the nation's councils, would not '. . . prepare them to give the most satisfactory advice'.[137]

NOTES

1 For numbers of country houses built see John Summerson, *The Classical Country House in Eighteenth Century England*, Thames and Hudson, London, 1990, pp. 82–5. For details of population see Michael Reed, *The Georgian Triumph*, Paladin Books, London, 1984, pp. 24–7 and 280–1. See also Edith M. Johnson, *Ireland in the Eighteenth Century*, Gill and Macmillan, Dublin, 1974, population charts.

2 Vicary Gibbs, *The Complete Peerage*, 13 vols, St Catherine's Press, London, 1912, II, p. 81. For numbers of peers see John Cannon, *Aristocratic Century*, Cambridge University Press, Cambridge, 1987, pp. 10–11.

3 G. E. Mingay, *A Social History of the English Countryside*, Routledge, London, 1992, p. 118 gives details of comparative wealth.

4 C. W. Chalkin and J. R. Wordie, *Town and Countryside: The English Landowner in the National Economy 1660–1860*, Unwin Hyman, London, 1989, p. 26. See also Lorna Weatherill, *Consumer Behaviour and Material Culture in Britain 1660–1760*, Routledge, London, 1988, pp. 169–70. The lesser gentry of whom she writes had considerable influence and social standing locally, but were less likely to be the owners of such items as china, pictures, looking-glasses and even pewter, than well-to-do tradesmen. Joan Johnson, *The Gloucestershire Gentry*, Alan Sutton, Gloucester, 1989, pp. 1–4 notes that the College of Arms, through the Visitation of Heralds, applied its own strict interpretation of what gentry status was before the eighteenth century. In the 1660s statutory rulings were made to define the situation, but the principal characteristic remained landownership and exploitation of estates. They were well established in the Home Counties and Gloucestershire, because land here formerly held by the Church and Crown was later dispersed to them as lesser owners.

5 *Ibid.*, p. 1.

6 G. J. Barker Benfield, *The Culture of Sensibility*, University of Chicago Press, London, 1992, p. 138.

7 Ray Kelch, *Newcastle: A Duke Without Money*, Routledge and Kegan Paul, London, 1974, pp. 167–8.

8 Barker Benfield, *Sensibility*, p. 97.

9 Karl Schweizer and John Osborne, *Cobbett in His Times*, Leicester University Press, Leicester, 1990, p. 6 and footnote 20.

10 Michael Fry, *The Dundas Despotism*, Edinburgh University Press, Edinburgh, 1992, p. 4.

11 Colin McWilliam, *The Buildings of Scotland: Lothian*, Penguin, Harmondsworth, 1978, pp. 158–62.

12 Fry, *Dundas*, p. 4.

13 R. F. Foster, *Oxford History of Ireland*, Oxford University Press, Oxford, 1989, p. 137.

14 Roderick Floud and Donald McCloskey (eds), *An Economic History of Britain Since 1700*, Cambridge University Press, Cambridge, 1994, pp. 98–9.

15 Paul Langford, *A Polite and Commercial People: England 1723–1783*, Oxford University Press, Oxford, 1990, p. 437.

16 Floud and McCloskey, *Economic History of Britain*, p. 99.

17 T. W. Bearstall, *A North Country Estate*, Phillimore, London, 1975, p. 80.

18 *Ibid.*, p. 84.

19 Roy Porter, *Coke of Norfolk: A Financial and Agricultural Study*, Clarendon Press, Oxford, 1975, p. 37.

20 *Ibid.*, p. 24.

21 *Ibid.*, p. 82.

22 *Ibid.*, p. 127.

23 *Ibid.*, pp. 116–17.

24 E. A. Wasson, 'A Progressive Landlord: The Third Earl Spencer', in Chalkin and Wordie, *Town and Countryside*, pp. 83–101.

25 Dorothy Stroud, *Henry Holland*, Country Life, London, 1966, p. 99.

26 Wasson, 'A Progressive Landlord', p. 93.

27 *Ibid.*, p. 83.

28 *Ibid.*, p. 93.

29 John Davies, *A History of Wales*, Penguin, London, 1994, p. 332.

30 Rosalind Mitchison, *Lordship to Patronage: Scotland 1603–1745*, Edinburgh University Press, Edinburgh, 1983, p. 155.

31 *Ibid.*, p. 154.

32 Johnson, *Ireland in the Eighteenth Century*, p. 86.

33 Langford, *Polite and Commercial People*, p. 594.

34 Bearstall, *North Country Estate*, p. 28.

35 *Ibid.*, p. 34.

36 James Macauley, *The Gothic Revival 1745–1845*, Blackie, London, 1975, pp. 8–9 and 315–17. Work was done by a number of architects, including Joseph and Ignatius Bonomi. £22,000 was spent on foundations for terraces between 1797 and 1801. Lambton was given battlements for the first Baron Durham, but had gas lighting. Castellation was favoured by northern coal owners: Nash designing Ravensworth Castle in this style for Lord Ravensworth in 1808 and Smirke building Lowther Castle, Westmorland, for the Earl of Londsdale, 1806–11.

37 Davies, *History of Wales*, p. 326.

38 *Ibid.*

39 J. R. Wordie, 'Aristocrats and Entrepreneurs in the Shropshire Mining Industry 1748–1807', in Chalkin and Wordie, *Town and Countryside*, pp. 192–3.

40 *Ibid.*, p. 200.

41 John Rule, *The Vital Century: England's Developing Economy 1714–1815*, Longmans, London, 1992, p. 295.

42 John Carswell, *The South Sea Bubble*, Cressett Press, London, 1960, pp. 273–81.

43 James Lees-Milne, *Earls of Creation*, Century Hutchinson, London, 1986, p. 37. Lord Bute, in a letter to Lord Stafford, expressed admiration for Bingley's knowledge of architecture in 1715.

44 Carswell, *South Sea Bubble*, p. 287.

45 Gibbs, *Complete Peerage*, p. 111.

46 *Ibid.*

47 David Green, *Sarah, Duchess of Marlborough*, Collins, London, 1967, p. 295.

48 Carswell, *South Sea Bubble*, p. 283. His gross assets in 1721 were £40,776.

49 Mark Bence Jones, *Clive of India*, Constable, London, 1974, pp. 188–9. A jagir was an assignment of the Government share of the produce of a particular district in the form of an annuity.

50 *Ibid.*

51 Michael Edwards, *Warren Hastings: King of the Nabobs*, Hunt, Davis, MacGibbon, London, 1976, pp. 180–1.

52 *Ibid.*, p. 180.

53 W. H. Doubleday and Lord Howard de Walden, *The Complete Peerage*, 13 vols, St Catherine's Press, London, VIII, p. 323.

54 George Taylor (ed.), *Plays of Samuel Foote and Arthur Murphy*, Cambridge University Press, Cambridge, 1989, pp. 12–13. Clive had been indicted of the misgovernment of Bengal in 1772, and Warren Hastings was prosecuted in the 1780s, a bill for the 'better regulation of the affairs of the East India Company' had been introduced in Parliament and nabobs were therefore the subject of satire. Foote's nabob was Sir Matthew Mite who, wanting an estate in Berkshire, told his agent to 'give the fellow four times the value and bid him turn out in a month'.

55 Christopher Hussey, *English Country Houses: Early Georgian 1715–1760*, Antique Collectors Club, London, 1986, p. 105. See also Nikolaus Pevsner, *The Buildings of England, Shropshire*, Penguin, Harmondsworth, 1974. Davenport House was designed in 1726 by Smith of Warwick. It had an extremely elaborate interior with its inlaid panelling in the saloon.

56 Christopher Hussey, *English Country Houses: Mid-Georgian 1760–1800*, Antique Collectors Club, London, 1986, p. 177. See also Bence Jones, *Clive*, p. 260.

57 Hussey, *Mid-Georgian*, p. 182.

58 Mitchison, *Lordship to Patronage*, p. 170.

59 Bruce Lenman, *Integration and Enlightenment: Scotland 1746–1832*, Edinburgh University Press, Edinburgh, 1981, p. 80.

60 Duncan Thomson, *Raeburn*, Scottish National Portrait Gallery, Edinburgh, 1997, p. 98.

61 J. H. Parry, *A Short History of the West Indies*, Macmillan Education, London, 1987, p. 151.

62 *Ibid.*, p. 155.

63 Mary Mauchline, *Harewood House*, David and Charles, London, 1974, p. 15. The Lascelles family did well out of West Indian affairs. Henry Lascelles had profited from the profits of colonial administration in government contacts and customs concessions and from the sugar crop. He set up a London West India merchant house to negotiate the commissions of planters in England, sell their crops, finance their loans and take over their mortgaged plantations. See also Hussey, *Mid-Georgian*, p. 61.

64 Parry, *West Indies*, p. 116.

65 *Ibid.*, p. 153.

66 Richard Pares, *A West Indies Fortune*, Longmans, London, 1950, p. 59.

67 *Ibid.*, p. 143.

68 Doubleday and Howard de Walden, *Complete Peerage VIII*, pp. 62–4.

69 Nikolaus Pevsner and John Harris, *The Buildings of England: Lincolnshire*, Penguin, London, 1989, p. 610. This was originally a Cistercian foundation of 1142. The seventeenth-century house enlarged by the Banks family was also named Revesby Abbey; they had bought it in 1714.

70 Bearstall, *North Country Estate*, p. 93.

71 *Ibid.*, p. 90.

72 Kelch, *Newcastle*, p. 73.

73 Porter, *Coke of Norfolk*, p. 24.

74 Mingay, *English Countryside*, p. 118. See also Gibbs, *Complete Peerage III*, p. 62. The second Marquess married Mary Ramsden who had a fortune of £60,000.

75 G. H. Collins Baker and Muriel Baker, *The Life and Circumstances of James Brydges, First Duke of Chandos*, Clarendon Press, Oxford, 1949, p. XIV.

76 Fry, *Dundas*, p. 4. See also Mitchison, *Lordship to Patronage*, p. 133. The 'Squadrone Volante' was the name of a party who were anxious for office at the beginning of the eighteenth century and were frustrated. It was led by the second Marquess of Tweedale.

77 Fry, *Dundas*, p. 4.

78 Heritors is a Scots term here used to mean proprietors of a heritable subject, especially heritors of the church who were responsible for each parish church and manse until 1925.

79 Fry, *Dundas*, p. 4.

80 Lenman, *Integration and Enlightenment*, p. 58.

81 Mitchison, *Lordship to Patronage*, p. 162.

82 Lenman, *Integration and Enlightenment*, p. 9.

83 Fry, *Dundas*, p. 1. Writes of 'The Great House of Arniston' (their seat in Midlothian), but challenges the idea that the Dundas family was corrupt or authoritarian in their use of power.

84 Lenman, *Integration and Enlightenment*, p. 93.

85 Hugh Montgomery-Massingberd, *Great Houses of Scotland*, Laurence King, London, 1997, pp. 83–91.

86 Doubleday and Howard de Walden, *Complete Peerage VIII*, p. 493.

87 John Gifford, *William Adam*, Mainstream Publishing, Edinburgh, 1989, p. 81.

88 Linda Colley, *Britons: Forging the Nation, 1707–1837*, Vintage, London, 1994, p. 166.

89 Johnson, *Ireland in the Eighteenth Century*, p. 53.

90 Lenman, *Integration and Enlightenment*, p. 112.

91 George Richardson, *New Vitruvius Britannicus*, 2 vols, J. Taylor, London, 1802–8, 1808–10, II, p. 8. The castle was designed by Archibald Elliot.

92 Gibbs, *Complete Peerage XII*, p. 410. See also J. O'Brien and D. Guinness, *Great Irish Houses and Castles*, Weidenfeld and Nicolson, London, 1992, pp. 158–61. Francis Johnston, James Wyatt and Thomas Hopper all worked at the Castle.

93 Peter Somerville-Large, *The Irish Country House: A Social History*, Sinclair Stevenson, London, 1995, p. 220.

94 Gareth Elwyn Jones, *Modern Wales: A Concise History*, Cambridge University Press, Cambridge, 1995, pp. 29–30.

95 E. D. Evans, *A History of Wales: 1660–1815*, University of Wales Press, Cardiff, 1993, pp. 10–11 and 151. The Wynns of Wynnstay and other families like the Morgans of Tredegar remained commoners, although they might have obtained peerages during the eighteenth century; but before the 1770s there were hardly any Welsh families in the peerage. The Wynns opened coal mines to provide for the needs of the iron industry and provided themselves with another source of income.

96 Green, *Sarah, Duchess of Marlborough*, p. 204.

97 Lenman, *Integration and Enlightenment*, p. 58.

98 *Orme's Graphic History of Life, Exploits and Death of Horatio Nelson*, Orme, London, n.d., p. 60.

99 Davies, *History of Wales*, p. 298. See for example Richard Haslam, *The Buildings of Wales: Powys*, Harmondsworth, Penguin, University of Wales Press, 1979, p. 58 and Edward Hubbard, *The Buildings of Wales: Clwyd*, Harmondsworth, Penguin, 1986, p. 59.

100 John Summerson, *Georgian London*, Penguin, Harmondsworth, 1978, pp. 191–7.

101 Bernard Falk, *The Berkeleys of Berkeley Square*, Hutchinson and Co., London, 1944, p. 118.

102 Chalkin and Wordie, *Town and Countryside*, p. 21.

103 *Ibid.*

104 Foster, *Ascendancy and Union*, p. 145.

105 Ian Lindsay and Mary Cosh, *Inveraray and the Dukes of Argyll*, Edinburgh University Press, Edinburgh, 1973, p. 171.

106 Thomson, *Raeburn*, p. 108.

107 T. C. Smout, 'The Landowner and the Planned Village in Scotland 1730–1830', in N. T. Phillipson and Rosalind Mitchison (eds), *Scotland in the Age of Improvement*, Edinburgh University Press, Edinburgh, 1970, pp. 77–107.

108 W. A. Maguire, *Living Like a Lord: The Second Marquis of Donegal*, Appletree Press and Ulster Society for Irish Historical Studies, Belfast, 1984, p. 12.

109 Paul Larmon, *Belfast: An Illustrated Architectural Guide*, Friar's Bush Press, Belfast, 1987.

110 Maguire, *Living Like a Lord*, p. 12.

111 Somerville-Large, *Irish Country House*, p. 81.

112 Langford, *Polite and Commercial People*, p. 410.

113 Bernard Falk, *The Bridgewater Millions* Hutchinson and Co. Ltd, London, New York and Melbourne, 1942, p. 103.

114 *Ibid.*, p. 175.

115 Doubleday and Howard de Walden, *Complete Peerage VIII*, p. 708.

116 Gibbs, *Complete Peerage III*, p. 329.

117 E. McParland, A. Rowan and A. M. Rowan (eds), *The Architecture of Richard Morrison and William Vitruvius Morrison*, Irish Architectural Archive, Dublin, 1989, p. 120.

118 Doubleday and Howard de Walden, *Complete Peerage VIII*, p. 493.

119 Jules Lubbock, *The Tyranny of Taste: The Politics of Architecture and Design in Britain 1550–1960*, Yale University Press, London, 1995, p. 97.

120 *Ibid.*, p. 105.

121 John Sekora, *Luxury: The Concept in Western Thought: Eden to Smollett*, The Johns Hopkins University Press, London, 1977, p. 80.

122 *Ibid.*, p. 69.

123 *Ibid.*, p. 81.

124 *Ibid.*, p. 70 quoting Bolingbroke, *The Idea of a Patriot King* (1749).

125 Keith Thomas, *Man and the Natural World: Changing Attitudes in England 1500–1800*, Allen Lane, London, 1983, p. 249.

126 John Brewer, *The Pleasures of the Imagination: English Culture in the Eighteenth Century*, HarperCollins, London, 1997, p. 431.

127 William Speck, 'Britain's First Prime Minister', in Andrew Moore (ed.), *Houghton Hall*, Philip Wilson, London, 1996, p. 16.

128 Moore, *Houghton Hall*, pp. 116, 117, 139 *passim*. See also Sekora, *Luxury*, pp. 88–9. Walpole was attacked as an agent of luxury. Bolingbroke's *Idea of the Patriot King* provided material on different types of English luxury. Walpole, he saw as the progenitor of selfishness and disruptive qualities that were changing the nation.

129 Sekora, *Luxury*, p. 117.

130 Lubbock, *Tyranny of Taste*, pp. 115–19.

131 Sekora, *Luxury*, p. 226.

132 Lubbock, *Tyranny of Taste*, pp. 121–43.

133 *Ibid.*, p. 135.

134 *Ibid.*, p. 126.

135 *Ibid.*, pp. 141–2.

136 Schweizer and Osborne, *Cobbett in His Times*, p. 8.

137 Donald Winch, *Riches and Poverty: An Intellectual History of Political Economy in Britain 1730–1834*, Cambridge University Press, 1996, p. 358.

2

The architecture of the country house

THE EIGHTEENTH-CENTURY COUNTRY HOUSE AS AN ARCHITECTURAL EXEMPLAR

The eighteenth-century British aristocracy and gentry had great political power, enormous wealth, and were able to take a lead in architectural patronage and taste. Their country houses were a vehicle for expressing their political, social and aesthetic dominance in every county. Through travel, publication of books of design, the increasing professionalism of architects, and the desire of patrons to express their power in solid forms, great houses were built. Lord Shaftesbury recognised the public and almost patriotic nature of building and architectural patronage. If '. . . instead of a beautiful pile [a man] raises at vast expence', he declared, 'such a false and counterfeit Piece of Magnificence as can be justly arraigned for is Deformity', then he might well be condemned not only by connoisseurs but by 'the whole People'.[1]

Architectural projects might be discussed and promoted in different societies and clubs which, in an informal way, took the place of an academy of architecture until the founding of the Royal Academy in 1768. Twenty gallons of claret were imbibed, on some occasions, at the Kit-Cat Club, where delicious mutton pies and talk about architecture also made for many convivial evenings. The members included Sir John Vanbrugh (1664–1726), architect and playwright; Sir Robert Walpole (1676–1745), Prime Minister and builder of Houghton Hall, Norfolk, a major and influential country house. The Kit-Cats were politicians, poets, country gentlemen and financiers. The presence of another dramatist, William Congreve, as well as Vanbrugh, may have lent an element of theatrical swagger to the taste for Baroque architecture.[2]

Another group of noblemen formed 'The New Junta for Architecture'; Lord Molesworth, a friend of Shaftesbury, Sir Thomas Hewett, Surveyor General of the Kings Works from 1719–26, and Sir George Markham Bt. were among its members. Their aim was to produce a new, more vigorous and archaeologically inspired classicism to breathe life into the spent Baroque forms in contemporary architecture.[3] They invited Florentine Alessandro Galilei (1691–1737) to England in 1714 and he also worked briefly in Ireland. Galilei worked at Kimbolton Castle, Huntingdonshire, in *c.* 1715 for the first Duke of Manchester and at Castletown, Co. Kildare, in Ireland.[4]

A later group which promoted a more ambitious examination of classicism and financed publications, was the Society of Dilettanti, founded in 1732. They too indulged in drunken dinners at the Star and Garter or Almacks and other London dives. They promoted classicism seriously through such works as James Stuart and Nicolas Revett's *Antiquities of Athens* (from 1762) and some of them built country houses. Sir Francis Dashwood rebuilt the west front of West Wycombe House, Buckinghamshire, between 1748 and 1771 with a reconstruction of the Temple of Bacchus at Teos by Revett; the first Earl Harcourt included new Greek decoration, by James 'Athenian' Stuart at Nuneham Park, Oxfordshire, in 1756, in the form of Serlian windows.[5]

As well as the work of groups, the architecture of country houses was promoted by great noblemen of political influence. Lord Shaftesbury was one of these, but Richard Boyle, third Earl of Burlington and fourth Earl of Cork (1694–1753) had even greater influence on the architecture of country houses. He was Treasurer of Ireland and Lord Lieutenant of the West Riding, a Knight of the Garter and a Fellow of the Society of Antiquaries. Burlington's villa at Chiswick stood as an example of the new purity in architecture which derived principally from the works of Andrea Palladio, and made the Baroque seem indulgent, incorrect and in need of modification. Count Algarotti wrote to Burlington in 1751 of his conversation with Frederick the Great: 'The name of My Lord Burlington came to be mentioned together with those of Jones and Palladio' and the King praised the Earl's work. Algarotti continued, 'Indeed, My Lord, your most noble example could be of the utmost use to the world . . . in order that the fine arts, so much abused in our days, could rise once more'.[6]

If Lord Burlington was regarded as an English Maecenas, Sir John Clerk of Penicuik was described as the Scottish Maecenas. Clerk admired Burlington and was entertained by him on a visit to England. He wrote *The Country Seat* in 1726, and like Burlington and Colen Campbell he felt the need for a purer taste, and the development of aesthetic judgement which he called 'Fine Genius'. Clerk also recognised the importance of a country seat as a power base, and in enumerating the different types of country house which might be built he mentioned 'the House of State' which was intended for a nobleman with a political career.[7]

Throughout the eighteenth century it became customary to praise the aristocracy for its taste. Much of this was, of course, flattery, but it is indicative of its position as leaders in the promotion of architecture in a country where academies were slow in developing and the monarch's patronage was often lacking. Lord Chesterfield deprecated Burlington's 'minute and mechanical'[8] knowledge of architecture, and it seems that the latter was often disinclined to discuss architectural matters. However, by the 1770s work at Chiswick was described as a 'Striking Instance of the great Abilities and reformed Taste of that illustrious architect',[9] and Burlington seemed to have attained expert status.

Often the praise was of a more general nature, playing upon the aristocrats' cultural superiority. George Lockart wrote in 1714 of the first Duke of Roxburghe, who was soon to employ William Adam at Floors Castle in Roxburghshire, that he was 'a Man of good sense improved by so much Reading and Learning, That perhaps, he was the best Accomplished young Man of Quality in Europe . . .'[10] Gradually, as descriptions of houses and estates became an aid to the polite traveller, a view of the mansion was accompanied by a paeon on its owner's connoisseurship. Watts in his *Seats of the Nobility and Gentry*, in describing and illustrating Sandbeck in Yorkshire, the house of Lord Scarborough, referred to its owner as 'a Nobleman distinguished by his fine Taste in the polite Arts'.[11]

The country house was developing as a leading examplar of taste. A gentleman owner must have some knowledge of architecture, as even Chesterfield acknowledged,[12] and because of his wealth and experiences on the Grand Tour he was in a position to lead. This was also aided by the publication of books, illustrating country houses. Most famous, as a volume illustrating classical houses (some of the Baroque, and some Palladian), was Colen Campbell's *Vitruvius Britannicus*, the first volume of which came out in 1715, and two more in 1717 and 1725 respectively. Burlington also promoted architecture through arranging with William Kent (?1685–1748) for the publication of the drawings of Inigo Jones, himself a promoter of classicism, in *Designs of Inigo Jones* in 1727.

Not all noblemen travelled or collected drawings and as James Gibbs observed, 'Gentlemen who might be concerned in Building'[13] needed information and guidance 'especially in remote parts of the Country where little or no assistance for designs can be procured'.[14] Gibbs's work was much more Baroque than anything by Campbell or Burlington, as he was trained in Rome by Carlo Fontana. Gibbs's *A Book of Architecture* (1728) provided a huge range of designs not only for country houses, but also chimney pieces, doorcases, balustrades, vases and sarcophagi and was immensely influential in spreading a recognisable decorative vocabulary all over the country.

If the initial impetus given to building by aristocratic patronage produced huge Palladian houses, the country house continued to be a pioneer of new style well into the Georgian period. Robert Adam (1728–92) and his contemporaries produced varied classical interiors, and a second wave of 'purity' in country house design came with austere Greek houses such as The Grange in Hampshire in 1804, and Belsay Hall, Northumberland, designed by another gentleman-connoisseur Sir Charles Monck Bt. between 1806 and 1817.[15] The designers of country houses then turned to Classical and Gothic asymmetrical picturesqueness, as owners discovered informality and a wish to evoke ancestral castles.

If the country house were to stand as an example of power and taste in the countryside, it had to be visible. Throughout the eighteenth and early nineteenth centuries visitors were allowed to see most houses. Books of views were published which were quite different from the architectural publications such as *Vitruvius Britannicus* or Gibbs's *A Book of Architecture*. The book of views showed the house 'with atmosphere', inhabited by the proprietor. W. Watts's *The Seats of the Nobility and Gentry in a Collection of the Most Interesting and Picturesque Views* of 1779 emphasised the grandeur of what might be seen. At Harewood, John Carr and Robert Adam's Neoclassical house near Leeds, Watts assured his readers, 'Mr Lascelles, the present possessor . . . has politely fixed every *Saturday* as a public viewing day for his House and Grounds, of which Permission the Nobility and Gentry, who frequent *Harrowgate* avail themselves with, the Slight Distance thereon being a most agreeable Excursion'.[16]

Some of the later books were full guides such as John Britten's *Illustrations of Fonthill* (1832). Apart from books, engravings were sold, such as John Rocque's *Engraved Survey of Chiswick* (1736) which popularised the novel idea of view boxes: that is to say a plan, with views of major buildings surrounding it.[17] John Donnell who showed views of the house in *c.* 1750 sold out his interest to print and booksellers who sold sets of views of Chiswick or single prints.[18] Most engravings show the house thronged with visitors, sometimes as many as thirty. Clearly the country house was open, to be admired, a place where polite society might congregate, as is apparent in the only view of the interior of the great Palladian house Wanstead in Essex, designed by Colen Campbell in 1723. Hogarth showed the richly furnished interior with the silver furniture in *The Wanstead House Assembly*.

It was not merely to the aristocracy and gentry that a country house might stand as an example of all that was to be imitated. During the period when the more lavish guides were being produced, Prince Puckler-Muskau commented in 1827: 'It requires a considerable fortune here to keep up a country house . . . according to the aspiring and imitative manners of the country as much . . . at the Shopkeeper's house as at the Duke's – a handsomely fitted up house, with elegant furniture, plate, servants in new and handsome liveries a profusion of dishes and foreign wines, rare and expensive dessert, and in all things an appearance of superfluity – "plenty" as the English call it.'[19] Merchants aspired not only to the architecture of the aristocracy but to its society. Prince Puckler-Muskau noticed that, 'It is an almost universal weakness of the unnoble in England to parade an acquaintance with the noble'.[20]

English aristocrats saw themselves as inheritors of the classical world. They believed their political system had an ancient nobility and virtue which could be proclaimed in architecture. They might indeed believe that their grand country houses were endorsed by the Ancients. A symbol of magnificence in such a house was a portico. To Aristotle the virtuous man was also a person of magnificence. Julius Caesar had been permitted to attach a portico to his own house.[21] The earliest portico on an English country house was affixed to an existing structure, the Vyne in Hampshire in 1654, but the most impressive new portico was a hexastyle designed by Colen Campbell for Wanstead in 1713, and signified his intention 'to introduce the Temple Beauties' to architecture.[22] Architects of the continuing Baroque tradition designed porticos too. John Vanbrugh provided one for Blenheim: the Duke of Marlborough noting that he had been 'advised by everybody to have the Portico, so that I have writt to Vanbrook to have itt'.[23] Vanbrugh himself observed of porticos in 1711 that 'No production in architecture is so solemnly magnificent'[24] and also introduced one into a later work at Seaton Delaval, Northumberland, in 1720. Some owners had to make do with a less expensive giant order of pilasters, but this was less impressive and not as visible.

The country house was promoted almost as an aspect of national good taste and as a showcase for architectural excellence throughout Britain by noblemen who built, designed and advised. This group included the 'Architect Earls', Bathurst, Pembroke and Leicester as well as Lord Bingley and in Scotland the sixth Earl of Mar.[25]

The country house was advertised through *Vitruvius Britannicus*[26] and other books such as James Paine's *Plans, Elevations and Sections of Noblemen and Gentlemen's Houses* (1767). It was also at the centre of artistic and architectural experience. William Kent (1685–1748), an apprentice coach painter, eventually became the architect of houses as well as their decorator. Initially he was sent to Italy by a number of country house owners (Sir William Wentworth of Bretton Park, Yorkshire, Sir John Chester of Chicheley Hall, Buckinghamshire, and Burrell Massingberd of Ormsby in Lincolnshire). Kent bought paintings and 'objects of virtù' for these country houses and eventually met Burlington and in time turned to architecture.[27] Lord Mar and a group of Scots nobles had similarly sent Alexander Edwards to France and the Low Countries in 1701 to 'view, observe and take draughts of the most curious and remarkable Houses, Edifices . . .'.[28] The country house, then, became an aesthetic exemplar. It brought architect and patron together, architects like Campbell and Gibbs produced books illustrating it and advertising their style. The country house incorporated copies of features from ancient buildings recently discovered. It was visited and admired, and guide books describing it and its contents were published.

IDEAS OF RANK

The idea that the architecture of the country house should emphasise rank was clearly an important one, especially in the first half of the eighteenth century. The Protestant monarchy of William and Mary, Anne and George I was established by a group of noblemen who were rewarded with peerages. By 1715 there were twelve new dukedoms – Brandon, Bolton, Buckingham, Montagu, Manchester, Devonshire, Leeds, Shrewsbury, Kent, Marlborough, Kingston and Ancaster.[29] These dukes tended to favour the Baroque style and several of them built houses well before the beginning of the eighteenth century. Vanbrugh had designed grand Baroque houses for Marlborough at Blenheim (1705–44), Ancaster at Grimsthorpe, Lincolnshire (1722–26) and for Manchester at Kimbolton, Huntingdonshire (1707–10).[30]

Rank was supported by a sense of dynasty, and this was frequently expressed through domestic rituals so that it became part of the fabric of the estate and the locality. At the beginning of the eighteenth century it might well appear in the grandest of forms in day-to-day matters. The 'Proud' seventh Duke of Somerset 'always delighted to live in Magnificence, Delicacy, Splendour, constantly preserving his Rank, like a Man of Birth and Fortune, ever moved in a Sphere above the Vulgar, thereby maintaining that just Order and Regularity which proceeds from a Distinction of Persons without which a State could not look comely nor government subsist'.[31] He achieved this, in part, through his domestic arrangements: 'His House was always kept with that grandeur and Decorum as formerly used by the *English* Kings and Men of Quality. Not as nowadays, when very little Distinction appears between a King's Palace and a private Gentleman's House, and often the latter is constructed with more Regularity in Appearance.'[32]

He was clearly more regal than the homely Hanoverians: 'His Grace's Entertainments were always noble and magnificent and his Sideboard was as richly adorned with Plate on such occasions as some foreign Altars; and what is now almost out of Fashion, all his Plate was of the finest Standard'.[33] He may even have felt himself somewhat above the upstart German Electors who had recently succeeded to the throne. It was written of him that his 'most princely spirit might be attributed to his priding himself in being descended in so many ways from the Blood-Royal of our ancient English kings'.[34] A visitor to Petworth in 1745 noted that the Duke spent most of his time on his estate 'in a grand retirement peculiar and agreeable only to himself'. Apparently he always came down to breakfast wearing his Garter ribbon and insisted on his children standing in his presence.[35]

Celia Fiennes (1662–1741) visited Beaudesert, Lord Paget's house in Staffordshire. Lord Paget, who had 'greate Command and Royalty in the county', was a figure a little like the Duke of Somerset. 'Most of the Gentlemen in the county pay him Chiefe rent and some hold the right in some of their land by waiteing on him on some solemn feast dayes in the yeare and bring up his dinner and wait on him as he eates . . .', Celia Fiennes noted. She also felt that the habit was beginning to die out and that 'these things are better wav'd'.[36]

This type of pride in family and lineage was expressed in other domestic ways. Lady Catherine Poulett, daughter of Earl Poulett, married a rich squire, John Parker of Saltram, in 1725. Her aristocratic connections were made apparent in a writing desk which was passed on to her through the Duchess of Montagu and Marlborough and was reputedly made for Louis XIV.[37] A generation later another earl's daughter, Theresa Robinson, whose father was the first Earl of Grantham, married another John Parker of Saltram as his second wife. Her brother, the second Earl of Grantham, was ambassador to Madrid and was able to send back paintings, especially Murillos, to adorn Saltram.[38] These women had access to illustrious objects of aristocratic taste which their rich but provincial husbands were eager to acquire to add a civilised splendour to their houses, just as their aristocratic wives gave grandeur to their dynasty. The reverse process might occur. When, in 1784, James Dutton was made Lord Sherborne, he gave the objects in his possession aristocratic lustre by having his crest engraved on existing family plate and painted on the panels of his coach.[39]

Family pride was also apparent in a taste for old and unfashionable houses. Horace Walpole certainly commented upon them, despite the fact that his own father had built a brand new, fashionable Palladian palace which contemporaries seem to have regarded as an art gallery. Walpole realised that family pride was not only something to be found in new houses and new collections. When he visited Navestock in Essex, the house of his niece and her husband the second Earl Waldegrave, in c. 1759, he clearly considered it old-fashioned. It seemed to suggest the age of the Stuarts to him, with its 'French allees of old limes' and 'a deal of noblesse à la St Germain, James II, Charles I, the Duke of Berwick . . .' Its furniture he described as having 'an air seigneurial'.[40] In 1763, he described Drayton, the seat of Lady Elizabeth Germain, as where the 'old furniture and customs' have been 'kept up most religiously'. The house was in the 'most perfect order and preservation': indeed there was, he wrote, 'scarce a House in England so entire in the old fashioned manner'. What Walpole admired was antiquity but also a sense that an ancient estate was still locally beneficial and alive. He observed that Lady Elizabeth Germain was in the habit of 'spending the whole income in the neighbourhood', although 'she has seldom lived there above six weeks in the year' and that she had 'scarce ever carried a Shilling to London'.[41] By comparison, when he visited Knole in 1780, although he admired 'all its faded splendour' and 'enjoyed' its preservation, he noted that 'it wants the cohorts of retainers, and the bustling jollity of the old nobility to disperse the gloom'.[42]

Frequently the houses of great noblemen were spreading, grandiose piles, sometimes masking older work. At Grimsthorpe [9] Vanbrugh completed only the massive north front with its bold ringed columns and huge forecourt. This hid the fifteenth- and sixteenth-century house, although Vanbrugh intended to reform the interior quadrangle and add a corridor round three sides. Sir Roger Pratt had recommended courtyards as suitable only for great noblemen.[43] Quadrangles and courtyards were both regarded as fitting for the more princely aristocrats. Badminton in Gloucestershire

9] Grimsthorpe Castle, Lincolnshire, architect Sir John Vanbrugh, 1723–24. The view shows the north front and forecourt. The earlier, east side of the house is just visible to the right

10] Badminton House, Gloucestershire, showing courtyard form

[10] had an old courtyard plan, as did Woburn in Bedfordshire. Badminton was embellished by a number of architects during the eighteenth and early nineteenth centuries. Francis Smith of Warwick worked there in 1725 and James Gibbs provided a splendid entrance hall and rusticated pavilions two years later, the latter being remodelled by William Kent.[44] Pavilions and towers seemed to suggest the castles of the ancient nobility. Grimsthorpe had massive square towers as did Seaton Delaval in Northumberland by Vanbrugh.

33

11] Castle Howard, Yorkshire, architect Sir John Vanbrugh, 1699–1726. The south front

Castles need not look medieval – Castle Howard in Yorkshire [11], for example, did not. Vanbrugh, with his background as a playwright, might have shared with Claude Lorraine (1600–83) a rather seventeenth-century theatrical sense of the past and a determination to make use of it. Claude enjoyed putting Renaissance buildings in his Biblical pictures. The distant past could be alluded to without a need for absolute precision. Claude did not use Palladio, despite being drawn in that scholarly-architectural direction by his patrons, and whilst Vanbrugh, later in his career, showed greater awareness of Palladio, he was not wholly affected. The English, considerable collectors of Claude's works during the eighteenth century, enjoyed his dream-like assemblies of classical elements and forms, and also the painterly possibilities of architecture.[45]

12] Wentworth Woodhouse, Yorkshire, architect Henry Flitcroft, c. 1734–70. View of the east front

13] Hopetoun House, West Lothian, architect William Adam. View of east front, 1721–46

The Palladian idea of a country house consisting of centre block, wings and end blocks had enormous influence in England and was popularised by Lord Burlington, Colen Campbell and William Kent. Houses such as Houghton and Holkham, both in Norfolk, are major surviving examples of this style. This expansive manner of designing suggested the dominance of the owner of an estate and the superiority of his rank.

One of the longest recorded fronts is of two hundred yards, and was designed for the first Marquess of Rockingham at Wentworth Woodhouse in the West Riding of Yorkshire [12] by Henry Flitcroft (1697–1769) in 1734. It was almost as though Rockingham sought to enhance his rank with Flitcroft's east front, for he had built a lighter hearted, more decorative west front from 1725–35. The east front, the plans of which were submitted to Lord Burlington, had a large centre block, with lower wings of eleven bays, connected by convex quadrants to higher square pavilions with domed roofs and lanterns.[46] This was a huge undertaking which took forty years to complete. The scale was tremendous, and, as was often the case, references

14] Castletown, Co. Kildare, architect Alessandro Galilei, 1722

to Stuart grandeur were made in the interior, especially appropriate here as Lord Rockingham was descended from the royalist Earl of Strafford, beheaded in 1641. On the *piano nobile* was the Marble Saloon, forty feet high with a balcony in the manner of Inigo Jones's hall at the Queen's House, Greenwich. The State Dining Room was hung with Van Dycks and had great architectural magnificence, with its coved and coffered ceiling. The west range of interiors suggested Venetian vivacity, but the Saloon declared the authority and nobility of rank.[47]

In Scotland William Adam added a huge eastern front to seventeenth-century Hopetoun House [13] between 1721 and 1746.[48] As in the case of Wentworth Woodhouse, what he produced was more self-confident than the original building. The outlying pavilions were single storeyed and gave a feeling of a spreading powerful building which claimed the land it required in an assertive fashion. Irish country houses such as Castletown, Co. Kildare [14], designed by Alessandro Galilei (1691–1737) for William Connolly in 1722 and Russborough, Co. Wicklow, for the first Earl of Milltown, built in 1741,[49] spread in a similar fashion with low wings and colonnades. Both houses take up the land and both have a complex of yards associated with farming and land ownership behind them, in exactly the way that Palladio had intended his designs to work. *Barchese* or farm buildings were arranged behind colonnades on either side of the central landowner's dwelling, as at Palladio's Villa Badoer (1554).

There were other aspects of the great noblemen's house which were also intended to suggest his rank; for example, at Badminton, the Duke of Beaufort emphasised his royal descent from Edward III. The fleur-de-lys of France was part of his ducal arms. The scale of architecture was massive, with a huge City of London-scale church attached to one side of the house.[50]

Horace Walpole complained that the fourth Duke and Duchess of Bedford were too conscious of their exalted rank.[51] They employed Henry Flitcroft (1697–1769) to turn their current house into a quadrangular one, whilst repairing some of the monastery buildings which had historical value. In 1733 the Bedfords enjoyed an almost royal progress through their estates, which covered nine counties. Their house at Thorney in the Fens had also, like Woburn, been an ancient abbey, whilst Stratton in Hampshire, was regarded as a place to stay between London and Bath. Each house seemed an essential part of the local community, despite the absence of the proprietor for much of the year. At Thorney the village women cleaned the house for thirty-four days before the Duke and Duchess's visit. At Crowndale in Devon, another of their houses, the tenants, according to the Duchess, showed 'the great value they have for the Duke' and all welcomed him warmly.[52]

Rank was also emphasised in the interior by a grand entrance hall, sometimes suggesting medieval architecture, as at Seaton Delaval and Grimsthorpe; it was used for entertaining tenantry. This led to a central saloon, a magnificent, lofty and richly decorated interior for much of the eighteenth century, and flanked by state apartments consisting usually of antechamber or drawing room, bedchamber and cabinet.[53] By the 1740s this pattern began to become unfashionable. Gradually it became common, as at Houghton Hall in Norfolk, to have separate units, one for public use and one for private.[54]

The modified system of apartments accompanied a change of room use. At Stowe in Buckinghamshire, the Duchess of Buckingham's drawing room was formed from the state bedchamber. Nevertheless, rank must still have been apparent. The Garter emblem appeared in the Duchess's dining room at Stowe[55] and in various other houses, including the ceiling of the stone hall at Houghton. Such decoration was required as a background not just for works of art, which many rich connoisseurs could acquire, but for items of special status. Family portraits, suggesting lineage, were important and might suggest the proprietors' place in history. Lord Lyttelton's house at Hagley, designed by Sanderson Miller in 1757, contained a portrait of Charles I's children over the saloon chimney piece. Indeed the rooms here suggest a link with the refinement of the Stuart court as at Wentworth Woodhouse, having busts of Rubens and Van Dyck and a plaster relief by Vassalli of *Pan Winning the Love of Diana* after Maratti.[56]

Grand houses which emphasised rank were the setting of many quarrels over precedence. Charles Townshend noted that at a Hagley ball to celebrate the completion of the house in 1760 'Lyttelton had classed the company according to their birth and reputed estates into three divisions'. One of his kinsmen insisted upon dancing with a village girl 'unknown in her birth, equivocal in her character, and certainly at the very tail of my Lord's third division'. Before dinner had ended everyone was discussing their pedigrees and 'Bacchus's hall was turned into the Herald's office'.[57] The idea of rank had therefore to be suggested in various ways. The country house might be a spreading pile, often with separate apartments – within the house many mansions. Reference to older architectural styles might be made, indeed vestigial medieval features were sometimes found. Links with former royal dynasties, accumulated honours, titles and offices were frequently to be seen in the decorative features of the house.

PALACES

Despite the efforts of William Kent and John Soane, British monarchs never fully succeeded in commissioning a great palace during the eighteenth and early nineteenth centuries. Certain country houses can be regarded as rural palaces although there is no sharp distinction between great house and palace, nor is it really possible to define precisely what a palace might be.[58]

Yet some country houses seem to be monuments to great national heroes, great dynasties, or simply self-aggrandising individuals who decided to build or at least plan vast houses. They were bigger than most other country houses, often more elaborately decorated, more often visited, or remarked upon in journals, and they were more controversial, built with strain and difficulty, demolished, burned or abandoned as paper schemes. During the eighteenth century the term 'palace' was used to describe some of them whereas by the nineteenth century the great house had become gradually much too private for this term, with its public connotations, to be appropriate.[59]

Blenheim Palace [15] was the great Baroque monument of the early eighteenth century.[60] It was begun in 1705 and was the gift of Queen Anne to the nation's hero, the first Duke of Marlborough, who had been victorious over Louis XIV at the village of Blenheim on the left bank of the Danube. The Duke died in 1722 and the house was completed by Sarah, Duchess of Marlborough, at a total cost of £300,000, one-fifth of this sum being paid by the Churchill family.[61] Sir John Vanbrugh was the architect and had shown Marlborough, a fellow member of the Kit-Cat Club, a model of Castle Howard, and then provided the Duke with the plan for Blenheim. Vanbrugh was then appointed architect by the Lord Treasurer Godolphin, a post to which he was perhaps entitled, as Comptroller of the Queen's Works and a representative of a government which had endorsed this generous present to the Duke.[62] Marlborough wished to erect a monument for posterity commemorating the achievement of his armies. It was hardly surprising that he

15] Blenheim Palace, Oxfordshire, architect Sir John Vanbrugh, 1705–20. The north front

should wish to build a palace, for his whole upbringing at the Courts of Whitehall and St James's Palace had made him the consummate courtier.[63] He had spent some time in Berlin and Hanover and had presumably seen the royal palaces there. Throughout his life he eschewed consideration of popularity or unpopularity and concealed his feelings behind a smooth, dissimilating courtly exterior.[64]

Vanbrugh believed in finding an architectural vocabulary suited to the type of building being erected. Whilst churches should be in '. . . a plain but Just and Noble Style', other buildings might require 'many Divisions and Breaks' or 'such Gayety of ornaments as may be proper to a Luxurious Palace'.[65]

Everything about Blenheim was as magnificent as Vanbrugh and Nicholas Hawskmoor, whom he employed to work with him, could make it. It was a vast pile with great 'arms' or wings engulfing the land before it, to create a grand court in the manner of Baroque palaces in other parts of Europe and especially Versailles.[66] These wings contained, on the east side, a vast kitchen court, and on the west a stable court. On the whole the original plan was adhered to, except that a portico was added to the south front. The ringed columns and rather French channel horizontal jointed rustication, together with the influence of Elizabethan houses like Wollaton (Nottinghamshire) on the design of the corner towers and the heavy and elaborate skyline lend Blenheim an air of triumphant strength.

The Duke, as hero, was celebrated everywhere in sculpture at great expense. Grinling Gibbons was paid more than £4,000[67] for carving the important statues, urns and trophies in stone. Over the portico on the south side a thirty-ton bust of Louis XIV, captured at Tournai, adorned the parapet. On the eastern clock tower the British Lion savaged the French Cockerel, whilst the eastern gate leading to the kitchen court was designed with Tuscan pilasters on stone cannon balls. An English general's triumph over the might of France was intriguingly suggested by ducal coronets over reversed fleur-de-lys. In order to provide a ceremonial route to the palace a vast bridge with thirty-three rooms and Michelangelesque windows was designed by Vanbrugh.[68] A column of victory with a lead statue of the Duke was designed by the Earl of Pembroke in 1730 and erected in the park, suggesting the great hero at the centre of his world.[69]

The interior was equally monumental. The arcaded stone entrance hall, with a ceiling painted by James Thornhill in 1716 showing the *Glorification of the Duke of Marlborough* was the setting for great tenantry dinners, and shared, originally, a balcony with the saloon beyond from which musicians performed.[70] Thus the gentry and nobility could also be entertained as they sat in Laguerre's magnificently decorated room with its figures surveying the assembled grandees from a giant *trompe l'oeil* Corinthian arcade. Marble doorcases framed *enfilades* creating a sense of endless space totalling 300 feet. A long gallery, two storeys in height was created for the Duke's pictures, and he also commissioned tapestries of his battles from Judocus de Vos in Brussels. These, and various silver and gold cisterns and ewers[71] together with full-length royal portraits and Rysbrack's statue of Queen Anne, gave the house a feeling of monumentality. Its scale almost set visitors trembling; Lady Lechmere wrote in *c.* 1720 '. . . some parts of Blenheim were so vast in ye designs that tho' they were form'd by a man, they ought to have been executed by ye Gods'.[72] Mrs Clayton anxiously observed that since she had never possessed such a house she had never experienced '. . . those uneasinesses that I believe always attend great Grandeur'.[73]

Wanstead House in Essex [16], built for Sir Richard Child, might be regarded as a palace expressing the new taste for Palladian purity and as a monument to the new urban wealth which Lord Shaftesbury had felt would stimulate the arts in Britain. W. Watts described it as 'one of the finest elevations in the country', and observed that it had 'furnished Hints to succeeding Architects'.[74] Being near London it was much visited, and the careful bands of channel joint masonry and smooth ashlar as well as the hexastyle portico, the roof of which went right across the house, were a model to other country house builders. It became 'the resort of princes and the seat of most splendid hospitality'.[75] Sir Richard Child, grandson of a merchant's apprentice who had married a daughter of the Duke of Beaufort, employed Colen Campbell in about 1715. The architect produced three plans and it was the second design essentially which was built, although the angle towers which Campbell proposed were never added.[76] There were many descriptions of the house and numerous illustrations. It had magnificent formal grounds planted in Richard Child's grandfather's time '. . . on a barren spot as oft times *these suddenly monied* men for the most part seate

16] Wanstead House, Essex, architect Colen Campbell, 1715

themselves'.[77] Child was created Viscount Castlemain and the house was further enriched by William Kent, Casali and Nollekens but demolished in 1822 and its contents dispersed due to the family extravagance.

Cannons in Middlesex was begun six years after Wanstead, but was in a richer, more Baroque style. It was the work of James Gibbs, whose Scottish background led him, like many of his countrymen, to establish connections with Holland, from whence he travelled through Europe to Rome, eventually entering the studio of Carlo Fontana. Cannons was built for James Brydges, first Duke of Chandos, who had made a vast fortune out of being Paymaster of the Forces from 1705 to 1713. He seems to have been encouraged in his career by Marlborough and was favoured by George I who for rather obscure reasons made Brydges a duke in 1719.[78]

Cannons was a vast project. Chandos was advised by amateur architect Lord Bingley and John Price the elder took over from Gibbs. It was regarded as a palace by contemporary writers. Samuel Humphreys wrote of 'The rich Profusions of a Royal Mind'[79] and John Macky, who linked it to Wanstead, believed that when completed it would 'be inferior to few Royal Palaces in Europe'.[80] Indeed Gibbs's plan has been likened to the Pavillon du Roi at Marly.[81] The house was deliberately exposed to view and two fronts appeared from the distance to be one vast front of twenty-two bays. The south elevation, as revised by Price, was of channel jointed Portland stone, of two storeys and a dominant attic and the central five bays were formed by giant Ionic attached columns.[82]

Perhaps contemporaries were over-impressed by Cannons, which may in fact have resembled Stoneleigh Abbey in Warwickshire. However, it was certainly sumptuous and it formed a court almost like that of a foreign princeling. Even in 1718 the household consisted of eighty-three persons. There was the Cannons Concert of twenty-four performers (of which Handel was Kapellmeister), and Franscesco Scarlatti, the brother of Alessandro, was among its members. The musicians each had their own table in the dining room at Cannons. There was a librarian and a Chaplain and corps of Chelsea pensioners with little houses and stables with carriages from Paris and Amsterdam.[83]

A full programme of decorative painting was devised for the rooms, and James Thornhill, Bellucci and Laguerre, amongst other painters, were employed. The saloon was decorated by Thornhill, with figures of Apollo and the Muses, with Peace, Plenty, Temperance, Fortitude, Justice and Prudence.[84] Perhaps they corresponded with the statuary on the parapet on the exterior of the building, where such figures as *History* with a table and pen and *Fame* Sounding a Trumpet were placed.[85] Chandos acquired through the Africa Company, ebony and other woods from the Gold Coast, and wood from Jamaica as well.[86] Doorcases were made of marble or of walnut or lime-wood; locks, doorhandles, fire-backs and grates were made of silver.[87] Outside there were terraces, pastures, lead and marble statuary, canals, a

17] Prior Park, near Bath, architect John Wood the elder, 1735–48

wilderness, a fruit and vegetable garden and eighty-three acres of walled pleasure gardens.[88] Cannons only existed for a little over twenty years, being demolished in 1747.

Another great house on the edge of a city was Prior Park [17], influenced by the first design Campbell made for Wanstead and consciously an attempt to outshine it.[89] It was built on the outskirts of Bath by John Wood in about 1735. Wood was employed by the remarkable Ralph Allen for five years to advise those who might wish to use the stone from Allen's Combe Down Quarries. The house would 'exhibit Bath Stone to much greater Advantage, and in much greater Variety of uses than it had appeared in any other Structure' according to Wood in his *Essay*. It was to be a commercial venture and was to show the orders of architecture 'in all their Glory'.[90] Allen's customers would progress through Doric stables, an Ionic gallery, a Corinthian portico, and they would also be able to inspect pedestals and vases 'as specimens of such kind of Things to recommend the Sale of them'.[91]

The Corinthian order of the chapel was to be the most splendid, with cherubim and palm trees as part of the decoration to conjure up 'the manner in which King Solomon finished the inside of the Temple of Jerusalem',[92] although this was not actually completed. In fact much of what Wood described in his 'perambulations for the curious'[93] was never actually executed.

'Low born Allen' as his friend Alexander Pope called him, did not have aristocratic tastes.[94] He was a man of obscure Cornish origins who

18] Worksop Manor, Nottinghamshire, architect James Paine, 1763–67.
Painting by William Hodges, 1777

came to Bath and made a fortune by reorganising the national postal system. He made himself even richer by developing the quarries on Combe Down.[95] Allen may have followed his immediate superior, Lord Lovell, the Postmaster General, in building a grand house. Indeed, Lovell, who became Lord Leicester, was originally advised to have Bath stone for Holkham, begun at the same time as Prior Park, by Kent and Burlington.[96] That a newly rich man should imitate a superior, as perhaps Chandos also did in following Marlborough's Baroque grandeur, was understandable. Certainly Allen followed the advice of Alexander Pope when decorating and buying pictures for his house.[97]

In many respects 'the comfortless Palace of Prior Park'[98] was a monument to Allen's extraordinary enterprise as a self-made man but also to his undoubted qualities as (in popular eighteenth-century terms), the 'Benevolent Man',[99] generous, benefactor of the poor, and an entrepreneur. He opened a new quarry to provide work for the distressed, especially those whose misery was made greater by the harsh winters. Pope said in 1739 that he had passed Christmas 'with the Most Noble Man of England'.[100]

The rebuilding of the Manor of Worksop in Nottinghamshire [18] was an enormous project of James Paine's (c. 1716–89) for the Duke of Norfolk in 1763. Paine had already refurbished the interior of old Worksop in 1761 but this was destroyed by fire[101] and a huge new courtyard palace was designed. 'This most magnificent palace'[102] was a vast scheme closer to the

43

unexecuted projects by Inigo Jones, William Kent and William Chambers for palaces at Whitehall and Richmond for the Stuart and Hanoverian monarchies. The Palace of Worksop would have been the largest country house commission for more than fifty years, since Blenheim. Worksop was a monument to the premier English ducal family, the Howards, who had married into the Tudor dynasty, but now stood somewhat apart form political affairs because of their Catholicism. The palace was in the form of a huge block,[103] with four facades three hundred feet long and with two internal courtyards, separated by an Egyptian Hall, one hundred and forty feet in length. The scale of the rooms in the state apartments was impressive, with a Great Dining Room one hundred and twenty feet long, and a library two hundred and six feet long.

The Duchess was responsible, as she had been at Norfolk House in London, for planning some aspects of the decoration, and supervised much of Paine's work. She designed the fireplaces, invited Theodore de Bruyn, a Flemish painter, to decorate the staircase with panels of the Arts and Sciences, and was presumably responsible for the careful matching of wallpapers, upholstery and fabrics in the family rooms. She was also the designer of the ornamentation of the exterior, including the *Vision of Solomon* in the south pediment, as well as other decorative features associated with the Howards. A view by William Hodges shows the great house with an unexecuted triumphal arch and screen surmounted by a figure of the second Duke of Norfolk as the hero of Flodden. Thomas Howard, the Duke's nephew and heir-presumptive, died on the Grand Tour, and another nephew and heir also died suddenly, and so all work on the building was stopped at a stage when only one-third of the palace was complete.[104] This vast project is an example of the way in which the aristocracy took over from the monarchy as patrons of the arts, for no royal palace on this scale was contemplated at the time. In fact the royal scale of Howard houses was clearly appreciated by royalty, as Frederick, Prince of Wales, borrowed Norfolk House as his London palace. Thomas Sandby observed in 1774 that had Worskop been completed it would have been 'too large for any subject'. W. Watts wrote, '. . . this Palace, if it had been finished agreeable to the intention of the Noble Founder, would doubtless have been unequalled by any in the Kingdom'.[105]

As Marlborough had been offered a vast house and an estate at the beginning of the eighteenth century, so was the Duke of Wellington in 1817, when the realm bought the Stratfield Saye estate in Hampshire for him at a cost of £263,000.[106] Benjamin Dean Wyatt (*c.* 1715–1850), its architect, had been employed as private secretary to Wellington in Dublin. He began his architectural career in 1809 after ceasing to be the Duke's Chief Secretary.[107] His designs for a Waterloo Palace dated from 1814–18 and were to replace the existing house at Stratfield Saye. The palace would have had a domed centre block, with the imposing qualities of the Pantheon, an oval forecourt with a colonnade rather like Bernini's at St Peter's, and a central gateway. There were almost windowless blocks, decorated by attached columns. The early nineteenth century was a time when domed, rather tomb-like interiors were in fashion, and were often to be found in schemes by John Soane. The entrance hall of Waterloo Palace would have been high and arched with a coffered saucer dome and a cupola which would have lighted the hall below. The hall itself was to be decorated with an upper screen of Corinthian columns, battle pictures and a sculptural frieze and was to have a grand double return staircase.[108] In fact it was reminiscent of some of the public buildings of the Regency period, and has something in common with unexecuted schemes for a National Monument in Edinburgh to commemorate the Battle of Waterloo.[109] This grand design was not executed.

In the first thirty years of the nineteenth century there were to be several schemes for Greek Revival galleries, museums and colleges, especially in Scotland. The style was sometimes applied to domestic architecture, as at Grange Park in Hampshire in 1804 by William Wilkins, and at Belsay Castle, Northumberland, in 1807. However, Wellington's palace would have been rather more imperial in style, almost 'English-Empire'.[110] It would perhaps, have echoed Versailles, like Marlborough's Blenheim, as another instance of the victor copying the vanquished.

Wyatt was not the only architect who produced plans for a palace for the Duke. Charles Cockerell (1788–1863), archaeologist and scholar of Ancient Greece, also made designs for a 'Wellington Palace' [19] which likewise remained unexecuted. Cockerell placed his palace on a 'gentle elevation to

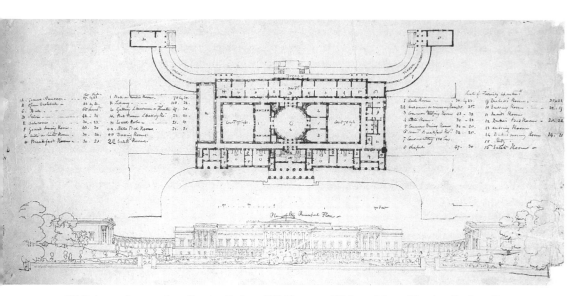

19] Scheme for a palace for the Duke of Wellington, 1816, architect Charles Cockerell

give greater grandeur to the situation and approach', something he felt that most country houses lacked. He gave the simple, grand design a central portico of eight columns derived from the Temple of Minerva at Athens and a second line of columns 'providing an extremely rich effect'. Like Wyatt he proposed a grand hall which would be monumental in character. There were to be statues of generals and officers 'most distinguished in the late wars' and between their pedestals a marble seat surrounded the wall. Above there was to be a frieze showing the principal actions of Wellington's battles and there were also to be fresco paintings of the main battles and portraits of heroes. The hall was to have a mosaic pavement patterned with the plans, fortresses and other subjects of the Duke's campaigns. In the centre of this hall, rather startlingly, was to be an open fireplace.[111] If we compare this to grand halls in earlier country houses, we see a new attempt to make antiquity serve contemporary life. Modern heroes adorn the room, whereas at Syon or Kedleston, the statuary was on the whole antique.[112]

Cockerell's father wrote to his son in 1816 warning him that such a project might not be worth his anxiety. He did not really believe that it would be possible to build a palace and maintain the hero in 'the Rank and State he is raised to'. It was natural to 'look to Blenheim for a suitable scale to work upon but such an Establishment', he wrote, 'would in this age swallow up above two thirds of the whole capital given by the public . . .'.[113] His prognostications proved to be correct: these great schemes were not executed, because although Wellington saw his estate as being potentially, as he said, 'a princely place'[114] he was not really interested in having a version of Blenheim.

A number of grand houses had been suggested as gifts to Wellington from the nation, before Stratfield Saye had been chosen.[115] These had included Uppark in Sussex and Houghton in Norfolk. It is significant that Wellington chose the simpler Hampshire house; perhaps because he had spent so much time campaigning, he preferred small-scale comfortable houses. At Stratfield Saye he installed hot-water heating and double windows, rather than spending £4,000 on gilding which the projected palace would have entailed.[116]

The Duchess of Wellington, used to Packenham Hall, her family house in Ireland, liked comfort, but visitors did not find either the refurbished Stratfield, or the Duchess agreeable. 'It is always cold there, and his wife is stupid',[117] wrote Princess Lieven, whilst acknowledging that Wellington found his house 'the most comfortable in the world'. She also thought the house ugly and the park barren.[118] There was a general feeling that it was not suitable for a great man. Sir Robert Peel who found it 'warm and not uncomfortable' thought it wretched and 'wretchedly furnished' and 'the drawing room very small and very low'.[119]

The early nineteenth century was a period of pride in urban elegance, with Nash's Regent Street and developments in Edinburgh's New Town. It was crescents and squares and city monuments which came to commemorate

20] Trafalgar (formerly Standlynch House), Wiltshire. Portico by Nicholas Revett, 1766

national heroes; the name Waterloo was applied to these, rather than to a palace, especially as the country house was becoming a more private place.

A dead hero provided a greater problem for the government than one who lived to be eighty-two. Nelson, unlike Wellington, could not be presented with a house. Rather unsatisfactorily, perhaps, the government decided to bestow the burden of dynastic heroism on his quiet clergyman brother who was created Earl Nelson and given Standlynch [20], a house and estate in Wiltshire. This was a 1730s house to which Henry Dawkins, one of the Dilettanti, had added wings and an imposing Greek Revival portico, four-teen columns wide (no doubt based on memories of his trip with Robert Wood to Baalbek and Palmyra in 1766), to the design of Nicholas Revett.[120] Standlynch was worth £90,000 and the Nelsons were presented with a per-petual pension of £5,000 a year, and £10,000 was to be set aside for repairs to the house, perhaps to make it more heroic.[121] In compliance with the terms of the will, the Earl renamed the house Trafalgar, but eventually abandoned it to his nephew and wife.[122] In a land where there were few magnificent royal palaces, the house as palace might be the dwelling of a remarkable public figure. He might be of as ancient and as splendid a dynasty as the one occupying the throne. It was possible for him to be a great military hero, or a new kind of man, unlike the great landowners in taste and background. He was often immensely rich even if only temporarily so, and his house might be of a more public kind in decoration, or it might pioneer a new style.

47

21] Antonio Pellegrini, *The Triumph of Caesar*, Kimbolton Castle, Cambridgeshire, 1711

THEMES OF INTERIOR SPLENDOUR

The interior of the great house of the early years of the eighteenth century was designed to impose upon the viewer a sense of the owner's status and personal magnificence. This was done through an elaborately decorated shell, making use of all kinds of Baroque *trompe l'oeil*, decorative effects which suggested the proprietor's knowledge of the antique, of mythology and some-times his role in national affairs.

This might be done through decorative painting. Mythology was fre-quently used to suggest the power and superiority of the protestant monarchy. Gerard Lanscroon was much patronised by the supporters of William III. At Powis Castle[123] he produced an apotheosis of the King, and he also worked at Drayton.[124] At Burley-on-the-Hill, Rutland,[125] in 1708, Lanscroon painted the *Life of Caesar* and Antonio Pellegrini depicted the *Triumph of Caesar* [21] at Kimbolton Castle in Cambridgeshire in 1711.[126] Again William was shown as protector of noble values, as Minerva points at him on the Kimbolton stairs. Perhaps James Thornhill's *Life of Achilles* at Hanbury Hall, Worces-tershire, of 1710 suggests William's heroic qualities as well. The proprietors

48

PLATE 1

Scone Palace, Perthshire. Drawing Room designed by William Atkinson in 1802. State portraits of George III and Queen Charlotte. Louis XV chairs with *chinoiserie* decoration by Pierre Bara

PLATE 2

Moor Park, Hertfordshire. The Hall, *c.* 1730–32

of these houses were making it clear that they, in inviting foreign Protestant princes to become Kings of England, were heroic too.[127]

Plasterwork might also be used to suggest political affiliation. At Cambo, in Northumberland, a team of Italian *stuccatori* was established in 1740 and its members worked at Callaly Castle between 1746 and 1757, possibly to the designs of James Paine. The saloon [22] which they created was a room of great richness. Medallions, possibly of George II and Frederick as Prince of Wales are placed to the right and left of the fireplace. Places of honour were left blank also, apparently for the Stuart Pretenders, by the Jacobite Clavering family who had commissioned the work.[128] The rather covert nature of their politics was further suggested by a false chimney flue in this room which was used as a priest hole.

Plasterwork might also have a mythological theme, through which family importance and political allegiance could be illustrated. The plaster could, of course, simply be inspired by details from a great temple or baths recently discovered.[129] Sometimes an engraving of a famous painting would be used as a basis for the plasterwork. At Clandon, Surrey, in 1730 Giovanni Bagutti and Guiseppe Artari used a print of the Carracci's Farnese Gallery ceiling showing Hercules and Iole.[130]

22] Callaly Castle, Northumberland, the Saloon, 1746–57

23] Ditchley House, Oxfordshire, *c.* 1725. The Hall

Even towards the end of the eighteenth century the celebration of dynasty was important. At Berrington Hall in Herefordshire, the heiress to the estate, Anne Harley, married Admiral Lord Rodney's son in 1781. As George Rodney was apparently to inherit the house, dolphins and seahorses were included in the frieze of the entablature on the staircase, and in the dining room were four putti and seahorses harnessed with blue ribbon – all in honour of the Admiral.[131]

Family magnificence was also apparent in projects to commemorate a Knighthood of the Garter. The Garter was found in various places in Guiseppe Artari's ceiling of the Stone Hall at Houghton, *c.* 1728,[132] and at Lumley Castle Francesco Vassalli was possibly the stuccoist who decorated a Garter Room there in 1730.[133] Massive plasterwork coats of arms were a feature of some halls, including that at Raynham Hall, Norfolk, *c.* 1730, attributed to Isaac Mansfield.[134]

Details of an ancient building might be produced in plaster or inspire a ceiling; or indeed other aspects of a room's decoration. Robert Wood's illustration of the Temple of the Sun (plate XIV from the *Ruins of Palmyra* (1753)) inspired the ceilings of rooms at Milton Abbey, Dorset, Drayton House, Northamptonshire, and Woburn Abbey, Bedfordshire, as well as the drawing room at Osterley.

Some rooms were an astonishing combination of features from ancient temples, plaster renderings based loosely on Baroque mythology and paintings or engravings from Cesare Ripa's *Iconologia*; emblems such as Britannia and military trophies suggested Britain's great power in the eighteenth century and love of national heroes.[135]

In the first part of the eighteenth century some rooms seemed to involve a number of different decorative effects. At Ditchley in Oxfordshire, by James Gibbs, most of the *stuccatori* working in England congregated in 1725 to work on the house for the second Earl of Lichfield. These were Francesco Vassalli (*fl.* 1724–63), the brothers Guiseppe (*d.* 1769) and Adalbertus Artari (1693–1751) and Francesco Serena (1700–*c.* 1730). The Hall [23] has an oval canvas on the ceiling of the Olympians by William Kent and the stuccoists produced grand reclining figures over the doorcases.[136] The chimney piece was also an ornate structure with two tiers and was carved by Christopher Horsenaile and Edward Staunton III.[137] Lichfield was a Catholic and so was his architect and the effect of this room is rich in incident even if it is produced in a somewhat staccato neo-Palladian manner, and in white and gold. It is difficult to analyse taste according to religious persuasion or political allegiance, although Roman Catholic patrons and architects had a greater opportunity, and inclination perhaps, to absorb the Catholic continental Baroque and use it at home.[138] At Moor Park in Hertfordshire,[139] a forty-foot cubic hall [plate 2] was executed for Benjamin Styles by a number of artists working under Giacomo Leoni (*c.* 1686–1746). This included four large paintings by the Venetian Jacopo Amigoni, stucco work by Giovanni Bagutti and some chiaroscuro decoration by Francesco Sleter to produce a rich and lively magnificence.[140]

Paulo and Filippe Lafranchini, born in Switzerland, came to Ireland in 1739 and appear to have introduced Baroque decoration in plasterwork. Carton, Co. Kildare, was remodelled in 1739 for the Duke of Leinster, and its Eating Parlour (now the saloon) [24] was given huge plaster figures representing the Courtship of the Gods, by the Lafranchinis.[141] They also worked at Russborough, Co. Wicklow, built like Carton by Richard Castle for the Earl of Milltown in 1741.[142]

Irish stuccowork was enormously exuberant but in Scotland there was, it would seem, a less lively manner in fashion before the advent of Robert Adam. His father employed Samuel Calderwood (c. 1689–1734) and Joseph Enzer[143] to work on a number of houses and together with Thomas Clayton they favoured martial trophies together with vases of flowers, urns, flower swags and cornucopia. Joseph Enzer also produced elaborate plasterwork [25] with a Jacobite message at the House of Dun near Montrose for

24] Carton, Maynooth, Co. Kildare. The Saloon, formerly the eating parlour. Paul and Philip Lafranchini executed the plasterwork of the ceiling depicting *The Courtship of the Gods*

25] House of Dun, Angus. The Saloon with plasterwork by Joseph Enzer,
1742–43

David Erskine between 1742 and 1743. The house, designed by William Adam,
was modest in scale, but the allegorical programme of decoration was highly
intricate involving allusions to European alliances as well as mythological
references.[144]

FRENCH TASTE

Palladio's architecture and the decoration of the Italian *stuccatori* were not the
only foreign influences on British interiors. The ideas of French architects

were transmitted through William Chambers who had attended J. F. Blondel's school of architecture in Paris. Some French architects also came to England; Pierre Patte was in London in 1768 and delivered a letter from Soufflot to Chambers.[145] Belanger came at the invitation of Lord Shelburne, returning to France with an interest in iron architecture and landscape gardening. Claude Nicholas Ledoux probably worked for Lord Clive at Styche in Shropshire.[146]

The influence of France on country house interiors was to be felt in different ways. It affected planning, and in 1725 Courtonne wrote of the 'new art of distribution' and J. F. Blondel expressed an interest in carefully worked out ground plans. Blondel also praised his contemporaries for the way in which they brought uniformity of design to a room and its furnishings, something which had 'aroused the interest of foreigners'. The French emphasised the importance of the *appartement de societé* which was to be used for entertaining family and friends. This was distinct from both the state apartments (*appartement de parade*) and the private apartments (*appartement de commodité*). The '*societé*' found favour in England, as increasingly reception rooms were required for entertaining, dancing, cards, collation and billiards.[147]

Robert Adam was instructed by Charles Louis Clérisseau, who had attended Blondel's Paris school. Robert was impressed by French planning; writing of Syon House, which he had remodelled for the Duke of Northumberland, he observed: 'A proper arrangement and set of apartments are branches of architecture in which the French have excelled all other nations: these have mixed magnificence with utility . . . and have rendered them objects of universal admiration'. To understand the art of living, it was necessary, he believed 'to have passed some time amongst the French . . .'[148]

French influence also affected decoration. Lord Burlington and the other Palladians had swept away much of the exuberance of the French Baroque. However, the influence of the lighter French Rococo was also felt in the embellishment of English country houses as well as their planning. The fifth Lord Baltimore had Rococo rooms at Woodcote Park and Belvedere, both in Kent. Some rooms at Woburn Abbey, Bedfordshire, were based on designs by Oppenord, and both Petworth in Sussex and Stratfield Saye in Hampshire had some rooms in a Rococo style. However, although English designers worked from French engravings to create rooms with white and gold *boiserie* and sheets of looking-glass, this style, so popular in France, was regarded as somewhat monotonous here.[149]

A taste for French luxury often came about through ambassadorial connections. The fourth Duke of Bedford was ambassador to France from 1762 to 1763, and brought back a Sèvres dinner service as a present from Louis XV.[150] The third Duke of Richmond, who was also the Duc d'Aubigny, was Ambassador Extraordinary from 1765–66. He brought back whiteground Gobelins tapestries depicting scenes from Don Quixote after Coypel, which were set in the tapestry drawing room at Goodwood in Sussex by Chambers.[151] The second Earl of Mansfield, who had been an attaché at the British Embassy in Paris in the 1750s and became Ambassador Extraordinary in 1772,[152] brought home Chinoiserie needlework panels. The fifth Duke of Argyll similarly ordered a set of Beauvais tapestries, *Les Pastorales*, after J. B. Huet's designs in 1784 for Inveraray Castle, Argyllshire.[153] Tapestries were a traditionally grand way of furnishing a room and were reminiscent of the castles of peripatetic feudal barons.

The 'bespoke' tapestry room was much in favour in expensive English interiors in the 1760s and 1770s. English buyers could visit the Gobelins works where there was even a model interior which showed the possibilities of such a room. Six tapestry rooms were created in England for Sir Lawrence Dundas, the Earl of Coventry, at Croome (1766–71), William Weddell at Newby (1766–71), Sir Henry Bridgeman at Weston Park (1766–71), Robert Child at Osterley (1775–81) [26] and the Duke of Portland at Welbeck, Nottinghamshire (1783).

Tapestries had been used extensively in bedrooms; now they were used for sitting rooms and their sale boosted the failing Gobelins factory, stricken by the Seven Years' War. These tapestries, which depicted subjects like the *Love of the Gods* by François Boucher, were devised by Soufflot and Maurice Jacques with the English market in mind. Although Rococo in some respects, they were often used, as at Newby in Yorkshire, with Neoclassical

26] Osterley Park, Middlesex. The Tapestry Room, 1773–81

plasterwork, and furniture.[154] Both William Weddell at Newby, with his Adam sculpture gallery and tapestry withdrawing room and Robert Child at Osterley with his Etruscan room and tapestry boudoir, were connoisseur-magpies, plucking out the most unusual modish interiors which indicated their cosmopolitan tastes.[155]

Another way of enlivening the interior was through the use of colour, often, from the 1750s to the 1770s, combined with Neoclassical ornament derived from ancient buildings. The Baroque rooms of the early eighteenth century depended on elaborate plasterwork and mythological decorative painting, but also upon carving and the use of fairly sombre colours sometimes combined with marbling or occasionally actual marble. These dark colours can be seen in the conversation pieces of William Hogarth and Arthur Devis.[156]

The neo-Palladian emphasis on simplicity led to the introduction of whites, creams and stone colours with much gilding.[157] The state rooms at Houghton were richly gilded, especially the Saloon, while the Stone Hall, with its paler creamy austerity, provided a prelude. The Marble Hall at Holkham, based upon Vitruvius's description of an Egyptian hall combined with the qualities of a Roman basilica by William Kent, was also in creams and veined buff marble.

Within the interior of the great house there tended to be a progression towards greater richness of colour and texture, whereas in circulation areas plainer, cheaper paints were used. Saloons were supplied with hangings, those at Houghton [27] being of cut velvet of rich crimson from Utrecht. Dining rooms too, like the Rococo one at Saltram, Devon, were given rich fabric wall hangings, this example having red velvet. Cabinets and closets were frequently very small but richly appointed, for example the Cabinet at Felbrigg [plate 3] with its crimson wall hangings was specifically designed as a picture room by James Paine in 1751.[158] Rich hangings in silk or velvet gave texture to a room, as did tapestries.[159]

By the 1750s bright colours began to be introduced into country houses.[160] The cool simplicity of some neo-Palladian rooms had usually meant that ceilings were painted white. However, William Kent in the cabinet at Houghton produced a coloured ceiling with a new emphasis on antique decoration.[161] This was taken up by James Stuart and Robert Adam.

Adam in *The Works in Architecture* (vol. 1) had claimed to have 'introduced a great diversity of ceilings, friezes and decorated pilasters, and have added grace and beauty to the whole by a mixture of grotesque, stucco and painted ornaments . . .' This 'beautiful variety of light mouldings' had replaced the 'ponderous compartment ceiling' and 'tabernacle frame' of the neo-Palladian.[162] Although Kent and Stuart had really been the pioneers in the application of the antique motif, Adam certainly popularised it and produced a series of startlingly elegant varied interiors in the 1760s and 1770s.

His earliest coloured, antique inspired, ceiling design was for Lady Scarsdale's dressing room in 1760 at Kedleston [plate 4]. Here his work was

27] Houghton Hall, Norfolk. The Saloon, *c.* 1728

influenced by the Palace of Augustus in Rome in both the dressing room and in the grotesque work on the dining room cornice in 1762.[163] The inset paintings by Antonio Zucchi in the corners were of the *Four Continents*. William Hamilton painted the *Four Seasons* and Henry Robert Morland painted *Love Embracing Fortune* in the centre.[164] At Syon House too he produced a design based on the House of Flora in Rome.[165]

To begin with Adam had experimented with the darker colours which appeared in illustrations of surviving Roman decoration.[166] Only at Harewood in 1765 did he begin to use the pastel colours, such as greens, pinks [plate 5] and occasional straw areas, which are popularly associated with his style. It has been suggested that his choice of a lighter range of colours, not obviously antique in spirit, might have been inspired by the writings of Edmund Burke,[167] who analysed Beauty as something which was delicate and had diversity. Clearly the 'picking in' of different light colours in Adam's work was in line with these theories.[168] Laugier's ideas concerning contrast in architecture may also have affected Adam.[169]

The pastel colours were to be found in a number of interiors including the Music Room at Harewood (1765–71), the ceiling of the Tapestry Room at Osterley (1772) and in the design for the Eating Parlour at Headfort

28] Kedleston Hall, Derbyshire. The Dining Room, architect Robert Adam, 1760

House, Co. Meath in Ireland (1771–72).[170] The colours were typically combined with swags, urns, twists, ribbons and anthemions; these formed raised plaster motifs on ceilings, but also in apses or friezes as in the dining room at Kedleston [28] and sometimes in wall panels as in the Eating Parlour at Headfort.

As with neo-Palladian houses the scale and type of decoration and colour varied. Large-scale and bold, rather martial trophies derived from Piranesi were used in the hall at Osterley and the ante-room at Syon House, Middlesex (1761). Flatter, more refined intricate decoration was used in the Red Drawing Room Ceiling and in the Gallery at Syon. The Red Drawing Room [29] with its coved ceiling, inspired by the Villa Madama in Rome, was a room for the ladies, or 'salle-de-compagnie, as it is called by the French',[171] Adam noted. The Gallery, with its closets at either end for china and miniatures respectively, was designed 'to afford greater variety and amusement'.[172]

Drawing rooms tended to contain elaborate decoration or pieces of furniture which could be admired in detail. The doorcases at Syon with sunken central panels in the early Renaissance style are fitted with gilded lead ornaments and the chimney piece has applied ormolu decoration by

Matthew Boulton, and at other houses there were fireplaces of equally intricate composition.[173]

The pale pinks and greens remained fashionable for some time, although by the 1780s the interest in intricate ceilings had waned and by the 1790s they were being repainted white.[174] Pinks and greens, although not archaeologically correct when applied to antique style decoration, may have been one aspect of Rococo lightness and luxury which continued until the end of the eighteenth century. They were also to be found in china, especially cups, saucers and teapots and in clothing, on women's dresses and, for example, men's waistcoats,[175] and may possibly be regarded as an aspect of variety in design of which Adam was a promoter.

There were occasions when in order to produce an impressive interior Adam emphasised unity and harmony of design. In 1774 he gave the drawing room at Osterley [30] a facelift to bring it in line with the state rooms. The ceiling, based on the soffit of the Temple of the Sun from Robert Wood's book *The Ruins of Palmyra* (1753) may originally have been painted white and gold in 1765, but was coloured to correspond with the newly-hung pea green damask when the room was remodelled in 1772. Adam also designed, in 1774, the floral 'mosaic' carpet made at Moorfields by Thomas Moore to be in the spirit of the pattern on the ceiling.[176] The chimney piece

29] Syon House, Middlesex. The Red Drawing Room, architect Robert Adam, 1765

had sphinxes supporting vases of flowers and the panels over the doors with medallions supported by griffins were added to correspond with the chimney piece. They were coloured to match the ceiling and a Greek anthemion frieze in a repeating pattern of arcades was also introduced.

Sometimes, however, Adam seems to have chosen discord, to give a more startling and memorable quality to the rooms he designed. The Red Drawing Room at Syon had Spitalfields damask which was chosen by the Duke and Duchess of Northumberland before the elaborate ormolu decorated fireplace was planned. As the ceiling in this room was so positively decorated in the manner of Raphael's Villa Madama, it might be felt that the hangings detract from the beauty of the room. However, this may be to misunderstand the nature of diversity in Adam's work where these very different elements might possibly represent a rich and exciting balance.[177]

Classical decoration became richer and darker at the beginning of the nineteenth century. Archaeology, a search for historical accuracy, and a greater knowledge of antique remains, led to Pompeiian and Gothic interiors being attempted. George Dance's Stratton Park, in Hampshire, had a Hall of Commemoration which, according to his drawings, was intended to have green faux-marble walls and pilasters also painted to resemble yellow-grey and white veneer marble. Here, apparently, Pompeiian and Egyptian works

30] Osterley, the Drawing Room, architect Robert Adam, *c.* 1772

31] Pitzhanger Manor, Ealing, Middlesex. The Breakfast Room, architect
Sir John Soane, *c.* 1802. The original decorative scheme was restored to the
room in 1986

were being imitated, although the direct influence came from Parisian Neoclassical taste. The Breakfast Room at Pitzhanger Manor at Ealing [31],
designed by Soane for himself, is a square room with saucer dome and
painted dark green marbling bordered by imitation blue-grey marble. There
were bronzed caryatids and a sky painted oculus.

The Gothic, too, produced a taste for darker, more intense interiors with
graining, heraldic devices and spots of colour from painted glass in windows.
Some of these effects could be found at Fonthill and Eaton Hall although the
principal rooms at Eaton were richly red and blue, rather like First Empire
colour and almost like the military uniforms of the Regency period.[178] The
country house interior, it will be seen, could express, through painted Baroque
mythology or intricate plasterwork, political achievements and allegories as
well as dynastic connections. French taste in the interior might suggest luxury
and sophistication, or sometimes the diplomatic career of the owner who had
collected objects as well as ideas whilst abroad. The influence of France was
one of high fashion, however; as we have noted when discussing rank, there
was sometimes an allusion to past aristocratic habits. Tapestry, for example,
was often from France in the eighteenth century; it had formerly been a movable kind of luxury and therefore echoed the habits of the feudal itinerant
nobility who moved from castle to castle, carrying their comforts with them.

Colour, often dark at the beginning of the century, became brilliant or pastel with the advent of the Rococo and continued so during the earlier part of the Neoclassical period. Only gradually did it conform to what was known of the antique interior or indeed the Gothic one, becoming richer or more sombre.

THE IDEA OF AGE

Country houses and villas built in the eighteenth century were intended to be new, fashionable and smart. Patrons sought, on the whole, sharp incisive stonework, brilliant rich colours, gilding that glistened in candlelight, and sumptuous Genoese velvet or Spitalfields silk. Old houses, if they were not demolished or abandoned, were drastically refurbished. Old styles, the architecture of Roman, Greek or even Goth, might be admired, but enjoyed as a source of inspiration. The patron built what he needed afresh, sometimes in loose imitation of what he had seen mouldering away in Italy.

Some architects were more sensitive to historical significance and to the association of ideas as they related to architecture. Vanbrugh pleaded for the preservation of the old manor of Woodstock at Blenheim because 'it was rais'd by One of the Bravest and most Warlike of the English Kings' and also because 'That Part of the Park . . . has Little Variety of Objects . . . therefore Stands in Need of all the helps that can be given'.[179]

Many patrons too, had a variety of historical interests. The Duke of Montague was a friend of the antiquarian William Stukeley who wrote of him in 1749: 'We had exactly the same taste for old family concerns, genealogy, pictures, furniture, coats of arms, the old way of building and gardening . . .' It was to Montague that the architect Batty Langley (1696–1751) dedicated his *Ancient Architecture Restored* in 1742.[180]

Despite an interest in the architecture of the past, architects seem barely to have distinguished between old and new. The Painted Breakfast Room at Kedleston, designed by Robert Adam in 1760 and extended by Agostino Brunias, was described in 1769 as 'finished with antique ornaments, after the Baths of Diocletian'. Yet Adam could write of it to his brother James as 'quite in the new taste'.[181] Syon might, as Adam wrote, 'be executed entirely in the antique style',[182] but its Saloon (unexecuted) could still be described as 'new and singular'.[183]

Adam was both archaeological and inventive. He drew and studied ancient Roman buildings such as the Baths of Caracalla, but he wanted to make something new from the old. He wrote to his brother James, 'I am to show the Baths in their present ruinous condition and from that to make other designs of them as they were when entire and in their glory . . .'[184] He saw himself as an innovator who had 'not trod in the path of others', only, he said, 'among architects destitute of genius and incapable of venturing into the great line of their art, [was] the attention paid to those rules and proportions . . . frequently minute and frivolous'.[185]

British architects and patrons came to enjoy Gothic and medieval castellated styles: gradually asymmetrical houses, whether medieval or Classical in inspiration became an aspect of picturesque variety in the late Georgian period.[186] Horace Walpole was a leader of taste in his appreciation of the Gothic. His Strawberry Hill at Twickenham, begun in 1749, was full of medieval associations. He wrote of 'gloomy arches' and described his house as 'so monastic'. It was in fact like the novel he wrote, *The Castle of Otranto* (1765), and reminiscent of a dream he described having in 1764: 'I had thought myself in an ancient castle (a very natural dream for a head filled like mine with Gothic story) . . . I saw a gigantic hand in armour'.[187]

Walpole had 'advanced' taste: most owners of houses still expected that their principal seat would be Classical.[188] Only if they were altering an ancestral house did they build or refurbish in the Gothic or castle style. James Paine was commissioned to reconstruct the keep [32] of Alnwick Castle in Northumberland in 1754. Paine did not alter the castle as much as later restorers, but he had little sympathy for its age: indeed he attempted to give the building symmetry by moving one of the towers of the curtain wall, and making storeys fit into a conventional Palladian arrangement of basement, *piano nobile* and attic.[189] Robert Adam designed seven interiors at Alnwick mostly in the Gothic style in the 1760s. All this work was done for

32] Alnwick Castle, Northumberland. The Gatehouse and
Keep, remodelled by James Paine in 1754

the first Duke and Duchess of Northumberland, who lived 'by the etiquette of the old peerage'[190] and wished to make clear, in architecture, that the blood of the ancient Percy family ran through their veins. Adam expressed their lineage for them by designing walls panelled with 'the whole pedigree of the Percys made out, showing them to be descended from Charlemagne'.[191] Yet the light columns, brittle decoration and mixture of Classical and Gothic forms did not really suggest age, or an old family, merely a use of the ornament of the past. Contemporaries made no distinction between old and new in their descriptions of the castle. W. Watts wrote in the 1770s, '. . . the present Duke and late Duchess . . . immediately began the necessary repairs, and with great taste and judgement restored and embellished it as much as possible in the style it had originally been, so that it may truly be considered as one of the noblest and most magnificent models of a great baronial castle'. He used the word 'ancient' three times, and spoke of 'dark dungeons' and 'original horror' despite Paine's efforts to regularise the castle.[192]

The Percys had inherited Alnwick, but the first Lord Milton bought his ancient pile and proceeded to tidy up its fabric with the help of several architects including John Vardy and Sir William Chambers. Horace Walpole described Milton as 'the most arrogant and proud of them, with no foundation but great wealth and a match in the Duke of Dorset's daughter'.[193] Chambers, the century's greatest classicist, designed in *c*. 1771 a regular symmetrical house with Tudor Gothic details.[194] Chambers swept away the village which had clustered around the original church. The old hall was retained as was the church itself. Again Watts saw little difference between the real old building which had been destroyed and the new, very rectangular, Georgian Gothic. He noted that Lord Milton had 'raised the present beautiful structure . . . in a Form expressive of its Name and former Application, and in a rich Style of Architecture corresponding to the venerable church'.[195]

Gradually although new Gothic was still produced in a rather flat and brittle form, it was invested with literary, philosophical and even political overtones. Like Horace Walpole, William Beckford (1760–1844) the author of *Vathek*, created a new Gothic house for himself. This was the soaring Fonthill Abbey in Wiltshire [33] created by James Wyatt (1746–1813) between 1796 and 1807. Its central octagon was intended to rival Salisbury Cathedral's spire in height, and it gave the house a feeling of the sublime. When entertaining Lord Nelson at Fonthill, Beckford tried to inject a medieval atmosphere into the reception for this great national hero. Like a stage set the architecture was enhanced by music, dramatic contrasts of light and shadow, and soldiers in armour carrying torches and moving across the parkland like minor characters in a lavish opera. The newness of the medieval walls was given character and patina by the deep shadows and lantern light.[196] Not only was Fonthill sublime, but there was an attempt to simulate age in a way which such writers as Uvedale Price had identified as characteristics of the picturesque.[197]

33] Fonthill Abbey, Wiltshire, architect James Wyatt, 1796–1807

At Arundel Castle in Sussex the eleventh Duke of Norfolk restored the structure in 1806,[198] in a mixture of perpendicular Gothic and Norman, which he associated with ancient liberty.[199] The foundation stone was dedicated 'to Liberty asserted by the Barons in the reign of John'. The theme of paintings, sculpture and stained glass has Liberty triumphing over monarchical autocracy. J. C. Rossi sculpted in the Coade stone 'King Alfred instituting trial by jury on Salisbury Plain'. The Great Norfolk Window in the Baron's Hall depicted *King John being forced to sign Magna Carta by the Barons*; the barons were, in fact, portraits of the Duke and his friends.[200]

Aristocrats at the beginning of the nineteenth century saw their houses as symbols of their old power which was threatened by the middle classes at home and by revolutionary ideas from abroad. Many aristocrats had, however, taken advantage of lucrative bourgeois enterprise such as coal mining, urban development and banking, and they were often enormously rich. A castle could be built with self-confidence, mingled with a certain nostalgia for the feudal power which was ebbing away.

James Wyatt remodelled Belvoir Castle in Leicestershire [34] for the Duke of Rutland between 1801 and 1813 and when it was refurbished after a fire, it became not only a symbol of medieval power but of the power and glitter of absolute monarchy.[201] Louis XV boiseries were bought in Paris and the general decoration seemed to have been inspired by Versailles.

William Porden (*c.* 1755–1822) designed Eaton Hall in Cheshire [plate 6] for Lord Grosvenor between 1804 and 1812. He chose the Gothic style because it helped in 'preserving that distinction to Rank and Fortune, which it is the habit of the age to diminish'. '. . . With regard to splendour', he added, 'it is far superior'.[202] Prince Puckler-Muskau, visiting England, and country houses especially, noted that 'everything is in the highest degree ultra aristocratic'.[203] He did not, however, admire Eaton, of which he wrote in 1827, 'In this chaos of modern gothic excrescence, I remarked, ill-painted modern glass windows and shapeless tables and chairs, which most incongruously affected to imitate architectural ornaments. I did not find one single thing worth sketching.'[204]

However, the new taste for asymmetrical country houses at the beginning of the nineteenth century allowed for variety that was 'infinite'[205] as Porden had suggested. Just as the architecture had become irregularly picturesque, so the furniture was now arranged informally in the centre of rooms rather than against the walls. Such informal arrangements and variety of architectural shape and planning denoted a more relaxed way of life. Even at older classical houses this seems to have occurred. Creevey, staying at Goodwood in Sussex in 1828 noted, 'There are quantities of visitors in the house many of whom, of course, one knows, as brother dandies. They are scattered about in the Libraries, Billiard Room, Hall and Drawing Room'.[206] Such informality allowed people to walk around the house almost as though it were a public place. Creevey noted of the hall at Goodwood that it '. . . has very handsome pillars in it, but they don't crowd it and darken it as they do

34] Belvoir Castle, Leicestershire. Principal architect James Wyatt, 1800–25

at Lowther, Thorndon, Wentworth, Raby. They are not in the way and it is a charming room or place to walk about in . . .'[207] Walking about seems to have been an English habit. As Puckler-Muskau observed, there was a delightful custom '. . . for men at English balls. After the conclusion of a dance, each takes his partner on his arm and walks about with her till the next begins'. This allowed a man 'time to conquer his timidity'.[208]

Castles in Ireland imparted a sense of age, rank and authority, especially at the beginning of the nineteenth century when a concern for coronets and Norman surnames was at its height.[209] Indeed James Wyatt, Francis Johnston, 'Capability' Brown and Thomas Hopper all played a part in turning back a 'Dutch Artisan Mannerist' style house, Slane, into a romantic version of the Pale fortress of Norman times.[210] The pediment and cupola of 1700 were removed and battlements introduced. Hopper, the Prince Regent's architect, designed a splendid Gothic Ballroom [35] for the Marquess of Conyngham, whose wife was 'Prinny's' mistress. John Nash built Lough Coutra Castle, Co. Galway for Lord Kiltarton[211] in 1811, arranging towers and castellated blocks in a picturesque fashion brought out so well in the many prints of distant romantic piles popular with travellers. Sometimes advancement in the peerage prompted reconstruction in castellated form. When the nineteenth Earl of Ormonde became a Marquess in 1825, William Robertson was commissioned to rebuild Kilkenny Castle on a larger scale.[212]

35] Slane Castle, Slane, Co. Meath. The Ballroom, architect Thomas Hopper, 1812

36] Seton Castle, East Lothian. Architect Robert Adam,
1789–91

In Scotland Robert Adam introduced his highly original castle style in the 1770s, and it was adopted by his successors, men such as John Paterson and Richard Crichton who continued to use it into the Regency period. The castle style was not necessarily intended to be wholly romantic and combined classical and medieval features, some of them like bartizans and crow-stepped gables, elegantly echoing the rude tower houses of the lairds who were ancestors of the polite aristocracy and gentry of late Georgian Scotland.[213]

In fact such houses had classical and medieval characteristics inter-woven in a skilful synthesis which came close to creating a new architec-tural vocabulary. There were a few large castles, such as Culzean in Ayrshire, built for the Earl of Cassillis in two stages between 1770 and 1790 with, as was common, an emphasis on orderliness and inside an urbane classicism derived from circular and apsidal spaces. Elsewhere, however, as at Seton Castle (1789–91) [36], Adam designed smaller fort-like castles for less aristo-cratic clients with classical, Romanesque and Scottish vernacular features.[214] Although Culzean was asymmetrical by the time Adam completed it, he seldom actually built castles as sublime or wildly rambling as those which

67

appear in some of his sketches of aged structures.[215] Indeed in his 1785 north elevation for Culzean he understated the height of the cliff upon which the castle stood, creating a very calm scene.[216]

Eighteenth-century Scotland witnessed a tension between the rationalism of the European Enlightenment and a yearning for its own national historic culture. This produced the cool Neoclassical architecture of Adam and the later Greek Revivalists as well as the sentimental Jacobitism of Robert Burns – Adams's own castles seem to combine the spirit of both.[217] It will be seen that for much of the eighteenth century most owners, except for a few connoisseurs, enjoyed what was new in architecture, and expected their main seat to be classical. Ancient families, proud of their lineage and inheriting a medieval castle, might repair it without too much regard for its ancient fabric, since patina was not highly regarded. Gradually, the medieval style came to suggest atmosphere, aristocratic authority, and their asymmetry led to greater informality of life within the country house.

VILLAS

Retreat from the city

The houses so far discussed have been large ones. The smaller house or villa was very common in England especially after about 1750. Charles Middleton writing in 1793 classified villas into three types: first, 'as the occasional and temporary retreats of the nobility and persons of fortune'; second, as 'the country houses of wealthy citizens and persons in official stations which also cannot be far removed from the capital . . .'; and third, as 'provincial hunting seats or the habitations of country gentlemen of moderate fortune'. They had to be compact rather than as extensive as a country seat.[218]

Perhaps the most characteristic villa which the mind can conjure up was that based directly upon the work of Andrea Palladio himself. Colen Campbell's Mereworth (1723), Lord Burlington's Chiswick (1725), and houses similar to it, were all derived from the Villa Rotunda at Vicenza. They were all richly decorated and small in scale. Such houses tended to be places of retirement, although not exclusively so; they were often luxuriously fitted out, and designed for entertainment.[219]

Such villas were often near cities and London's wooded environs, especially the banks of the Thames, were studded with them. The most famous of these villas was Lord Burlington's at Chiswick, which he built in 1727, and attached to his existing late Tudor house. The latter was demolished in 1788, when two wings were added to the east and west of the villa. This was 'a complete and desirable residence',[220] not simply a place to hang pictures, and after Lord and Lady Burlington had given up their court appointments in 1735, it became their home in the south.

Chiswick[221] had an impressive central domed octagonal saloon with rectangular suites on three sides. It was richly decorated with, on the west front, the Red and Blue Velvet Room and the Red Closet. William Kent provided historical and mythological ceiling paintings, and perhaps the richest of his rooms was the Blue Velvet Room. It had a heavy ceiling with an allegorical scene of architecture and may have served as a Grand Cabinet for Burlington where his close friends could congregate. Perhaps it copied the famous *Chambre Bleue* of the Marquise de Rambouillet (1588–1663) at the Hotel de Rambouillet which she remodelled for her literary soirées.[222] Certainly Chiswick had a large library in the rustic.

The Thames-side villa was a favourite of politicians and literary figures. Before Burlington's activities as an architect had begun, James Gibbs designed a villa for Alexander Pope at Twickenham in 1719. Dawley, some distance from Twickenham, was remodelled in an Antique fashion rather than a strictly Palladian one for Henry St John, Viscount Bolingbroke, a Tory minister of Queen Anne, in 1728. It was to be 'a Ferme ornée' with, as Bolingbroke wished, a 'country hall [painted] with Trophies of Rakes, Spades, Prongs &c' and 'all the Insignia and Instruments of Husbandry'.[223]

There were many splendid villas built for successful professional men and merchants: Carshalton House was built for a rich tobacco merchant, Edward Carleton, at Salton in 1714; Mount Clare at Roehampton [37] for George Clive, a banker; and Eagle House, Mitcham, was the home of Fernandez Mendez, physician to Catherine of Braganza. These houses were not at the centre of great estates; they were not 'squirearchical' but elegant and sometimes plainly decorated residences for men who might have a house in the City of London but who wished for the fresh air of the country close at hand.[224]

There was a carefree, boisterous atmosphere around many of these Thames-side villas. William Hickey remembered as a small boy in 1756 sitting on his godfather's knee at Sir William Stanhope's villa which had been Pope's property. Watching Sir William, Lord Cholmondeley (Hickey's grandfather) and Lord Carhampton quaffing claret in the garden, young Hickey said he wished to be a man 'that I might drink two bottles of wine everyday'.[225] Hickey observed Thomas Hudson, the portrait painter, with his 'uncommonly low . . . stature . . . [and] prodigious belly . . .' resting all his weight on his walking stick which Hickey kicked away and sent poor Hudson tumbling. The boy Hickey was sternly rebuked but gradually forgiven.[226]

The habit of building and refurbishing villas continued in the later Georgian period. Sir John Soane had definitive views about villas and discussed them in his Seventh Lecture, stressing the importance of seclusion from the city and from intrusion of callers.[227] He remodelled his own villa, Pitzhanger Manor at Ealing, in *c.* 1800–3 with a new facade reminiscent of the style of the Bank of England, and a fitting introduction to his collection of pictures, Etruscan vases and casts from the Antique.

In other parts of the United Kingdom, villas outside cities were also important.[228] Edinburgh's accommodation, until the building of the New Town in 1769, was largely in the spine running from the Castle to the

37] Mount Clare, Roehampton, 1770

Palace of Holyrood House, and since this Old Town was insanitary in the summer months, the desire for a villa outside its malodorous confines was natural. Inveresk and Morningside were considered healthy and suitable. Whilst Viscounts Tarbat and Dundas were grandly housed at Caroline Park and Melville Castle, later in the period Sir Walter Scott spent his summers at Barony House, Lasswade. In the summer games were played and gardens inspected and aristocrats mingled with lesser gentry and ambitious lawyers.[229] The merchants of Glasgow also invaded the countryside around their city, often setting their villas in ornamental woods.[230]

The influence of the villa on the great house

Sarah, Duchess of Marlborough, unappreciative of Vanbrugh's genius, preferred simple houses to the grandeur of Blenheim. Of Windsor Lodge, which she loved, she wrote, 'I have everything convenient and without trouble'.[231] Holywell, her house in Hertfordshire, she would never part with, despite its being ordinary. She liked houses which were 'strong, useful and plain'.[232] The Baroque gesture of the bridge at Blenheim led her to observe that 'Tis time to put a stop to such maddnesse'.[233]

The formality of early eighteenth-century life in country houses, like Blenheim, began to disappear. Baroque houses and Palladian ones such as Wanstead or Wentworth Woodhouse had sets of apartments, including bedrooms and dining rooms on either side of a central hall and saloon, running along the principal front of the house. The owner of the house usually had his own apartment and so did his wife. However, there were no state apartments at Houghton or Ditchley[234] and gradually the double circuit plan, with rooms arranged around two staircases, as at Holkham, became fashionable. The influence of the compact villa was felt on the architecture even of the great houses[235] – the family seat. Architects such as James Paine and Sir Robert Taylor had begun to devise large elegant villas in the 1750s. Taylor's villas such as Harleyford, Buckinghamshire (1755) described as a convenient house[236] were usually arranged around a central staircase which was top lit. Although classically proportioned, such houses were often astylar, with a centred bay and they were set in a commanding position with excellent views.

James Paine (1717–89) and Isaac Ware (d. 1766) also produced designs for villas in the 1750s. Paine's Gosforth Hall, Northumberland, was built for Sir Charles Brandling[237] on a site north of the Tyne and in more pleasing country than the old family house in Felling on the south banks. When it was completed in 1764 it was the largest of the villa country houses built. Although Gosforth had wings and end pavilions, the main house still functioned as a compact unit with main rooms distributed around the staircase and on the *piano nobile*. Stockeld Park (1758–63)[238] in Yorkshire was a villa of great originality with bold triple pediments. It was a typical villa plan with a very grand central staircase and principal rooms on the ground floor [38].[239]

Paine's compact villas still gave a sense of the building spreading in the landscape. In Ireland the same desire to contain the main rooms in a single unit, but give movement and presence to the house, was apparent from the middle of the century. At Florence Court, Co. Fermanagh, David Ducart was probably responsible for adding arcades and pavilions to the 1730s house in about 1770.[240] These mark simpler service blocks and courts. Despite maintaining very grand Dublin houses, many country gentlemen were living in uncomfortable older tower houses in the 1750s.

Some minor gentry families were prudent enough to realise that they could not afford both a grand Dublin house and a wholly new Palladian country one. After the death of Edward Lovett Pearce and Richard Castle there were no architects of similar status to take over.[241] However, lesser architects could give Palladian grandeur to older unprepossessing houses with the addition of curtain walls and end pavilions to suggest a spreading, dominant effect, as at Rathbeale Hall, Co. Dublin.[242]

GENDERED SPACES IN THE COUNTRY HOUSE

The Duchess of Marlborough's hostility towards Vanbrugh's schemes for Blenheim were based upon a dislike of heroic architecture. Heroism was for field-marshals and generals, and it led, in architecture, to discomfort. This might lead one to wonder whether areas of the country house were designed for women who seldom had a role as national warriors or even political figures. Did architects design parts of houses in a style considered appropriate for women?

Vanbrugh's architecture emphasised masculinity and this seemed to be the way he viewed it himself. This is despite the fact that at Kimbolton Castle in Huntingdonshire, it was Lady Manchester, whose husband was in Venice, who asked Vanbrugh's advice. Vanbrugh was all for massive display in his scheme.[243] 'I'm sure this will make a very Noble and Masculine Shew' and later he wrote of the exterior that people would 'See a Manly Beauty in it when tis up . . .'.[244]

When French habits of planning began to lend greater comfort and subtlety to the country house, Robert Adam did make some distinction between rooms for men and those for women in his designs. At Syon he remodelled the gallery 'in a style to afford greater variety and amusement; and it is, for this reason, an admirable room for the reception of company before dinner and for the ladies to retire to after it'.[245] The little closets, one for china and the other for miniatures at either end of the gallery also suggest a space for women to retire to. These small rooms and the gallery were separated by a drawing room from the eating room, and this, as Adam observed 'prevents the noise of men from being troublesome'.[246] Adam, however, seems to have given less privacy to the Duchess of Northumberland's dressing room, making

38] Stockeld Park, Yorkshire, the south front. Architect James Paine, 1758

it an integral part of the circuit of rooms of parade, whereas the Duke's private apartments formed a separate unit with access by private staircase.[247]

The idea of a first-floor boudoir may have been of some importance for women. At Heaton Hall, Lancashire, the Dowager Lady Egerton had a dressing room in the Pompeiian style in the 1770s [39], designed by James Wyatt, who also created the Etruscan Room at Heveningham in Suffolk. It was decorated with a pattern of triumphal arches, embellished with *grotteschi* on paper panels fixed to the pilasters. The furniture originally consisted of gilt and painted sofas and chairs, torchères, window seats and a circular carpet. Biagio Rebecca painted the dome of the dressing room with allegorical subjects – the outer area showing *The Virtues* and the inner *The Elements*. *Sigismunda Weeping over the Ashes of Tancred* (a symbol of virtuous widowhood) was placed over the fireplace and symbolised the widowhood of Lady Egerton, wife of the sixth baronet.[248]

Warren Hastings's wife Marion had a first-floor boudoir at Daylesford in Gloucestershire[249] which was splendidly enriched and like the Duchess of Northumberland, she had a collection of Worcester, Wedgwood, Derby and Dresden porcelain.[250] Another circular boudoir was designed for Attingham, Shropshire, in the Louis XVI taste by George Stewart in the 1780s. It was probably painted by Louis-André Delabrière, who worked at Southill in Bedfordshire as well, and its decoration has been likened to the arabesque work

39] Heaton Hall, Lancashire, Lady Egerton's Dressing Room, 1772

73

of the Rousseau brothers in the Queen's *cabinet de toilette* at Fontainebleau of 1785. Such small-scale richly subtle rooms as these for women suggest something of the intimacy of villa architecture transported to the great house.[251]

COMFORT AND ASYMMETRY

Many of the grand country houses and villas which have been discussed were dramatic pieces of architecture of great presence in the landscape, and with richly decorated interiors. Even if small, they were often exotic and fanciful. However, some houses were essentially built for comfort and convenience or simply altered to suit the new owner. By the early nineteenth century such ideas were becoming more important to architects and affected the development of Victorian middle-class taste.

Some eighteenth-century industrialists were keen to develop their estates to make fortunes for themselves, but might well have a house on the site near their works. They did not necessarily regard industry as ugly and to be kept separate from their domestic life. Responding to the great demand for Queen's Ware, Josiah Wedgwood bought the Ridgehouse Estate[252] and began to build a large manufactory on the banks of a proposed canal. The grounds were laid out with the advice of Capability Brown who, through his patron Lord Gower at Trentham Hall, became interested in using Wedgwood's jasper ware tablets for fireplaces.[253] Wedgwood laid out a village for the workers of his factory which he called Etruria in honour of the Ancients,[254] and Wedgwood also built Etruria Hall for himself in 1770. The Wedgwood family had a number of other houses in the vicinity. Josiah had, for a time, rented Ivy House in Burslem from John and Thomas Wedgwood who themselves lived in the Big House erected in 1750 next to the earthenware factory in Burslem.[255]

The third Duke of Bridgewater, who built the canal named after him from his estates at Worsley to Manchester, had extensive properties and business interests in different parts of England and Wales.[256] Eventually he decided to build himself a new hall at Worsley in the classical style. This was on the edge of a ridge so that he had good views over the canal from his windows. James Brindley, his engineer, had free board and lodging at Worsley Hall for some time.[257]

A view which provided a mixture of ancient buildings and modern industry seems to have been appreciated. Watts, writing of Hooton Hall in Cheshire, house of Sir William Stanley, observed, 'Very few Villas can boast of a situation comparable to Hooton . . .' The Mersey river ran close to the house, '. . . and all vessels trading from Liverpool to Warrington, Manchester and the Duke of Bridgewater's canal pass in full view of the House. The Principal towers and spires of Chester can be seen'.[258]

Busy statesmen and national heroes also enjoyed convenient houses which were not necessarily architecturally striking or stylishly decorated.

The Younger Pitt bought Holwood House in Kent in 1785. It was a small early seventeenth-century brick lodge and Pitt did little to alter it at first although he made additions later. Altogether there were six bedrooms and five more in the back quarters as well as garrets and servants' quarters. Downstairs was a dining room, drawing room and study – the latter hung with Gillray's prints. Although small, the service quarters included still room, dairy, laundry, coachmen's room, grooms' room and two bedrooms over the stables.[259] Pitt could accommodate a small party of friends and some of them came to watch him work with great enthusiasm on his land. Lord Melville reported to Lord Wellesley in 1806: 'Often have I seen him working in his woods and gardens with his labourers for whole days together undergoing considerable fatigue, and with so much eagerness and assiduity, that you would suppose the cultivation of his villa to be the principal occupation of his life.'[260]

Lord Nelson enjoyed a similarly simple life at Merton Place, Surrey [40], which he bought in 1801. Merton, or 'Paradise Merton',[261] as Nelson called it, was seven miles from London. It had a Palladian north front with central pediment and wings which had been built in the early eighteenth century. The main entrance was on the east side, where there were the bow windows of the dining room and drawing room. A free planted lawn surrounded the dining room. Inside there were plenty of glass doors to make the house light and two large drawing rooms, a dining room, a library, five bedrooms with dressing rooms, eight servants' rooms, excellent cellars, a detached dairy and an ice house. There was a pleasure garden, greenhouse, kitchen garden, an orchard and paddock – in all twenty-two acres.[262] Nelson seemed to revel in the suburban ordinariness of his life at Merton. He wrote to Emma Hamilton in 1800: 'To be sure we shall employ the trades people of our village in preference to any others in what we want for common use . . . Have we a nice church at Merton?'[263] His neighbours included James Perry, the editor of the *Morning Chronicle*, who lived at Wandlebank House; Abraham Goldsmid of Morden Hall and Benjamin Goldsmid of The Grove.

40] Merton Place, Surrey, altered by Lord Nelson, *c.* 1801

The Goldsmids were bullion brokers, brothers who commuted every Monday morning from the comfort of the Home Counties to their offices in Fenchurch Street, in the City.[264]

By the end of the century architects were designing and publishing books about small, compact houses which seem like the semi-rural paradises that Pitt and Nelson had contrived for themselves. One example of this was Seton Castle, Tranent in East Lothian (see [36]), designed in 1789 by Robert Adam for Alexander Mackenzie of Portmore. Mackenzie was a lieutenant in the Twenty-First Dragoons and was only twenty-two years old when this Adam castle-style house was completed. It had some traditional Scottish features such as a crow-stepped gable, which took the place of a pediment, and a rather sophisticated classical entrance with a fanlight that might have been found in the New Town of Edinburgh. Adam provided Mackenzie with a drawing room, dining room, principal bedroom, two dressing rooms and smaller bedrooms in the main house. He gave the house a wonderful curving forecourt and in the courtyard buildings designed a dairy, laundry, slaughterhouse, hen house, stables, sculleries, kitchen, business room and butler's room. The house was self-sufficient, compact and a combination of Neoclassical and Neo-medieval features, in a synthesis which was new – a new domestic vocabulary.[265]

In Ireland Richard Morrison (1767–1849) published in 1793 *Useful and Ornamental Designs in Architecture*. He, too, designed country houses in modified Neoclassical, Neo-Gothic and Neo-Tudor styles. Morrison designed five types of house from 'Parsonage or Farmhouse' (costing £762) to grandest villas which were 'A Temporary Residence for a Nobleman whose Principal Residence is in England'. His proposed villa or country house, which cost £1,100, was suitable for a country gentleman of modest means and was to be found all over the Irish countryside. The basement contained the kitchen, servant's hall and cellars. The ground floor had a study and breakfast parlour off the square hall to left and right, and at the back were longer identical rooms, a dining room and a drawing room. There were seven bedrooms on the first floor and seven garret rooms for servants above that, with windows in the valleys to light them.[266] The 'Parsonage or Farmhouse' combined something of the Palladian notion of hiding the wash house and stables behind, in this case very short wings, with Adam's sense of practical self-contained, small-scale design.[267]

Regency design was often exuberant, and there were also huge serene Greek houses like Belsay [41] in Northumberland, which were like vast temples. There was, however, a rather virtuous, even straightlaced quality about the attempts of Sir Robert Smirke (1781–1867) and Charles Cockerell (1788–1863) to plan new classical country houses in a style often shorn of Greek Revival characteristics.[268] The moral virtues of the classical age were emphasised and morality and sensible restraint seemed to go hand in hand. Charles Cockerell was sure, he said, that 'Temples were never adopted to

41] Belsay Hall, Northumberland, architects Sir Charles Monck, Sir William Gell and John Dobson, 1810–17

Houses' and that 'space and commodiousness' were the objects of the domestic planning of the Ancients.[269] Smirke fulminated against luxury which was bad for the character, he claimed, as an 'excess of ornament is . . . the symptom of a vulgar and degenerate taste'.[270]

'The New Square Style of Mr Smirke',[271] as Pugin called it, was expressed in an unadorned, practical plan for Whittinghaeme, East Lothian, where accommodation was divided up into several self-contained areas. Although the ground floor was composed of long public rooms, there was a separate family wing; James Balfour and his wife each occupied their own dressing and sitting rooms off a shared bedroom, above which were day and night nurseries and another bedroom. The house was well supplied with water closets and Lady Eleanor Balfour had a fixed bath as well.[272]

John Dobson (1787–1865) of Newcastle also designed well-planned country houses and villas for the gentry, manufacturers and professional men of the north-east. At Longhirst (1828) in Northumberland he designed a splendid sandstone house [42] with a stone oval hall, stair and galleries, surmounted by a coffered stone dome [43]. The masonry had a beautiful severity and precision about it which almost suggested superior cabinet making. However, the feeling of classical restraint was tempered by a love of smooth bows, with low windows, linking, in typical Picturesque fashion, an asymmetrical house with its garden.[273] Dobson was critical of certain architects such as Vanbrugh and Paine who did little, in a practical way, to make

77

42] Longhirst Hall, Northumberland, architect John Dobson, 1825

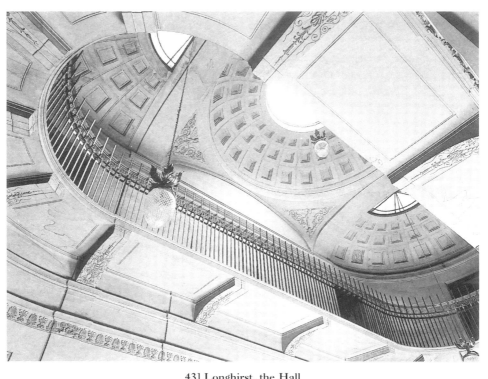

43] Longhirst, the Hall

houses comfortable. Vanbrugh's Seaton Delaval was so cold that visitors told Dobson they always needed an extra cloak.[274]

THE TASTE OF THE NABOBS

The employees of the East India Company seem to have favoured very lavishly decorated houses and often quite unusual ones. Robert Clive, whose family had been gentry from the south-west,[275] was particularly keen to acquire land and eventually owned estates in Monmouthshire, Radnor, Devon and Shropshire. He was interested in agricultural experiment and presented prizes to his tenants for their turnips and cattle. Okehampton, his estate in Devon, also provided him with an extra seat in Parliament.[276]

Claremont in Surrey [44] was Clive's most lavish estate. 'This Villa', wrote W. Watts, 'has received from Nature and Art such liberal Advantages as have brought it the nearest to perfection of any in this kingdom.' It was, he continued, '. . . an Instance where great Expense has produced Grandeur, Convenience, Firmness, Delight and Enjoyment'. Like many new villas it was 'Happily designed and situated, as to command fine views from the four Fronts',[277] and replaced Vanbrugh's old house, which stood on low ground. Lancelot Brown was the architect and work began in 1769.[278] The main body of the house, a rectangular block, was built of white brick with a Portland Stone Corinthian portico, balustrade and window surrounds. It was simple and elegant in style with an emphasis on practicality and luxury

44] Claremont, Surrey, architects Lancelot Brown and Henry Holland, 1769

within a compact plan. The basement service rooms and kitchens had a wide area around them so that they were light and airy, and the principal rooms, as in many villas, were arranged around a central staircase hall. Henry Holland also worked on the interior of Claremont and the painter Benjamin West was consulted about the decoration of the Eating Room. This was to contain the paintings of Clive's career in India which would have made it, had it been executed, an extraordinary room for its period. West was to have filled it with vast canvases of battles, treaties, scenes of the Far East, all to be framed with gilded plasterwork.[279] Clive had everything that was fine and practical elsewhere in the house. There were water closets, and an immense grey marble sunken bath which had taps and pipes. Clive's collection of deer, antelope, different kinds of Cape geese, Guinea hens and large Cyrus birds were kept in the parkland by the newly raised fence, which locals claimed kept the devil from seizing this wickedly rich man.[280] Clive owned five other houses, but on the whole he had little time for Palladian grandeur. Claremont had no colonnades or pavilions, and it was certainly not a palace. The aristocracy judged men like Clive harshly: 'General Clive is arrived all over estates and diamonds',[281] reported Horace Walpole. He was critical too of Clive's choice of pictures referring sarcastically to him as one of 'those learned patrons of taste . . . Lord Clive or some Nabob'.[282]

Thomas Rumbold, Clive's ADC at Plassey in 1757 also built himself a stylish house in the way of rich nabobs. Thomas Leverton (1743–1824) designed Watton Wood Hall (now Woodhall Park), Hertfordshire (see fig. 4) between 1777 and 1782, for Rumbold who was Governor of Madras by 1778. Leverton worked in the Adam manner and employed Joseph Bonomi, their pupil, as his assistant. Woodhall had much Neoclassical decoration in the style of Adam and Wyatt as well as a splendid print room, for which a plan exists. Rumbold's widow sold the house to another nabob, Paul Benfield, in 1794, who added three large rooms, but he became bankrupt in 1801, after which the house was sold to a banker, Samuel Abel Smith. Its slim vertical proportions gave it a metropolitan air and judging by its purchasers, it was considered a modish, rich man's dwelling.[283]

Warren Hastings, too, had a considerable taste for fine luxurious houses. Like Clive, he was of minor landed stock, but by 1715 the family estate had been sold off and the manor house demolished.[284] Hastings was determined to regain the family estates at any price. He reacquired Daylesford in Worcestershire (now Gloucestershire) with only 650 acres (1785), but he began to buy back land around it at inflated prices. Hastings employed Samuel Pepys Cockerell (c. 1754–1827) to build him a new house between 1790 and 1796.

Cockerell, who became the East India Company Surveyor[285] in 1806, had built Sezincote near Daylesford for his brother Charles, a retired East India Company official, which was much influenced by Indian buildings.

PLATE 3

Felbrigg, Norfolk. The Cabinet, architect James Paine, 1751

PLATE 4

Kedleston Hall, Derbyshire. The Painted Breakfast Room. Design for the ceiling, 1760, architect Robert Adam executed by the artist Agostino Brunias. The room was dismantled in 1807

Sezincote was modelled directly on drawings made in India. Daylesford, however, was much more English looking and like Claremont, a luxurious house. Hastings had built himself a splendid house at Alipore in India in the 1770s, and also owned eight paintings by William Hodges, who published *Travels in India* in 1793.[286] At Daylesford the grounds were laid out in the fashion of those at Alipore. Cockerell designed a dome for Daylesford and an elongated pinnacle. The interior of the house was richly decorated in silver and crimson, with 'oriental alcoves' and in the basement, an Eastern gaming room. Thomas Bankes provided the fireplaces in the early 1790s and the one in the west drawing room was decorated with Indian women as caryatids returning from the Ganges. Bankes also adopted harem life as the subject matter of the central panel of the chimneypiece.[287] Hastings furnished his drawing room and library with ivory furniture from India which he described as 'not designed for fat folks or romps'.[288] He also had a collection of Mughal miniatures in these rooms. His Persian silver chain armour was hung on the library walls, and his European paintings, including a Rembrandt and a Correggio, hung in a separate picture room.[289] Like Clive he was inclined to illustrate his exotic life: he owned Johann Zoffany's painting of *Colonel Mordant's Cock Fight at Lucknow* and William Hodges's painting of a terrible storm which had wrecked Mrs Hastings's boats on a rock at Calcutta. Hastings, like Clive, had the latest modern sanitary arrangements, including Joseph Bramah's water closet.[290]

Those returning from India continued to bring wonderful objects home. Prince Puckler-Muskau noted in 1826 that he had seen '. . . the sale of an Indian Cabinet, the property of a bankrupt Nabob, which contained some curios and beautiful works of art'.[291]

Sir Charles Cockerell, for whom Sezincote [45] was remodelled, had made a fortune in the East India Company and wished to become a country gentleman at home. Thomas Daniell, the Indian topographical artist, who had considerable experience of Indian architecture, helped Cockerell, and Humphrey Repton advised Cockerell about the park.[292] The architecture, through Daniell's advice about details perhaps, was convincingly Mogul rather than Hindu, and all was executed in an orange-stained stone which was intended to resemble that of India. The house had a copper onion shaped dome, but the interior of the house was classical, just as the Adam-style castles in Scotland of this period often had classical interiors. As at Daylesford, the planning of the house was unusual, with the principal reception rooms on the first floor and the family rooms on the ground floor.

The taste of the nabobs was of a fabulous nature. It was almost as though England seemed too quiet and faded on their return. When the Marquess of Wellesley came back to England, the reception at Portsmouth was polite but it was a great change from the solemn pageants of the East. He was apparently a very public man who found it difficult to establish a domestic life for himself. Despite the arduous sea trip out to India, made

45] Sezincote House, Gloucestershire, architect Samuel Pepys Cockerell, 1805

worse for Wellesley by his being a bad sailor, he had insisted upon the pomp of office. 'He dresses for dinner as if he were at home', *The Morning Chronicle* noted, and the frigate he sailed in was packed with his carriages and accoutrements.[293]

This taste for the exuberant was to be enjoyed in India and brought to Regency taste, at home, the raffish variety of Empire. William Hickey wrote that 'Lord Wellesley was in no way sparing with the Company's cash.[294] His lordship's own embellishment of servants' equipages etc, were extravagant in the superlative degree, not only in point of number, but splendour of dress.' He had had ideas of embanking the River Hooghley on the Calcutta side in the style of the Adelphi or Somerset House and building himself a palace.[295] English eighteenth-century aristocrats could rarely resist the temptation, whether in Britain or abroad, to become princelings, and Wellesley was greatly disappointed, on his return, that a dukedom was not created for him.[296]

THE LUXURY COTTAGE

Rich men could afford variety from nabob orientalism to the Royal Pavilion. Beckford enjoyed both the Turkish and the Gothic styles.[297] All these broke from the formality of classicism and curiously another such break was a taste for cottages – almost a rejection of nouveau riche luxury.

In Ireland the younger sons of minor gentry frequently resided in cottages. Lord Lisle's kinsman William Lysaght, wrote in his journal, 'In 1749 I built a pretty little thatched house at Clogheen, a parlour, kitchen, cellar, dairy and little hall, three lodging rooms over and garrets'. This little house in County Cork was humble by English standards, even though its owner was connected by marriage to Lord Blakeney, the Governor of Minorca, as well as other members of the gentry. Edmund Burke, son of an attorney, was brought up in a thatched cottage in County Leitrim.[298]

The cottage in Ireland might have had a shabby genteel quality, but it was hardly the chosen abode of the rich. The cottage in England might well be very grand like the Prince Regent's.[299] Wales, the Wye Valley and the Peak District of Derbyshire were favoured places for *cottages ornés*. However, the Isle of Wight and various seaside places also saw the development of the marine villa [46]. The south coast of the island, known as Undercliff, seemed to combine elements of Picturesque variety and Sublime grandeur. In 1770 the Governor of the island, Sir Hans Stanley MP, built Steephill, with white walls and roofs of thatch, and thatched bay windows. These houses were very luxurious and Rousseauesque in their provision of a retreat. Steephill was inherited by the sixth Earl of Dysart and had everywhere 'the appendages of junket and good living'.[300] John Wilken's Sandham Cottage, leased in 1788, had a fashionable canvas pavilion, providing extra accommodation for entertaining and was decorated as an Etruscan Room filled with Etruscan vases.[301]

46] The Isle of Wight, the southern coast. The view shows the Earl of Yarborough's villa, Captain Pelham's cottage and Steephill Castle. Engraved by G. Brannon, 1843

47] Chiswick, Middlesex. The main front begun in 1725

Sir Richard Worsley built Sea Cottage as an alternative to his Baroque seat Appuldurcombe Park which housed his collection of Greek sculptures and other objects of virtu. The small house was used as a refuge from public life after Sir Richard had resigned from Comptrollership of the Royal Household rather in the way that other public figures such as Burlington and Bute found solace in building after their retreat from public appointments. Worsley kept his principal collection at his main seat, whereas Burlington, on the other hand, always regarded Chiswick [47] as the perfect place, where he could embellish his garden, entertain his friends and ultimately house his cherished possessions. The country house could therefore be a building of many guises, a place of unadorned carefree retreat, or an exquisite box of private aesthetic and intellectual delights.[302]

THE COUNTRY HOUSE, ARCHITECTURAL PROFESSIONALISM AND THE SPREAD OF TASTE

At the beginning of this chapter the convivial relationships between architect and patron were discussed. However, there were frequent and sometimes violent quarrels between the two. Out of this acrimony a new architectural professionalism was born, and because the architect had a more recognisable and public role, the opportunity to allow an ever wider audience to see new styles arose. The quarrels could persist for many years. The first Earl of Fife commissioned William Adam to design Duff House in Banff in 1730 but considered himself greatly overcharged and halted building, leaving his house unroofed for nine years. Lord Fife was so angered by Adam that he drew down his carriage blinds when he passed Duff, and the case was only settled, in Adam's favour, in the Court of Session in Edinburgh.[303]

John Gwynn believed that patrons had little understanding of architectural procedure and this led to serious problems. Although it was too much to expect 'that every Person of great Fortune should be a practical Surveyor', he wrote, to 'plan his own Estate and draw . . . the . . . Elevation of his own Mansion' would give 'satisfaction and Delight'. Patrons he considered, would only be properly informed if chairs in the fine arts, including architecture, were established at Oxford and Cambridge.[304]

As matters stood at the beginning of the eighteenth century, some patrons imagined that they could dispense with an architect altogether, despite their meagre knowledge. Sarah, Duchess of Marlborough, who had quarrelled with Vanbrugh, wrote in 1732 that she knew of no architects who were 'not mad or ridiculous'. 'I really believe', she added, 'that anybody that has sense with the best workmen of all sorts could make a better house with no architect . . .'[305]

Architects were therefore much dependent upon the goodwill and condescension of potential patrons, there being few other opportunities of advertising their skills. In 1761 George Dance met the Duchess of Bridgewater, Sir George Lyttleton and Mr Pitt (nephew of, as Dance recorded, 'the Great Minister'). He reported to his father, 'they received me very politely and Mr Pitt, who is a great Lover of Architecture desired me to make him a Drawing of the famous Gallery at the Colonna Palace'.[306]

Despite friendships formed on the Grand Tour, the architect's commission was often uncertain and he might find himself no longer in command of work at a country house where he had been superseded by a new favourite. The first Lord Scarsdale employed at Kedleston in the 1750s, Matthew Brettingham, James Stuart, James Paine and Robert Adam, each producing elaborate schemes, some of which were ultimately rejected.[307]

Friendships and family connections between architect and patron could not always be relied upon to cement a businesslike partnership, although they might be important. Sir John Vanbrugh, a distant relation of the first Duke of Ancaster, formed a friendship with him and eventually became the architect of Grimsthorpe, although his scheme remained incomplete.[308] Colen Campbell, looked to the second Duke of Argyll as a patron for, as he wrote, '. . . it's my greatest Honour, to receive my Blood from his August House'. Clan loyalty seemed to have little effect, however, and it was to James Gibbs that Argyll gave his patronage, the architect designing Adderbury and Sudbrooke for the Duke in the 1720s.[309]

The architects' status improved gradually. The establishment of the Royal Academy in 1768 was important in developing academic training but also in allowing for the exhibition of drawings.[310] Many designs for country houses were exhibited at the annual exhibitions of the Society of Artists and the Free Society from 1760 to 1778; these and drawings of country houses shown at the Royal Academy between 1769 and 1799 amounted to 324 in number compared with 99 for different types of public building.[311] Thomas Sandby, the first Professor of Architecture at the Royal Academy, noted, in 1794, that the 'perspective view is much more Picturesque than a Geometrical Elevation and will show its parts to better advantage'.[312] Interiors particularly looked realistic, as three-dimensional views, which showed the atmosphere of rooms much better than the earlier flattened models.[313]

The Copyright Act of 1735 had encouraged the spread of decorative Rococo print.[314] Increasingly, during the eighteenth century expensive folio works by architects such as those of Robert Adam, published at first in parts during the 1770s,[315] not only established the status of the architect, but displayed his skills and spread ideas about the design of country houses and of the individual items of which they were composed, such as fireplaces, doorcases and furniture.

During the 1780s English paper mills began to be developed successfully.[316] This permitted the spread of pattern books as well as allowing the architect to produce endless drawings and gain a firm and direct control over any building project. Between about 1780 and 1815, very large numbers of pattern books spread ideas about designing in the Greek, Roman, castellated and Gothic styles. Four new books alone came out in 1807. Whereas in the earlier period major architects of country houses, such as Gibbs, Paine or Adam had published works to establish their status and spread their style, in the late eighteenth and early nineteenth centuries the important men, such as Wyatt, Holland, Dance, Nash and Smirke no longer felt the need to promote themselves in this way. However, minor architects tried to make their reputations through books. These architects, men such as Robert Lugar or Robert Mitchell produced many designs for smaller houses, 'within the reach of moderate fortunes' as Soane observed. Indeed his own *Plans, Elevations and Stations of Buildings*, published in 1788, was for the gentry rather than great noblemen.[317]

Professionalism, new ideas and expertise were also spread through the developments of large offices after 1750 by Chambers, Adam, Robert Taylor, Holland and Dance. Ten architects worked for Chambers at different times, twenty for James Wyatt, and the Adam brothers had the biggest architectural practice in Britain with offices in London and Edinburgh.[318]

Concepts of heroic grandeur, a sense of dynasty, expressions of extreme wealth, a growing taste for elegant comfort or a romantic feeling for history – all might govern the architecture of country houses in the period under consideration.

NOTES

1 Howard Stutchbury, *The Architecture of Colen Campbell*, Manchester University Press, Manchester, 1967, p. 21.

2 J. D. Stewart, *Sir Godfrey Kneller*, G. Bell and Sons Ltd, London, 1971, Appendix IX, pp. ii–xviii.

3 Toby Barnard and Jane Clark (eds), *Lord Burlington Architecture, Art and Life*, The Hambledon Press, London, 1995, p. 163.

4 James Lees-Milne, *English Country Houses: Baroque*, Country Life, London, 1970, p. 12.

5 Giles Worsley, *Classical Architecture in Britain: The Heroic Age*, Yale University Press, London, 1995, pp. 258–9. Stuart's first Grecian motif in England was derived from the Hellenistic Aqueduct of Hadrian at Athens used at Nuneham in the form of windows.

6 John Harris, *The Palladian Revival: Lord Burlington, His Villa and Gardens at Chiswick*, Yale University Press, London, 1994, p. 31.

7 Howard Colvin (ed.), *The Country Seat: Studies in the History of the British Country House*, Allen Lane, The Penguin Press, London, 1970, pp. 110–17; S. Piggott, 'Sir John Clerk and the Country Seat', in *ibid*.

8 Barnard and Clark, *Burlington*, p. 132.

9 W. Watts, *The Seats of the Nobility and Gentry from a Collection of the most interesting and Picturesque Views*, 1779, Plate XXX.

10 Colvin, *Country Seat*, p. 84.

11 Watts, *Seats*, Plate X.

12 Barnard and Clark, *Burlington*, p. 132, quoting B. Dobrée (ed.), *The Letters of Lord Chesterfield*: Chesterfield wrote to his son, 'You may soon be acquainted with the considerable parts of civil architecture'.

13 Terry Friedman, *James Gibbs*, Yale University Press, London, 1984, p. 257.

14 *Ibid.*

15 J. Mordant Crook, *The Greek Revival*, John Murray, London, 1972, p. 126.

16 Watts, *Seats*, Plate VII.

17 Harris, *Palladian Revival*, p. 218.

18 *Ibid.*, p. 258.

19 E. M. Butler (ed.), *The Letters of Prince Pückler-Muskau*, Collins, London, 1957, p. 60.

20 *Ibid.*

21 Richard Riddell, 'The Palladian Portico' in Charles Hind (ed.), *New Light on English Palladianism*, The Georgian Group, London, 1988, pp. 81–93.

22 *Ibid.*

23 David Green, *Sarah, Duchess of Marlborough*, Collins, London, 1967, p. 132.

24 Riddell, 'The Palladian Portico', p. 81.

25 James Lees-Milne, *Earls of Creation*, Century Hutchinson, 1986, discusses the careers of Bathurst, Pembroke and Leicester in detail. Bingley and Mar are introduced.

26 Stutchbury, *Colen Campbell*, p. 55. For example, Campbell was far from modest about his designs for Mereworth, Kent, 1723, for the Hon. John Fane. In *Vitruvius Britannicus* he gave more than half a page of text and claimed to have found rendering of chimney stacks unnecessary.

27 Howard Colvin, *A Biographical Dictionary of Architects*, John Murray, London, 1954, p. 341.

28 Worsley, *Classical Architecture*, p. 75.

29 Lees-Milne, *Baroque*, p. 9.

30 *Ibid.*, Blenheim, pp. 166–84; Grimsthorpe, pp. 191–201; Kimbolton, pp. 102–12.

31 Anon., *Memoirs of the Life, Family and Characters of Charles Seymour, Duke of Somerset*, p. 65.

32 *Ibid.*

33 *Ibid.*

34 *Ibid.*, p. 64.

35 *Petworth House*, National Trust Guide, p. 43.

36 Christopher Morris (ed.), *The Illustrated Journeys of Ceilia Fiennes 1685–1712*, Macdonald, London, 1982, p. 229.

37 Trevor Lummis and Jan Morris, *The Woman's Domain: Women and the English Country House*, Viking, London, 1990, p. 66.

38 *Ibid.*

39 Joan Johnson, *The Gloucestershire Gentry*, Alan Sutton, Gloucester, 1989, p. 222.

40 Violet Biddulph, *The Three Ladies Waldegrave*, Peter Davies, London, 1938, p. 35.

41 Paget Toynbee (ed.), *Horace Walpole's Journals of Visits to Country Seats*, vol. 16, Walpole Society, Oxford, 1927–28, p. 55.

42 W. S. Lewis (ed.), *The Yale Edition of Horace Walpole's Correspondence*, Oxford University Press, London, 1965, 33, II, p. 224.

43 Gervase Jackson-Stops, 'Badminton House, Gloucestershire II', *Country Life*, CLXXXI, 16 April 1987, pp. 136–9.

44 Gervase Jackson-Stops, 'Badminton', *Country Life*, CLXXXI, 9 April 1987, pp. 128–33.

45 I. G. Kennedy, 'Claude and Architecture', *Journal of the Warburg and Courtauld Institute*, 35, 1972, pp. 260–83.

46 Nikolaus Pevsner and Enid Radcliffe, *The Buildings of England: Yorkshire, The West Riding*, Penguin, Harmondsworth, 1974, p. 541. John Carr of York altered the house in 1782–84 giving giant Doric columns and three bay pediments to the wings of the east front.

47 Unknown Author, 'Wentworth Woodhouse, Yorkshire', *Country Life*, XIX, 31 March 1906, pp. 450–61.

48 Hugh Montgomery-Massingberd, *Great Houses of Scotland*, Laurence King, 1997, pp. 132–43. Hopetoun's entrance front of 1727 by William Adam gives the feeling of a Baroque palace, but screens the more modest garden (West) front by Sir William Bruce. Adam's scheme included a central portico and curved double staircase which were not executed.

49 Jacqueline O'Brien and Desmond Guinness, *Great Irish Houses and Castles*, Weidenfeld and Nicolson, London, 1992, p. 52.

50 Jackson-Stops, 'Badminton', 9 April 1987.

51 I. L. Ingram, 'John, Fourth Duke of Bedford, 1710–1771', *Apollo*, CXXVII, June 1988, pp. 382–6.

52 Marie Draper, 'Houses of the Russell Family', *Apollo*, June 1988, pp. 387–92.

53 Mark Girouard, *Life in the English Country House*, Yale University Press, London, 1978, p. 158.

54 Worsley, *Classical Architecture*, p. 234.

55 John Cornforth, *English Interiors: The Quest for Comfort*, Barrie and Jenkins, London, 1978, p. 45.

56 John Cornforth, 'Hagley Hall, Worcestershire I', *Country Life*, CLXXXIII, 27 April 1989, pp. 136–9.

57 Cornforth, 'Hagley Hall, Worcestershire, II', *Country Life*, CLXXXIII, 4 May 1989.

58 John Harris, *The Palladians*, Trefoil Books, London, 1981, p. 55. Harris discusses the general influence of Kent's engravings and illustrates his engraving of Inigo Jones's scheme for a vast Whitehall Palace.

59 James Lees-Milne, *The Country House*, Oxford University Press, Oxford, 1982, p. 16; extract from Arthur Young's *A Southern Tour* 1767. Young writes of Blenheim as 'that celebrated palace, which has been by some so excessively abused, and so praised by others'.

60 John Harris, *Sir William Chambers*, Zwemmer Ltd, London, 1970, p. 13. Chambers referred to Blenheim as a palace in a letter to the Reverend Mr Weston in July 1772.

61 Lees-Milne, *Baroque*, p. 183.

62 *Ibid.*, p. 50.

63 J. R. Jones, *Marlborough*, Cambridge University Press, Cambridge, 1993, p. 224.

64 *Ibid.*, p. 99.

65 Worsley, *Classical Architecture*, p. 100.

66 The Schönbrunn Palace in Vienna by Fisher von Erlach (1696–1713) had such a forecourt, and the Oriente in Madrid was given one by J. B. Sacchetti in 1738: Hugh Montgomery-Massingberd, *Royal Palaces of Europe*, Chartwell Books, London, 1983.

67 Lees-Milne, *Baroque*, p. 169.

68 *Ibid.*, p. 170.

69 Girouard, *English Country House*, p. 156.

70 *Ibid.*, p. 158.

71 Green, *Duchess of Marlborough*, p. 216.

72 *Ibid.*, p. 221.

73 *Ibid.*

74 Watts, *Seats*, Plate LVI.

75 Stutchbury, *Campbell*, p. 28.

76 *Ibid.*, p. 28.

77 *Ibid.*, p. 27. Watts, *Seats*, Plate LVI noted that the gardens 'partake of a greater formality than is constant with present Taste', 1779.

78 C. H. Collins Baker and Muriel Baker, *The Life and Circumstances of James Brydges, First Duke of Chandos*, Clarendon Press, Oxford, 1949, p. 307.

79 Friedman, *Gibbs*, p. 111.

80 Collins Baker and Baker, *Chandos*, p. 308.

81 Friedman, *Gibbs*, p. 111.

82 *Ibid.*

83 Collins Baker and Baker, *Chandos*, pp. 127–9.

84 *Ibid.*

85 *Ibid.*, p. 142.

86 *Ibid.*, p. 147.

87 Friedman, *Gibbs*, p. 113.

88 *Ibid.*, p. 357.

89 John Summerson, *Architecture in Britain 1530–1830*, Penguin, Harmondsworth, 1977, p. 325. Allen was conscious of rivalling Wanstead and had the diameter of his columns made $1^{1}/_{2}$ inches greater.

90 Benjamin Boyce, *The Benevolent Man: A Life of Ralph Allen of Bath*, Harvard University Press, Cambridge, Massachusetts, 1967, p. 100.

91 *Ibid.*

92 *Ibid.*, p. 101.

93 Tim Mowl and Brian Earnshaw, *John Wood, Architect of Obsession*, Millstream Books, Bath, 1988, p. 115.

94 *Ibid.*, p. 116.

95 Richard Morris and Ken Howard, *The Buildings of Bath*, Allan Sutton, Stroud, 1993, p. 3.

96 Boyce, *Benevolent Man*, p. 99.

97 *Ibid.*, p. 109. Allen seems to have enjoyed the moral content of his paintings, many of which were not original. Boyce writes, 'Allen might compete with Lovell and Child in stone, but his fortune was not sufficient . . . to allow him to become a collector. George Vertue and Horace Walpole therefore felt it unnecessary to include Prior Park in their country house tours'.

98 Mowl, *Wood*, p. 116.

99 Boyce, *Benevolent Man*, p. v.

100 Mowl and Earnshaw, *Wood*, pp. 116–17.

101 Marcus Binney, 'Worksop Manor Nottinghamshire I', *Country Life*, CLIII, 15 March 1973, pp. 678–82.

102 Watts, *Seats*, Plate XIII.

103 Binney, 'Worksop'. The ranges were 300 feet in length. The author considers Worksop a contribution to palace, rather than country house design.

104 John Martin Robinson, *The Dukes of Norfolk*, Oxford University Press, Oxford, 1982, pp. 159–64, deals with the scheme for rebuilding by Paine.

105 Watts, *Seats*, Plate XIII.

106 Elizabeth Longford, *Wellington: Pillar of State*, Weidenfeld and Nicolson, London, 1972, p. 44.

107 Colvin, *Dictionary*, p. 720.

108 John Martin Robinson, *The Wyatts: An Architectural Dynasty*, Oxford University Press, Oxford, 1979, p. 105.

109 A. J. Youngson, *The Making of Classical Edinburgh*, Edinburgh University Press, Edinburgh, 1966, pp. 159–60.

110 Robinson, *Wyatts*, p. 121. Philip Wyatt designed Wynyard Park, Co. Durham, for the Marquess of Londonderry using a scheme based on many of B. D. Wyatts's ideas for Waterloo: p. 122. Princess Lieven reported that the Marchioness's bed was surmounted by 'a coronet the size of the crown of the King of Württemberg on the Palace at Stuttgart – red velvet, ermine, everything that goes with it'. It actually sounds like the Empress Josephine's bedroom at Malmaison.

111 David Watkin, *The Life and Work of C. R. Cockerell*, Zwemmer, London, 1974, pp. 26–32.

112 Modern heroes adorned the Temple of Liberty at Woburn, but this was more in the nature of private devotion and they were not displayed in a grand central hall.

113 Watkin, *Cockerell*, p. 25: letter, 7 May 1816.

114 Longford, *Wellington*, p. 44.

115 Neville Thompson, *Wellington after Waterloo*, Routledge and Kegan Paul, London, 1986, pp. 8–9. Wellington had little interest in country life but enjoyed life at Walmer Castle, his official residence as Lord Warden of the Cinque Ports. His wife regarded Stratfield Saye as her principal residence.

116 Longford, *Wellington*, p. 325.

117 Peter Quennell (ed.), *The Private Letters of Princess Lieven to Prince Metternich 1820–1826*, John Murray, London, 1937, p. 19, letter 1 March 1820.

118 *Ibid.*, p. 25: letter, 1 April 1820.

119 Longford, *Wellington*, p. 89.

120 Worsley, *Classical Architecture*, p. 306.

121 *Orme's Graphic History of the Life, Exploits and Death of Horatio Nelson*, Orme, London, n.d., p. 60.

122 Winifred Gérin, *Horatio Nelson*, Clarendon Press, Oxford, 1970, p. 224. George Bolton, nephew of Enid Nelson, married Harriet Eyre of Downton.

123 Lees-Milne, *Baroque*, p. 101 for Lord Rochford.

124 Lanscroon worked at Drayton in 1712. He showed *Hercules and Justice Striking Down Envy and Malice, whilst Minerva and the Arts are Glorified*. All this alluded to William III's attributes.

125 *Ibid.*, p. 118. In the Great Room.

126 *Ibid.*, p. 111.

127 *Ibid.*, p. 130.

128 Christopher Hussey, 'Callaly Castle, Northumberland, II' in *Country Life*, CXXV, 9 February 1959, pp. 358–61.

129 Like the version of the *Temple of the Sun*. See p. 44.

130 Geoffrey Beard, *Craftsmen and Interior Decoration in England 1660–1820*, Bloomsbury Books, London, 1981, Plate 72. This had been produced as an engraving in 1757 by Carlo Cesio. Engravings of the Palazzo Pitti ceiling were also used in English stuccowork.

131 Dorothy Stroud, *Henry Holland*, Country Life, London, 1966, p. 56.

132 Andrew Moore (ed.), *Houghton Hall*, Philip Wilson, London, 1996, p. 26.

133 Geoffrey Beard, *Decorative Plasterwork*, Phaidon, London, 1975, Plate 61.

134 *Ibid.*, Plate 71.

135 Beard, *Decorative Plasterwork*, Plates 88 and 89 show mixed effects of coffering and mythological figures at Lytham Hall, Lancashire, 1760. Plate 90 shows Elemore Hall, Durham, 1757, with a Neptune panel, suggesting perhaps Britain's naval dominance. All these are the work of Giuseppe Cortese.

136 Beard, *Craftsmen*, pp. 176–7.

137 *Ibid.*, Plate 68 illustrates the equally ornate saloon chimneypiece with a medallion of Cybele, goddess representing the fecundity of nature. A similar medallion appeared thirty years later at Hagley Hall, Worcestershire. Beard observes how dependent stuccoists were on engravings and this must be true of Scottish work also: see Blair Castle and The Drum, p. 47.

138 *Ibid.*, p. 180 and Plates 38 and 39. Mawley Hall in Shropshire was built by Sir Edmund Blunt in 1730, the executant architect being Francis Smith. Ornate plasterwork by Italian *stuccatori* and intricate woodwork included displays of tools, symbols of music and painting on the staircase. Mrs Lybbe Powis observed in 1771, 'a thousand nick-nacks from abroad . . . as one generally sees with these Catholic families'. See Christopher Hussey, *English Country Houses: Early Georgian, 1715–60*, Antique Collectors Club, London, 1986.

139 Beard, *Craftsmen*, p. 39. The room was very richly decorated with four large pictures by Jacob Amigoni. Giovanni Bagutti provided stucco overdoor figures.

140 *Ibid.*, p. 99. Francesco Sleter was commissioned to paint *trompe l'oeil* figures in the niches in the gallery of the hall and Gaetano Brunetti to create an elaborately carved illusionistic dome in 1732. Bagutti supplied trophies in stucco.

141 O'Brien and Guinness, *Irish Houses*, pp. 72–7.

142 *Ibid.*, pp. 81–5. See also Peter Somerville-Large, *The Irish Country House: A Social History*, Sinclair Stevenson, London, 1995, p. 163. At Russborough their highly ornamented saloon may have inspired native plasterers in other rooms. The ceiling of the saloon was coved, with large scrolls and leaves as well as cupids.

143 John Fleming, *Robert Adam and His Circle*, Harvard University Press, Cambridge, Massachusetts, 1962, p. 43.

144 Christopher Hartley and William Kay, *House of Dun*, National Trust for Scotland, Edinburgh, 1992, pp. 8–9. The most elaborate work is in the saloon which was designed for banquets. Bacchus and Apollo, typically, appear on the ceiling. The overdoors display urns filled with the products of the estate, and laid-up arms and trophies suggesting peace and plenty. Two fireplaces are dominated by Mars and Neptune. The Earl of Mar, who was a kinsman of Erskine, is celebrated as Sword Bearer to the King of Scotland. In the role of Mars he guards the Scottish crown surrounded by emblems of the traditional accord between Scotland and France. Neptune appears as the god of the waters, suggesting Erskine's (Lord Dun) fishing rights and also the Jacobite toast to the 'King over the Water'. Venus and tritons appear, and the scene above them shows a hound bringing a stag to bay. George I banned hunting in Scotland, otherwise the house might have served as a hunting lodge. The Earl of Mar gathered men together, in the guise of a hunt, in 1715 when he attempted to capture the English throne for the Old Pretender. Minerva appears opposite Mars in the coving as a warrior goddess and as Goddess of Wisdom – the suitable goddess in a judge's house. She holds a Medusa headed shield and points to the entrance hall. There are captive figures at Minerva's feet representing the enslaved Scots. Minerva points to the arms of the Erskine clan and medallions portraying Lord Dun and the Earl of Mar. Above the windows are ancestral busts festooned with fruit, flowers and vines, and beside them are pastoral trophies which celebrate viticulture and agriculture. There are musical instruments including bagpipes which derive from Watteau's engravings.

145 Allan Braham, *The Architecture of the French Enlightenment*, Thames and Hudson, London, 1980, p. 78.

146 *Ibid.*, p. 172.

147 Peter Thornton, *Authentic Decor – The Domestic Interior 1620–1920*, Weidenfeld and Nicolson, London, 1984, p. 93.

148 Robert Oresko (ed.), *The Works in Architecture of Robert and James Adam*, Academy Editions, London, 1975, p. 48.

149 Gervase Jackson-Stops, 'Living with the Louis', *Country Life*, CLXXXVI, 1 October 1992, pp. 68–9.

150 Ingram, 'Duke of Bedford', pp. 382–6, and Geoffrey Beard and Helena Hayward, 'Interior Design and Furnishings at Woburn Abbey', *Apollo*, June 1988, pp. 393–400.

151 Gervase Jackson-Stops, 'A Ducal Shopping Spree', *Country Life*, CLVXXVI, 13 February 1992, pp. 34–7.

152 Montgomery-Massingberd, *Houses of Scotland*, p. 88. The seventh Viscount Stormont was a diplomat in Dresden, Vienna and Paris. Basil Skinner, *Scone Palace*, Guide, 1966, discusses and illustrates furniture and porcelain collected during a diplomatic career. These included Rococo chairs in the drawing room by Pierre Bara and Sèvres and Dresden porcelain.

153 John Cornforth, 'Inveraray Castle, Argyll I', *Country Life*, CLXIII, 18 June 1978, pp. 1619–22.

154 Edith Standen, 'Tapestries in Use Indoors', *Apollo*, CXIII, July 1981, pp. 6–15.

155 Lindsay Boynton, 'Sir Richard Worsley's Furniture at Appuldurcombe Park', *Furniture History*, 1, 1965, pp. 39–58. Another set of these tapestries seems to have been made for this house. Its owner Sir Richard Worsley's mother-in-law, Lady Harewood, may have seen the Newby tapestries, as she was a neighbour.

156 Ian Bristow, *Architectural Colour in British Interiors 1615–1840*, Yale University Press, London, 1996, p. 60. Hogarth's *The Wollaston Family* (1731) and *The Assembly at Wanstead House* (1731), show dark coloured rooms, and since they appear in Arthur Devis's *Mr and Mrs Richard Bull in their House at Ongar* painted in 1747, it is clear that they were popular well into the century.

157 *Ibid.*, pp. 71–5.

158 Gervase Jackson-Stops and James Pipkin, *The English Country House: A Grand Tour*, Weidenfeld and Nicolson, London, 1984, p. 190.

159 Lees-Milne, *Baroque*, p. 163. The Tapestry Room at Castle Howard was supplied by John Vanderbank of Soho with a series of *The Seasons* after Terriers.

160 Bristow, *Architectural Colour*, p. 69.

161 *Ibid.*, p. 93. William Kent used polished blue granite for some of the coloured grotesque decorations on the flat ceiling compartments leaving others white in the manner of later eighteenth-century decoration.

162 Oresko, *Works of Adam*, p. 46.

163 Bristow, *Architectural Colour*, p. 83.

164 Leslie Harris, *Robert Adam and Kedleston*, The National Trust, London, 1987, p. 33.

165 Bristow, *Architectural Colour*, p. 85.

166 *Ibid.*, p. 89.

167 *Ibid.*, p. 98.

168 *Ibid.*, pp. 97–8. In marble work raised ornament was carved in pure white, but laid in a coloured ground. This ornament on ceilings was treated in this way. So the whole of the ceiling was painted white and then the coloured background 'picked in'. Today the process is reversed but the modern effects are less lively, Bristow believes.

169 *Ibid.*, p. 99. Laugier believed that a sweet harmony of columns 'is not at all incompatible with some bold contrasts or, rather, becomes more masked when among the complementary colours there are some which upset the tranquillity through the effect of dissonance'. Bristow feels this gave Adam authority for using the blue, bright red and dark brown found in Roman ceilings.

170 John Harris, *Headfort House and Robert Adam*, RIBA, London, 1973, Plates 20–30, work by Robert Adam for the first Earl of Bective.

171 Oresko, *Works of Adam*, p. 49.

172 *Ibid.*

173 Alistair Rowan, 'Wedderburn Castle, Berwickshire', *Country Life*, CLVI, 8 August 1974, pp. 354–7. At this house there is a fireplace supplied by Piranesi, originally for Lord Arundel, which was decorated with cameos.

174 Bristow, *Architectural Colour*, p. 122.

175 Paintings of continental palace interiors sometimes showed courtiers in brilliantly coloured and elaborately embroidered clothes against grand rooms with white backgrounds – the paintings of Martin Van der Meytens (1695–1770) at the Schönbrunn Palace, Vienna, show this. The smaller rooms such as cabinets, in which fewer people could be accommodated and therefore could not form a separate, human display, are more elaborately decorated. The British conventions, if they existed, are difficult to determine. See also Anna Somers Cocks, 'The Nonfunctional Use of Ceramics in the English Country House During the Eighteenth Century' in Gervase Jackson-Stops (ed.), *The Fashioning and Functioning of the British Country House*, National Gallery of Art, Washington, 1989, pp. 195–215, but especially pp. 207–8.

176 Eileen Harris, *Osterley Park*, The National Trust, London, 1994, p. 56.

177 'The Redecoration of Adam Interiors', The Traditional Paint Forum in Collaboration with the Georgian Group Conference, November 1997; Eileen Harris, 'A Harmony of Many Contrasts', lecture.

178 Bristow, *Architectural Colour*, ch. 6, *passim*.

179 John Dixon Hunt and Peter Willis (eds), *The Genius of the Place*, Paul Elek, London, 1975, p. 122.

180 Worsley, *Classical Architecture*, p. 184.

181 Harris, *Adam and Kedleston*, p. 52.

182 Oresko, *Works of Adam*, p. 47.

183 *Ibid.*, p. 49.

184 Fleming, *Adam and His Circle*, p. 217.

185 Oresko, *Works of Adam*, pp. 45–6.

186 For example Cronkhill, Shropshire, is an Italianate asymmetrical villa for Lord Berwick's agent at nearby Attingham Park, 1802.

187 J. M. Crook, 'Strawberry Hill Revisited I', *Country Life*, 7 June 1973, pp. 1598–1602.

188 Francis Russell, 'Luton House Bedfordshire, I', *Country Life*, CLXXXVI, 16 June 1992, pp. 44–7. Here Robert Adam's castle-style project for the house is discussed. This would not have been an addition to a medieval house but a replacement of a non-castellated seventeenth-century original house.

189 Peter Leach, *James Paine*, Zwemmer, London, 1988, p. 140.

190 James Macaulay, *The Gothic Revival 1745–1845*, Blackie, London, 1975, p. 60.

191 *Ibid.*, p. 75.

192 Watts, *Seats*, Plate LVII.

193 Harris, *Chambers*, p. 59.

194 Giles Worsley, 'The Villa and the Classical Country House', in John Harris and Michael Jardin (eds), *Sir William Chambers*, Yale University Press and Courtauld Institute of Art, London, 1996, pp. 77–85. Chambers disliked Lord Milton and the Gothic style. It appears, according to Worsley, that John Vardy had produced the design for the house and Chambers only took over after the death of Vardy.

195 Watts, *Seats*, Plate XXXIII.

196 H. A. N. Brockman, *The Caliph of Fonthill*, Werner Laurie, London, 1956, p. 124.

197 Dixon-Hunt, *Genius of the Place*, p. 355 quotes Uvedale Price (1747–1829), *An Essay on the Picturesque* (1794). Picturesqueness was associated with age and variety, roughness of effect, whereas according to Burke the sublime was 'founded on principles of awe and terror'.

198 Robinson, *Dukes of Norfolk*, p. 180.

199 As at, for example, the Gothic Temple, or Temple of Liberty at Stowe, Buckinghamshire.

200 Robinson, *Dukes of Norfolk*, p. 181.

201 Robinson, *Wyatts*, p. 107.

202 Cornforth, *Quest for Comfort*, p. 47.

203 Robinson, *Wyatts*, p. 109.

204 Butler, *Letters of Pückler-Muskau*, p. 135.

205 Cornforth, *Quest for Comfort*, p. 47.

206 John Gore (ed.), *Creevey's Life and Times*, John Murray, London, 1934, p. 270.

207 *Ibid.*

208 Butler, *Letters of Pückler-Muskau*, p. 277.

209 Brian de Breffny and Rosemary Ffolliott, *The Houses of Ireland*, Thames and Hudson, London, 1975, p. 193.

210 O'Brien and Guinness, *Irish Houses*, p. 158.

211 de Breffny and Ffolliott, *Houses of Ireland*, p. 193.

212 *Ibid.*, p. 197.

213 Alistair Rowan, 'Robert Adam's Last Castles (1778–1792)', *Country Life*, CLVI, 22 August 1974, pp. 494–7.

214 Culzean was designed for the 10th Earl of Cassillis. Apart from Seton, which was designed for Alexander Mackenzie of Portmore, the smaller castles included Oxenford (1780–82) for Sir John Dalrymple Bt., Airthrey (1790–91) for Robert Haldane, and Maudsley (1791–92) for the 5th Earl of Hyndford.

215 A. A. Tait, *Robert Adam: The Creative Mind*, Sir John Soane's Museum, London, 1996, p. 29. One of twenty-one compositions of ruined castles in mountainous scenery, it is an extreme version of the castle style in Scotland with an element of artistic licence.

216 David King, *The Complete Works of Robert and James Adam*, Butterworth, London, 1991, p. 167.

217 David Daiches, *The Paradox of Scottish Culture: The Eighteenth Century Experience*, Oxford University Press, London, 1964, p. 15.

218 Marcus Binney, *Sir Robert Taylor*, George Allen and Unwin, London, 1984, p. 40.

219 Stutchbury, *Campbell*, p. 56. Colen Campbell's Mereworth was the earliest of these, dating from 1723. It was used largely for the lavish entertainment of modish friends who were visiting Tunbridge Wells, although after its owner John Fane became 7th Earl of Westmorland and married, accommodation was extended by the addition of pavilions quite detached from the house. Other villas of similar design were Isaac Ware's Foot's Cray Place in Kent (*c.* 1754) and Thomas Wright's Nuttall Temple, Nottinghamshire (1754).

220 Watts, *Seats*, Plate LXI.

221 T. S. Rosoman, 'The Decoration and Use of the Principal Apartments at Chiswick House 1727–1770', *The Burlington Magazine*, CXXVII, October 1985, pp. 663–70.

222 Peter Thornton, *Seventeenth Century Interior Decoration in England, France and Holland*, Yale University Press, London, 1981, pp. 7–8.

223 Friedman, *Gibbs*, p. 141.

224 Giles Worsley, 'Jewels in a Rich Coronet', *Country Life*, CLXXXXVII, 14 October 1993, pp. 68–71.

225 Alfred Spencer (ed.), *Memoirs of William Hickey*, 4 vols, Hurst and Blackett, London, 1913, II (1749–75), p. 8.

226 *Ibid.*, p. 27.

227 David Watkin, 'Soane's Concept of the Villa', in Dana Arnold (ed.), *The Georgian Villa*, Allan Sutton, Stroud, 1996, p. 95.

228 Ian Gow, 'The Dining Room', in Annette Carruthers (ed.), *The Scottish Home*, National Museum of Scotland, Edinburgh, 1996, pp. 129 and 134 discusses Mavisbank, Midlothian. It was a villa of character and quality, consisting of a high mansard-roofed Baroque block with rusticated pilasters and a pleasingly crusted and crowded facade of swags and segmented pediments, linked by carved colonnades to low Dutch-looking pavilions. The interior, as Gow says, had impressively decorated state apartments, despite the small scale of the house.

229 Ian Gow, 'The Edinburgh Villa Revisited: Function and Form', in Arnold, *Georgian Villa*, p. 150.

230 Michael Davis, 'The Villas of Scotland's Western Seaboard', in *ibid.*, p. 139. Typical was Greenbank, of dressed stone work, built in 1763 for a Virginia merchant Robert Allason.

231 Green, *Duchess of Marlborough*, p. 297.

232 Giles Worsley, 'Wicked Woman of Marl', *Country Life*, CLXXXV, 14 March 1991, pp. 44–7.

233 Green, *Duchess of Marlborough*, p. 204.

234 Worsley, *Classical Architecture*, p. 234.

235 *Ibid.*, p. 228.

236 Binney, *Taylor*, p. 41.

237 Leach, *Paine*, pp. 64–5 and 186.

238 *Ibid.*, p. 210.

239 *Ibid.*, p. 72.

240 O'Brien and Guinness, *Great Irish Houses*, p. 89.

241 de Breffny and Ffolliott, *The Houses of Ireland*, p. 129.

242 *Ibid.*, p. 131.

243 Kerry Downes, *Vanbrugh*, Zwemmer, London, 1977, p. 48.

244 Gervase Jackson-Stops, 'A British Parnassus: Mythology and the Country House', in Jackson-Stops, *Fashioning and Functioning of the British Country House*, pp. 217–37. Halls were masculine with collections of armour, or plaster military trophies of the kind that Adam designed for Osterley Park. However, femininity, and the power of love overcame the martial spirit in other rooms. Again at Osterley the Loves of the Gods was the theme of the Gobelins tapestries in the antechamber.

245 Oresko, *Works of Adam*, p. 49.

246 *Ibid.*

247 Gill Perry and Michael Rossington (eds), *Femininity and Masculinity in Eighteenth-Century Art and Culture*, Manchester University Press, Manchester, 1994; Colin Cunningham, 'An Italian House is My Lady: Some Aspects of the Definition of Women's Role in the Architecture of Robert Adam', in *ibid.*, pp. 63–78.

248 James Lomax, 'Heaton House', *Transactions of the Lancashire and Cheshire Antiquarian Society*, 82, 1983, pp. 77–9.

249 Nikolaus Pevsner and David Verey, *The Buildings of England: Gloucestershire*, Penguin, Harmondsworth, 1978, pp. 208–9.

250 Lindsay Boynton, 'The Furniture of Warren Hastings', *The Burlington Magazine*, CXII, August 1970, pp. 508–20.

251 *Attingham*, National Trust Guide, London, 1997, p. 13.

252 Somers Cocks, 'The Non-functional Use of Ceramics in the English Country House, pp. 195–214. The intimacy of rooms was enhanced by collections especially of china. Landscape gardening and collecting and the arrangement of ceramics in small private spaces was feminine on the whole. Josiah Wedgwood said that his life 'was devoted to the service of the Lady', whereas Capability Brown's, he told the gardener, 'was to that of the Noblemen and Gent': Samuel Smiles, *Josiah Wedgwood: His Personal History*, Plutarch Press, Ann Arbor, 1971, p. 85.

253 Dorothy Stroud, *Capability Brown*, Faber and Faber, London, 1975, p. 150.

254 Llewellyn Jewitt, *The Wedgwoods*, Virtue Bros, London, 1865, p. 196.

255 Smiles, *Wedgwood*, p. 10.

256 Hugh Malet, *The Canal Duke*, Phoenix House, London, 1961, p. 10.

257 *Ibid.*, pp. 71–81.

258 Watts, *Seats*, Plate XXIII.

259 John Ehrman, *The Younger Pitt: The Years of Acclaim*, Constable, London, 1969, pp. 590–2.

260 *The Wellesley Papers*, Herbert Jenkins, London, 1914, p. 193.

261 George Naish (ed.), *Nelson's Letters to His Wife and Other Documents*, Navy Records Society, London, 1958, p. 567.

262 Gérin, *Horatio Nelson*, p. 37.

263 *Ibid.*, p. 33.

264 *Ibid.*, p. 35.

265 Alistair Rowan, *Designs for Castles and Country Villas by Robert and James Adam*, Phaidon, Oxford, 1985, pp. 134–7.

266 de Breffny and Ffolliott, *Houses of Ireland*, p. 170.

267 *Ibid.*, p. 169.

268 Giles Worsley, *Architectural Drawings of the Regency Period*, André Deutsch, London, 1991, p. 65.

269 Thornton, *Authentic Decor*, p. 142.

270 *Ibid.*

271 Worsley, *Regency Period*, p. 78.

272 *Ibid.*, p. 64.

273 Lyall Wilkes, *John Dobson*, Oriel Press, Stocksfield, 1980, p. 26.

274 *Ibid.*, p. 106.

275 Mark Bence-Jones, *Clive of India*, Constable, London, 1974, p. 1.

276 *Ibid.*, p. 265.

277 Watts, *Seats*, Plate VI.

278 Stroud, *Brown*, p. 142.

279 Bence-Jones, *Clive*, p. 297.

280 *Ibid.*, p. 257.

281 *Ibid.*, p. 188.

282 *Ibid.*, p. 268.

283 Christopher Hussey, *English Country Houses: Mid-Georgian 1760–1800*, Antique Collectors Club, London, 1986, p. 177.

284 Michael Edwards, *Warren Hastings: King of the Nabobs*, Hart Davis, MacGibbon, London, 1976, p. 20.

285 Pevsner and Verey, *Gloucestershire*, p. 392.

286 David Watkins, *Thomas Hope and the Neo-Classical Idea*, John Murray, London, 1968, p. 234.

287 *Ibid.*, p. 234.

288 Boynton, 'Furniture of Hastings', pp. 508–20.

289 Bence-Jones, *Hastings*, p. 182.

290 *Ibid.*

291 Butler, *Pückler-Muskau*, p. 102.

292 Pevsner and Verey, *Gloucestershire*, p. 392. See also Christopher Hussey, *English Country Houses: Late Georgian*, Antique Collectors Club, London, 1986, p. 68.

293 W. H. Hutton, *The Marquess Wellesley KG*, Clarendon Press, Oxford, 1893, p. 19.

294 Spencer, *Memoirs of Hickey*, 4, p. 236.

295 *Ibid.*, p. 237.

296 Hutton, *Wellesley*, p. 54.

297 Watkin, *Hope*, p. 235.

298 de Breffny and Ffolliott, *Houses of Ireland*, pp. 115–17.

299 Terence Davis, *John Nash*, David and Charles, Newton Abbot, 1973, p. 81. The King's Cottage (1812–14), later rebuilt as the Royal Lodge, was in the Picturesque style of Blaise Hamlet. It was gabled and thatched, but spacious with a service wing hidden by a shrubbery. It probably cost £200,000.

300 Lindsay Boynton, 'The Marine Villa' in Arnold, *Georgian Villa*, pp. 120–1.

301 *Ibid.*, p. 121.

302 *Ibid.*, p. 126.

303 Fleming, *Adam and His Circle*, pp. 52–4.

304 Frank Jenkins, *Architect and Patron*, Oxford University Press, London, 1961, p. 76.

305 *Ibid.*, p. 45.

306 *Ibid.*, p. 97.

307 Peter Leach, 'James Paine's Designs for the South Front of Kedleston Hall: Dating and Sources', *Architectural History*, 40, 1997, pp. 159–70.

308 John Lord, 'Sir John Vanbrugh and the 1st Duke of Ancaster: Newly-Discovered Documents', *Architectural History*, 34, 1991, pp. 136–44.

309 Stutchbury, *Colen Campbell*, pp. 22–3.

310 Charles Saumarez Smith, *Eighteenth-Century Decoration, Design and the Domestic Interior in England*, Weidenfeld and Nicolson, London, 1993, p. 291.

311 Damie Stillman, 'The Neoclassical Transformation of the English Country House', in Jackson-Stops, *The Fashioning and Functioning of the British Country House*, pp. 75–93.

312 Worsley, *Architectural Drawings of the Regency*, p. 23.

313 Saumarez Smith, *Eighteenth-Century Decoration*, p. 23.

314 Michael Snodin, 'English Rococo and Its Continental Origins', *Rococo Art and Design in Hogarth's England*, Victoria and Albert Museum, London, 1984, pp. 27–32.

315 Saumarez Smith, *Eighteenth-Century Decoration*, p. 297.

316 Worsley, *Architectural Drawings of the Regency*, p. 32.

317 Sandra Blutman, 'Books of Design for Country Houses 1780–1815', *Architectural History*, 11, 1968, pp. 25–33.

318 Worsley, *Architectural Drawings of the Regency*, p. 1.

3

Role and rank: family and servants

Seventeenth-century writers seeking to support the Divine Right of Kings likened monarchy to the family: the authority of kings was as that of fathers.[1] John Locke redefined the notion of family authority: parental power must be absolute in infancy but was to be reduced as children developed independence and marriage itself was a voluntary contract. In the early eighteenth century, even a Tory writer such as Lord Bolingbroke who might have been expected to support royal authority, did not see a paternal role for the king, but he continued to think of the family as the first political society, and to give fathers the role of magistrates.[2]

In the country, especially, where landowning activities were distinctly masculine, the hierarchical paternalism and somewhat authoritarian notion of the family persisted more than in London, where, for example, it might be challenged by society ladies who were far from subservient, and where there might be greater scope for the power of matriarchs and heiresses. The position of the men, women and children who owned the country house, the importance of marriage, and the position of country house servants, deserves consideration.[3]

MEN

It was the first-born male offspring to whom the country house and estate normally descended. When the owner of the estate had a peerage, he also had noble status and a seat in the House of Lords. The family house and estate descended by arrangements which were extremely complex and known as the *strict settlement*. A deed of settlement was signed which secured house and estate for the heir, often on his marriage.[4] This meant that he was unable to sell the estate or to mortgage it, and it required a private Act of Parliament to break the settlement. An aristocratic family might attempt to

arrive at a position whereby the title and land were inherited by one person
– the eldest male. This arrangement of the nobility, a system of primogeniture,
was quite unlike that adopted by small peasant landowners, who preferred
equal distribution.[5] Entailment of an estate through the strict settlement largely
excluded wives and daughters, making it possible for most of the land to go
to a distant male kinsman who might have inherited the family title. Sometimes, however, land and titles were separated. When the second Earl Ferrers
died without sons, his brother inherited the earldom and other titles, but 'his
Lordship having the misfortune to be a lunatic', the lands passed again to a
younger brother. In 1745, the lands and titles were reunited, but the estates
were temporarily forfeit afterwards because the new Earl murdered his steward
in a violent rage and was condemned to death.[6] Land conferred political power
and patronage and a seat in the House of Lords. Families feared extinction
and were anxious to see their estates enlarged through judicious marriage.
They were also concerned that an ancient name and title should not disappear. The dukedom of Newcastle was recreated four times between 1690
and 1780, no duke being the son of the previous one, the only connection
being a vast set of estates throughout many counties.[7]

A position like that of the Newcastles bestowed real political power
and great social prestige. The Duke of Marlborough, most unusually, was
able to ensure that his titles were inherited by a daughter when no sons were
borne to him. More often a son-in-law was persuaded to merge his identity
in that of his wife's family. As we shall see, this allowed the Percy line to be
recreated in 1750, having become virtually extinct in *c*. 1670. As another
example, the Duke of Newcastle's neighbour, the ninth Earl of Lincoln,
married the duke's daughter, inherited the Newcastle estates and eventually
became Duke of Newcastle of the fourth creation, but his independent identity as Earl of Lincoln disappeared.[8] The smaller gentry did not necessarily
adopt the practice of strict settlement and quite often considerable areas of
land were excluded from the settlement.[9]

Primogeniture and the entailed estate gave great powers to one man;
his brothers and sisters, after some bequests, had to find their own way
in the world. The owner of estate and country house was, with his great
authority, often in several counties, like a kind of 'super-father'. Yet it was
during the first years of the eighteenth century that writers began to question
the idea of the patriarch in a political and social sense. Mary Astell asked, in
Reflections on Marriage (1731), 'If absolute sovereignty be not necessary in a
state, how comes it to be so in a family? Or in a family why not in a state'.[10]
In 1705, Bishop Fleetwood in *Relative Duties of Parents and Children, Husbands and Wives, Master and Servant* had set out to challenge the traditional
absolute role of husband and father. 'There is', he wrote, 'no relation in the
world either natural or civil or agreed upon but here is a reciprocal duty
obliging each party'.[11] Despite these ideas, the notion of the country house,
its estates and servants, as the 'Great Family' and by contrast the children

of the landowner as the 'Little Family' was maintained for much of the century. Even Bishop Fleetwood believed in hierarchy and in the idea of providing 'for our own', that is, 'For such as have any relation to and dependence upon us'. This was the role of the owner of the country house, at home and in his neighbourhood.[12]

Rich aristocrats acquired vast estates in several counties and their titles sometimes at an early age. This was true of both the Dukes of Newcastle and Wharton, although they were to have very different lives. Thomas Pelham Holles (1693–1768) inherited title and lands from both his father and his uncle, from whom the dukedom actually descended. Although his uncle's will was disputed by female relations, Thomas was probably left with £35,000 a year in interests from these properties alone. He also inherited estates in eleven counties: Dorset, Wiltshire, Hertfordshire, Derby, Kent, Suffolk, Middlesex, Sussex, Lincolnshire, Nottinghamshire and Yorkshire.[13] Although a number of country houses had passed to him, his political concerns made it necessary for him to have a house near London. Vanbrugh built Claremont, notable for its arcaded wings and Great Room, for him in 1714.[14] This house was constantly embellished. William Kent designed the park, and the gardens were known for their fruit trees which provided cherries, peaches, apricots and strawberries. It was a house for entertaining the great and although a refuge from London, it was only two hours from Parliament.[15] The Duke was also fond of Halland in Sussex, perhaps because it emphasised ancestry, indeed having some of the qualities of a museum, with its armour, tapestries and herds of deer. He had three other residences in Sussex, including Laughton Place, the traditional family seat, and Bishopstone, a hunting lodge. Nottingham Castle and Clumber Park, also in Nottinghamshire, were his, but they were too far from London and fell into decline, having, in the case of the castle, been maintained for decades by a small staff.[16]

The first and only Duke of Wharton also inherited great wealth when young. He too owned estates in different parts of England. Winchendon, his estate in Buckinghamshire, had fine agricultural land; he had Wooburn in the same county, Old Wharton Hall in Westmorland and Rathfarnham Castle near Dublin. Whereas Newcastle's career was soon devoted to politics, Wharton was rather spoiled in youth, surrounded by the political and literary elite who were his father's friends, and given his own stud when he was twelve years of age. Newcastle became Prime Minister, whereas Wharton died in exile at the age of twenty-two, with only the Order of the Garter from the Old Pretender.[17]

If eldest sons could expect vast riches, younger brothers had more varied circumstances. Newcastle's brother, Henry Pelham, entered Parliament in 1717 and eventually he too became Prime Minister. His career was supported by the Duke, who provided him with an annuity of £1,000 and later added Sussex estates worth £1,500 a year. Henry found, as was customary for the successful younger son, an heiress, Lady Katherine Manners, daughter of the Duke of Rutland, whom he married in 1726. More land was given to Henry Pelham by his brother and from these estates and from some which he purchased, his income was about £3,000 a year. Pelham and Lady Katherine had William Kent remodel Esher Place near Claremont, in a Gothic style. Their daughter married Henry Fiennes Clinton, second Earl of Lincoln, and an elaborate dynastic pattern was created.[18]

Not all great landowners who acquired several estates and country houses did so with the ease that Newcastle did. Sir Hugh Smithson married, after some family difficulties, Lady Elizabeth Seymour, granddaughter of the seventh Duke of Somerset. Lady Elizabeth's mother was the daughter of the last Percy, Earl of Northumberland. Suddenly, Lady Elizabeth's brother, Lord Beauchamp, died of the smallpox at the age of twenty. He had been heir to vast estates, including Petworth, Syon and Alnwick Castle. The old Duke was horrified that the upstart Smithson, whose forebears had been drapers in the City, might eventually inherit. With great effort, Sir Hugh contrived to have the Earldom of Northumberland, a new creation, bestowed upon his wife's father, with remainder to him. In 1750, his father-in-law died and Sir Hugh became second Earl of Northumberland, his wife inheriting the Barony of Percy from her mother's family. By Special Act of Parliament, Smithson assumed the name and arms of Percy. He eventually became Lord Lieutenant of Ireland, was honoured with the Garter in 1756 and eventually a dukedom was bestowed upon him. No dukedom had been created for fifty years. It had been suggested by Lord Chatham that, because of his great estates, he should press for a marquessate, but Smithson (or Percy) dreamed of recreating the Dukedom of Brabant, because of his wife's descent from the princely house of Lorraine. Eventually he settled for the titles of Duke of Northumberland, Earl Percy and Viscount Lorraine.[19] The Duke improved his Northumberland estates with vigour. He imported fruit trees, repaired properties, opened mines and created a system of drainage. Between 1749 and 1778 the rent roll jumped from £8,607 to £50,000 a year.[20]

An estate and title were the basis of political power in the eighteenth century. Philip Yorke, who became Lord Chancellor and first Earl of Hardwicke, bought Wimpole Hall in Cambridgeshire as his seat as well as considerable estates. He had a distinguished legal career and believed that his lands and country seat were essential to his line and family dignity. He wrote, 'In my opinion . . . a person, who takes a title of honour from the Crown, ought in duty to the Crown, to the public and his family, to transmit a competent estate to the heir of the title'.[21]

These men were all aristocrats (although Smithson was only a baronet) and they all married into the aristocracy. Perhaps no man in the eighteenth century moved directly from a humble background to a country house and a peerage.[22] However, it was possible in one generation to take a step up the ladder and acquire the house and the land, if no more. Indeed, Daniel Defoe, in *The Compleat English Gentleman* (*c.* 1728) discussed the rise of the 'gentleman by breeding', as opposed to the 'gentleman by birth'. The gentleman bred rather than born was gentle, according to Defoe, because of his immense wealth and his good education. Defoe saw the merit in such a man and invented one, Sir A. C.,[23] who was, like Sir Hugh Smithson, a baronet and whose father had been Lord Mayor of London. Sir A. C. was more plebeian than Sir Hugh, for it was his father who kept a shop, not a more distant ancestor. Whereas the two younger brothers in this family were 'brought up to their father's trade',[24] and his shop was left wholly to them, Sir A. C., who inherited the baronetcy normally bestowed on London's Lord Mayor, had been sent to Eton and to a university. He was not bred for business. When he returned from the Grand Tour, he inherited his father's recently acquired country estate in Hampshire, which brought an income of £3,000 a year. The young man had also inherited 'a vast stack of money' in the Bank of England,[25] and the South Sea Company. Sir A. C. improved his estate almost immediately. He raised cottages for poor tenants, replaced decayed paling with a new park wall, built stables, coach houses, offices and a 'large dog-kennel and a little dwelling-house for his huntsman'.[26] When some traditional country gentlemen, 'gentlemen by birth' rather than by breeding, in Defoe's terms, came to visit Sir A. C., they were astonished by his being able to act as his own architect or 'Surveyor Generall': 'Why, they say he was bred a trades-man, a mere citizen. His father was a . . . grocer'. The second visitor interrupts him, saying 'Let his father be what he will, 'tis apparent he understands very well how to be a gentleman'.[27]

William Beckford (1760–1844) was the son of a rich Lord Mayor of London. Beckford senior, an alderman and a friend of John Wilkes and a supporter of the liberty of the people, complained to George II personally about a false return made at the Middlesex election.[28] He was a sugar tycoon with rough manners and a strong colonial accent who had married a granddaughter of the Earl of Abercorn.[29] He built himself a huge Palladian house, Fonthill Splendens in Wiltshire, with a portico and a lake to set it off. Like Sir A. C., the young Beckford was brought up a gentleman. He was not sent to Eton, but educated by a tutor, and, famously, the nine-year-old Mozart taught the five-year-old Beckford musical composition. Like Sir A. C., young William developed an interest in architecture and was trained in its principles by Sir William Chambers. When Beckford went on the Grand Tour he used his father's immense fortune to collect more objects and eventually to pull down his father's 'palace' and employ James Wyatt to create the sublime and soaring Fonthill Abbey.[30] The young Beckford, it is clear, was in a different position from the solid gentlemanly founder of a dynasty whose country house was an aspect of patriarchy or of political significance. Beckford always fulfilled the role of connoisseur, the exotic and the leader of taste.

Apart from grandees the country gentleman of more modest means played an important role in the county where his land lay. In Gloucestershire, for example, the great – the Dukes of Beaufort and the Earls of Berkeley – had control of county seats in parliamentary election.[31] To be in the Commons was extremely beneficial to landowners, since much legislation was concerned with turnpikes, enclosures and canals; it was the county and borough members who saw bills through the House of Commons, and made sure their friends and family connections in the House of Lords turned bills into Acts of Parliament.[32]

Some of the gentry, however, preferred, often for financial reasons, to act locally rather than nationally. Frequently they became justices, claiming only four shillings a day in expenses for attending the Sessions and Assizes. They were required to travel to formal meetings with the other magistrates, perhaps at a nearby inn. Quarter sessions were held in March and August, when judges, accompanied by much ceremony, were present; from the landed gentleman's point of view it was also an occasion to meet other gentry and discuss agricultural and rural issues.[33] Some legal matters were considered insignificant enough to be dealt with in a magistrate's own home. James Leigh, a Gloucestershire magistrate, was always concerned that the value of stolen items should be fixed at less than one shilling, so that the felon should not have to be referred to a higher court, where a savage sentence of death or transportation might be inflicted. Knowing families and their circumstances, he was able to take a gentler view of petty crimes. Justices were required to ensure that the local population maintained roads before the introduction of turnpikes. They also managed the regulation of the Poor Law, enforced the Corn Laws and investigated incidents of highway robbery.[34]

The local gentry served as Sheriffs and especially Deputy Lord Lieutenants. They trained and drilled the local militia, increasing its numbers when necessary. Country gentlemen in Gloucestershire supported the Hanoverians against the Jacobites in 1715 and again in 1745. William Blathwayt of Dyrham paid for the Dyrham Volunteers to be equipped with swords, silk sashes and feathers.[35] By contrast, in Northumberland in 1715 the Jacobite cause seemed at first to prosper and it was only later that the local gentry who were Catholic or Tory were forced into hiding to avoid arrest. This included the third Earl of Derwentwater, the fourth Lord Widdrington and two MPs, Thomas Forster of Adderstone and Sir William Blackett of Wallington. It was probably John Bacon, High Sheriff of Northumberland, who hid the fleeing Lord Derwentwater at Staward Manor.[36]

Some country gentlemen who confined themselves to the country had the reputation of being wholly uncivilised. In *The Young Gentlemen's New Year Gift* a 'Gentleman of the Middle Temple' wrote in 1729, 'There is not a more worthless despicable animal than a true country booby, who, calling himself a country gentleman, spends his life only eating, drinking and sleeping; and distinguishes himself in nothing from the brutes, but only that, whereas they keep within the bounds of nature, he prides himself in the excess of it'.[37] Lady Theresa Parker of Saltram thought her neighbours, Sir

John Chichester of Arlington and Sir Thomas Ackland of Killerton, dull company when she had to entertain them and she disliked cockfighting and other rustic amusements. Writing to her brother Lord Grantham in 1774, she asked '. . . can anything be worse than to be reduced to such company and such amusements?' The fifth Duchess of Devonshire described Theresa's husband, when she stayed at Saltram, as being 'dirty, as comical and talking as bad English as ever'.[38]

The younger sons of country houses frequently occupied an important position in the Church of England. The pulpit could be an important seat of power, providing the clergyman preached the correct Hanoverian sentiments, which included only moderate piety and a dislike of enthusiasm. Some noblemen's sons rose high. Brownlow North, son of the Earl of Guildford and brother of the Prime Minster, had three important promotions from the Bishop of Lichfield to Bishop of Worcester and finally Bishop of Winchester, with a salary of £5,000 a year. Through the ownership of advowsons the aristocracy had very great influence over the Church. A *Survey of the Cathedrals of England* of 1727 estimated that of the 9,800 churches visited, 1,200 (or 12 per cent) were presented by a peer. The Duke of Norfolk was patron of twenty-one livings and the Duke of Devonshire of twenty-nine and a half. Some peers' sons benefited directly from the father's holding many livings; Lord William Somerset, son of the fifth Duke of Beaufort, held five listings in the Beaufort gift in the 1820s. He never wrote a sermon and preached in Bristol Cathedral only twice in twenty-three years, but he built splendid stables for himself. Clergymen were patronised for political purposes. They knew the locality well and were good arguers and frequent visitors of parishioners who might also be electors.[39]

WOMEN

Because of the emphasis on primogeniture in handing on the country house and estate, women often suffered economically and socially. Frequently their interests were set aside by fathers and brothers and they were 'controlled' in order that the eldest male heir should inherit almost everything. Sir William Blackett (d. 1728) whose estate was unentailed, left it in his will to his nephew, Sir Walter Calverley, on condition that he married Sir William's illegitimate daughter, Elizabeth Ord, and took the name of Blackett.[40] This, of course, provided for her financial security, for she was able to become mistress of the Wallington estate in Northumberland. Compared with many illegitimate women, she was fortunate, although her future was entirely ordered for her, in a way which was common in the eighteenth century.

Lady Mary Campbell, daughter of the Duke of Argyll, married Lord Coke, son of the Earl of Leicester, in 1747. Lady Mary had £20,000 of her own, which, however, seems to have given her little pleasure or independence during her marriage.[41] Lord Coke treated his wife very badly, leaving her on their wedding day and devoting himself to the gaming tables. Horace Walpole wrote of him that he 'has lost immense sums at play and seldom goes home to his wife till eight in the morning. The world is vehement on her side and not only her family but his own give him up'.[42] At first Lord Leicester supported his daughter-in-law. He wrote to her in 1747 in amazed anger that her husband 'should not come to his senses but still continue brute enough not to prize as he ought the great jewel he has in you'.[43] Later he changed sides, sensing, perhaps, that Lady Coke was a shade more independent than his own wife: 'Lady Leicester', wrote Lady Louisa Stuart, 'is a peaceable, inoffensive woman, long endured to obedience, who, as the father was yet more ill-tempered than the son, and addicted to the same vices, had borne submissively for thirty years the trials that exhausted Lady Mary's scanter stock of patience in three months'.[44] When the latter was at Holkham both Lord Leicester and Lord Coke encouraged the servants to be rude to her and call her 'Our Virgin Mary'.[45] Divorce proceedings began, but eventually the case collapsed. It was at last arranged that Lady Coke should live separately with her mother at Sudbrooke, a handsome Baroque villa near Richmond on condition that she should withdraw her charges, never go to London and live on her pin money.[46] Apparently she eventually had £2,000 a year rent charge and was 'absolute mistress of herself'.[47]

That Lady Coke was rich in her own right was something which her friends often stressed when writing about her. Women, however, apart from being socially restrained, were often seen as a drain upon a country house and estate. Property constantly needed consolidating, it was believed, and women 'took it away' from the estate and the heir. When Eleanor Brownlow of Belton married Sir John Cust in 1712, her portion of her father's wealth passed to her husband for his use during his lifetime.[48] Dowagers as well as daughters were regarded as a drain upon resources. The second Duchess of Manchester was a widow for forty-seven years, drawing more than £80,000 from the estate.[49] It was not uncommon for mothers to leave to daughters whatever private fortune they could, which entailment could not claw back to the estate. Dame Alice Brownlow, mother of Eleanor, left diamonds to two of her daughters and granddaughters and £1,000 to Eleanor and another sister.[50] Since 25 per cent of all upper-class young women remained unmarried during the eighteenth century, it became acceptable for the daughters of landowners to seek some kind of employment. Mary Wollstonecraft noted that the daughters of the lesser gentry might become companions or governesses and sometimes they were employed as housekeepers. Otherwise they faced life on a small pension in crowded lodgings.[51]

William and Elizabeth Chute of the Vyne, being childless, chose the daughter of a cousin, Caroline Wiggett, whose father was a Norfolk clergyman, to live with them. Ultimately, Caroline's brother became heir to the state. Caroline had few prospects; it was envisaged that she would stay at home and be a companion to the aunt. She and her aunt shared a bedroom and in the same corridor were the housekeeper's bedroom, the under-servants' room and the lady's maid's room, in a kind of women's wing.[52] Caroline Wiggett's life was rigidly circumscribed: she could not travel by herself and required the Chutes' permission and their money. In any case, women were always escorted on journeys by a kinsman or a servant. All her expenditure was subject to the scrutiny of a male relation and she had no income of her own. Her rank in society did not allow presentation at court, but she came out at the age of seventeen at a ball in Winchester and had a coming-of-age party. She had certain domestic responsibilities despite her lowly position. She was left in charge of the family house when she was twenty-four and had to interview and engage servants and supervise laundry.[53]

Women like Caroline Wiggett were often groomed for the comfort of others. In 1825, when Sir Harry Featherstonhaugh of Uppark was seventy, he married, to her great surprise, Mary Anne Bullock, an eighteen-year-old dairy maid. He was lonely and perhaps did not wish to marry a self-confident social equal who would change his ways or his house. She was 'coached' in polite manners and deportment by a governess – possibly an illegitimate daughter of Sir Harry's – and spent some time in Paris. Mary Anne did not really go into society or even have imposing portraits of herself painted. She and her younger sister, Frances, who also, as a child, came to live at Uppark, simply soothed Sir Harry Featherstonhaugh's last years. However, since there were no legitimate heirs, Mary Anne, and later Frances, inherited the estate.[54]

Sir Harry Featherstonhaugh had had Emma Hamilton as his mistress and by tradition housed her in a cottage near his estate by the time she was fifteen years old, in 1780.[55] Emma Hamilton was the daughter of a colliery blacksmith, but many women who became mistresses of noblemen were from a merchant or professional background. The fifth Duke of Bedford's mistress was the daughter of a bankrupt physician, and the mistress of the Earl of Surrey was the daughter of a bankrupt attorney.[56] Such infidelities meant that at some country houses the children in the 'family' were only half-brothers or sisters, or even unrelated. At Chatsworth in the 1790s there were five children. Three were children of the fifth Duke of Devonshire and Georgiana, Duchess of Devonshire, and two were children of the Duke and Lady Elizabeth Foster; one child of the Duke and Charlotte Spencer and another of the Duchess and Lord Grey were not, it seems, housed at Chatsworth.[57]

However, it has been argued that a new kind of domestic woman emerged: a powerful figure who could challenge aristocratic culture, as the new bourgeois 'economic' man was also doing. This new domestic woman was supported by much advice from sermons, domestic manuals and periodicals.[58] Such a woman was Elizabeth Shackleton (1726–81) who was born in London, the daughter of a linen draper. When her widowed father inherited Browsholme Hall in Yorkshire, she organised and supervised its smooth running. Later in the 1750s, as the wife of Robert Parker of Alkincoats (d. 1758), she had again an important domestic role on his Lancashire estate. After her husband's death she married John Shackleton, a wool merchant and eventually, when Thomas Parker, her eldest son, married in 1778, he as ultimate inheritor of the estates, moved to Alkincoats and she departed for a modest manor house. In leaving familiar surroundings she felt a sense of regret, disliking her daughter-in-law's new decorations, and she also lost status. Nevertheless, she had controlled and managed land and house for about three decades. Housekeeping and shopping were important; she graded her possessions carefully. She repaired and made new use of household linens, but she was also an important customer of firms both locally and in London. She wrote, for example, of buying a new mahogany table from Gillows of Lancaster. 'It is in three parts, the middle square and two ends which are half rounds – all put together makes an elegant oval. The wood very handsome 16 feet long all very strong and made neat, it cost only . . . in all £5:8:6d'. It could be argued that the well-to-do houses of the lesser gentry had a greater impact on trade, if not on taste, than immensely rich aristocrats who commissioned items from Kent or Adam. Mrs Shackleton and her kind made the wheels of consumerism move. Unable to inherit land, she, like other gentlewomen, attached much importance to personal, movable goods. She shopped in Preston, Warrington, Chester, Wrexham, Wakefield, Pontefract and York and, although she gave up visiting London after 1757, she had a London newspaper sent to her. From the metropolis came the fine china which gave elegance to her supper and tea parties.[59]

Charitable acts were another way of establishing women's independent activity, although writers usually assumed in sermons and essays that acts of benevolence were perpetrated largely by rich, well-educated men. Throughout the eighteenth century, to feel another's suffering and to react generously and unselfishly were believed to give great pleasure. The development of sensibility brought tears, trembling, blushing and fainting at the woes of the unfortunate. Women were admired especially for their capacity for grief, and women living in country houses were frequently engaged in charitable acts.[60] Celia Fiennes's will specified that the income from £40 per year should continue to fund her charitable causes after her death in 1741.[61] When she reigned over the Holkham estates Lady Leicester raised the rents of her tenants, but was generous in her charities. She maintained vagabonds throughout Leicestershire and in 1755 she endowed six picturesque almshouses which were to be built on either side of the main entrance to the park. In 1767 she wholly refurnished and restored a local church. A year later, she created a fund of £21,300 for the maintenance of three men and three women, who were to receive six pence a day, coal annually and new clothes once every two years.[62] At Melbury, the kitchens were very spacious and near them a cell was built by Mrs Horner 'to receive beggars', Horace Walpole reported. He also noted that the chatelaine gave £3,000 a year in charity.[63]

In the last quarter of the eighteenth century something more fundamental than sensibility was affecting attitudes towards suffering. Anglican Evangelicalism was converting the middle classes to a new revival of religious fervour, due in part to the fears for the future of Christianity brought on by the French Revolution.[64] Elizabeth Fry always remained faithful to Quakerism, although both Anglicans and Quakers of her youth were similarly spontaneous and passionate in their religion. Although her father, John Gurney, was a successful Norwich merchant, he had as his country house Earlham Hall in Norfolk. In 1811, Elizabeth participated in the founding of the Norwich branch of the British and Foreign Bible Society. The Gurneys entertained prominent Anglican and Dissenting visitors at Earlham after the public meeting. Elizabeth broke through the normal conventions of a country house dinner and the restrictions set upon charitable and religious women by kneeling in prayer, dominating an essentially masculine occasion with her zeal and piety.[65]

Some women managed to establish a literary career despite little opportunity in early life for education. Sarah Fielding (1710–68), sister of Henry Fielding, grew up in the country. Her mother died when she was eight, but family friends appear to have helped in her education, and she learned Latin from Dr Arthur Collier. She had an annuity from her father and some money from her brothers, but she also depended on the proceeds from writing. Elizabeth Robinson (1720–1800) married Edward Montagu and apart from becoming a leading bluestocking hostess, she organised charities and managed her husband's farms. Catherine Sawbridge (1731–91), whose mother died when she was young, educated herself in the library of her father, a well-to-do squire. Elizabeth, Countess of Craven (1750–1828), daughter of the Earl of Berkeley, of Berkeley Castle in Gloucestershire, became a successful playwright and Maria Edgeworth (1767–1849) was educated by her father, who encouraged her interest in politics, and for whom she managed the family estates in Ireland.[66]

MARRIAGE

An important aim of a great house and estate during the eighteenth century was to ensure that the owner's eldest son, and indeed all his children, had careful, advantageous marriages. The Gower family, who became Dukes of Sutherland in 1833, were particularly fortunate in this respect. In 1744, when the family were only barons, the third Lord Gower married the daughter of an MP who brought them £16,000. She died within eighteen months and he married the daughter of the first Duke of Bridgewater, eventually bringing his family estates worth £75,000 a year inherited from the third Duke of Bridgewater, who died without heirs of his own. In 1785, the family acquired more than a million acres in Scotland, through the marriage of the fourth Baron Gower to Elizabeth, Countess of Sutherland in her own right.[67]

Other families made good marriages of this kind. The Grosvenors, who became the Dukes of Westminster in 1874, acquired estates which eventually became Belgravia through judicious careful marriage. The Cecils, Earls and Marquesses of Salisbury, acquired Liverpool property in 1821 through marriage into the Gascoyne family.[68] By the nineteenth century the family name of the Dukes of Buckingham was Plantagenet-Temple-Nugent-Brydges-Chandos-Grenville. These names represented pride in dynasty and a union of fortunes.[69]

When the heir married whom he pleased, there was every chance that the estate might go into a decline. Lydiard Tregoze, the house of the Viscount Bolingbroke, was lost to the family through several injudicious marriages throughout the eighteenth and nineteenth centuries. This began with the second Viscount divorcing his wife in 1767, with the idea of marrying a 'rich monster', who would 'retrieve his affairs' and replenish a fortune lost on cards and horses. His heiress escaped from his clutches, as did a second, pursued in Bath and worth £43,000; the desperate peer died insane.[70]

It would be wrong to imagine that financially advantageous marriages were necessarily unhappy ones, and it is interesting to see how they were negotiated. Unusually, Sir Hugh Smithson proposed to Lady Elizabeth Seymour without speaking to her parents first. Since she was the grand-daughter of a duke, although not then the great heiress she subsequently became, and since his own paternal descent was plebeian, he asked the Duke of Leeds to write to her formidable grandfather on his behalf, stressing that he was a gentleman and had a fortune. Sir Hugh had £4,000 a year practically unencumbered and was heir to another property worth £3,000 annually. However, the Duke of Somerset, Lady Elizabeth's grandfather, replied to Leeds in a manner which was certainly haughty if not high-handed. He wrote 'that he did not know Sir Hugh Smithson or his fortune, but that if upon enquiring he should find out that his family was Gentlemanly and respectable and that his fortune would allow of his settling £2,000 a year Rent charge on his Granddaughter, by way of joynture, and £500 a year for pin money, that he should not object to it'. But Somerset would not receive Sir Hugh, nor correspond directly with him.[71]

Sometimes the preliminary legal negotiations for marriage settlements involved endless investigation into roll rents. On occasion, an independent suitor acted quickly. The Duchess of Northumberland reported in 1767, that 'Lord Thanet was married to Miss Sackville: Beauty without Art had in this case its reward; he had never spoken to her when he wrote to her mother following the proposal: 800 a year for Pin Money, 5,000 joynture and 5,000 for younger Children'.[72] Clearly money was not the only concern when the daughter of the Duke of Richmond married Henry Fox against her parents' wishes. Lord Carteret mocked deep family shock: 'I thought', he wrote, 'our fleet or our army were beat or Mons betrayed into the hand of the French'.[73]

Divorce was not common among the landed classes in the eighteenth and early nineteenth centuries. The only type of divorce which allowed remarriage had to be obtained through a private parliamentary bill and only twelve of these took place. The Church in England accepted divorce *a mensa et thoro* (from bed and board), or judicial separation, but marriage partners were allowed to remarry by the late seventeenth century with a civil divorce *a vinculo* (from bond); this was brought in to ensure legitimate heirs and to protect property.[74] If a woman was being divorced on the grounds of her adultery, an action for damages against the co-respondent was undertaken first. In this the woman was not represented, which indicated that women were still held legally to be property. These proceedings took place in public and were known as 'crim-con', an abbreviation of 'criminal conversation' or connection. Jack Parker, the first Earl of Morley of Saltram had a liaison with Lady Elizabeth Monck, daughter of Lord Arran, who was married with children. She bore three of Lord Morley's sons and he proposed marriage to her, but she dismissed such ideas, saying 'It would be too hard on my daughters and poor Henry (her husband) to obtain a divorce'.[75]

Marriage was regulated by Lord Hardwicke's Marriage Act of 1753, which made marriage for those under the age of twenty-one illegal without the consent of father or guardian.[76] The landed classes saw it as a way of ending 'clandestine' marriages which might threaten their estates, since a husband would have control of his wife's fortune at least for life. Some believed the fathers of heiresses would now only allow them to marry peers, and John Shebbeare thought that it would allow the nobility to consolidate wealth and political power. He feared that they would attempt to purchase boroughs with their now closely guarded fortunes and would 'choose what Commons they please'. This, he considered, would mean that the House of Commons would in reality represent the wishes of the House of Lords and not the people and that the king would become a 'mere cypher, a kind of pensioner of the Lords'.[77] Increasingly, however, towards the end of the eighteenth century, ideas of romantic love, of companionship, of freedom and individuality came to influence marriage more than dynastic or financial considerations alone. The Duke of Newcastle married Henrietta Godolphin in 1716 and, although this was an arranged marriage (for she wished to be a duchess and he felt in need of her fortune), they developed the greatest affection. After a quarrel in 1759, he wrote to her, 'For God's sake, my dear, consider the many happy years we have, by the mercy of God, had together, how much our mutual happiness depends on each other. You know, you must know, how sincerely I love and esteem you'.[78]

Throughout the century the idea of marrying to produce a male heir and finding a second partner for love, sexual pleasure and companionship changed, and the roles fused. Of course there was a rise in aristocratic adultery. Charles II had set a precedent, indeed had expanded the peerage with several dynasties of ducal bastards. Throughout the eighteenth century men of rank kept mistresses. Nevertheless, there might also be a spirit of domesticity as well as libertinism on the country estate. Lady Sarah Napier perceived it in her nephew when she wrote '. . . his amiable little wife adores him and he doats on her and six pretty girls: its quite charming to see them all together, and they are so domestick you scarce seem them separate'.[79] Since women were taking over much of the work formerly done by men, the mistress of the house began to direct them and to take a greater part in domestic organisation. 'The government of your house, family and children', Lord Halifax told his daughter, 'is the province allotted to your sex'.[80]

Domesticity within aristocratic circles might well provide romantic rather than dynastic affection. If it did not, the nobility might temporarily or permanently abandon their class. The fifth Earl of Berkeley married a Gloucester butcher's daughter.[81] The Earl of Tankerville eloped with a New-castle butcher's daughter, although they eventually returned to Chillingham Castle in Northumberland and she was made a lady of the bedchamber by Queen Caroline.[82] Lady Harriet Wentworth, the Marquess of Rockingham's sister, 'a Girl of admirable good sense and unblemish'd character' eloped with her own footman in 1764. When he came into her service, he was unable to write his name, but she saw that he was taught mathematics, grammar and music. When she married him she parted with all her fine clothes, believing that, as his wife, 'she should for the future wear only Washing Gowns as was fit for his wife'.[83] It was this romantic attachment to a partner of lower caste which Lord Hardwicke's Act had been designed to prevent. It was also an aspect of upper-class behaviour which Sheridan satirised in *The Rivals*, where Lydia Languish, a young woman devoted to novels of sensibility, believes herself to be illicitly in love with penniless Ensign Beverley.[84]

One country gentleman whose properties in East Anglia brought him in £350 a year and whose arranged marriage gave a larger fortune, and a twenty-five-bedroomed Buckinghamshire country house, was John Wilkes.[85] Would he have claimed that a dull, fat wife and a Calvinist mother-in-law led him to preach libertinism in his *Essay on Women* and to become a member of the Hell Fire Club, with its appetite for sexual freedom? Libertinism has been associated with both sexual and political radicalism. It is apparent that, after Waterloo, the landed aristocracy became politically and sexually more conservative and in retrenching their position to save their estates from being ravaged as they had been on the continent, they adopted more bour-geois habits in forging matrimonial alliances.

CHILDREN

Children born in a country house were important, not least because they were heirs to historic names, ancient titles, lands and fine architecture. Be-cause of family settlements and marriage contracts, some aristocratic women were only sixteen or seventeen when they gave birth and a long period of bearing children might lie before them. Lady Bristol had seventeen pregnancies in twenty years. She preferred to live at court and her husband in the country, although this meant looking after endless children. He wrote to her, 'If you knew what full employment this family keeps me in, you would rather wonder how I had the time from it to correspond'.[86]

Keeping an heir alive in infancy was difficult, and smallpox and rickets were the greatest threat to life, especially for children aged nine to eighteen months. Cold bathing was thought to prevent rickets in babies' limbs. Aristocratic children began to be inoculated against smallpox in the early part of the eighteenth century. Lady Mary Wortley Montagu had her five-year-old son inoculated in 1711, having come across the Turkish method, and Lord Berkeley had his heir and daughter inoculated in 1722, although frequently it was the younger sons who had the treatment.[87] The death of children, although common, may have changed the attitude of parents. Because of serious illness and death among their other children, Charles James Fox's parents lavished immense amounts of affection upon him. His charm and intelligence captivated them. His father wrote: 'Charles is playing by me and surprises me with the *eclat* of his beauty ev'ry time he looks me in the face'. Later he wrote: 'I dined at home today, *tête-à-tête* with Charles, intending to do business, but he has found me pleasanter employment, and was very sorry to go away so soon'. Charles's own letters were intelligent and mature, showing how he had benefited from adult attention. In 1757, before he was seven, he wrote to his brother: '. . . The king of Prussia has beat the French and the Germans. I shall take it very ill if you don't write to me next Post. FitzGerald desires that you would send him the Cricket Ball which you promised him a half year ago'.[88]

The death rate among aristocratic children fell after 1750 by 30 per cent for those under five years of age and the life expectancy of the nobility was far greater than for the rest of the population.[89] Nevertheless, heirs still died off. Lord Beauchamp, heir to the Duke of Somerset and vast estates in Sussex and Northumberland, died on the Grand Tour in 1744 from smallpox.[90] Pompeo Batoni's glossily elegant portrait could not disguise the valetudinarian Marquess of Monthermer, whose death in 1770 brought to extinction the Dukedom of Montagu.[91]

Great preparations were made for the birth of a child and especially of an heir. Lace and linen costing £130, a coral teething necklace and expenses for lodging the 'Little Master', Edward, Viscount Coke, were recorded in 1749.[92] In April 1772, when Theresa Parker of Saltram gave birth to a boy, her brother, Lord Grantham wrote: 'Certain it is, a son extends our worldly views and prospects, strengthens the bonds of domestic dependence'.[93] By his time, the idea of maternal tenderness was developing. French visitors observed it in '. . . the English Ladies of all ranks'.[94] Clothes were less constricting and children's cheeks were ruddy with health. Theresa Parker's children were brought up by their aunt at Saltram after their mother's death

Harewood House, Yorkshire. The Music Room, architect Robert Adam, 1765–71

Eaton Hall, Cheshire, the Drawing Room. Architect William Porden, 1804–12

PLATE 7

The Fourth Duke of Atholl and family by David Allan

in 1775 and they were allowed to express their emotions more openly. 'Jack', Anne, his aunt noted, 'is easier managed by indulgence than severity'. When he left school in Hammersmith at seven years old, she wrote, '. . . he behaved at parting with his usual propriety, though I believe there was a shower [of tears] in the chaise'.[95]

The sixth Countess of Portarlington, daughter of Lord Bute, admired the freedom of Irish ways with children, after she went to live at Dawson Court, Co. Leix, in 1778. She wrote to her sister: 'I must admire the Irish way of bringing up children for in all the families I have happened to know there seems the most perfect ease and confidence . . . even the Duke of Leinster, where there is a good deal of state, I could not help noticing the grown up girls stealing an opportunity when they thought the company did not mind them to go to their father and mother with an appearance of affection that did them good. I will adopt this comfortable fashion if I can with my own children in spite of the vulgarity of it, for I am convinced familiarity with one's children is looked upon in that light by a great many of the English'.[96]

Children at large country houses had greater opportunities than many others to express their feelings and energy, in wild games which could take place in the fine landscapes and shrubberies their families owned. In the 1790s, Ralph Verney of Claydon House, Buckinghamshire, was in the charge of the Rector of Claydon, whilst his parents were in London. His pleasures were simple: '. . . after prayers and dressing, between the Book and the top, and other diversions', the clergyman wrote, 'the Hours pass smoothly and not unprofitably away so tho' he is everyone's care and Concern he is trouble to none. He pleases himself with imagination of his Brothers being cooped up in a little house, while he has the liberty of ranging the Gardens and Fields and on Church-Days has the sole ringing of the Bell and the whole property of the News papers'.[97] Marjory Fleming, who was born in 1803, kept her own diary of visits to the country houses around Edinburgh. She wrote, when about seven years of age, 'Now I am quite happy for I am going tomorrow to a delightful place Braehead by name, belonging to Mrs Craford, where their [sic] is ducks, cocks, hens, bubbly jocks, 2 dogs, 2 cats & swine'.[98] Though all was not farmyard pleasure, as she also noted: 'Here at Braehead I enjoy rurel filisty to perfection, content, retirements, rurel quiet friendship books all these dwell here . . .'[99]

Members of the Society of Friends were interested in the upbringing of children and, indeed, infant mortality rates among their offspring were very low.[100] Elizabeth Fry wrote of a free and happy childhood at Earlham Hall in Norfolk, running wild over garden and fields and drinking syllabub through the straw (and probably made straight from the cow).[101] There were many outdoor and indoor games of a more organised kind, although these were not peculiar to country house life. Whist (or whisk, as it was sometimes called), piquet, nap, loo, chess, draughts and backgammon were popular, and Oliver Goldsmith enjoyed hunt-the-slipper. Hide-and-seek (called Harry Racket sometimes) and see-saw (known as Titter-totter, or Tittermetotter) were also enjoyed.[102]

Childhood was short and, after infancy, children's dress was the same as that of adults in the first half of the eighteenth century. The lack of separate image is apparent in Gawen Hamilton's portrait of 'The Third Earl of Oxford and His Family' (1736). Marriage often took place when the participants were barely out of childhood: a grandson of William Penn's married at thirteen. At fifteen, girls were often brought out into society.[103] It is sometimes claimed that because their childhood was cut short, the upper classes often behaved childishly.[104] Perhaps intensive labour forced the urban poor and the lower middle classes to regard certain aspects of play as something which children alone might be allowed, briefly, to engage in. The aristocracy with plenty of time and space did not necessarily abandon play: fancy dress, masquerades, playing with baby (doll's) houses and a general taste for pranks remained with them in later life.

The education of children, at least during their early years, often took place within the country house itself. There was a common belief that private education by a tutor produced a more virtuous child. Tutors and governors were required by writers in the early years of the eighteenth century to be virtuous above other qualities.[105] John Locke's *Some Thoughts Concerning Education* was published in 1693, but was of influence for some time after that; in it Locke stressed the importance of teaching children the need for kindness, especially if they were cruel to animals or birds. One might, however, wonder how much effect this had upon the more ruthless country men, who developed more efficient methods of killing wild creatures for sport.

Locke also believed that parents should remove their children from the influence of servants.[106] A tutor should be carefully chosen and paid about £20 a year to teach his pupils in a well-informed and kindly way. Most boys were taught Greek and Latin, but little time was spent on other aspects of education, such as geography, history or elementary science. Locke approved of games and play, but felt that children should make their own rather than be supplied with expensive ones.[107]

Writers were critical of the complacent attitude of the landed aristocracy, which led them to undervalue education. Writing of the son of rich parents, Jonathan Swift observed: 'He is taught from the nursery, that he must inherit a great estate, and hath no need to mind his book, which is a lesson he never forgets to the end of his life'.[108] In *The Compleat English Gentleman*, Daniel Defoe (c. 1728) described arrogance as well as complacency among the gentry. He was critical of the 'lady-mothers' and 'lady-aunts' of a boy, 'those directresses in his early years', who left him so uneducated that he was unable to use his great wealth properly. They relied on inadequate teaching at home because they did not wish the boy to be taught at school by a social inferior. Defoe imagined these domestic harridans angrily asking:

'Shall *my son be sent to school to sit* bareheaded and say a lesson to such a sorry . . . rascal as that, be browbeaten and hector'd and threatn'ed with his authority and stand in fear of his hand! my son! . . . Let the Latin and Greek go to the D-! My son is a *gentleman* and he sha'n't be under such a scoundrel as that'.[109] Defoe observed elsewhere, 'The young gentleman has a tutor bestow'd on him to teach him at home, 'tis taken for a scandal to the heir of the family to be under the power and coercion of a sorry pedagogue: No, he shall have a tutor'. However, his tutor was often a 'playfellow', who taught him inadequately until he was thirteen.[110]

Defoe invented a conversation between a country gentleman and a visitor about the lack of books at his house. The country gentleman said he and his friends valued 'a good table and good champaign'. When visitors come, he added, 'I show them some good sport'. If he had bookish visitors, he took them to the parsonage, where there was a good library. However, he realised that his sons must have access to books; 'I'll be the last dunce of the race', he claimed.[111] Two other country gentlemen of Defoe's creation lamented the lack of education among them. One, who came from an old-fashioned landed family, whose younger brother had been educated and had become a lawyer, sadly admitted: 'But I have no learning. I was an unhappy dog. I was born to the estate or else I had been taught, but I must be a blockhead forsooth, because I am to be a gentleman'.[112]

The system of primogeniture made the treatment of children highly selective; some were inoculated (against diseases such as smallpox) to survive and inherit, while some were educated to find their own way in the world. Defoe's traditional countrymen, in conversation, admired the new merchant rich, who bought estates but still educated the eldest son, whose trained mind enabled him to run his property successfully. Speaking of such an acquaintance, they noted that he had had five years at Cambridge and three years on the Grand Tour, yet, despite this, he wore his learning easily, not speaking endlessly of the pictures and buildings he had seen, nor filling his conversation with scraps of Latin and Italian.[113]

Later in the eighteenth century, there was a positive interest in improving education. Mrs Coke of Holkham was in correspondence with Dr Samuel Parr, who in 1785 presented her with his *Discourse on Education*.[114] She believed in his sound experience and hoped that he might come to Holkham to see how well she had been able to educate her daughters. Mrs Coke was less impressed by Jean-Jacques Rousseau, who was not possessed with 'the superior advantage of experience'.[115] However, Rousseau had captured the attention of the landed classes. Lady Kildare and her sister had read *Emile*, the 'Childrens Charter', when it appeared in 1762. Rousseau advocated noise, laughter and games as approaching the idea of the unspoiled Noble Savage, although he thought it more suitable for boys than girls to be unconstrained. Lady Kildare asked Rousseau to be her children's tutor, but although this never happened, she developed a programme for her children based on his ideas.[116] They were out of bed by five and engaged in weeding and making bonfires in the winter and making hay during the summer months. Older children had lessons early in the morning and at nine breakfast was served to all; then the younger children played wild games.[117] From one to three o'clock they had more exercise, then dinner, play and bathing, and more school work until five, supper at seven thirty and bed an hour later. In 1766, Lady Kildare acquired a boating lodge at Black Rock called Frescati which overlooked the Irish Sea. Since Rousseau had declined the post of tutor, a Dublin Scots teacher, William Ogilvie, was appointed. He was a mathematician, a French speaker and a good classical scholar. Unlike Defoe's arrogant 'lady-mothers', Lady Kildare was almost willing to treat him as a gentleman and companion of her sons. There was the agonising problem, much discussed, of whether, if he were a gentleman, he should have wax or tallow candles.

Ogilvie was established at Black Rock, teaching a Rousseauesque range of exercises and some intellectual activities to Charles Fitzgerald, Lady Kildare's eldest son. He learned Latin verse and grammar, he read Ovid's *Metamorphoses* and, in French, *Gil Blas*. He also studied some English history and Fielding's *Tom Thumb*. The daughters of the Kildare family were given some knowledge of the classics and of mathematics and were taught with their brothers by Ogilvie. Lady Kildare felt that it was necessary for girls to have additional lessons in singing and deportment.[118] The education of girls gradually improved in general, although needlework, a little French and some slight skill with a harpsichord to lull a husband to sleep after dinner and port were still regarded as important.[119] Some girls struggled to teach themselves Latin, but there was considerable opposition to this. Fanny Burney's father forbade her to learn,[120] and Fielding became jealous when his sister proved to be rather good at classics. It has been suggested that women were discouraged from learning classical languages because they were crucial to higher education.[121]

Maria Edgeworth, of Edgeworthstown, Co. Longford, had much to say about country estates and managed her father's after his death. She also wrote *Essays on Practical Education* in 1811. She believed that 'the superintendence of the education of young ladies in the higher ranks of life, the daughters of our affluent nobility ought to be considerably greater than it is already'. It should, she felt, take twelve to fourteen years, and a governess, learning herself as she taught her pupil, should be paid £300 a year. It was essential for girls to be taught about literature.[122] By contrast young men needed to have some understanding of estate improvement before they went into the world. She wrote that 'A father who is building or improving grounds . . . can easily allot some portion of the business to his son, as an exercise in judgement and prudence'. Men needed to know about the architectural orders, and to have developed taste in order to choose wallpaper, and must study classical objects, such as gems or ancient medals. No doubt she was not alone in expressing these ideas about the suitable education of the 'Regency man of taste' whose house and grounds were on show and could indicate his aesthetic judgement. However, she did not believe that aristocrats had natural good taste: it had to be cultivated.[123]

On a less elevated level, women in country houses sometimes tried to offer some kind of education, often religious, to local village children. This was frequently in the form of a social event. Mrs Montagu seems not to have provided much in the way of intellectual fare in August 1795: 'I had last Thursday a fine party of Sunday School Girls form Newbury to dinner in my grove, and all my poor neighbours and labourers to sup there. I hope there are few persons who do not assist the distressed in these miserable times. It is a great crime not to do it'.[124] Elizabeth Chute of the Vyne encouraged local children to go to the Sunday School which she had founded. Caroline Wiggett, her niece, tried to make it more agreeable, spending her own money on a dinner at the Vyne of roast beef, plum pudding and gooseberry pies; there were games and dancing with a band. Each week the girls in the group came up to the big house to practice their singing.[125]

SERVANTS

A country house was supported by its servants, without whose work the estate could not have functioned.[126] Servants usually signed contracts when they entered into employments and were organised into upper and lower groups. By 1720, the upper group had ceased to include gentlemen or gentlewomen who had formerly been employed as state servants or as ladies and gentlemen-in-waiting. As late as 1702 Lord Derby had six officers who were members of the gentry in his employment. Many noblemen continued for some time to have a chaplain, although this post also gradually disappeared.[127]

After the departure of 'gentle' servants the household was under the authority of the steward, who controlled butler, valet, groom of chambers, clerk-of-the-kitchen and gardeners. The steward organised household matters, kept the accounts, paid for food, wages and provisions and oversaw the rents of the estate.[128] The order of the landowner would be passed on to the steward or agent as at Erddig in the 1770s, when John Caesar the elder conveyed orders about receiving the local militia to Betty Jones, a trusted housemaid.[129]

The clerk-of-the-kitchen had an important role in seeing that food arrived as it was needed by the cook. He also organised the menus, times of meals, the conveying of courses to his lord's table and presided over the lower domestics. His role began to change as confectioners and chefs, especially foreign ones, became important. By the 1770s the clerk-of-the-kitchen had frequently disappeared, as in the case of Lord Stanhope's household.[130]

The butler looked after plate, glass, the wine cellar and sometimes, where he was the principal male servant, he controlled the footmen at table

117

and other male servants. The role of the butler was not always sharply defined in the eighteenth and early nineteenth centuries which meant that a variety of talents was demanded. In Suffolk, in 1775, one employer required 'a Butler that can shoot and shave well'.[131] The butler and a footman had to wash and polish the silver and arrange it in the strongroom after the family dinner. At Erddig the silver was guarded by a footman who slept in a bed in front of the only door to the safe, which contained baize-lined shelves upon which sat splendid late seventeenth-century Monteith and silver sauceboats, as well as about twenty other pieces.[132] Footmen were often kept for largely ornamental purposes and their presence became increasingly expensive. In 1777, Lord North put a tax of one guinea per head a year on male domestics and in 1786 a duty on hair powder was also introduced, so that servants in full livery were becoming a great extravagance.[133] Footmen, of whom there might be between four and seven, had to be tall and fairly good-looking and were well paid.[134] Philip Yorke of Erddig paid Edward Allen, a footman, twelve guineas a year in 1785.[135] The groom of chambers looked after the furniture: for example moving chairs back into position against the wall and restoring the architectural appearance of a room after visitors had disturbed it. He also waited at table when there were visitors and maintained the fires around the house.[136]

Outside, in a traditional household, the clerk-of-the-stables organised the coachmen, the grooms and the stable boys. He had to have a knowledge of horses of different kinds and purposes.[137] The coachman was also a liveried servant, and an important one, bringing the family over treacherous roads to their estate. In 1776, Philip Yorke who employed a variety of liveried staff, including grooms, footmen, postilions and coachmen, provided Ambrose Campion, his coachman, with a full uniform, in addition to his wages.[138] This consisted of plush breeches, one pair of buckskin breeches, waistcoat, frock greatcoat and boots in every second year. He was allowed an extra jacket, but had to buy himself a frock coat for common wear.

The housekeeper, the ladies' women and the cook were the other principal upper servants. During the eighteenth century, the household became predominantly female and women held responsible positions within it. In the earlier part of the century, the lady of the house would be responsible for organising the supply of dairy produce, poultry and also for the supervision of baking, pickling and preserving. Sometimes this was in the hands of a trusted female servant, such as Mary Covey at the Vyne in Hampshire, who controlled expenditure to the sum of six shillings a week for fish and other items from the market. By the end of the century, the lady of the house had withdrawn somewhat from this intricate involvement. The Chute family at the Vyne consumed much food produced on the estate in the 1740s. Gradually more food came from markets and shops; as the consumption of expensive foods increased, so more food had to be locked in the housekeeper's room.[139]

The housekeeper was an important figure and played a major part in running the great house. In the 1780s, the Parkers of Saltram in Devon employed a housekeeper of a rather 'middling background', 'a remarkable, well-behaved decent woman' who had previously been employed by Lady Dundas.[140] The housekeeper had to manage the maids; she often controlled the kitchens, supervised the meals and looked after the footmen. She also seems to have been a figure of moral authority, sending the housemaids to church. At Claremont, in Surrey, the housekeeper was required to supervise seven housemaids and three laundrymaids.[141] In a smaller house, where there were fewer upper male servants, the housekeeper had an even more important role. Mary Salusbury was housekeeper at Erddig from 1798 to 1804. She and her successor were responsible for buying in luxury items such as, in 1798, ducks, lobsters, salmon, eels, muffins and cakes. Housekeepers dealt with the household linen in large quantities and prepared for, and cleared up after, visitors. They covered furniture and partially dismantled state rooms when families were away from the estate and paid serving women and washerwomen.[142]

The lady's maid had always to be at hand. At Erddig, there is evidence that personal servants slept in passages on the first floor in order to be instantly available to their employer. Elizabeth Ratcliffe was, as a lady's maid, of considerable support to her widowed employer, Dorothy Yorke, between 1768 and 1788. She was the daughter of a Chester clockmaker who had supplied his wares to Erddig. She was an extremely talented young woman, who could draw and model. She copied mezzotints and produced a version of a Chinese pagoda, based on an engraving in William Chambers's *Gardens and Buildings at Kew* (1763).[143]

Among the lower servants there were a great many chambermaids, laundrymaids and scullery maids. It would be wrong, especially in the earlier part of the eighteenth century, to define the various tasks narrowly.[144] In the Victorian period a parlour maid might well have an entirely different role from a housemaid, but in the Georgian period servants were expected to work inside or outside the house, wherever they were most needed.[145] Nicholas Blundell of Crosby Hall near Liverpool often employed either a cook or a housekeeper, but once, for a period of several months, he employed both. He spoke of his 'wife's maid', whether she was the chambermaid or an additional servant.[146]

The keeping of a black servant was extremely fashionable, as is apparent from Hogarth's work. In the 1730s a black coach boy was employed even at remote Erddig [48]. He was painted in his scarlet livery with its silver buttons, holding his horn.[147] He appears to have been treated well, but many were not. Very often they were regarded as slaves and paid no wage. Once they had reached adolescence and ceased to be appealing as diminutive fashion accessories, they were often sold back into slavery on a plantation. When he reached the age of nineteen, Sambo, the Duchess of Kingston's black servant was sent 'home' to plantation slavery.[148] Some remained as faithful family retainers. Horace Walpole wrote of his relations, the Misses Philipps, having a 'favourite Black who has lived with them a great many years and is remarkably sensible'. On one occasion, when he heard a visitor saying that the British were sending a ship to the Pelew Islands in the Western Pacific, the servant exclaimed: 'Then there is an end of their happiness!' 'What a Satire on Europe', Horace Walpole added.[149] Many black servants almost seemed anonymous pieces of property to their employers. The Duchess of Devonshire offered her mother an eleven-year-old black boy, because 'the duke don't like me having a black, and yet cannot bear the poor wretch being ill used. If you like him instead of Michel I will send him, he will be a cheap servant and you will make a Christian of him and a good boy, if you don't like him they say Lady Rockingham wants one'. Anonymity

48] Erddig, Clywd. Portrait of John Mellers, coach boy. One of a series of portraits of servants

was forced upon black servants. At Knole, in Kent, there was a succession of them, who regardless of their real names, were known as John Morocco.[150]

Numbers of servants employed in country houses varied considerably although the numbers fell during the Georgian period. A rich peer might have from twenty-five to fifty people in his household.[151] At Erddig in the 1770s, the full complement of staff was about twenty-five to thirty,[152] whereas in 1742, Lord Petre's household at Thornden in Essex numbered thirty-three.[153] Sir Edward Knatchbull of Mersham-le-Hatch in Kent had about twenty-four servants in 1767. James and Susanna Whatman of Turkey Court near Maidstone had thirteen in 1778,[154] and at Hatfield Lord Salisbury had thirty-six in 1797.[155] Stockeld Park in Yorkshire, a large villa designed by James Paine, was maintained by thirteen servants in 1791. By 1825 a manual describing the household of 'a respectable Country Gentleman with a young family' recommended hiring twenty-five servants.[156]

Male servants were gradually replaced by female in the second half of the eighteenth century.[157] Great households employed male cooks, as did any householder who could afford to employ them for such work as was 'performed in the presence of guests'.[158] The income of the country house owner was clearly an important factor: when he was fifteen years old, Thomas Coke had an income of £10,000 with which to support Holkham (and go on the Grand Tour with highly paid servants), while Parson Woodforde had £300 a year. Out of this the latter was able to employ two housemaids, a footman, a boy for certain rough work about the house and a farm labourer. Besides their keep, he gave them £30 12s a year between them.[159] By 1791 the Middletons of Stockeld, with an income of £4,000 a year, were employing six male and seven female servants.[160]

Wages varied considerably as did the number of servants. They were not especially low compared with other forms of manual work.[161] The highest pay was awarded to male cooks, who might earn about £50 and £80 a year, but were only kept by the grandest of families.[162] In the middle of the eighteenth century, butlers were paid about £9 or £10 a year and housekeepers, at least in the earlier part of the century, about £10 a year.[163] Salaries were often not increased over the years: some maids were paid only £6 a year in a senior position in the household between the 1770s and the 1790s. Odd sums were paid to workers who came into the great house from the locality. In the 1790s a woman who did two days' sewing was paid one and fourpence at Erddig and a harpsichord tuner was paid 10s 6d.[164] Some servants were very badly paid, but seem to have performed few tasks. John Nicholas, a kitchen man at Erddig was paid 8d a day in his old age.[165] Indoor staff were housed and provided with some clothing and it was perhaps the footmen, paid between half a crown and six shillings a week, who had the least arduous existence.[166]

Servants certainly expected to receive various allowances and prerequisites over and above their wages. Normally they were provided with food and lodging and some clothing, which some of them came to regard as their right. Will Gates was employed as a footman at Hickstead Place in 1704.[167] Apart from a salary of fifty shillings, he was to be supplied with 'a hat, a coat and breeches once every two years'. However, he was not to retain the clothing if he were dismissed in the first year of employment. Elizabeth Shackleton of Alkincoats in Lancashire provided clothing over a period of time for her maids. In 1773, Nanny Nutter received a pair of black silk mitts and there seem to have been regular presents to various maids of handkerchiefs, necklaces, shoe buckles and other trifles. Female servants did not have clothes given to them as part of their contract of employment, unlike men, and sometimes the expense of their clothing was deducted from their wages.[168] Tea was often provided as part of the servants' agreement of employment: in the *London Advertiser and Guide* of 1786, John Tucker recommended that tea and sugar should be given to them.[169]

The term 'vails' usually referred to tips given to servants by visitors. There were many attempts to abolish this practice, although there was a belief that wages would have to be increased if these gratuities disappeared. Parson Woodforde gave the servants of friends with whom he dined two shillings each in 1770.[170] Housekeepers received considerable sums on occasion.[171] The housekeeper at Heythrop in Oxfordshire once received sixteen shillings. Of course it was always possible to turn presents of clothing into cash, despite the fact that employers who passed it on did so in order to give their servants a genteel air.[172] Under normal circumstances faithful servants would expect to be rewarded with some kind of pension. Sometimes they would receive accommodation on the estate.[173] Certainly, they could hope to be remembered in wills. Horace Walpole noted in 1789 that General Fitzwilliam left £3,000 a year to his late wife's maid, 'a very meritorious servant', and, astonishingly, a lump sum of £45,000 pounds to his own manservant: 'a prodigious recompense'.[174] Walpole was shocked when staff were not remembered. Fitzroy Scudamore of Holme Lacy in Herefordshire had 'not left a farthing' to 'two or three very old servants' in 1782. Walpole added: 'it is no excuse that the will is of ancient date – why did he not make a later?'[175]

One of the problems of employing servants was that, although essential, they could deprive the great house of privacy and intimacy. In 1732, a visitor to Erddig noted that the then owner, John Mellor, was suspicious of his servants: he did not wish to employ only local people on his staff, as he did not want them to discuss his affairs in Welsh out of his presence.[176] Richard Lovell Edgeworth, who had been an absentee landlord, returned to his remote Irish estate, Longford, Co. Longford, in 1782. He found his front lawn crowded with lawyers and petitioners, 'tenants, undertenants and drivers' and came to dislike his servants and dependants in general.[177] Servants had control over possessions, they had the freedom of the house in their employer's absence and could help themselves to food and drink, or even order unnecessary amounts in order to sell it. Female servants themselves were extremely vulnerable. They often worked far away from the rest of the household, slept in attic rooms which could not be locked and were regarded by the master and sons of the house as sexually available.[178] At the same time, female servants were sometimes idealised as virtuous and perfect women. The simplicity of ordinary life was thought to be improving. Rousseau had suggested that boys should be brought up to understand at first hand the work of the manual labourer. The idea that happiness was to be found not in the larger country house, but in the very small one, was not uncommon. Fanny Burney wrote in *Camilla*: 'The romantic sound of love and a cottage, she considered such a habitation as a bower of eglantine and roses in which she might repose and be adored all day long'.[179] The Duchess of Devonshire dressed for a masquerade as a housemaid in 1786 and Marie Antoinette played the dairymaid at Rambouillet.[180] Sir Harry Fetherstonhaugh went further and at the age of seventy, as we have seen, married an eighteen-year-old dairymaid, Mary Ann Bullock, in 1825.[181] Increasingly, however, servants were separated from their employers.[182]

The community in the country house was a complex one. Rank gave proprietors a position of authority in the countryside, yet a means of belonging elsewhere – to distant estates and to the metropolis. Men, women and children had prescribed roles and the whole structure of the property was supported by a tied separate 'family' of servants dependent on the great house and close to their employers.

NOTES

1 Susan Dwyer Amussen, *An Ordered Society: Gender and Class in Early Modern England*, Colombia University Press, Oxford, 1988, pp. 61–5 *passim*.

2 *Ibid.*, p. 65. Locke's ideas were expressed in *Two Treatises on Civil Government* (1690) and Bolingbroke's in *Letters on the Spirit of Patriotism and On the Idea of the Patient King* (1799). Amussen observes that although Bolingbroke did refer to the King as a father, he did not develop this analogy, and believed that the law should govern a good king (Amussen, footnote 84).

3 Roy Porter, *English Society in the Eighteenth Century*, Penguin, London, 1990, p. 25. See also Amussen, *An Ordered Society*, p. 65, footnote 83, which quotes Hilda Smith, *Reasons Disciplines: Seventeenth Century English Feminists*, Illinois University Press, Urbana, 1982, which discusses the unpopularity of Locke's ideas on the family amongst feminists, as it undermined the informal family power of upper-class women.

4 H. H. Habakkuk, 'England', in Albert Goodwin (ed.), *The European Nobility in the Eighteenth Century*, Harper Torchbooks New York and Evanston, and Adam and Charles Black, London, 1967, p. 2.

5 Randolph Trumbach, *The Rise of Egalitarian Family: Aristocratic Kinship and Domestic Relations in Eighteenth Century England*, Academic Press, London, 1978, p. 41.

6 Mary Abbott, *Family Ties: English Families 1540–1920*, Routledge, London, 1993, p. 42.

7 Trumbach, *Rise of Egalitarian Family*, p. 50.

8 *Ibid.*, pp. 46–9.

9 Goodwin, *European Nobility*, p. 3.

10 Lawrence Stone, *The Family, Sex and Marriage in England 1500–1800*, Weidenfeld and Nicolson, London, 1977, p. 240.

11 *Ibid.*

12 Trumbach, *Rise of Egalitarian Family*, p. 129.

13 Reed Browning, *The Duke of Newcastle*, Yale University Press, London, 1975, pp. 2–5.

14 Kerry Downes, *Vanbrugh*, Zwemmer, 1977, pp. 100–1.

15 Browning, *Newcastle*, p. 6.

16 *Ibid.*, p. 5.

17 Mark Blackett-Ord, *Hell Fire Duke*, Kensal Press, Windsor, 1982, pp. 11–13.

18 Browning, *Newcastle*, p. 40.

19 Gerald Brennan, *A History of the House of Percy*, 2 vols, Fremantle and Co., London, 1902, II, p. 436.

20 *Ibid.*, p. 446.

21 Philip Yorke, *The Life and Times of Philip Yorke, Earl of Hardwicke*, 3 vols, Cambridge University Press, Cambridge, 1913, p. 571.

22 John Cannon, *Aristocratic Century*, Cambridge University Press, Cambridge, 1984, pp. 1–34, provides a detailed discussion of the composition of the peerage of eighteenth-century England.

23 Daniel Defoe, *The Complete English Gentleman* (with an introduction by Karl Bulbring), David Nutt, London, 1890, p. 268.

24 *Ibid.*

25 *Ibid.*

26 *Ibid.*, p. 270.

27 *Ibid.*, p. 272.

28 H. A. N. Brockman, *The Caliph of Fonthill*, Werner Laurie, London, 1956, p. 21.

29 Elizabeth Mavor, *The Grand Tour of William Beckford*, Penguin, Harmondsworth, 1986, p. 15.

30 Brockman, *Caliph of Fonthill*, p. 24.

31 Joan Johnson, *The Gloucestershire Gentry*, Alan Sutton, Gloucester, 1989, p. 137.

32 *Ibid.*, p. 142.

33 *Ibid.*

34 *Ibid.*, pp. 143–4.

35 *Ibid.*, p. 137.

36 Frances Dickinson, *The Reluctant Rebel: A Northumbrian Legacy of Jacobite Times*, Cresset Books, Newcastle, 1996, p. 29.

37 Defoe, *English Gentleman*, p. lxxxii.

38 Trevor Lummis and Jan Morris, *The Woman's Domain: Women and the English Country House*, Viking, London, 1990, p. 68.

39 Cannon, *Aristocratic Century*, pp. 63–8.

40 Lummis and Marsh, *Woman's Domain*, p. 168.

41 A. M. W. Stirling, *Coke of Norfolk and His Friends*, The Bodley Head, London, 1908, p. 62.

42 *Ibid.*, p. 54.

43 *Ibid.*, p. 53.

44 *Ibid.*, p. 62.

45 *Ibid.*, p. 53.

46 *Ibid.*, p. 59.

47 *Ibid.*, p. 62.

48 Lummis and Marsh, *Woman's Domain*, p. 47.

49 Cannon, *Aristocratic Century*, p. 126.

50 Lummis and Marsh, *Woman's Domain*, p. 45.

51 Stone, *Family, Sex and Marriage*, p. 384.

52 Lummis and Marsh, *Woman's Domain*, pp. 97–8.

53 *Ibid.*, pp. 107–8 and 110.

54 *Ibid.*, pp. 129–30.

55 *Ibid.*, pp. 124–5.

56 Stone, *Family, Sex and Marriage*, p. 531.

57 *Ibid.*, p. 533. See also Arthur Calder-Marshall, *The Two Duchesses*, Hutchinson, London, 1978, p. 9. Family relations were extremely complicated: Lady Elizabeth Foster gave birth to the Duke's illegitimate daughter, Caroline St Jules, three weeks before the Duchess was delivered of the Duke's second legitimate daughter. Eventually Lady Elizabeth became the Duke's second wife.

58 Vivien Jones, 'The Seduction of Conduct: Pleasure and Conduct Literature', in Roy Porter and Marie M. Roberts (eds), *Pleasure in the Eighteenth Century*, Macmillan, London, 1996, pp. 109–13.

59 Amanda Vickery, 'Women and the World of Goods: A Lancashire Consumer and Her Possessions 1751–81', in John Brewer and Roy Porter (eds), *Consumption and the World of Goods*, Routledge, London, 1994, pp. 274–301.

60 Carolyn Williams, 'The Luxury of Doing Good: Benevolence, Sensibility and the Royals Humane Society', in Porter and Roberts, *Pleasure in the Eighteenth Century*, pp. 77–107.

61 Christopher Morris (ed.), *The Illustrated Journeys of Celia Fiennes 1685–1712*, Macdonald and Co., London, 1982, p. 25.

62 Stirling, *Coke of Norfolk*, p. 69.

63 Paget Toynbee (ed.), *Horace Walpole's Journals of Visits to Country Seats*, vol. 16, Walpole Society, Oxford, 1927–28, p. 48.

64 John Kerr, *Elizabeth Fry*, B. T. Batsford, 1962, p. 17.

65 *Ibid.*, p. 31.

66 Katherine Rogers, *Feminism in Eighteenth Century England*, Harvester Press, Brighton, 1982, pp. 251–73.

67 Cannon, *Aristocratic Century*, p. 72.

68 *Ibid.*

69 Abbott, *English Families*, p. 44.

70 Cannon, *Aristocratic Century*, p. 71.

71 Brennan, *House of Percy*, pp. 434–5.

72 James Greig (ed.), *The Diaries of a Duchess: Extracts from the Diaries of the First Duchess of Northumberland 1716–1776*, Hodder and Stoughton, London, 1926, p. 76, entry for 3 August 1767.

73 Goodwin, *European Nobility in Eighteenth Century*, p. 19.

74 Lummis and Marsh, *Woman's Domain*, p. 87.

75 *Ibid.*, p. 86.

76 Porter and Roberts, *Pleasure in the Eighteenth Century*, pp. 112–13.

77 Trumbach, *Rise of Egalitarian Family*, p. 107.

78 Stone, *Family, Sex and Marriage*, p. 368.

79 *Ibid.*, p. 527.

80 Trumbach, *Rise of Egalitarian Family*, p. 132.

81 Cannon, *Aristocratic Century*, p. 77.

82 *Ibid.*, pp. 73–4 and footnote 12, p. 74.

83 Greig, *Diaries of a Duchess*, p. 59, entry for 25 October 1764.

84 Richard Brinsley Sheridan, *The Rivals* (1775), ed. Elizabeth Duthie, A and C Black, London, 1994, p. 14. Fag, young Captain Absolute's servant, says that his master is in love with '. . . a lady who likes him better as half pay ensign than if she knew he was the son and heir of Sir Anthony Absolute, a baronet with three thousand a year'. Footnote 43 points out that an ensign in the 1770s earned about £65 a year, whereas a captain would have earned £190 per annum.

85 Louis Kronenberger, *The Extraordinary Mr Wilkes*, New English Library, London, 1974, pp. 5–6 and footnote 1, p. 6.

86 Trumbach, *Rise of Egalitarian Family*, p. 187.

87 *Ibid.*, pp. 193–4. For details of Lady Mary Wortley Montagu's son see Jonathan Curling, *Edward Wortley Montagu 1713–1776*, Andrew Melrose, London, 1954, pp. 33–5.

88 Loren Reid, *Charles James Fox: A Man for the People*, Longmans, London, 1969, p. 9.

89 Trumbach, *Rise of Egalitarian Family*, p. 187.

90 Geoffrey White, *The Complete Peerage*, St Catherine's Press, London, 1953, XII, p. 81. Lord Beauchamp was born in 1725 and died in Bologna on his nineteenth birthday.

91 W. H. Doubleday and Lord Howard de Walden, *The Complete Peerage*, St Catherine's Press, London, 1936, IX, p. 108.

92 Stirling, *Coke of Newcastle*, p. 47.

93 Lummis and Marsh, *Woman's Domain*, p. 74.

94 Desmond Shawe-Taylor, *The Georgians: Eighteenth Century Portraiture and Society*, Barrie and Jenkins, London, 1990, p. 191 quoting Anne-Marie Lepage Breuge, *Letters Concerning England and Holland*, 1770.

95 Lummis and Marsh, *Woman's Domain*, pp. 78–9.

96 Peter Somerville-Large, *The Irish Country House: A Social History*, Sinclair-Stevenson, London, 1995, p. 175.

97 Rosamund Bayne-Powell, *The English Child in the Eighteenth Century*, John Murray, London, 1939, p. 175.

98 Frank Sidgwick, *The Complete Marjory Fleming*, Sidgwick and Jackson, London, 1934, p. 61.

99 *Ibid.*, p. 22.

100 Trumbach, *Rise of Egalitarian Family*, p. 187.

101 Bayne-Powell, *English Child*, p. 189.

102 *Ibid.*, p. 190.

103 *Ibid.*, p. 16.

104 *Ibid.* William Windham and fellow MPs threw stones at each other after leaving the House of Commons; later, in St James's Street, they threw oranges.

105 George Brauer, *The Education of a Gentleman: Theories of Gentlemanly Education 1660–1775*, Bookman Associates, New York, 1959, p. 22.

106 Trumbach, *Rise of Egalitarian Family*, p. 130.

107 Bayne-Powell, *English Child*, pp. 49–50.

108 *Ibid.*, p. 2.

109 Defoe, *English Gentleman*, pp. 6–7.

110 *Ibid.*, p. xvi.

111 *Ibid.*, pp. 135–6.

112 *Ibid.*, p. 274.

113 *Ibid.*, p. 272.

114 *Dictionary of National Biography* notes that Dr Samuel Parr (1747–1825) was a master at Harrow in 1766. He then started his own rival school at Stanmore in 1771, then becoming in 1777 Headmaster at Colchester Grammar School. In some respects he had liberal ideas on education, encouraging meetings of a social nature with the boys and promoting literary discussions as well as athletics and cricket. He had the support of aristocratic patrons including the Earl of Dartmouth, and Lady Trafford, mother of one of his pupils, presented him with a perpetual curacy in Warwickshire.

115 Stirling, *Coke of Norfolk*, p. 234, letter from Mrs Coke to Samuel Parr, 1785.

116 Trumbach, *Rise of Egalitarian Family*, p. 214.

117 *Ibid.*

118 Stella Tillyard, *Aristocrats: Caroline, Emily, Louisa and Sarah Leanox, 1740–1832*, Vintage, 1994, pp. 244–6.

119 Bayne-Powell, *English Child*, p. 13.

120 Rogers, *Feminism in Eighteenth Century England*, p. 27.

121 *Ibid.*, p. 29.

122 Maria Edgeworth, *Essays on Practical Education*, 2 vols, J. Johnson and Co., London, 1811, II, pp. 205–15.

123 *Ibid.*, p. 403 and pp. 279–82 *passim*.

124 Reginald Blunt, *Mrs Montague 'Queen of the Blues'*, 2 vols, Constable, London, 1923, p. 319.

125 Lummis and Marsh, *Woman's Domain*, p. 107.

126 Lorna Weatherall, *Consumer Behaviour and Material Culture in Britain 1660–1760*, Routledge, London, 1988, p. 139. The author considers that servants '. . . were not a luxury or a form of conspicuous consumption: they were a fundamental part of domestic life'.

127 Trumbach, *Rise of Egalitarian Family*, p. 135.

128 *Ibid.*

129 Merlin Waterson, *The Servants' Hall*, The National Trust, London, 1990, p. 10.

130 Trumbach, *Rise of Egalitarian Family*, p. 136.

131 Bridget Hill, *Servants: English Domestics in the Eighteenth Century*, Clarendon Press, Oxford, 1996, p. 23 quoting the *Ipswich Journal* for 1755.

132 Waterson, *Servants' Hall*, p. 176.

133 *Ibid.*, p. 170.

134 Trumbach, *Rise of Egalitarian Family*, p. 136.

135 Waterson, *Servants' Hall*, p. 170.

136 John Fowler and John Cornforth, *English Decoration in the Eighteenth Century*, Barrie and Jenkins, London, 1974, p. 76. Rooms were 'dressed' by the Groom of Chambers especially in a large house, that is to say he replaced the furniture which family and visitors had moved. See also Trumbach, *Rise of Egalitarian Family*, p. 136.

137 Trumbach, *Rise of Egalitarian Family*, p. 136.

138 Waterson, *Servants' Hall*, p. 169.

139 Lummis and Marsh, *Woman's Domain*, p. 96.

140 *Ibid*. See also Christine Hardyment, *Behind the Scenes: Domestic Arrangements in Historic Houses*, The National Trust, London, 1997, pp. 49–67. The housekeeper controlled the stillroom with its own fireplace, small oven and boiler as well as charcoal stoves, where preserves were made as were soaps, medicines and cosmetics. She also supervised a storeroom for such items as candles, soap and sugar, a china closet and a linen closet. (Those who were conscious of their social success always had fine linen.) The housekeeper also oversaw the work of the housemaids.

141 Trumbach, *Rise of Egalitarian Family*, p. 137.

142 Waterson, *Servants' Hall*, p. 77.

143 *Ibid.*, pp. 35–8.

144 Trumbach, *Rise of Egalitarian Family*, p. 137.

145 Ronald Fletcher, *The Parkers at Saltram*, BBC Publications, London, 1970, pp. 44–5. The term menial means *intra mura*, 'within walls', according to the law. Although servants were expected to work in different places, rules were laid down for them in works by writers such as Hannah Gasse who wrote *The Art of Cookery* (1747) and *The Servants' Directory* (1760).

146 Hill, *Servants*, p. 155.

147 Waterson, *Servants' Hall*, p. 33.

148 Gretchen Gerzina, *Black England: Life Before Emancipation*, John Murray, London, 1995, pp. 53–4.

149 Lewis, *Walpole's Correspondence*, 34 (III), p. 29, letter to Lady Ossory, 19 October 1788.

150 Gerzina, *Black England*, p. 53.

151 Mark Girouard, *Life in the English Country House*, Yale University Press, London, 1978, p. 208.

152 Waterson, *Servants' Hall*, p. 30.

153 Girouard, *English Country House*, p. 328, footnote 34.

154 Hill, *Servants*, p. 28.

155 Girouard, *English Country House*, p. 328, footnote 34.

156 Hill, *Servants*, quoting Samuel and Sarah Adams, *The Compleat Servant*, 1825.

157 *Ibid.*, p. 37.

158 *Ibid.*, p. 30. La Rochefoucauld, writing in 1789, said that male servants were 'employed only for such duties as are performed in the presence of guests'.

159 Jean Latham, *Happy Families: Growing Up in the Eighteenth and Nineteenth Centuries*, Adam and Charles Black, London, 1974, p. 159.

160 Hill, *Servants*, p. 28.

161 Lummis and Marsh, *Woman's Domain*, p. 81.

162 Hill, *Servants*, pp. 25–6.

163 Waterson, *Servants' Hall*, p. 76.

164 *Ibid.*, p. 77.

165 *Ibid.*, p. 101.

166 Lummis and Marsh, *Woman's Domain*, p. 81.

167 Hill, *Servants*, p. 69.

168 Vickery, 'Women and World of Goods', p. 283.

169 Hill, *Servants*, p. 70.

170 *Ibid.*, p. 80.

171 *Ibid.*, p. 81.

172 Brewer and Porter, *Consumption*, p. 284.

173 Cornforth, *English Interiors 1790–1848*, p. 134, Plate 173 illustrates the cottage at Marton in Yorkshire of Nurse Dodwell. Her sitting room is shown in a watercolour of 1846, but the style reflects George Smith's work as a decorator. The room is in the form of a tent and looks surprisingly like an interior which might have belonged to her employers, the Chichester Constables at Burton Constable.

174 Lewis, *Walpole's Correspondence*, 34 (III), pp. 59–60, letter to Lady Ossory, 4 August 1789.

175 *Ibid.*, 33 (III), p. 354, letter to Lady Ossory, 3 August 1782.

176 Waterson, *Servants' Hall*, p. 26.

177 Somerville-Large, *Irish Country House*, p. 197.

178 Hill, *Servants*, pp. 47–9.

179 Shawe-Taylor, *Georgians*, p. 200, quoting Fanny Burney, *Camilla* (1766), Book IX, ch. II. See also World's Classic edition, ed. Edward and Lillian Bloom, Oxford University Press, 1983, p. 719. Melmond says 'O Fair and angelic Indiana! In a cottage with you would I have dwelt, more delightedly, and more proudly, than any potentate in the most gorgeous palace!'. The footnote on p. 953 says this is a version of the proverb 'Love lives in cottages as well as in courts'.

180 *Ibid.*

181 Lummis and Marsh, *Woman's Domain*, p. 125.

182 Leonore Davidoff and Catherine Hall, *Family Fortunes: Men and Women of the English Middle Class 1780–1850*, Hutchinson, London, 1987, p. 377. By the 1770s servants were summoned from bare premises, by bell and no longer infringed family privacy. Even on ordinary farms, labourers were separated from the family at their own table at the midday meal. Employers feared that their servants, if not separated from them, might act as spies and blackmail them: see Porter, *English Society in the Eighteenth Century*, p. 89.

4

Landscapes, follies and villages

by Pat Gardner

INTRODUCTION

The character of the British landscaped park and garden in the eighteenth century is a complex one. It ranged from ultra-formal terraced gardens to studied naturalism, and all points in between. Although general trends such as the breakaway from formality in garden design can be discerned, it is too simplistic to regard this as a steady linear progression via Bridgeman and Kent to Capability Brown and Humphry Repton and beyond. As Boris Ford reminds us, the English garden's journey during the eighteenth century: 'is as serpentine as some of its paths and lakes, covering several different movements and detours such as Rococo and the ornamented farm'.[1]

Much depended upon the wishes of the patron; their ideas, politics, education and social class all had a bearing on the final design. In some cases the patron demanded a highly individualistic design which did not conform to current 'fashionable' taste. George Booth, second Earl of Warrington, for example, went against prevailing trends when he laid out his park at Dunham Massey, Cheshire, between 1720 and 1748 [49]. He used the straight, radiating lines of the *patte d'oie* or 'goose-foot' formation popular in grand schemes, such as Louis XIV's Versailles. Even by the 1720s formality such as this was starting to fall out of favour – by the late 1740s it was woefully antiquated. An even more extreme example of the disregard for changes in garden fashion is at Stradbally, Co. Leix, in Ireland. As late as 1740 it retained a formal layout in the compartamentalised, Dutch-influenced style of the seventeenth century. Indeed, in the case of the Earl of Warrington, there is no evidence that he actually employed a designer at all – this was partly due to financial constraints, but mainly because he had his own preferences for the layout of the park. He supposedly planted some 100,000 trees on his land; which aside from aesthetics were planned as a source of income for later generations. His reply to claims of extravagance in his planting showed this: 'Gentlemen, you may think it strange that I do these things; but I have the

49] Dunham Massey, Cheshire, from the north. Painting by John Harris, *c.* 1750

inward satisfaction in my own breast; the benefit of posterity; and my survivors will receive more than double the profit, than by any other method I could possibly take for their interest'.[2]

The designs chosen for landscaping commissions often reflected the patron's personal wishes and ideas. The type of garden or park (whether 'formal' or 'natural'), the type of statuary and buildings within the landscape were all subject to his intervention. Nowhere is this more evident than at Stowe in Buckinghamshire.

Envisaged as a political statement from the start, the East Garden was, according to John Martin Robinson, 'a carefully conceived iconographical programme that incorporated political allusions'.[3] Dedicated in large part 'to the Liberty of Great Britain', the layout of the grounds expressed Viscount Cobham's political independence. The Elysian Fields, with their resonances of antiquity, were filled with monuments and statuary which demonstrated Cobham's libertarianism. The Temples of Ancient Virtue and British Worthies contrasted with the Temple of Modern Virtue – designed as a ruin – with a headless statue said to be of Sir Robert Walpole, Cobham's political enemy. One cannot doubt that the ideology expressed here was Cobham's own, rather than that of the designer/architect William Kent [50].

Similarly, the opposite political view was illustrated by the designs chosen by Tory patrons. A famous example was Lord Bathurst's estate, Cirencester Park, in Gloucestershire. Coming from a staunch Tory family, long-time Stuart courtiers, Lord Bathurst was denied office by Walpole and the Whigs. Therefore, in political retirement, he turned his attentions towards developing his estate.

Unlike Stowe and other Whig estates which tended to be isolated in their own grounds away from centres of population, Tory estates such as Cirencester Park were often still part of the village. It accorded with Tory ideas about the role of the landowner as inheritor of ancient paternalistic traditions. They saw themselves as the custodians of traditional values in land and people management. Their use of native craftsmen over foreigners, and the traditional styles they chose, demonstrated this. Lord Bathurst's park also incorporated symbols of his political beliefs. Much was made of the historical associations of the Cirencester area with King Alfred and his defeat of the Danes locally.

Alfred and the Saxons were viewed as quintessentially 'English' – supposed originators of many of the rights 'free-born Englishmen' enjoyed. Bathurst strengthened the connection between the Saxons and Tory belief in tradition by constructing 'Alfred's Hall', formerly 'Wood House' (c. 1721)

50] Gothic Temple (Temple of Liberty) at Stowe, Buckinghamshire

in the middle of his new plantation. Built in a deliberately archaic style, it recalled the great feasting halls of Saxon times. According to Mrs Pendarves (later Mrs Delany) the building was 'now a venerable castle and has been taken by an antiquarian for one of King Arthur's – which apparently gave Lord Bathurst great pleasure'.[4]

The antiquarian can be forgiven his mistake, when we realise that Lord Bathurst 'recycled' medieval and Tudor stone and facings from nearby Sapperton Manor giving the impression that the building had been there centuries. It also gave cachet to Bathurst's extensive plantations – mediating the rawness and implying a traditional landscape. By association it also hinted at an ancient pedigree for Lord Bathurst's family which was not founded in reality.[5]

By the 1740s Bathurst was more overt in his political affiliations – erecting a memorial in his grounds to Queen Anne, last of the Stuarts – an implicit criticism of both the Hanoverian kings and the Whig oligarchy.[6] With the failure of both the 1745 Jacobite rebellion and hopes of a Stuart restoration, Jacobitism was regarded as less politically sensitive and the monument lost much of its impact.

The downfall of the Jacobites had even greater effects on Scottish landscaping. Always poorer than England, with a harsher, colder climate, some of Scotland's landscape designs were also restricted by fines on Jacobite landowners. The fourth and fifth Earls of Traquair, for instance, suffered both personally and financially for their part in the Jacobite Rebellions.[7] In addition, the family was Catholic, incurring heavy fines, which meant that the estate was never rich and landscaping improvements were piecemeal at best. The fourth Earl was responsible for the Long Avenue, a French-style plantation, but was mainly restricted to minor alterations due to impecunity. His elaborate plans for rebuilding the entrance front and landscaping by James Smith were shelved.

Some families, such as the Murrays of Blair Castle and the Dukes of Atholl, had divided loyalties which affected their landscaping style. Following 1745 the anglophile, pro-Hanoverian, second Duke of Atholl altered the old castle and grounds, creating what Mark Girouard calls 'a modern country house surrounded by an English style park'.[8]

The dilemma faced by chieftains such as Atholl was choosing between the stability of Hanoverian rule and older, atavistic links to clan and the Stuarts. The second Duke chose the Hanoverians and his house and park reflected this choice. The third Duke was apparently anglophile too, being painted with his family by Johann Zoffany, then the height of fashion in England [51]. The scene is accordingly cosmopolitan in feel. The family are in current English fashions and there is no specific Scottishness apparent in the painting. The landscape has been softened and 'civilised' – the mountains are less rugged and deciduous rather than fir trees abound. The water-feature looks like an English-style lake rather than a *loch*; the placid scene

51] The third Duke of Atholl and family by Johann Zoffany

accentuated by a swan swimming serenely by. There is no sign of indigenous wildlife, the only animal being the children's pet raccoon from the West Indies. The Duke himself is shown fishing, an altogether less dangerous and more passive activity than hunting.

His successors, though, 'began to go back to Scottish themes and traditions'; the fourth Duke, for instance, is shown in full Highland rig in a painting by David Allan.[9] The background landscape is that which we associate with Scotland-fir trees and moorland – and within its ring of mountains, Blair Castle itself [plate 7]. The wearing of the kilt heightens the feeling of 'Scottishness' without the political sensitivities of the past. One could be proud of Scottish heritage *and* be loyal to the Hanoverians; indeed George IV wore the tartan himself on a visit to Scotland in the 1820s.

The 'wildness' of the landscape is apparent in the Allan picture – the terrain is rugged, apparently without artifice, fitting in with current Romantic thought about the sublimity of the natural world. 'Accessories', such as a gnarled old ghillie and wolfhound, and local game such as a dead stag and blackcock, accentuate the cultural differences between an English and Scottish landscape. It is hardly a typical 'hunting' subject – no riding to hounds here – even if the terrain allowed it.

The contrast between two pictures of the same scene illustrates not only how fashion and cultural changes affected landscape design itself, but how the owner perceived his role in managing the land and how he wanted it to be depicted. This complex process was informed by factors as disparate as political affiliations, cultural hegemony, fashionableness and personal taste.

INFLUENCES ON GARDEN DESIGN: THE FORMAL GARDEN

The patron's input into the final plan was not the only influence on Georgian gardens and parks. The impact of fashion, which often started on royal or the larger aristocratic estates, was responsible for radical changes in landscaping. The 'naturalness' of the *jardin anglais* from the mid-century onwards, was both an English innovation and a reaction to the formality of the French and Dutch models so popular before.

Louis XIV's court at Versailles was the epicentre of the landscaping innovations which spread throughout Europe [52]. The work of André Le Nôtre at Vaux le Vicomte and Versailles was widely copied, albeit less grandly, all over the continent and Britain. The French style was formal – laid out with avenues, fountains and ornamental parterres. Order and symmetry were stressed and nature was 'tamed'; trees were planted in straight rows or 'rides' and water-features tended to be manufactured and contained within straight-sided boundaries.

Similarly, the Dutch fashion was for uniform planting with parterres and topiary. The Dutch style gained currency with the accession of William III, a Dutchman, to the English throne in 1689. William III was a keen

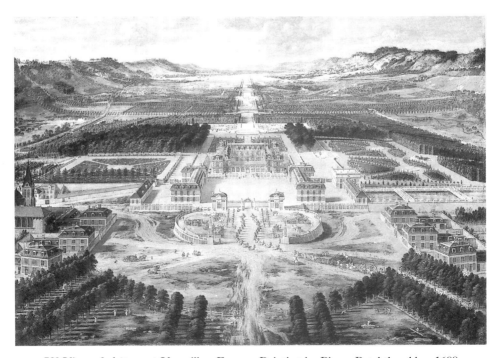

52] View of *château* at Versailles, France. Painting by Pierre Patel the elder, 1688

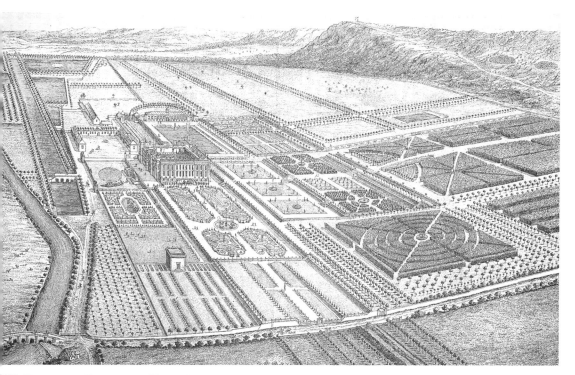

53] Chatsworth, Derbyshire. View of formal gardens taken from Kip and Knyff's *Britannia Illustrata*, *c.* 1711

gardener and garden innovator.[10] The king's ideas for Kensington Palace gardens reflected the formality of French and Dutch gardens, with geometrical parterres, avenues of trees and clipped topiary. It was a style of garden which indicated wealth, power and conspicuous consumption, as the owner had to be sufficiently affluent to employ teams of gardeners to maintain it.[11]

By the time of Charles Bridgeman and Henry Wise's report on *A State of the Royal Gardens from the Revolution to the Year 1727*, this style of garden was seen as old-fashioned and artificial, with a more naturalistic style taking over. Nonetheless, the formal style of landscaping reigned supreme for over thirty years, and houses with such different terrain as Badminton House in Gloucestershire and Chatsworth in Derbyshire both followed an essentially formal layout.[12] The topographical features of the terrain were not allowed to interfere with this process – hills were levelled and the course of streams altered to run along allotted courses [53]. The landscape outside the garden or park was untamed, but within all was order and symmetry, the triumph of man over nature.

In Scotland the legacy of the *Auld Alliance* with France meant French taste was particularly popular, although it had to be adapted to the Scottish climate. For example, the grounds of the sixth Earl of Mar's palace at Alloa

135

were gargantuan in size.[13] Formal features such as 'canals, parterres, ornamental trees and statues' were part of the scheme.

Irish landscaping was also affected by the formal style brought across from England. Later Irish commentators such as Joseph Cooper Walker of the Irish Royal Academy considered this to be yet another aspect of English colonisation.[14] For it involved the eradication of an organic, natural style for the sake of expensive artificiality. The early eighteenth century saw a succession of formal gardens laid down, with English gardeners imported to do the specialised work. Burton House, Co. Cork, for instance, incorporated 'English' pleasure grounds within the fortifications, which had been so necessary until the 1690s.

Wales too, although influenced by the formal style, tended to adapt it into a smaller, cheaper version. As in Scotland and Ireland there were often economic constraints on 'improvements', and the mountainous terrain of much of Wales meant that formal schemes were difficult to implement. Seventeeth-century gardens such as Tredegar and Llanerch were 'relatively modest in size',[15] but by the 1690s some grand formal schemes were being laid down. Those at Chirk Castle in Clwyd and Powis Castle in Powys dated from this time. Powis Castle, a genuine medieval building, had three long terraces built around 1697. An orangery and aviary were added and 'an enclosed valley; laid out initially with lawns and formal pools' which was later described as in a great state of decay.[16]

In garden design the hegemony of England, especially southern England, was absolute. Sometimes provincial English, Scots, Welsh and Irish designs were years behind those of the English *beau monde*. Powerscourt, Co. Wicklow, for instance, had a formal terraced scheme with parterres, laid out as late as 1731–41 – long after the style was outmoded in England.

BREAKDOWN OF FORMALITY

But what had replaced the grand formal style and what were the causes of change? The usual reference point for the rejection of formality in landscaping is Joseph Addison's articles for *The Spectator* in 1712, which advocated a return to 'the Pindaric Manner' which was 'irregular', but imitated 'the beautiful Wildness of Nature, without affecting the nicer Elegancies of Art'.[17] It would be simplistic to assume that Addison advocated a clean break with formality; in these articles there was an awareness that there were 'as many kinds of Gardening as of Poetry'.[18] The monumental and *formal* work of George London and Henry Wise, at Kensington Palace, won them the title of 'Our Heroick Poets' from Addison.[19] In his essay in *The Spectator* of 6 September 1712, Addison developed this connection between landscaping and poetry, where the 'Makers of Parterres and Flower Gardens' are equivalent to 'Epigrammists and Sonneteers'. He judged each style on its merits and its appropriateness for the site.

Addison's own taste was for 'the beautiful Wildness of Nature': appreciation of the natural characteristics of a landscape, enhancing nature rather than eradicating it (as happened in the formal schemes). One must be wary of exaggerating the extent of 'wildness' intended, though, as Addison's own garden at Bilton, Warwickshire, was, apparently, quite formal with parterres and flower gardens.

Although influential, Addison's ideas did not mark the end of formal gardens. However, by the 1730s there was a gradual loosening of formality in design. Symmetry became less important to a scheme and paths became serpentine and meandering, often leading to an interesting garden feature such as a pavilion, cave or grotto.

In England formal designs were associated with French autocracy, which caused ambivalence – on the one hand, admiration for the elegance of the style, on the other, dislike of the political system it represented. The artificiality of the style, with nature clipped and trimmed to extremes, was seen as a signifier of absolute royal power, such as that of Louis XIV at Versailles. This did not accord with Whig ideas of liberty and benevolence; nor did the link with French Roman Catholicism find favour. The sheer size of these gardens and the amount of expenditure needed often meant that British schemes were on a smaller scale. Furthermore, differences in climate and topography between Britain and France meant that wild northern landscapes, such as at Castle Howard in Yorkshire and Chatsworth in Derbyshire, accentuated the difference between 'nature' inside and outside the park.

THE GENIUS OF THE PLACE

Generally speaking, English formal schemes were less rigid than French examples. Quite early on there was an awareness of what Pope later called 'the genius of the place'; a taking account of the topographical and historical features particular to an area.[20] In 1705 John Vanbrugh was in the vanguard of changing taste, with his scheme for Castle Howard. Although keeping some formal features, such as a parterre and regular avenues, he incorporated a curving path around wooded Ray (or Wray) Hill on the east side, in order to conserve it. Henry Wise's orginal suggestion was to clip it into a star shape. There is evidence that the patron, Charles Howard, third Earl of Carlisle, was involved in the preservation of the site, so the star-shape plan was unexecuted.[21]

Vanbrugh's interest in conservation was even more marked at Blenheim where he attempted to retain old Woodstock Manor within his scheme [54]. It had historical and romantic associations as the site of Henry II's *pied-à-terre* for his mistress, 'Fair Rosamund' Clifford. Vanbrugh would have been aware of the historical significance of the manor, but also wanted to preserve it for the practical purpose of being a focal point or 'eyecatcher'

137

54] View of 'Old' Woodstock Manor, near Blenheim, Oxfordshire. This building
was demolished during Vanbrugh's remodelling of the estate, *c.* 1710

for the design. As he pointed out: 'that part of the New Building (Blenheim) has little Variety of Objects. Nor does the Country beyond it Afford any Vallue (sic). It therefore stands in Need of all the helps that can be given, which are only two; Buildings and Plantations. These rightly dispos'd will indeed supply all the wants of Nature in that Place'.[22]

He proposed mixing the old manor house with trees 'Promiscuously set to grow up in a Wild Thicket', thus the semi-ruinous manor house would blend in eventually, making 'one of the most Agreeable Objects that the best of Landskip Painters can invent'. If the house was destroyed, he warned that nothing would be left 'but an Irregular, Rugged, Ungovernable Hill'.[23]

Planting with 'a painterly eye' became increasingly common as the vogue for 'naturalness' took hold. Vanbrugh was somewhat ahead of his time in 1709 with his advocacy of old Woodstock Manor. This was a trend which was to grow, with the work of later landscapers, into a style which incorporated historical and topographical features in a naturalistic landscape.[24] Addison went further than Vanbrugh when he declared that there should be no artificial divide between the garden or park and the surrounding country-side. 'Why may not a whole Estate be thrown into a kind of Garden by Frequent Plantations? . . . Fields of Corn make a pleasant Prospect . . . (and with) the natural Embroidery of the Meadows . . . some small Additions of Art . . . Trees and Flowers . . . a Man might make a pretty Landskip of his own Possessions'.[25]

Addison's use of the term 'Landskip' here suggests a deliberate scene-setting of nature, in the way that an artist composes the elements of a landscape painting. He asserted that nature's works were 'more delightful than artificial shows' and that there was a correlation between 'Art and Nature'. A landscaping which resembled a painted landscape, with all its elements in proper proportion, was better than a random planting.[26]

During his Grand Tour to Italy (1699–1704), Addison had seen the wonders of ancient and Renaissance Italy for himself. Although his interests were primarily antiquarian and historical, he had first-hand knowledge of how ancient buildings had blended in with, and been softened by 'nature'. The landscapes of Claude Lorraine with their inherent affection for the Roman Campagna and its classical past were in sympathy with the theme of a 'Golden Age' – when Man and Nature had been in harmony. Also apparent was an awareness of the transience of humanity's achievements, as in the topographical *capriccios* of Giovanni Battista Piranesi. Although the sheer scale of ancient buildings was evident in these works, as they dwarfed modern bystanders, their severity was tempered by the organic outcrops that colonised them, softening the chiselled outlines. Ultimately the greatest works of art and architecture are overcome by nature – which will not be denied.

The strands of historical and antiquarian interest combined as time progressed, with a love and awe of the wildness and grandeur of the natural world. Ashley Cooper, third Earl of Shaftesbury, had earlier in the century asserted his enthusiasm for 'Nature' which he felt had a 'genuine order'.[27] Accordingly, 'rude rocks' and 'mossy caverns' among other features, as they represented 'Nature', were 'the more engaging, and appear with a Magnificence beyond the formal mockery of Princely Gardens'. Shaftesbury contended that it took both 'Taste and Morals' to achieve human perfection. Taste was attained by the acquisition of correct feelings or 'the polite imagination'.[28] His ideas proved influential, and the combination of the intellect and taste engaging with the natural world was a theme repeated in various guises throughout the period.

THE INFLUENCE OF ALEXANDER POPE

In his garden at Twickenham, the poet Alexander Pope appreciated both intellect and passion. He broke down formality and valued 'natural' features such as the grotto he constructed from a subterranean passage which joined the house to the garden, which was separated by the Hampton Road.[29]

Pope's layout was original in several ways. When he purchased the land in 1719 it was a small, bare area of five acres – tiny by comparison with the vast estates of his aristocratic friends such as Lords Bathurst and Burlington. Small though it was, Twickenham was to fulfil many purposes for Pope. It was a 'test-site' which enabled him to put into action his ideas about laying out gardens in harmony with nature. Also it was near enough to the capital to be a commutable country retreat. It fused the practical function of providing breaks from metropolitan life with the classical ideal of retreat to the country.[30] Classical texts such as Virgil's *Georgics* – on farming

– and his '*Eclogues*' – pastoral poems – accorded with contemporary ideas about the countryside, the natural world and man's interaction with them. In Pope's case it is important to notice the slippage between this rural idyll and reality – far from being just a place of solitary 'communing with nature', Twickenham was the site of elaborate parties for Pope's *literati* friends from London.

Despite the small site, Pope was nothing if not inventive. Unlike a formal scheme, the focal point of the garden was not the house itself. Instead the eye was drawn to different garden features: an orangery, orchard, kitchen garden, garden house and, of course, the grotto. This was achieved by the judicious planting of belts of trees to hide the boundaries of the land, without recourse to walls or fences.[31] A central lawn or bowling green gave a feeling of spaciousness. Artificial 'mounts' were added to give height, acting both as vantage points and as screens to various areas of the garden. Meticulous care was taken in devising sightlines and vistas with the use of urns and statues, which led the eye away from the confined space. A line of cypresses was used formally, both to give the garden length and to lead the eye to the funerary obelisk to Pope's mother, which itself acted as a focal point [55].

Although Pope was in overall charge of the design of the garden, he was helped by William Kent and Charles Bridgeman and others within Lord

55] William Kent's drawing of Pope's garden at Twickenham, showing the Shell Temple and other features, *c.* 1730

Burlington's circle, which ensured a broader vision. Pope's fame as a poet and wit combined with his knowledge of horticulture meant that he was popular as a house guest and amateur landscaper. His contribution to Ralph Allen's Prior Park, for instance, appeared to be that of a mentor and guide to good taste. He suggested the use of several of the features present in his own garden.[32]

Pope's relationship with Lord Bathurst of Cirencester Park was more volatile – with Bathurst accusing Pope of unworthy criticism of his schemes whilst drawing up grandiose plans of his own. Despite this, Pope was almost certainly responsible for encouraging Bathurst in his large-scale planting.[33]

LORD BURLINGTON AT CHISWICK

Pope's writing about gardening and taste was influential, but his contribution is one of several which would determine the direction of the British garden. The scheme of Richard Boyle, third Earl of Burlington, at Chiswick, for instance, was innovative and won praise from Pope himself.[34] Burlington had been greatly influenced by his Grand Tour of Italy and by his study of the works of Palladio and Inigo Jones. Burlington designed most of the garden layout at Chiswick himself – with later contributions from his protégé William Kent, who was also influenced by his own Italian travels [56].

Burlington's early landscaping, was predominantly formal, comprising three avenues with a building or monument as their focal point. Until the 1730s the garden buildings were intended as a homage to antique and Palladian models (the Ionic Temple, for instance) set in a formal landscape. From the early 1730s, Kent's landscaping was looser and more organic. The formal canal on the western side of the house was made serpentine and natural-looking, and an area of lawn was introduced between the canal and the straight avenues. Kent also built the first artificial ruin – the 'Ruined Cascade' of 1738 was, from its inception, battered and delapidated, giving an air of naturalness and long-standing establishment to the canal/'lake'.[35]

WILLIAM KENT AT ROUSHAM

Kent's comparatively small *oeuvre* as a landscaper does not detract from his contribution to the development of the English style. Rousham, near Oxford, for General Dormer, is often considered his finest work [57]. His task there was to rework Bridgeman's formal scheme from the 1720s. In comparison with his work at Holkham in Norfolk and Badminton in Gloucestershire, Rousham is small, but Kent was able to use the constricted site to his advantage in creating his preferred 'carefully contrived succession of spatial experiences'.[36]

Kent's genius lay in creating landscapes with a classical feel, but which blended disparate and anachronistic elements. At Rousham, for example, he remodelled the house in a Tudor or Gothic style, whilst the gardens are

141

Italianate and classical. Features such as the Vale of Venus and Praeneste Terrace recall antiquity, whilst statuary such as Scheemakers's *Lion Attacking A Horse* is influenced by Renaissance Italy.[37] Kent used his sources eclectically, for instance a classical gate, complete with pediment and rustication, abuts on a castellated 'Gothic' seat. Ornamental features such as this were used in conjunction with the topography of the site.

Together with an 'eyecatcher' Triumphal Arch in Aston Field, a Gothic corn mill, called rather grandly the Temple of the Mill, took the viewer's eye beyond the confines of the park into the countryside beyond. The river Cherwell provided a natural barrier against the encroachment of agriculture (rather as the ditch-like ha-ha had been used elsewhere) without breaking up the feeling of continuity with the natural landscape. Kent's use of the Gothic rather than Classical architecture here is an evocation of a native 'English' style. It was a style which was to overtake the Classical in popularity as time went by, but never entirely superseded it.

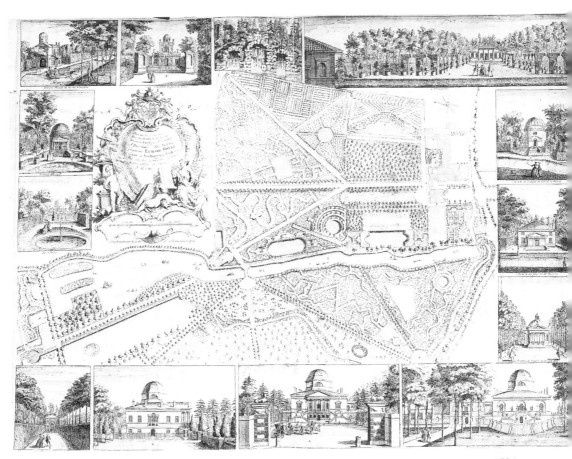

56] Chiswick, Middlesex. Engraved plan of house and gardens by John Rocque, *c.* 1736

57] Rousham, Oxfordshire. View of the Cascades designed for General Dormer by William Kent

WILLIAM SHENSTONE AND THE LEASOWES

Another 'literary' garden of the period was The Leasowes – laid out by William Shenstone, the poet, in mid-century on the relatively small income of £300 p.a. Situated near Halesowen in Worcestershire, the gardens had a blend of urns, statuary and architectural features combined with a freedom of treatment of the landscape intended to engage the viewer's emotions and intellect. In his treatise *Unconnected Thoughts on Gardening* of 1764, Shenstone divided gardening into three types – 'kitchen-gardening – parterre gardening – and landskip or picturesque gardening: which latter . . . consists in pleasing the imagination by scenes of grandeur, beauty, or variety. Convenience merely has no share here; any farther than it pleases the imagination'.[38]

The concept of an emotional response being evoked by the association of objects and the landscape itself was increasingly found as the century progressed. Shenstone suggested that as well as acknowledging the natural topography of the site, the landscaper should 'strengthen its effect' rather than seek to change it. For example, the accompaniments to 'the lover's walk' were 'assignation seats with proper mottoes – Urns to faithfull lovers – Trophies, garlands, &c. by means of art'.[39] Shenstone's ideas, like Pope's, were to influence thought about landscaping far beyond his modest plot.[40]

CHANGES IN IRISH GARDENING

As in England, Irish writers and literary circles were involved in the 'loosening up' of formal gardening in Ireland. Jonathan Swift, author of *Gulliver's Travels*, was in contact with Pope and had stayed with him at Twickenham in the 1720s. Whilst there he visited several of Pope's landscaping friends: Lord Bathurst at Cirencester Park and Lord Bolingbroke at Dawley with its *ferme ornée*. Swift was also aware of the trend towards informality in landscaping, through the work of Addison and Lord Shaftesbury. In 1721 Swift acquired his own garden in Dublin, part of his prebend as Dean of St Patrick's Cathedral. Called, ironically, 'Naboth's Vineyard' – as Swift had appropriated adjoining land to extend his plot which was very small (less than two acres in total). Nonetheless, he incorporated an orchard which produced over 1,200lbs of apples in 1724.[41]

Among Swift's circle were Dr Patrick Delany, a fellow of Trinity College, Dublin, and his wife Mary (formerly Mrs Pendarves). She was particularly interested in landscaping and when in England had visited many of the great estates – from Lord Bathurst's Cirencester to Sir Richard Grosvenor's formal estate, Eaton, in Cheshire. Mrs Delany was an influential figure in Irish landscaping – living long enough (1700–88) to see the changes from the formal style to the picturesque. As a practical gardener, painter and builder of gardenalia such as shell grottoes, she was important in that she used the idea of 'landscape as painting', common to Pope and his circle and adapted to the Delany estate at Delville, outside Dublin [58].

Once again this was a small estate, comprising only 11 acres. To give a feeling of space the Delanys made the most of the surrounding scenery – the Wicklow mountains to the south and the remains, on a hill, of an old castle.[42] Mrs Delany's taste was less formal than her husband's and her innovations at Delville included an elaborate shell grotto 'all fitted up and painted by her own hand'.[43]

Dr Delany's bent was for a more practical use of the landscape – making as Addison called it 'a pretty Landskip of his possessions'. Delany grew oranges, 'melons, beaury pears, grapes, filberts and walnuts' amongst others and had deer grazing in the grounds. However, Delville was not a true *ferme ornée*, such as that at Woburn in Surrey. The latter, the first of its kind, was developed by Philip Southcote in 1735; Southcote incorporated agricultural and horticultural areas into the 'garden' itself, in an encompassing perimeter walk. Mrs Delany's drawings of Delville show a far less agricultural scene, although certain features of the *ferme ornée* were used, such as the perimeter walk taking in the 'working' side of the grounds. The walk also gave fine views of the small deer park and of the countryside beyond. As it was such a small site it could not be viably farmed in the way that the

PLATE 8

Allan Ramsay, *John Stuart, 3rd Earl of Bute*, 1758

PLATE 9

Pompeo Batoni, *Thomas Dundas, later 1st Baron Dundas*, 1764

58] Delville, near Dublin. Reproduction of *Ye Swift and Swans Island* by Mary Delany, 1745

larger English versions were, but Delany was successful in adapting these ideas to suit his circumstances.[44]

The Swift/Delany nexus was important in that it influenced larger landowners such as Lord Orrery in landscaping his estate at Caledon, Co. Tyrone.[45] Lord Orrery incorporated the informal with the classical – antique statues of Minerva and Diana were set in naturalistic groves. Garden buildings included a lodge and 'at the expence of five pounds, a root house, or hermitage to which on Sunday, the country people resort, as the Londoners to Westminster'.[46] Another unusual feature at Caledon was a 'bone house' constructed of thousands of animal bones to make what Lord Orrery called 'an ossified edifice', the purpose of which was to 'strike the Caledonians with wonder and amazement by affixing an ivory palace before their view'.[47]

The hermitage at Caledon was in a clearing surrounded by indigenous trees and shrubs. Built of tree roots and bark, it contained everything necessary for the life of a contemplative hermit. Containing simple, handcrafted furnishings, evidence of erudition was present in manuscripts and mathematical instruments. Although popular in England, too, hermitages seemed particularly apposite in Ireland, with its past history of hermit monks working as illustrators and historians. The lush natural terrain created the illusion of naturalness and historicism more easily.

INFLUENCE OF OSSIANISM

In 1760 James Macpherson published *Fragments of Ancient Poetry collected in the Highlands of Scotland* and later two works, *Fingal* (1761) and *Temora* (1763) which he claimed were the work of the third-century Celtic bard Ossian. Although later largely discredited as forgeries, these works were influential in the development of Romanticism in Britain and Europe. More importantly, though, they told of a unifying mythic past for the countries of the 'Celtic Fringe' – Ireland, Scotland and Wales – then all effectively under English control. It was a theme which some of the non-English landowners used on their estates. In Scotland in 1783, for instance, the viewing pavilion overlooking the River Braan and its waterfall was transformed into 'Ossian's Hall'. Spectacular effects were achieved by the use of mirrors to reflect the falls.[48]

'CAPABILITY' BROWN

In England the landscape park was probably the most important development in garden design. The best-known practitioner of the style was Lancelot 'Capability' Brown who 'improved' almost 200 estates during his long career. His vision, following in Kent's wake, was for serpentine paths and streams, open parkland, rounded hills and naturalistic groves. The landscape park itself was an open expanse of grassland, often with isolated clumps of trees in the middle distance. The parkland advanced up to the house itself and was not artificially compartmentalised by terraces or flower gardens. Critics of Brown's style said that the houses were 'adrift in a sea of turf'.

Brown's aim was to create a sort of Arcadia – a scene of apparent simplicity which engaged both the mind and the emotions. The style was associated with Whig ideas of liberty and free trade – such as at Stowe, where Brown was assistant to William Kent. Indeed, there is evidence that the final scheme was partly Brown's. This is particularly so in the case of the Grecian Valley, which demonstrated some of Brown's ideas about increasing naturalism in the landscape.

The new landscaping ideas were generally unpopular in Tory circles, where the 'perfection of Nature' was regarded as a specious ideal if it broke down the old order of society, isolating landowners from the common people. By surrounding the house with grassland, often itself surrounded by a perimeter wall, the social gulf between the classes was supposedly emphasised. Also the open aspect of the parkland allowed the owner's house and grounds to be displayed in a very conspicuous way, leading to further alienation. Tory critics such as Dr Johnson and Oliver Goldsmith thought that the appropriation of tenants' homes and land, merely to build a bigger park was unacceptable and an abuse of power.

Brown's improvements were nothing if not sweeping; rivers were dammed, water features created, hillsides levelled and trees planted in naturalistic clumps. At Blenheim, Brown dammed the river Glyme to create a spectacular lake. Among other innovations, he demolished parterres dating from Wise's time. At Burghley he destroyed the formal garden and replaced it with a lawn which reached the house itself. Further improvements included a new lake and stone bridge with extensive tree planting behind it. At Longleat, Brown eradicated the old layout and built the Pleasure Walk which featured trees, shrubberies, lawns and a lake. This work cost some £6,000 in 1759.

To achieve this new, apparently simple look was very labour intensive and costly. Brown's commission for Lord Bute at Luton Hoo, Bedfordshire, required over ten years work and cost over £10,000. It involved major landscape changes, among which the valley near the house was dammed and flooded with the river Lea to form an enormous lake, approximately a quarter of a mile across. Brown added interest to the lake by the construction of artificial islands which he planted to give a natural look. This was so successful that when Arthur Young saw it a few years later he declared it 'the finest water I have anywhere seen'.[49]

From the late 1750s Brown's influence was immense. He was a practical businessman as well as a landscaper, employing a skilled team of draughtsmen, surveyors, foremen and gardeners. Brown was the 'ideas man' who made the initial visit (at a fee of 10 guineas a day!) on site and described to potential clients the 'capabilities' (hence his nickname), or potential, of the estate to gain a commission. His team of assistants and foremen oversaw the work whilst he moved on to the next job.[50]

It would be incorrect to imagine that Brown and his men were responsible for all, or even most, of the landscape improvements so fashionable from the 1750s onwards. It has been estimated that there were some 4,000 landed estates at the time of Brown's death in 1783, therefore 'even Brown and his busy team can hardly have been responsible for more than 5 per cent of these'.[51] In reality the situation was complicated; although many parks did have Brown's personal input, others were the work of talented nurserymen such as Richard Woods, who had several important commissions such as Cannon Hall Park and Harewood House both in Yorkshire. Brown's former assistant William Emes was responsible for innovative schemes in the Midlands and Wales – especially at Erddig, Denbighshire, where he remodelled the formal gardens.

GENTLEMEN IMPROVERS

Many of the improvements to estates were planned and executed by the landowners themselves – 'Gentlemen Improvers' – either for reasons of personal taste or economy. If the landowner had a ready workforce on the estate and perhaps a capable land agent to oversee the work, why pay to have a professionally-designed scheme? The apparent simplicity of Brown's style lent itself well to amateur versions, and texts like Thomas Whateley's

Observations on Modern Gardening (1770) gave detailed advice about achieving variations of colour, texture and perspective.

The larger estates became sites of tourism for garden planning, as road improvements encouraged travelling. Like Elizabeth Bennett and her party visiting Pemberley in Jane Austen's *Pride and Prejudice*, genteel visitors were allowed to tour houses and grounds. Some enterprising landowners, such as the Earl of Carlisle at Castle Howard, built inns near their estates to handle the influx of these 'tourists'. Such visitors tended to be from the smaller gentry estates, and after collecting ideas from the show gardens, adapted them to their own situation.

SIR WILLIAM CHAMBERS AND EDMUND BURKE

The Brownian landscape park remained influential, but even in Brown's lifetime it met criticism for being unimaginative. Foremost among the critics was Sir William Chambers with his controversial *Dissertation on Oriental Gardening* (1772). This was a seminal work which argued against the Brownian viewpoint, and advocated a variety of gardening styles. Chambers cited the case of gardening among the Chinese where 'Nature is their patron, and their aim is to imitate her in all her beautiful irregularities'.[52]

Chambers divided Chinese gardens into three types 'the pleasing, horrid and enchanted'. Personally he was fascinated by the 'horrid' category of landscape or scenery; a view that was to become increasingly fashionable among the *cognoscenti*. Edmund Burke's *A Philosophical Enquiry into the Origins of our Ideas of the Sublime and the Beautiful* (1757) gave a theoretical framework for examining popular trends such as Ossianism, the 'Gothic' in both architecture and writing, and an appreciation of the wildness of the natural landscape which prefigured Romanticism.[53]

For Burke, however, natural phenomena such as precipices, mountains and waterfalls should inspire terror, admiration, dread and 'a delightful horror' in the beholder. The main characteristics of the sublime were 'Vastness of Dimension in Depth or Height or Length' which was 'most awe inspiring, especially with rough or broken surfaces'. Another characteristic of the sublime was 'Infinity – a Uniformity with no boundary'. Similarly, edifices such as Stonehenge display another characteristic – 'Difficulty' – being difficult to transport and erect – which should inspire awe – but which are 'artless' in the creative sense. Another category was that of 'Magnificence and Darkness' – where the sombre and rich colours of nature were a cause of admiration.[54]

WILLIAM MASON AT NUNEHAM COURTENAY

Sir William Chambers's call for 'scenes of terror' – a landscape 'half-consumed by fire or swept away by the fury of the waters', caused controversy. It is

59] Nuneham Courtenay, Oxfordshire, showing 'Mason's Garden' by Paul Sandby, 1788

doubtful whether Chambers seriously expected such an inhospitable land-scape to be created in Britain; but it serves as an example of complete antithesis to Brown's ubiquitous smoothness of terrain. Chambers's work, although impractical, stimulated interest in other styles of landscaping. A rebuttal by the poet William Mason, *An Heroic Epistle to Sir William Chambers*, followed in which the sublimity suggested by Chambers was mocked. Mason was also inspired to create a new style of garden (called 'Mason's Garden') on Lord Harcourt's estate at Nuneham Courtenay [59]. Secluded among a thicket of trees and shrubs, it was small – comprising approximately two acres. Here Mason incorporated the classical fondness for urns, temples and statuary with the more radical landscaping of informal flowerbeds and shrub-beries. The 'flower garden' as an area had never entirely died out, even under Brown, but was usually kept at the back or side of the house – out of view. Mason's garden prefigured the later schemes of Humphry Repton *et al.* with its larger-scale informal planting of flowers within the landscape.

WILLIAM GILPIN AND THE PICTURESQUE

From the 1760s the Reverend William Gilpin (1724–1804) had promulgated his ideas of the picturesque. Between 1768 and 1776 he made his 'pictur-esque travels' across many areas of Britain. Starting with the southern counties of Kent and Essex, he eventually visited South Wales (1770), North Wales (1773), the Lake District (1772) and the Highlands of Scotland (1776).

Gilpin recorded his travels in a journal accompanied by his own drawings. After publication his work became extremely popular and raised public awareness of the delights of touring amongst rugged, natural terrain. By 1792 he had turned his attention to the aesthetics of the picturesque in landscape design. His *Three Essays: On Picturesque Beauty: On Picturesque Travel: And On Sketching the Landscape* (1792) attempted to define the picturesque as a mode of beauty.[55] Gilpin defined the picturesque as combining 'roughness or ruggedness of texture, singularity, variety, irregularity, *chiaroscuro* and the power to stimulate the imagination'.

Gilpin's ideas were the starting point for both Uvedale Price and Richard Payne Knight, who took up the cudgels against Brown's successor Humphry Repton (1752–1818).

HUMPHRY REPTON

Following a chequered career as, *inter alia*, textile merchant, small-scale farmer, antiquarian author, political agent and Chief Secretary to the Lord Lieutenant of Ireland, Repton set himself up as a landscape designer in 1788. To gain experience he visited many of the major sites designed by Kent and Brown, and by 1795 he had had over fifty patrons ranging from East Anglian Whig landowners to Nottinghamshire Tories.

Like Brown, Repton was a prodigious salesman. His marketing innovations included the famous 'Red Books', made specifically for his commissions. The Red Books were 'before' and 'after' illustrations of the proposed improvements. By means of sliding tabs or partial overlays, he demonstrated how a property could be transformed. Bound in red morocco leather and containing his own watercolour sketches and text detailing proposed changes, the Red Books were an effective sales enhancer. In addition, Repton's prolific writing on landscape ensured the spread of his ideas. From *Sketches and Hints on Landscape Gardening* (1795) to *Observations on the Theory and Practice of Landscape Gardening* (1803) and, finally, *Fragments on the Theory and Practice of Landscape Gardening* (1816), his books ensured that his ideas were always kept before the public eye.

Repton's earlier work had an awareness of 'appropriation' – by which he meant that the area surrounding the estate appeared at one with the house and park. To achieve this effect he suggested that key buildings in the adjoining villages reflected the style of the 'big house' and that the family coat of arms should be on everything from 'the market-house' to the local milestones. Such devices gave a pleasing first impression of homogeneity to the passing traveller whether owned by the estate or not.

Similarly, Repton attached much importance to the entrance to the estate and the drive leading to the house. Repton attempted to match lodge buildings at the park entrance to the style of the house and park. At Prestwood House, Staffordshire, for example, he suggested a lodge: 'partaking of the stile *(sic)* in which the house itself is built; this Lodge will be so placed as to meet the Eye and become a very picturesque object from both roads'.[56]

PAYNE KNIGHT AND PRICE ON THE PICTURESQUE

Just what constituted the picturesque was a source of increasing controversy in the 1790s. Uvedale Price and Richard Payne Knight, both Herefordshire landowners and amateur landscapers, built on Gilpin's work on the picturesque to produce a critique of the Brownian view of landscaping. Payne Knight's work *The Landscape; A Didactic Poem* and Price's *Essay on the Picturesque* (both of 1794) criticised Brown 'and his imitators' for the unnaturalness of their landscaping, calling it flat and insipid.[57] Brown *et al.* were accused of having no clear distinction between the house and the park, with the lawn rolling right up to the house itself (*cf.* [60] and [61]).

Both Price and Payne Knight preferred the roughness of a landcape created over centuries by rural agricultural processes than by artificial landscaping. Ancient hedgerows, rutted roads, ditches and pollarded trees appealed because of their naturalness within the countryside. Buildings which looked 'antiquated' or were in the vernacular style were preferred to 'foreign' looking ones.[58]

Price's stance was more conservative and paternalistic. Apart from his interest in landscaping, he was concerned about the living conditions of labourers. He saw enlightened estate management, which improved the lot of the ordinary people, as a way of curbing social unrest. Not such a strange idea at a time when the French Revolution was destroying France and threatening the social order in Britain.

REPTON'S LATER STYLE AND PATRONS

Eventually, even Repton's ideas had to change along with society. Like Price he was aware of social changes such as land enclosure and the development of 'new-monied' estates for the merchant classes, which affected traditional rural life. Appropriation *per se* no longer seemed right – it had to include paternalism to materially improve the life of the rural population.[59]

In his later work Repton developed gardens, terraces and pleasure grounds near to the house itself. Rather than occupying one single expanse of parkland, the house and park were now once again clearly divided by formal, often geometric, gardens.[60] Repton's landscape design at Ashridge, Hertfordshire, was self-consciously 'antiquarian', in keeping with the Gothic style residence built by Wyatt. He was aware of the importance of striking the right balance and tone between the style of the house and garden.[61]

Historicism and a harking back to the paternalistic land ownership system of the past appealed to a society which was becoming increasingly industrialised. Smaller-scale 'villa estates' owned by merchants and the rising

60, 61] Contrasting views from Payne-Knight's *The Landscape*, 1794, which
show a 'Brownian' landscape compared with a *picturesque* remodelling of the
same scene

middle classes necessitated a different approach from the large aristocratic
estates.[62] However, Repton found that his commissions were increasingly
coming from this type of estate. To make the best of them required highly
detailed planting schemes rather than an expanse of greensward, which would
only draw attention to their lack of size.[63]

Later landscapers increasingly designed for the smaller estate. J. C. Loudon wrote the extremely successful *Encyclopedia of Gardening* (1822) which dealt with all aspects of gardening for the inexperienced gardener. The title of Loudon's last book, *The Suburban Gardener and Villa Companion* (1838), shows how far landscape and garden design had travelled from early large aristocratic schemes such as Stowe, Cirencester Park and Castle Howard, to include modest middle-class commissions in the early nineteenth century.

LAND USE AND CLASS DIFFERENCES IN LAND OWNERSHIP: STEPHEN SWITZER AND 'RURAL AND EXTENSIVE GARDENING'

An important aspect of landscaping was of linking beauty with practicality. Stephen Switzer (1682–1745) was a major influence on this trend. A nursery-man and garden designer by profession, he endeavoured to promote what he called 'Rural and Extensive Gardening' in publications such as *The Nobleman, Gentleman and Gardener's Recreation* of 1715. This was an important work which suggested leaving 'the Beauties of Nature . . . uncorrupted by Art.[64]

Switzer was also being practical when he suggested the opening up of the garden on to the countryside, as it would lengthen the view of the onlooker and 'make an additional Beauty to the Garden, and by an easy, unaffected manner of Fencing, shall appear to be part of it, and look as if the adjacent Country were all a garden'. These suggestions were commonplace with the advent of the naturalistic style, but were considered radical in 1715 when formal gardens were fashionable.

In his writings Switzer drew on his experience of working at both Castle Howard and Blenheim under Henry Wise and Vanbrugh. As early as 1710 he worked with Vanbrugh at Grimsthorpe in Lincolnshire. At Grimsthorpe Switzer had altered the gardens to include military-style bastions which encouraged looking outward to the surrounding countryside rather than creating introverted exclusive formal gardens.

Switzer also drew on the work of the classical pastoral poets such as Virgil, and, above all, Horace for his ideas. Horace's *Ars Poetica* with its stress on the combination of the beautiful and the useful was an inspiration for Switzer. His work of 1715 was so popular that it was expanded into a three-volume set entitled *Ichnographica Rustica* in 1718, which ran to three editions.[65]

It seems probable that Switzer knew of Addison's influential *Spectator* articles of 1712 with regard to opening up the landscape, and was giving Addison's suggestions a practical slant. Like Addison, Switzer saw no mismatch between the 'practical' rural landscape outside the park and the ornamental walks within. 'And why, is not a level easy Walk of Gravel or Sand shaded over with Trees, and running thro' a Corn Field or Pasture Ground a pleasing as the largest Walk in the Most Magnificent Garden one can think of?'[66]

By the time of the enlarged edition of *Ichnographica Rustica* in 1742, many of Switzer's earlier ideas had been adopted by others.

62] Woburn Park, Surrey. Philip Southcote's *ferme ornée* from an engraving by Luke Sullivan, 1769

BOLINGBROKE, SOUTHCOTE AND THE *FERME ORNÉE*

Following his move to London in 1727, Switzer came into contact with Lord Bathurst and Viscount Bolingbroke. Bolingbroke, a Stuart supporter, had been in exile in France for his beliefs. After his return he bought Dawley in Middlesex as a retreat from inimical Whig-dominated politics. He removed the huge expanse of parkland, let a substantial amount to tenants and renamed the estate Dawley Farm. Apart from making a *ferme ornée* at Dawley, Bolingbroke was making a political statement about his retirement from politics (a covert comparison with the Roman general Cincinnatus, who retired to his farm at the end of his career).[67]

Lord Bathurst, Bolingbroke's friend and fellow Tory, developed a similar system on his estate at Riskins (or Richings) in Buckinghamshire. In fact Riskins was chosen by Switzer in his *Ichnographica* as an example of the *ferme ornée* or 'ornamented farm'. Although sheep might graze in the parkland and there was 'a Cart, Coach or Chaise Road round the whole Plantation', in order to view the rural scene, Riskins was far from an un-structured mish-mash. Switzer's plan of Riskins in the 1742 edition of *Ichnographica* shows a landscape which was still formal, but unifying the agricultural and the aesthetic.

An early follower of Switzer's ideas was Philip Southcote, who made a famous *ferme ornée* at Woburn, Surrey, in 1735 [62] comprising just under 120 acres.[68] At Woburn, Southcote's original idea for 'a garden on the middle high ground and a walk all around my farm, for convenience as well as pleasure' was altered because of advice from his cousin Lord Petre and members of Lord Burlington's circle.[69] Lord Petre advised Southcote on planting schemes, especially for the flower garden. The first recorded example of a herbaceous border was planted as part of the 'belt' or perimeter planting. The walk around the estate took in both 'the areas adorned to the highest degree' and the farmland proper. The two areas complemented each other and were linked by the use of 'decorations which are communicated to every part'. These decorations included shrubs, flowering borders and small trees which gave a continuity throughout the grounds. Woburn was a forerunner of the later 'circuit gardens' which combined a perimeter walk with carefully selected vistas of the estate and of the countryside beyond.[70]

THE MIDDLE-CLASS 'ESTATE'

The flexibility of the *ferme ornée* idea meant that it could be used on smaller properties as well as on large estates. This ensured its popularity from the 1750s among the middle classes who aspired to a country retreat on a small scale.[71] These social aspirants included affluent merchants, bankers or even *nabobs* – expatriates who had made their money in India, in service with the East India Company. Their 'country estates' often met with ridicule, as certain aspects of the large aristocratic estate, such as the landscape park, were not successful 'in miniature'. In 1753 Francis Coventry wrote a famous piece, which mocked 'Squire Mushroom' for his pretensions to grandeur.[72] The size of Mushroom's estate – 'less than two acres', with its 'yellow serpentine river, stagnating through a beautiful valley, near twenty yards in length' – illustrates the absurdity of applying naturalistic landscaping to such a small area [63].

Nonetheless, large numbers of pattern books were published, giving details of proposed 'farm' layouts and architecture, many aimed at middle-class patrons. Isaac Ware's encyclopedic *Complete Body of Architecture* (1756) contained designs for smaller estates, for which he suggested following the example of 'the villas of the ancient Romans'. This was influential, and many middle-class estates were called villas – especially those on the out-skirts of towns and cities. Pattern books from William Halfpenny's *Twelve Beautiful Designs for Farmhouses* (1750) and John Miller's *The Country Gentleman's Architect* (1787) to J. B. Papworth's *Designs for Rural Residences* (1818) all catered for the middle-class market.[73]

The layout of middle-class gardens tended to be symmetrical with formal elements, although the planting could be more naturalistic and paths and hedges might be serpentine. Although many of the professional classes were keen gardeners and planned their own gardens, a number of them employed professional landscapers such as Humphry Repton. Indeed, one of Repton's first commissions (1788), was for the merchant Jeremiah Ives,

63] The Hermitage, North End Road, London. Painting, *c.* 1770, by Theodore de Bruyn, showing a typical middle-class garden 'estate'

owner of Catton Park, outside Norwich. Despite its grand name, Catton Park was a small estate, comprising just a few acres. To make it appear more spacious, Repton planted with extreme care. Belts of trees excluded the nearby village from view – allowing glimpses of the spire – and elsewhere opened up to give the impression of a large, sprawling estate. Small but intricate pleasure grounds were laid out near the house; the approach to the house was enlarged by elaborate screens of shrubs and a winding drive. The drive led out to a 'thatched cottage' lodge which served the dual purpose of an eyecatcher from the house.

The trend towards smaller garden schemes grew as ever more of the clientele of professional landscapers came from the professional classes rather than the landed interest. Towards the end of his career, Repton's commissions were increasingly of this type.[74]

AGRICULTURAL IMPROVEMENTS AND
THE RISE OF THE PATTERN BOOK

The interest in gardening and 'improvement' of one's land was not confined to the middle classes. Proprietors of large tracts of land, such as Coke of Norfolk (regarded as a model improver on his estate at Holkham in Norfolk), also had a host of agricultural pattern books aimed just at them. The needs of a growing population meant that large expanses of agricultural land were not just aesthetically pleasing to the landowner, but necessary for crops. To bring this land under cultivation meant buying up or even just appropriating small farms and common land.

Until the end of the eighteenth century each enclosure required an individual Act of Parliament and investigation by a team of commissioners. Permission to enclose land was costly and time-consuming to obtain. Nonetheless, the number of enclosures rose rapidly during the course of the century.[75] The parliamentary system tended to be heavily weighted in favour of the landowners, however, as to keep their rights to the land cottagers were required to pay for fencing it off and to contribute towards the legal costs of enclosure.

In practice, the majority sold up, giving the large landowner sole control of vast areas of land. Estates were rationalised and consolidated, which made large-scale agricultural methods possible and crop rotation could be more flexible, ensuring greater yields. Larger landowners often went to great lengths to achieve a consolidated estate. Coke of Norfolk, for example, sold off his lands in Lancashire and Oxfordshire in order to enlarge his 'powerbase' – Holkham in Norfolk – by buying up surrounding land.

Pattern books and agricultural manuals aimed at the large landowner abounded. Nathaniel Kent's *Hints to Gentlemen of Landed Property* (1775) was particularly important. Aimed at disseminating practical ideas and scientifically based farming methods, Kent's work influenced patrons such as Coke at Holkham, the Duke of Bedford at Woburn and Lord Brownlow at Belton in Leicestershire. Kent's most important patron was 'Farmer George' himself – George III at Windsor.[76]

At Windsor, he was allowed to put his theories into practice when the king commissioned two experimental farms – the Norfolk Farm and the Flemish Farm – which adapted farming methods to soil type. On the light soil of the Norfolk Farm, over 1,000 acres were cultivated on a five-year crop rotation plan. The heavier soil of the Flemish Farm required a four-year rotation plan and was much smaller – only 400 acres.

Another idea which Kent advocated was the use of 'skill and frugality' in farm building. He advised that agricultural buildings should be useful rather than ornamental. The farm layout should be compact and uncomplicated – Kent particularly favoured square designs – around a courtyard. Above all the buildings should be solid, well built and use serviceable materials. This seems obvious advice now, but in the 1740s and 1750s more and more outlandish designs for farm buildings had appeared. Rococo- and Gothic-inspired outbuildings were fashionable, although the subject of mockery.[77]

This fashionable taste seems laughable now, as Thomas Wright's rural designs for Badminton, Gloucestershire, show. For the fourth Duke of Beaufort, Wright included designs for castellated barns with arrow slits. Sometimes agricultural buildings were deliberately ornamented to act as 'eyecatchers' from the main house.[78]

The eleventh Duke of Norfolk improved his estate at Greystoke in Cumberland with an eclectic mix of Gothic detailed buildings, the names of

157

which reflected his pro-American political stance during the 1770s. Fort Putnam – a half-octagonal building – was named after the American Revolutionary General Putnam, and Bunker's Hill commemorated the first American victory of the War of Independence.[79] At Arundel Castle, Sussex, the Duke's main seat, he designed a 'Tudor' style Home Farm which was made on the former parkland at Rewell Wood. The sale of some of his other lands enabled the consolidation of the Arundel estate by the purchase of some 800 acres to the north of the castle which was made into the new park.

The most popular architectural styles for farms and offices on the new consolidated estates were Classical, Neoclassical and Gothic. Often intended to tone in with the style of the main house, they were sometimes grand edifices in their own right. Other, less well-used styles included the 'Indian', 'Moorish' and 'Chinese' (under the influence of Sir William Chambers's work at Kew for the royal family). Richard Bateman, a 'Gentleman Improver', had a small *ferme ornée* at Grove House, Old Windsor, in the 'Indian' style – which comprised a pagoda-style roof and oriental tiled recesses. Sezincote, Gloucestershire, had a 'Moorish Dairy' within an overall 'Indian' theme designed by Cockerell, *c.* 1808 [64]. The new buildings were to replace earlier outbuildings which spoilt the view from the house, and to act as a focal point for landscaping. Famously at Woburn Abbey, Bedfordshire, Henry Holland designed a 'Chinese Dairy' for the fifth Duke of Bedford in 1791.

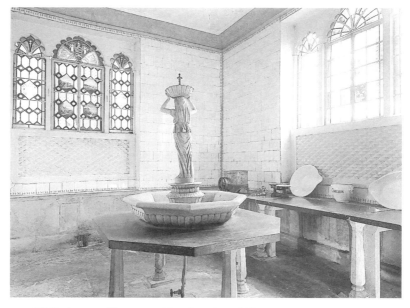

64] Sezincote, Gloucestershire. Interior of Moorish Dairy designed by Cockerell in 1808

ORNAMENTAL DAIRIES

Dairies were often sites of innovation and ornamentation. Prince Puckler-Muskau in his *Tours in England* (1832) described the dairy as 'one of the principal decorations of an English park and stands by itself, quite away from the cow-house'. Apart from their practical purpose of supplying dairy produce to the main house, dairies were considered suitable projects for the involvement of the ladies of the house.[80] Furthermore, the dairy – with the emphasis on extreme cleanliness – was a pleasant place to visit in comparison with other farm buildings, such as the byre and pigsty.

Placed well away from the more mundane farm buildings (on occasion within the confines of the park itself), the dairy was also a site of leisure for landed females. Walks or drives were constructed around the estate with the dairy as the destination or as a stopping-off point. Tea rooms such as the Strawberry Room at Hamels Park, Hertfordshire, were often part of the dairy, or nearby, and provided the ladies with light refreshments.[81]

Other ladies were involved with the design and construction of the dairy itself. There is evidence that the second Countess Spencer designed the rustic dairy at Althorp, Northamptonshire, with the assistance of the architect Henry Holland during the 1760s. The fifth Duchess of Rutland was credited with the design and layout of the farm buildings at Belvoir Castle, Leicestershire. The patronage of the dairy at Frogmore, Windsor, by Queen Charlotte was to prove a counterpart to her husband's agricultural experimentation in the Great Park.[82]

Keeping the produce free from dirt and cool enough to prevent 'turning' was a problem faced by dairymaids. The advent of tiles and ceramic dairyware which did not taint the milk, and was easily washed and sterilised, made their job much easier. Josiah Wedgwood, the ceramics manufacturer, was quick to see a potential market in dairyware and tiles for his Queensware – cream-coloured earthenware.[83]

AGRICULTURAL IMPROVEMENTS AND ENCLOSURE

The life of the female aristocrat was much more circumscribed than that of her male counterpart. Where she was confined to decorous pursuits such as walking, sketching and painting the landscape, men were much more active. Apart from conducting estate business with stewards and land agents, the landowner was the instigator of agricultural improvements to his estate [65]. Farms on large consolidated estates were often not farmed directly by their owners, but rented out to progressive tenant farmers. Tenants were encouraged to use the new agricultural methods and selective stockbreeding, all of which was a far cry from the old, open-field system of smallholders and squatters.[84]

Norfolk, from Holkham to Houghton, had been nothing but 'a wild sheep-walk before the spirit of improvement seized the inhabitants', according

65] *The Woburn Sheep Shearing* by George Garrard, 1804. Such gatherings were encouraged by aristocratic 'improvers' such as the Duke of Bedford at Woburn Abbey, Bedfordshire, to disseminate new agricultural ideas

to Arthur Young, writing in 1768.[85] 'Inclosure', he added, had led to the land being 'cultivated in a most husband-like manner'. Similarly, Sir Christopher Sykes of Sledmere in Yorkshire was responsible for bringing vast tracts of the 'Yorkshire wolds' into production.[86]

Landowners also gave a lead to the large numbers of agricultural societies which sprang up from the 1770s to pass on the new ideas. Coke of Norfolk, for example, held annual meetings at Holkham to demonstrate the new techniques in agriculture and stockbreeding. At the end of his life he claimed to have spent over half a million pounds on estate buildings alone. However true this is, during his tenure the annual estate rental was increased from just over £2,000 to £20,000 – a tenfold increase which would justify his initial outlay.

FORESTRY

Another essential ingredient of the Georgian estate was the planting of great numbers of trees. This brought several benefits to the landowner. First, as in the case of the second Earl of Warrington (1675–1758) at Dunham Massey,

66] Caversham Park, Oxfordshire. Drawing by Dayes showing tree-felling and forestry, an essential part of park management. Engraved by W. and I. Walker, 1773

they provided a profitable income when felled.[87] Oak was particularly valued as the multi-purpose wood of the age. The Royal Navy used it in shipbuilding and it was used in house frames. Second, forestry was combined with landscaping aesthetics, since trees in the landscape softened and naturalised new layouts [66]. Third, trees and shrubs provided a covert for game birds and foxes during field sports such as hunting and shooting, which were extremely popular among landowners.

Landowners planted vast numbers of trees apart from oaks; beech and elm were also popular but in practice many varieties were planted. Coke was said to have planted some forty-nine species at Holkham, for example. Aside from indigenous varieties, trees were imported in great numbers; for example, the Cedar of Lebanon from Asia Minor and the Lombardy Poplar from Italy. Trees from North America included the Weymouth Pine (named after Viscount Weymouth of Longleat), the Virginia Dogwood, the American Lime and the Canadian Poplar. The sheer number of saplings planted was vast. Coke was said to have planted over two million at Holkham, in twenty years. The first Baron Yarborough was even more ambitious and planted over twelve million trees on his estate at Brocklesby, Lincolnshire, during his lifetime.

FIELD SPORTS

The upper-class passion for field sports altered the landscape even further. Aside from the planting of coverts, which served an aesthetic as well as a

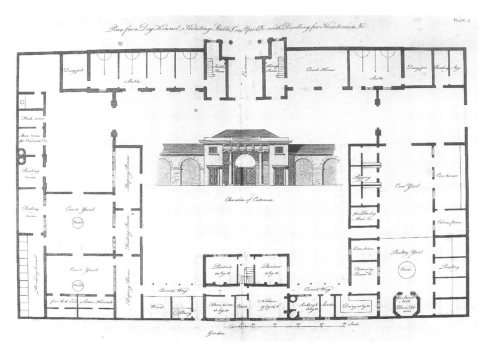

67] Robert Lugar's design for a dog kennel and hunting stables from *The Country Gentleman's Architect*, 1815

practical purpose, field sports required a new form of rural architecture – kennels for the hounds and stables for the hunt horses. Robert Lugar's *The Country Gentleman's Architect* of 1815 had plans for a classically-inspired 'Dog Kennel, Hunting Stable, Cow Yard etc. with Dwelling for Huntsmen &c. proper for a Nobleman or Gentleman' [67]. What is surprising is the extent of the space devoted to the hounds. Lugar advocated a suite of separate rooms for them, including 'a breeding kennel with a feeding room, and another smaller for sick and lame hounds'. There were spacious 'sleeping rooms' which were to be washed out regularly for the comfort of the hounds and to preserve 'their exquisite sense of smelling (on which alone the sport they yield depends)'.[88] That well-known architects such as Lugar and James Wyatt should take such commissions so seriously speaks volumes about the importance of hunting to the upper classes.

RURAL HOUSING AND EMPARKMENT

Whether so much care was lavished with regards to the accommodation provided for farm labourers and cottagers is debatable [68]. The consolidation of the estates, although not the only cause of rural poverty, made life harder for the ordinary people. Enclosure of what had previously been common land and emparking – bringing land within the boundaries of the park itself – led to a 'closed' parish, where the landowner was the only or main landlord. Smallholders and cottagers were encouraged to leave, and their houses pulled down or left to rot. Workers were employed from the 'open' parishes outside the area instead. Arthur Young wrote in 1774 that:

> when a whole parish becomes one farm, under one landlord, the power over both the poor and their habitations will centre in such a landlord and tenant. The tenant pays the poor rates, and perhaps as part of his agreement repairs the cottages here therefore are two strong reasons why he should drive the people away, and let their houses go to ruin, or perhaps advise his landlord to pull them down; first, he eases himself of rates, and secondly he gets rid of repairs.[89]

In 1761 Lord Harcourt replaced the old village of Newnham Courtenay with semi-detached brick cottages placed on the main Oxford to London road. The proximity of the original village to his new Palladian mansion had spoilt the view from the house. The impulse to replace the old cottages with

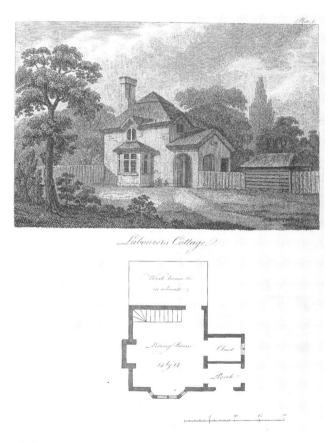

68] Robert Lugar's design for a labourer's cottage from *The Country Gentleman's Architect*, 1815

new 'two-up-and-two-down' houses, complete with dormer window, was less to do with the welfare of the villagers than with a wish to improve the approach to the main house and park. Although the cottagers were described by the pro-Harcourt faction as being fortunate to enjoy 'the comforts of industry under a wholesome roof', the scheme received criticism. For example, Oliver Goldsmith's poem *The Deserted Village* (1770) referred obliquely to Nuneham Courtenay, as 'Sweet Auburn' – in an idealised picture of the pre-enclosure landscape and the effect that enclosure had had on it.[90] Lord Harcourt's scheme was also criticised on aesthetic grounds by advocates of the picturesque such as William Gilpin and Uvedale Price. For Price, the 'methodical arrangement' of two parallel lines of houses, identical in every way, was 'formal and insipid'.[91]

Other landowners built terraces of cottages for the workers. The Earl of Harewood incorporated rather grand terraced cottages along the approach to Harewood House, Yorkshire, in the 1760s, for example.[92] At around the same time Lord Lowther commissioned the Adam brothers to design a new village at Lowther, Cumberland. The layout was somewhat eccentric, using as it did, 'the grandest features of city architecture . . . the crescent and the square upon the mean scale of a peasant's cottage'.[93] Only ever partially completed, this grandiose scheme was never popular with the inhabitants.

MODEL VILLAGES AND PATTERN BOOKS FOR COTTAGES

A famous case of emparkment and relocation of inhabitants was that of Milton Abbas in Dorset. Lord Milton, later Earl of Dorchester, was successful in rerouting three major roads away from his estate in the 1760s. Over the course of twenty years he bought up all the leases of the adjacent town of Milton Abbey to achieve his desire for a solitary grand mansion set in extensive grounds. The town was demolished and Capability Brown was commissioned to design a landscape park on the site.

The majority of townsfolk moved away and Lord Milton engaged Sir William Chambers to design a 'show village' to house the remainder. The scheme was to a uniform plan, but some concessions to the picturesque, such as sympathetic planting near the cottages and a naturally attractive site softened the regularity. The cottages themselves look strong, sturdy and spacious; it is surprising to realise that they were each intended to house more than one family.[94]

Apart from the convenience of the landowner, there was a growing appreciation of the plight of the rural poor. Nathaniel Kent's *Hints to Gentlemen of Landed Property* (1775) was amongst the first to highlight the atrocious living conditions of agricultural workers: 'The shattered hovels which half the poor of this kingdom are obliged to put up with, is truly affecting to a heart fraught with humanity'.

Apart from appealing to the landowners' humanitarianism, Kent added that it was in their financial and social interest to provide decent accommodation for their workers. People living in salubrious surroundings would be healthier and therefore able to work harder, and also greater numbers of their children would survive infancy to service the estate in the future. As the cottages were often 'tied', i.e. the tenants depended on working on the estate to keep their homes, landowners were assured of a relatively compliant workforce.[95] *Hints to Gentlemen of Landed Property* also included plans for suitable cottages which provided plain but adequate housing. Kent estimated that the initial cost of a two-bedroom house was £58 for wooden-built and £66 for one of brick. Kent's book was ground-breaking and several landowners implemented his ideas, such as Lord Brownlow at Belton in Leicestershire.

Another influential work was John Wood's *Series of Plans for Cottages or Habitations of the Labourer* (1781). Wood, the architect of many of the finest buildings in Bath, apparently had humanitarian aims in mind with this book. It was the first publication to concentrate solely on cottage architecture. Wood aimed to improve the lot of those living in 'shattered, dirty, inconvenient hovels'. His designs are a combination of practicality, and the symmetry and regularity found in his grander commissions.

The growing influence of the picturesque was to have its effect on cottage building also, and pattern books for vernacular-style cottages appeared from the 1780s onward. For example, James Malton's *Essay on British Cottage Architecture* (1798) gave advice on conservation and picturesque building.[96] Richard Elsam's *Hints for Improving the Conditions of the Peasantry* (1816) was another work which encouraged better conditions for the labouring classes. Bodies such as the Board of Agriculture, set up in 1793 to establish standards of good agricultural practice, also disseminated the idea of humane living conditions. Their *Communications to the Board of Agriculture* (1797) contained seven chapters concerned with cottage building. The Board's interaction with landowners led to basic standards for cottages being laid down in 1804, which influenced later designs.

INNOVATION AND PATERNALISM

Apart from living accommodation, some enlightened schemes allowed for cottage gardens or allotments (as at Harewood) and others incorporated a common pasture which enabled tenants to graze their own cows (Belton). Coke's estate at Holkham was once again a paradigm of good agricultural practice. His model village, designed by Samuel Wyatt, was considered one of the best of its kind. An innovative feature was single-storeyed cottages for the elderly, which allowed those too old or infirm to work to be part of the community.

Similarly, Blaise Castle Hamlet, near Bristol, was an extension of this idea of charity for the aged or deserving poor. Designed by John Nash in 1811, it comprised ten picturesque cottages around a village green. They were commissioned by John Harford, a Quaker banker and landowner, as 'retreats for aged persons, who had moved in respectable walks of life, but had fallen under misfortunes' and Blaise residents lived rent-free. The quaint style of the houses – all designed to be slightly different – ensured the fame of the hamlet. Thus, in some fifty years since the laying-out of Nuneham Courtenay the balance was redressed, away from housing purely for the landowner's convenience, to a more humane (albeit not totally altruistic) approach.

IRISH AGRICULTURE

The situation regarding land ownership and paternalism was different in other parts of Britain. Ireland, in particular, suffered from absentee landlords who spent their time (and money) away from their estates. As a result, their estates were left in the hands of 'middlemen who relet the lands and live upon the produce, not only in idleness, but in insolent idleness', according to the novelist Maria Edgeworth.[97] Other families, such as the Beresfords of Curraghmore, were semi-nomadic – in their case spending seven years at a time alternating between London and their estate in Ireland. There were all too few 'improving landlords' such as Mr Bernard of Castle Bernard, Co. Cork, who won John Wesley's approval for spending 'his time and fortune in improving his estate and employing the poor'.[98]

Arthur Young itemised the waste of the Irish system in *A Tour of Ireland* (1783). Young had first-hand experience of it as the land agent for the large, but delapidated, Mitchelstown estate in 1777. He was that rare thing, a conscientious agent – in contrast to his predecessors who rarely visited the estate, leaving the administration to a clerk 'who had a summer house in the castle garden for his office'.[99]

Living conditions on the Irish estates were generally worse than in England. Cottages were made of mud rather than brick, for example.[100] Generally, however, conditions were basic until the vogue for model villages arrived in Ireland in the nineteenth century. Irish landowners tended not to be so fussy about the impression delapidated cottages gave of their estate as their English counterparts were.[101]

As in England, timber was valued in Ireland as a source of income. Estates such as Curraghmore, Co. Waterford, had huge tracts of forestry. Elements of the *ferme ornée* proved popular here, too – deer parks, parkland with cows and sheep and cornfields were all within the desmesne lands. Field sports were popular as well, and coverts and lakes were constructed which provided hunting and fishing. There were agricultural improvements – landlords such as Sir James Caldwell of Castle Caldwell, Co. Fermanagh, who introduced different crops, such as new strains of potato. However,

69] Hafod, Cardiganshire, 1792, by John Warwick Smith. Thomas Johnes's estate at Hafod showed the influence of the *picturesque* ideas of Payne-Knight and Price

Irish agriculture tended to be a more makeshift affair than its mainland counterpart.

AGRICULTURAL IMPROVEMENT IN WALES

The situation in Wales was not dissimilar to that in Ireland. A wild mountainous terrain for the most part, it was not fully appreciated until the picturesque came into fashion. A famous Welsh garden-cum-*ferme ornée* was that made by the Ladies of Llangollen at Plas Newydd. Lady Eleanor Butler and Sarah Ponsonby set up home there in 1788 and over the next thirty years or so developed their small estate. Influenced by The Leasowes, Gilpin's tours and Mason's garden at Nuneham, Plas Newydd contained flowers, fruit trees and an ornamental dairy. Another section of their land was kept as a wilder, 'Sublime' area overlooking the surrounding mountains.

Similarly, Thomas Johnes was influenced by both Mason and Gilpin when laying out his grounds at Hafod, Cardiganshire. A cousin of Richard Payne Knight, Johnes established one of the greatest picturesque schemes of the time [69]. Using the natural ruggedness of the terrain as a starting point, he planted over two million trees between 1795 and 1801. His work there 'improved' the natural surroundings; for example, he developed the area around the Cavern Cascade to enhance the view.[102]

167

Johnes also had a social agenda in his planting schemes. Hafod was intended to house a community of contented inhabitants living at one with nature, though due to the intransigence of the tenants, this was never achieved. Living conditions for cottagers in Wales were basic, with the one-storeyed, two-room cottage being commonplace. The ruggedness of the Welsh terrain meant that improvement schemes were more common nearer the coast, often on land which was drained or reclaimed from the sea. Lord Penrhyn, the North Wales slate magnate, had an estate at Penrhyn Castle in which he utilised slate. Apart from the conventional slate roofs, the floors of farm buildings were made of slate and his wife's ornamental dairy was lined with sheets of polished slate from his mine.

SCOTTISH AGRICULTURE

The situation in Scotland was very different from either Wales or Ireland. Unlike them Scotland had no history of absorption, marginalisation, conquest and suppression until after the time of the Jacobite rebellions of 1715 and 1745.[103] Although a colder and poorer country than England, during the course of the eighteenth century Scotland managed to become one of the foremost nations in Europe in the field of agricultural reform. With the defeat of Jacobitism in 1745, the Scottish upper classes turned their attention to building a 'polite society' – based on notions of taste and philosophical ideas thrown up by the Enlightenment. Philosophers such as David Hume, architects such as the Adam brothers and political thinkers such as Adam Smith, all had their roots in a rationalist Scotland.[104]

As in England, improvement and enclosure replacing the old strip-farming system (called runrig in Scotland) had been taking place for many years, albeit at a slow pace. During the eighteenth century the process of change speeded up markedly. The middle of the century saw the general enclosure of the lowland estates, followed later by enclosure in the Highlands themselves. Large-scale agricultural improvements were undertaken by major landowners such as the Earl of Hopetoun at Hopetoun, West Lothian, and the Duke of Argyll at Inverary Castle, Argyll. In both these cases improvement schemes were carried on over several generations.

The third and fourth Dukes of Argyll built improved farm buildings such as the dairy at Tombreac in the 1750s and rationalised the core of the estate.[105] Land was reclaimed or drained, new farmsteads built, barns erected and a new road system laid out in the 1790s. Forestry at Inverary was on a vast scale with upward of 2 million trees planted. Different breeds of livestock were introduced, including a herd of 600 Highland cattle. As at Hafod in Wales, the experiment at Inverary ultimately failed due to the intractability of the local community who preferred traditional farming practices such as crofting to the great agricultural changes which enclosure and increasing mechanisation brought. Nonetheless, in Scotland generally, vast tracts of land were rationalised, their inhabitants displaced and new farming methods and machinery introduced.[106]

The consolidation of large estates such as this were made possible by two Acts of Parliament. The first, passed by the Scottish Parliament in 1695 – 'Act anent Lands lying runrig' – enabled landowners to circumvent the ancient runrig or strip-farming system in order to rationalise their estates. The second act, passed at Westminster in 1770, enabled Scottish entailed estates to be developed and improved. Estimates rate the proportion of entailed estates as up to one-third of the total, so the effects of the act were far-reaching.The resulting large tracts of land were often given over to grazing or planted for timber. There are several well-known examples of comprehensive planting: from Sir John Clerk of Penicuik, Midlothian, who planted over three million trees, to James Farquarson of Invercauld who planted sixteen million. Probably the most famous of all was the fourth Duke of Atholl, who planted over twenty-seven million trees on his estate at Blair Atholl.

Animal husbandry was important, too; native Scottish beasts were crossbred with English breeds to develop new strains, such as the Aberdeen Angus and the Ayrshire cow. This led to changes in the landscape, as new buildings were needed to house the animals and land was set aside for grazing. Cattle breeding and grazing were profitable areas of development for landowners.[107]

THE HIGHLAND CLEARANCES

The removal of crofters from the Highlands to free the land for sheep-grazing was a source of controversy. After 1746 and the defeat of Jacobitism the old system of clans started to break down. Many lairds became absentee landowners or even sold up to outsiders, who did not want to continue the traditional crofting rights of the locals. As many as 20,000 inhabitants of the Highlands and Islands emigrated to America and Canada between 1763 and 1775 alone, a trend which was to continue into the nineteenth century.

The first Duke of Sutherland and his land-agent John Loch planned a new system at his Sutherland estate which was to break down the old pattern of subsistence farming. The inland area was to be turned over to grazing and agriculture where possible and the crofters were to be relocated nearer the coast in purpose-built fishing and coal-mining villages. Thus there was to be a total break with their past as subsistence farmers. The former crofting areas were replaced by large-scale farms with the latest agricultural machinery. Large farmhouses were built to house the affluent tenant farmers, such as at Inverbrora on the Sutherland estate.[108]

DEVELOPMENTS IN AGRICULTURAL EDUCATION

Many of these tenant farmers were educated men who were well aware of the latest developments in stockbreeding and agriculture. The rationality of the Scottish approach was such that many tenants had even studied agriculture at Edinburgh University (where a chair in agriculture was set up in the 1790s). The educated tenant farmer required better accommodation than his predecessors and was more involved in decision-making about the farm. Good tenants were innovative and hard-working and worth the landowner making an effort to keep. The tenant was of a higher social caste than the crofters and there was social interaction between him and the landowner. Given the depopulation of the area caused by the formation of the large tenant farms, the social mix of the area was changed irrevocably.

Pattern books and treatises on agriculture were published to meet the demand from landowners and tenant farmers alike.[109] An early work on enclosure was *An Essay on Ways and Means for Inclosing, Fallowing, Planting etc. in Scotland* by William Mackintosh (1729), and Lord Kames's *Gentleman Farmer* (1776) proved influential later in the century. Lending libraries were established to meet the thirst for instruction and education among the middle classes and agricultural and gardening books proved popular.

As in England agricultural bodies existed to promote and disseminate new ideas about farming. The Edinburgh Society for Encouraging Arts, Sciences, Manufacturing and Agriculture was set up in 1755 and the Highland and Agricultural Society followed in 1784.

CONCLUSION

Traditional histories of landscaping for the period 1700–1830 have usually undertaken a linear approach, with each style neatly superseding its predecessor. Although there are clearly discernible trends such as the breakdown of formality in landscaping and the development of the *jardin anglais* it would be simplistic to assume that these trends were rigidly adhered to. The finances, terrain and, above all, the personal taste of each individual patron would determine the extent fashionable landscaping was followed on his land.

Early in the century Lord Shaftesbury, Joseph Addison and Alexander Pope were influential in changing ideas about the beauty of natural scenery, bringing the surrounding countryside within the scope of the garden. Addison's notion of incorporating agricultural scenery within the bounds of the estate was novel and widely copied in the idea of the *ferme ornée*, such as Philip Southcote's Woburn and Lord Bolingbroke's Dawley Farm.

Combining practical, agricultural landscape with the ornamental park was an idea which continued throughout the century; it brought together the rationalist approach of the Enlightenment and the appreciation of natural beauty found in Brown's ideas and those of the followers of the picturesque. An adjunct of this appreciation of the natural world was an increasing interest in landscaping, gardening and in agricultural improvement. Landscape 'improvers' included George III and his experimental farms at Windsor, through the far-reaching innovations of great landlords such as the Duke of Sutherland, down to the 'villa estate' of the rising middle classes.

Changes in society itself brought about changes in landscaping. The rise of middle-class professionals and their aspirations to an 'estate' meant that the rolling landscaping of Brown *et al.* was unsuitable on a small scale. Professional landscapers such as Repton had to change their style as, by the turn of the nineteenth century, they had a mainly middle-class clientele.

Pattern books and treatises abounded to advise both the middle classes and the 'gentleman improver'. The sheer variety of these works testifies to the growing interest in landscaping. Early works such as Stephen Switzer's *Ichnographica Rustica: Or the Nobleman, Gentleman and Gardener's Recreation,* (1718 – extended 1742), were principally aimed at the aristocratic or the professional landscaper; but later texts such as Thomas Whateley's *Observations on Modern Gardening* (1770) and J. C. Loudon's *Enclyclopedia of Gardening* (1822) also catered for the middle-class market.

Changes to the landscape such as enclosure, emparkment and the development of large areas of land in 'closed parishes' ensured that the landowner's ideas predominated. It is important to stress, however, that the process of enclosure had been going on since the Middle Ages, and that though the eighteenth century saw a rapid increase in the amount of land enclosed throughout the country, it was not uniform, either in acreage or its effect on the local population. For some countryfolk, such as the crofters on the Duke of Sutherland's estate, their traditional way of life was destroyed by the innovations the landowner brought in. Villages or settlements were relocated or rebuilt according to his plans, which had a permanent effect on the social mix of the area.

The introduction of the 'model village' to house dispossessed tenants, served several functions. Landowners such as Lord Milton at Milton Abbas and Lord Harcourt at Nuneham Courtenay rehoused locals for their own convenience, removing encroaching dwellings from their park gates. The model village also served as a site of patronage and munificence. As the housing was 'tied' to the estate the landowner exerted a benevolent paternalism, which acted as a form of social control. Later in the century, an awareness of the dangers of mob rule (as had happened in France) and a genuine interest in humanitarianism following a religious revival, meant that these housing schemes became more attuned to the needs of their inhabitants.

A burgeoning population and drift to the towns and cities permanently altered the way agricultural land was used. To meet increasing demand new methods of farming and crop varieties were introduced, aided by institutions such the Board of Agriculture. For most of the period, agriculture was booming and provided a good return on the landowner's initial outlay. This motivated innovators such as Coke of Norfolk and the Duke of Bedford not only to improve their own lands to the utmost, but to encourage smaller

171

producers with the sheep shearing and agricultural displays which developed into 'agricultural shows'.

The different strands of landscaping, garden design and agricultural improvement during the eighteenth century are difficult to consider in isolation, tied in as they are with notions of fashionability, taste, education and national identity. Functions intertwined; thus a *ferme ornée* could be both a viable farm and an aesthetic statement and an ornamented farm building could be both a practical building and act as an 'eyecatcher' from the main house. In addition, the style chosen for landscaping, garden and farm buildings could reflect the owner's political affiliations as at Cirencester Park and Stowe, as well as current fashionable taste. However, the complexities of Georgian politics and an individual's personal beliefs within the political system make any generalisation regarding 'political landscaping' fraught with danger. For example, the independent Whig politics of George Booth, second Earl of Warrington, are not discernible in the French-style formal parkland he laid out at Dunham Massey in Cheshire up to the 1740s.

Although one can follow the serpentine route of garden design and landscaping through trends and fashions, it is important to remember that each region and estate was different and responded to individual circumstances.

NOTES

1 Boris Ford, *Cambridge Cultural History*, Cambridge University Press, Cambridge, 1992, p. 261.

2 See unpublished M.A. thesis of P. A. Gardner, *Last of the Booths: Patronage and Investment at Dunham Massey Hall 1694–1772*, Manchester Metropolitan University, 1996, p. 15.

3 John Martin Robinson – *Temples of Delight: Stowe Landscape Gardens*, George Philip Ltd (for the National Trust), London, 1990, p. 84.

4 Mrs Pendarves (later Mrs Delany), letter to Dean Swift at St Patrick's Cathedral, Dublin, from Cirencester dated 24 October 1733.

5 The family rose through the ranks of society, generation by generation. Lord Bathurst was only the first Earl Bathurst, his father was only a knight and his great-grandfather only an alderman, so there is some 'slippage' between the image of them as feudal landlords and the reality.

6 There was also a personal dimension to his commemoration of Queen Anne. He had served her at Kensington Palace, and had been there on the day she died in 1714.

7 Mark Girouard, *Historic Houses of Britain*, Artus, London, 1979 (2nd edn 1981), p. 57. There is a tradition at Traquair House that the Great Bear Gates were locked after the departure of Bonnie Prince Charlie and 'would never be opened again until a Stuart king was crowned in London' (*ibid.*).

8 *Ibid.*, p. 77.

9 *Ibid.*, p. 78.

10 According to Daniel Defoe: 'His Majesty was particularly delighted with the decoration of evergreens, as the greatest addition to the beauty of a garden, preserving the figure of the place, even in the roughest part of an inclement and tempestuous winter.' See Christopher Thacker, *The Genius of Gardening: The History of Gardens in Britain and Ireland*, Weidenfeld and Nicolson, London, 1994, p. 158.

11 In 1727 Bridgeman and Wise produced a report for George II – *A State of the Royal Gardens, from the Revolution to the Year 1727* – a cost-cutting exercise which recommended,

among other measures, putting 'the several kinds of clip'd Evergreens out of the gardens' on the grounds that keeping them in trim 'yearly increases the labour and expence [sic] in keeping'.

12 The Duchess of Beaufort was also a keen garden improver, and is recorded as paying large sums to Mansfield in the 1690s for garden design.

13 Tim Buxbaum, *Scottish Garden Building: From Food to Folly*, Mainstream Publishing Ltd, Edinburgh, 1989, p. 9. He mentions a visit to Alloa by John Macky in 1729: 'the plantation is the largest and finest of any in Britain. It far exceeds Hampton Court or Kensington, the gardens consisting of two and forty acres; and the wood with vistas cut through it of 150 acres . . . To the south of the house is the parterre, spacious and finely adorned with statues and vases, and from the parterre to the River Forth runs a fine Terras or Avenue; from whence and from the parterre, you have 32 different vistas; each ending on some remarkable seat or mountain at some miles distant'.

14 Joseph Cooper Walker of the Irish Royal Academy described the transformation of Irish gardens under English influence in the late seventeenth to early eighteenth centuries in his *Essay on the Rise and Progress of Gardening in Ireland*, 'as soon as the English subdued the martial spirit of the Irish . . . they introduced the formal style of gardening, which then and for some years before, prevailed in England'. He mentions Ballybeggan (Co. Kerry) for its 'fine avenues of walnut, chestnut and other trees'; Bangor (Co. Down) had 'gardens which are large and handsome, and filled with noble evergreens of a great size, cut in various shapes'. Water features such as *jets d'eau* and canals existed at Listerne (Co. Waterford) and Thomastown (Co. Tipperary) was terraced 'and filled with statues as thick as trees'. None of these changes met with Cooper Walker's approval, however, as by then naturalism and nationalism had coloured his view – 'Thus did our ancestors, governed by the false taste which they imbied from the English, disfigure with unsuitable ornaments the simple garb of nature': *Transactions of the Irish Royal Academy, Dublin*, 1790, vol. iv, *Antiquities*, pp. 3–19.

15 See Thacker, *The Genius of Gardening*, p. 150.

16 *Ibid.*

17 Thacker, *The Genius of Gardening*, p. 160.

18 *The Spectator*, no. 477, 6 September 1712.

19 *Ibid.*

20 Thacker, *The Genius of Gardening*, p. 161, makes the interesting point that both Addison and Pope were both 'profoundly city-centred, involved in the carefully contrived artificialities of social and cultural life', rather than natural country-dwellers.

21 Edward Malins, *English Landscaping and Literature, 1660–1840*, Oxford University Press, Oxford, 1966, p. 17, about Wise's plan to clip the wood into an ornamental star shape. Here Vanbrugh is bending the rigidity of the formal style to suit his historical bent and the terrain.

22 Vanbrugh wrote a paper called *Reasons for Preserving Part of the Old Manor, 11th June, 1709*, in the hopes of persuading his patroness, Sarah Churchill, Duchess of Marlborough, to no avail!

23 *Ibid.*

24 *Ibid.*

25 *The Spectator*, no. 414, 25 June 1712.

26 See Malins, *English Landscaping and Literature*, p. 22, where Malins suggests that Addison's position is 'a restatement of Longinus . . . For art is perfect just when it seems to be nature and nature successful when the art underlies it unnoticed'.

27 Ashley Cooper, 3rd Lord Shaftesbury, *Characteristicks, vol. II*, London, 1732, p. 231.

28 See Malins, *English Landscaping*, pp. 20–1, on the importance of the acceptance of 'passion' as well as intellect in the creation of taste. Shaftesbury advocated the setting up of busts and statues of abstract qualities such as 'virtue, fortitude and temperance, hero's busts, philosopher's heads; with suitable mottos and inscriptions . . . with all those symmetrys which silently express a reigning order, peace, harmony and beauty'. Malins

comments that 'In placing Man first and Nature's harmony and order as a means to his attaining virtue, Shaftesbury states one of the themes which were constantly repeated throughout the century' (p. 21). We find echoes of it in gardens as disparate as Stowe and Stourhead, The Leasowes and Twickenham.

29 Dr Johnson famously decried this feature: 'but Pope's excavation was requisite as an entrance to his garden, and as some men try to be proud of their defects, he extracted an ornament from an inconvenience, and vanity produced a grotto where necessity enforced a passage'. Dr Johnson is being a little unfair on Pope, who right from the start envisaged the grotto as being an atmospheric retreat rather than just a passageway.

30 As the country was regarded as the repository of purity and innocence in comparison with the corruption of the town, it proved attractive to more than Pope: Viscount Cobham's withdrawal from public life to develop his estate at Stowe was another example of this type of 'retirement'. In addition, one of Pope's finest mature works is his *Imitations of the Satires of Horace* (1733–38), so he would be well aware of the classical author's 'little Sabine farm' as a country retreat – which perhaps influenced the layout of his own estate.

31 Pope had taken painting lessons, *c.* 1713 from his friend, Charles Jervas, so was cognisant of how effects of light and shade were achieved with paint. In fact he looked on landscaping as analogous to painting, and aimed at achieving painterly effects in his planting, such as 'disposing the thick grove work, the thin and the openings in the proper manner'.

32 Letter from Pope to Ralph Allen of Prior Park, 15 May 1740, 'It is my firm resolution . . . to see your garden finish'd (ready for Mrs Allen's grotto and cascade the following year). I must enquire next after hers and your health, after that of the Elms we planted on each side of the lawn? And of the little Wood-work to join one wood to the other below which I hope that you planted this Spring'.

33 In a letter to Robert Digby in May 1722, Pope described himself as 'the Magician appropriated to the Place, without whom no mortal can penetrate into the Recesses of those Sacred Shades'.

34 Alexander Pope's *Epistle to Lord Burlington*, 1731.

35 The source for the cascade was said to be Italian – the 'rustic' cascade at Villa Aldobrandini – which Kent may have seen on his Grand Tour.

36 John Dixon Hunt, *William Kent; Landscape Garden Designer: An Assessment and Catalogue of his Designs*, A. Zwemmer Ltd, London, 1987, p. 78.

37 According to the gardener John Macclary, Scheemakers' horse sits on top of 'a very fine concave Slope, at the bottom of which runs the beautiful river Charvell (*sic*) . . . at this time you have the prettiest view in the whole world, 'tho the most extensive part of it is but short, yet you see from hence five pretty Country Villages and the Grant (*sic*) Triumphal Arch in Aston Field, together with the naturial (*sic*) turnings of the Hills, to let that charming River downe to butify (*sic*) our gardens, and what stops our Long View is a very pretty Corn Mill, built in the Gothick manner': Mavis Batey, 'The Way to View Rousham by Kent's Gardener', *Garden History*, 11 February 1983, pp. 125–32.

38 Shenstone says that the imagination is pleased by 'the great, the various and the beautiful', but some objects and views do not fit neatly into these categories: 'a ruin, for instance, may be neither new to us, nor majestick (*sic*), nor beautiful, yet afford that pleasing melancholy which proceeds from a reflexion on decayed munificence. For this reason an able gardiner should avail himself of objects, perhaps not very striking; if they serve to connect ideas, that convey reflexions of the pleasing kind': William Shenstone, *Unconnected Thoughts on Gardening*, 1764.

39 Similarly, 'wherever a park or garden happens to have been the scene of any event in history, one would surely avail one's self of that circumstance to make it more interesting to the imagination. Mottoes should allude to it, columns, &c. record it; verses moralise upon it; and curiosity receive its share of pleasure': *ibid*.

40 *Ibid.*

41 Although there is no detailed planting scheme extant for Naboth's Vineyard, Swift appears to have assisted friends with landscaping. Knightley Chetwode's scheme at

Woodbrook, near Portarlington, won Swift's approval for its 'winding and meandering riverside walk'. This would appear to indicate a sympathy with a less formal approach to landscaping: see Edward Malins and the Knight of Glin, *Lost Desmesnes: Irish Landscape Gardening 1660–1845*, Barrie and Jenkins Ltd, London, 1976, p. 36.

42 'from whence there is an unbounded prospect all over the country'.

43 Letter from George Montagu to Horace Walpole, 1 October 1761.

44 Cooper Walker attributed to Delany the introduction of the 'modern' style of gardening to Ireland (see Malins and Glin, *Irish Landscape Gardening*, p. 37): 'a style by which Pope, with whom he lived in habits of intimacy, taught him to soften into a curve the obdurate and straight line of the Dutch'.

45 Lord Orrery was also influenced by the large English showgardens at Stowe and Stourhead, the banker Henry Hoare's *tour de force*. Stephen Switzer, a prime influence behind the *ferme ornée* with his seminal work *The Nobleman, Gentleman and Gardener's Recreation* (1715), later enlarged and called *Iconographica Rustica*, 1718, worked on Lord Orrery's English estate at Marston in Somerset, and possibly at Caledon itself.

46 From the Orrery Papers, Houghton Library, Howard College, MS Eng 218.2, vol. 5, p. 55. See also Malins and Glin, *Irish Landscape Gardening*, p. 55.

47 As Lady Curzon had built a similar building at Kedleston, Derbyshire, Lord Orrery wrote to friends in England for construction advice.

48 See Buxbaum, *Scottish Garden Buildings*, p. 150. Dorothy Wordsworth visited the falls with her brother William and described the visit in *Recollections of a Tour Made in Scotland*, of 1803. Entrance to the waterfall room was, according to Dorothy Wordsworth, via a painting of Ossian which parted in the middle revealing the waterfalls beyond.

49 Arthur Young, *A Farmer's Letters to the People of England*, 1768. See also Edward Hyams, *Capability Brown and Humphrey Repton*, J. M. Dent Ltd, London, 1971, p. 55.

50 Several of Brown's assistants eventually set up on their own account and spread the 'natural style' far and wide. Robert Robinson, for example, set himself up in Scotland in 1761 and laid out the grounds of Duddingston House, near Edinburgh, and numerous others in a very Brownian way. David Jacques makes the point that 'his (Robinson's) styles of design and draughtmanship proved to be very similar to Brown's which was not always appropriate in the more rugged Scottish countryside' – another example of fashionability overcoming natural topography: see David Jacques, *Georgian Gardens: The Reign of Nature*, Batsford Ltd, London, 1983, p. 81.

51 Tom Williamson, *Polite Landscapes: Gardens and Society in Eighteenth Century England*, The Johns Hopkins University Press, Baltimore, 1995, p. 82.

52 See Malins, *English Landscaping and Literature*, p. 190.

53 Burke was not alone in his appreciation of the natural landscape; earlier commentators had included Lord Shaftesbury, Joseph Addison and Alexander Pope, and the cult drew inspiration from Longinus (AD 213–273), a Greek philosopher thought to be the author of a treatise on the sublime.

54 Burke, *A Philosophical Enquiry* ... Dr Hugh Blair, Regius Professor of Rhetoric and Belles-Lettres at Edinburgh University from 1762, gave Burke's ideas an Ossianic, Celtic feel – 'the hoary mountain, and the solitary lake; the aged forest, and the torrent falling over the rock' – which inspired mixed emotions, of delight tempered with 'a degree of awfulness and solemnity even approaching to severity ... very distinguishable from the more gay and brisk emotion raided by beautiful objects'.

55 It was through the work of Gilpin that the rarefied ideas of the intelligentsia filtered to a more general audience.

56 From Prestwood House Red Book, 1791. See also Tim Mowl and Brian Earnshaw's *Trumpet a Distant Gate: The Lodge as a Prelude to the Country House*, Waterstone, London, 1985, p. 209.

57 Payne Knight felt that Brown's work lacked the proper painterly division into foreground, midground and background. Repton was accused of falling into the same error by following Brown's style 'without any attention to the natural or artificial character of a place'.

58 Payne Knight put some of his own ideas into practice on his own estate at Downton, where he built a picturesque bridge over a gorge combined with 'eyecatchers' – decorative focal points *en route.*

59 Landscaping should not cut the house off from the rest of the countryside, by 'surrounding a house by a naked grass field'.

60 For example Repton's proposed scheme for Ashridge, Hertfordshire, in 1813 included fifteen different gardens, some of which were very formal in appearance. There was a return to the elaborate rose gardens of the past with a rosarium with roses trained over trelliswork around a central fountain and rosebeds.

61 In his *Fragments on the Theory and Practice of Landscape Gardening* of 1816, Repton claimed that he 'ventured boldly to go back to those ancient trim Gardens, which formerly delighted the venerable inhabitants of this curious spot': *ibid.,* p. 69.

62 The difference in scale between the smaller 'villa estates' and the traditional landed estate meant that practices such as appropriation of the surrounding area were not possible.

63 The period from the turn of the century to the 1830s saw a proliferation of garden designs for the middle-class villa garden or small estate. Landscapers such as William Sawrey Gilpin (1762–1843), nephew of William Gilpin, and John Claudius Loudon (1783–1843) catered for this growing market.

64 'the immuring, or as it were, the imprisoning by Walls . . . too much us'd of late, . . . but Where-ever Liberty will allow, would throw my Garden open to all View to the un-bounded Felicities of distant Prospect and the expansive Volumes of Nature herself': Stephen Switzer, *Ichnographica Rustica, Volume III,* 1718 and 1742.

65 Its aims were to give 'Directions for the Surveying and Distributing of a Country-Seat into Rural and Extensive Gardens, by the Ornamenting and Decoration of Distant Prospects, Farms, Paddocks, etc.'

66 Switzer's vision in *Ichnographica Rustica* of a less formal garden blending with agriculture was to prove influential.

67 Bolingbroke continued the agricultural theme inside the house itself with paintings of farming implements on the walls. His sister, Lady Luxborough, mentioned this in a letter to William Shenstone, dated 28 April 1748. 'When my brother Bolingbroke built Dawley, which he chose to call a Farm, he had his hall painted in Stone-colours, with all the implements of husbandry': Lady Luxborough's *Letters* of 1775, p. 22.

68 This, of course, was much bigger than the Delany estate at Delville in Ireland which was arranged on similar lines.

69 Lord Petre had already improved his own estate at Thorndon Hall in Essex and was an acknowledged botanist, plant collector and landscaper.

70 Estates as disparate as Delville, The Leasowes and Stourhead were all influenced by Woburn, although grand Stourhead could never be called a *ferme ornée!* Robert Castell's *Villas of the Ancients,* 1728, was also influential in landscape design. It contained a layout for Pliny's Tuscan villa which showed the surrounding countryside as well as the villa and its grounds.

71 Alleged social emulation meant that; 'while the nobleman will emulate the grandeur of a prince, and the gentleman will aspire to the proper status of a nobleman; the tradesman steps from behind his counter to the vacant place of the gentleman': Henry Fielding, *Enquiry into the Causes of the Late Increase in Robbers,* Oxford edn, 1988, p. 77.

72 The 'Squire' was an archetype of middle-class emulation of the aristocracy. 'Squire' (a title borrowed from the gentry) implied a long-standing Tory paternalism which was at odds with the reality of *nouveau riche* owners.

73 Lack of space on the smaller estates meant that the planting had to be far more detailed – with flowers, hedges and shrubs – than that of the landscape park. The expanses of rolling turf of the large estates were not feasible, so the middle-class estate contained more decorative planting to make the garden more interesting. Seed-shops were set up in the cities and towns and nurseries on the outskirts to meet the growing demand for

plants and seeds. This would argue for a large, mainly urban, middle-class clientele rather than a select aristocratic one.

74 In Repton's *Fragments* ... of 1816 he mentions that: 'It seldom falls to the lot of the improver to be called upon for his opinion of places of great extent ... while in the neighbourhood of every city or manufacturing town, new places as villas are daily springing up, and these, with a few acres, require all the conveniences, comforts and appendages of larger and more sumptuous, if not more expensive places. And ... these have of late had the greatest claim to my attention'.

75 In 1700–10, for example, there had been only one enclosure, whereas from 1800–6 there were 906.

76 In 1790 Nathaniel Kent was commissioned by the king to design farm and planting layouts on the royal estate in Windsor Great Park. Kent's main aim in estate management was (according to his book) 'to discover and adopt all practicable modes of improvement upon the land'.

77 Robert Morris in his *Architecture Improved*, 1755, scoffed at 'beautiful Henhouses and delightful Cow Cribs, superb Cart-Houses, magnificent Barn Doors, Variegated Barn Racks and admirable Sheep-Folds; according to the Turkish or Persian manner'.

78 Castle Farm at Coleshill, Berkshire, had castellations, arrow slits and a stepped gable which from a distance gave it the appearnce of a medieval building.

79 Although Francis Hiorne of Warwich probable assisted the Duke architecturally, the design of the estate carries Norfolk's idiosyncratic brand of humour, arguing for a large amount of personal input by the patron.

80 Among the reasons for this involvement was the historical tradition – outmoded by the eighteenth century – of the chatelaine of an estate personally supervising the work of the dairy.

81 The ninth Duchess of Norfolk took comfort one step further when she added a library of agricultural books for her visits to the tea pavilion at Worksop Manor, Nottinghamshire.

82 Frogmore was considered innovative, incorporating features such as a decorative fountain, tiled surfaces and ceramic dairyware.

83 From the late 1760s Wedgwood supplied patrons ranging from Queen Charlotte to the Spencers at Althorp, to the Dukes of Marlborough at Blenheim with his products. See also John Martin Robinson, *Georgian Model Farms: A Study of Decorative and Model Farm Buildings in the Age of Improvement, 1700–1846*, Oxford University Press, Oxford, 1983, p. 97.

84 Many modern commentators, such as Frank O'Gorman, take the view that enclosures were not necessarily 'the heartless expropriation of the English peasantry' but part of a long-term agricultural and social process of change. Urban drift and an increased population required the land to be farmed more intensively and effectively than ever before and previously infertile land was brought into production: see Frank O'Gorman, *The Long 18th Century: British and Social History 1688–1832*, Arnold, London, 1997, p. 331.

85 Arthur Young, *A Six Weeks Tour through the Southern Counties of England and Wales*, 1768, p. 21.

86 One of the most ambitious English schemes was the transformation of part of Exmoor by John Knight, a Worcestershire iron-master, and his son. Previously the land had been unusable and did not contain even the most basic infrastructure. Knight invested large sums of money in draining and improving the land and providing farm buildings and roads, gradually creating productive land where none had existed before.

87 Mary, Countess of Stamford, daughter of the second Earl of Warrington, purchased Caverswall estate in Staffordshire in 1759. Unusually for a woman at this time, she guarded her rights as a landowner assiduously, keeping a running correspondence with her solicitor John Jackson regarding Caverswall. The life tenant, Lord Vane, was restricted in the number and location of trees which he was allowed to fell. In 1765, for example, the Countess agreed to Lord Vane felling trees on condition that 'timber near the castle or growing timber is not felled': correspondence between Mary, Countess

Stamford (*née* Booth) and John Jackson, regarding tree felling at Caverswall, Staffordshire, Dunham Massey Papers, ref. EGR/3/7/1/48 at John Rylands University Library, Manchester.

88 Robert Lugar, *The Country Gentleman's Architect*, J. Taylor, London, 1815, p. 16.

89 The exclusion of the poorest people removed the expense of the Poor Law from the shoulders of the landowners and affluent tenant farmers. The power held by landlords in the closed parishes was immense. Whole villages were demolished or moved away from the owner's mansion.

90 The man of wealth and pride
Takes up a space that many poor supply'd
Space for his lake, his park's extended bounds
Space for his horses, equipage and hounds . . .

91 Later critics such as J. C. Loudon found fault with Nuneham for being built 'too like rows of street houses', the biggest mistake being building the village parallel with the main road.

92 The architect, John Carr of York, added Palladian detailing such as arches, pediments and entablatures to give a feeling of unity with the main house.

93 Richard Warner, *Tour through the Northern Counties*, 1812.

94 By the nineteenth century, with the scarcity of rural housing, as many as four families (up to 36 people) were recorded as living in these houses.

95 This form of social control was increasingly valued when the English upper classes saw the aftermath of the social upheaval during the French Revolution.

96 'to perpetuate in Principle that Peculiar mode of Building which was originally the effect of chance'. His own designs aimed for this effect by using uneven walls and vernacular detailing such as dormer windows. Apart from housing estate workers some of the designs were intended for grander *cottages ornées* – as rural retreats for the upper classes.

97 Her own father Richard Lovell Edgworth had, in fact, been an absentee landlord himself before returning to improve his estate in Co. Westmeath.

98 A more common example was the young Lord Donegal, who drew an income of some £31,000 *per annum* from his Irish lands – and spent it all in England.

99 This ramshackle system was made worse by the Irish tenants paying their rents 'in a constant succession of driblets the whole year round'.

100 There was the occasional exception – Cootehill, Co. Cavan, was described as being 'like a pretty English village' by Mrs Delany.

101 Although some, such as the Earl of Orrery, owned estates on the mainland too.

102 Like William Beckford at Fonthill in Wiltshire – a garden which is often compared to Hafod – Johnes used unusual plantings of native American shrubs.

103 Scotland became part of Britain through the Act of Union of 1707, and although influenced by England, retained its own culture, laws and traditions.

104 Alongside ideas of taste and rationality there was a strong practical streak. Indeed, after the 1750s the Scots began to outstrip the English in agricultural developments.

105 The fifth Duke famously continued their work and spent over £50,000 during the 1770s.

106 At Hopetoun (West Lothian) the fifth Earl of Hopetoun spent large sums of money on farm buildings. Always in the forefront of new technology, the Earls of Hopetoun installed new machinery on their farms. A steam threshing machine is recorded as being installed as early as 1839, for instance.

107 'Scotch Beef' had increasingly become synonomous with quality in England, and cattle drives from Scotland down to market in southern England were lucrative.

108 As in England the tenant farmers were men of substantial capital and the farms they controlled were extensive. The average size of a Scottish tenant farm was around 500–700 acres which rivalled the larger English examples.

109 Similar books had been published in Scotland since the late seventeenth century, but it was the latter part of the eighteenth century which saw a vast increase in agricultural works.

5

A temple to the arts

In 1797 a French visitor to James Wyatt's Castle Coole in Co. Fermanagh described it as 'un palais superbe',[1] but also considered it too much like a temple in its chaste classical beauty. Temples, he felt, should be left to the gods.

In the eighteenth century the paintings and sculpture in a country house often made it seem like a temple to the arts and sometimes, through the arts, a temple to certain social and political ideals. Painters, sculptors and architects created actual garden temples within the idealised landscape at Stowe: the Temple of Ancient Virtue and the Temple of Concord celebrated the triumph of Whig policies and the Temple family who lived there.

Country houses seemed to visitors to have something of the aura of temples where the gods might reside. Richard Sullivan in his *Observations* wrote of the hall at Kedleston: 'Here indeed the senses become astonished. In one word, the whole strikes you as if it were designed for more than a mortal residence' [70].[2] A visitor to Newby at the beginning of the nineteenth century described the experience of looking from the dining room to Adam's sculpture gallery as 'into the penetration of the Temple'.[3]

Travellers expected to be able to see the paintings in country houses. Arthur Young wrote of his irritation at having to make an appointment, believing that it was his right to have this important experience.[4] Certainly special arrangements were made for visitors, especially foreign ones, to see the collections at Houghton and Holkham. When Sir Robert Walpole's paintings at Houghton were sold in 1774 there was a public outcry, as though they were a national collection, and John Wilkes demanded that a National Gallery be formed.[5]

Neoclassical architects on the continent designed national galleries which were temple-repositories of art, often enshrining ideas about national identity, as did the classical edifices of Schinkel and Klenze in Germany. Some eighteenth-century English country houses looked like temples and

70] Kedleston, Derbyshire. The Hall, architect Robert Adam, *c.* 1765

were decorated like galleries or museums. Writing to a friend in 1796 about his new house, Ickworth, a great classical pantheon in Suffolk, Lord Bristol described his intention as 'To have a few pictures but choice ones, and my Galleries to exhibit an historical progress of the art of Painting both in Germany and Italy – and that divided into its characteristic schools – Venice, Bologna, Florence, etc. . . .' In fact he seems to have thought of it more as a gallery than a house, and living there was not something he anticipated with pleasure. He went on: 'When that house is finished I hope to make some residence at Ickworth, tho' its vicinity offers nothing . . .'[6]

We must look at the contents of these temples and analyse the way in which the art displayed within enshrined the beliefs and taste of their owners.

SCULPTURE

One of the principal collectors of sculpture at the beginning of the eighteenth century was the eighth Earl of Pembroke (1664–1723). His collection was enhanced, from about 1720, by the addition of 1,300 busts and other sculptures from the Giustiniani Palace in Rome, from the Valetta family of Naples and by works formerly owned by Cardinal Mazarin.[7] Lord Pembroke was principally interested in objects which would illustrate ancient history and literature. 'Busts', observed one writer, 'he was particularly fond of, as they expressed with more strength and exactness the lineaments of the face.' Looking back into history, through collecting not only sculpture but coins, medals, busts and engraved portraits was enough to 'persuade a man he now seeth two thousand years ago'.[8] Lord Pembroke's collection, which took about fifty-five years to amass,[9] was housed in the state rooms at Wilton, although by 1801 James Wyatt had been commissioned to design Gothic cloisters for the display of the collection, which was arranged by Westmacott. Lord Pembroke also, through a desire to make the public aware of his collection, had it catalogued by Count Gambarini.

There was no great public display of sculpture at the beginning of the century in Great Britain. The marble copies made for Louis XIV in Rome of all the finest statues in Italy were the envy of Europe and certainly had no counterpart in this country. Some attempts were made to remedy this situation. Foreign craftsmen began to produce lead garden statuary and plaster copies after about 1700. There were, however, few casts in country houses at the beginning of the century.[10] As these were apparently so hard to come by, patrons had to be satisfied with grisaille painted versions of famous antique sculpture as at Houghton, Moor Park (see [plate 2]) and Raynham.

The Duke of Marlborough had four bronze copies of Soldini in c. 1714 and Lord Stafford at Wentworth Castle also had four marble copies in his gallery.[11] Not to be outdone, his magnificent kinsman, the first Marquess of Rockingham, began ordering sculpture through Lord Malton, his son, who was in Rome in 1749. He wrote to his son, 'If when at Rome you chuse to lay out 4 or 500£ in Marble Tables, statues, as you Shall judge agreeable to you I will answer your Bills to that summ'.[12] A taste for marble was certainly common amongst those who were furnishing country houses, whether in the form of sculpture or furniture. Lord Malton wrote to his father to tell him that he was ordering Sienna marble tables and marble copies of the best antique statues. Seventy years on, the sixth Duke of Bedford was not only a connoisseur of sculpture but became fascinated by specimen marbles, and used those from his Devon estates to enhance his gallery.[13]

One problem encountered by the rich milordi like Lord Malton was having to advance large sums to sculptors, since as he noted, 'the people here are so poor . . . that if one did not advance money, the Greatest Sculptors would starve before it [the work] was finished'. Eventually four works by leading Roman sculptors and four by British artists working in Rome were sent back to Wentworth Woodhouse. Apart from admiring the antique, the English aristocracy had also begun, in a rather uninformed way, to admire some High Renaissance and Mannerist sculpture.[14]

Lord Rockingham had been most concerned that the sculpture should be of particular measurements so that it would fit into the hall. This was a common attitude for much of the eighteenth century: sculpture was regarded as part of an imposing architectural setting by many patrons, and individual pieces had to be suited to an overall scheme. Often plaster casts were considered desirable. Matthew Brettingham the Younger (1725–1803) was in Rome from 1747 to 1754, acquiring antique marble sculpture for the gallery at Holkham, as well as plaster casts. After a time it seems to have occurred to him that it would be to his advantage to buy the moulds from which he could cast several statues once he had returned to England. He created a new way of designing halls, and brought back with him an Italian craftsman, Bartolomeo Matteral, to produce the casts, which he was able to sell to Nathaniel Curzon and Lord Leicester.[15]

Sir Nathaniel Curzon furnished his saloon at Kedleston initially with twelve statues in groups of three, and in the hall by 1760 four of the niches at the north and south ends were to be so embellished, with statues of Antinous, Mercury, Apollo Belvedere and Meleager. Later, in the 1770s, when he had altered the saloon, he removed the statuary from it and put eight of the saloon statues in the hall niches.[16] Brettingham was also able to provide busts of Greek philosophers and poets. Homer, Sappho, Socrates, Virgil, Pindar, Anacreon and Horace were supplied to Kedleston, and this became a fashionable way of introducing sculpture into libraries in the eighteenth century. The heavy pedimented doors – with broken pediments in the case of Holkham – were particularly suited to this type of decoration, whilst Adam's thinner, flatter style offered fewer opportunities. Nevertheless, some of the spaces at Kedleston continued to provide the opportunity to display sculpture. At the foot of the great staircase was the sub-hall, later known as

Caesar's Hall, because of the bronzed plaster busts of Roman emperors displayed around the walls in niches.[17]

At Newby Hall [71], Robert Adam designed a gallery for William Weddell's collection of antique sculpture. Basing his scheme on drawings he had made of Hadrian's villa at Tivoli and of catacombs during the 1750s, he looked also to Charles Louis Clérisseau's work and to the designs of Piranesi. He created a gallery in three sections with a central rotunda for Weddell's collection, which had largely been acquired from Thomas Jenkins. It included the 'Jenkins Venus' which had been sold to Weddell for a vast but undisclosed sum in 1765.[18] These two rooms were lit by windows on one side and the rotunda between them was top-lit. The solemn, tomb-like quality was emphasised by the large *pavonnazzo* sarcophagus in a niche at the far end of the gallery, as well as the Adam-designed cineraria which were provided as pedestals.[19]

Gradually a change was taking place between the 1740s and the 1770s in the way in which sculpture was displayed. At Kedleston statuary was arranged in a setting which suggested, in the columned entrance hall and Pantheon-style saloon, the vestibulum and atrium of ancient Roman domestic

71] Newby Hall, Yorkshire. The Sculpture Gallery, architect Robert Adam, 1767–72

architecture.[20] There was little that was scholarly about this approach, yet English patrons were often keen that sculpture should provide lessons and academic standards to contemporary artists. The Duke of Richmond established a gallery in his house in Whitehall, filled with casts: it was intended to provide an academy of sculpture for students. Between 1771 and 1773 Gavin Hamilton supplied Lord Lansdowne with antique statuary, busts and bas-reliefs for Lansdowne House in Berkeley Square, which was regarded as a major project. Hamilton wrote to Lord Lansdowne, 'The use of this gallery is to be a receptacle of fine antique statues. I should therefore advise throwing our whole strength on this point. I don't mean a collection such as has been hitherto made by myself and others. I mean a collection that will make Shelburne House famous not only in England but all over Europe'.[21] Joseph Bonomi designed a gallery for Townley Hall to house Charles Townley's collection of sculpture in about 1789. This was still decorative and the objects were arranged symmetrically within a rotunda and, although the statues were displayed in a looser way, an attempt seems to have been made at classifying them.[22]

Charles Townley had visited Rome with Henry Blundell in 1776. Blundell, encouraged by Townley, built two galleries to house a very large collection of sculpture.[23] The first of these buildings was a garden edifice turned into a temple, whilst the second was a small-scale replica of the Pantheon [72], which was completed in 1809, at his country house, Ince Blundell in Lancashire. There were five hundred pieces of sculpture in his collection by the time of his death in 1810. Townley had died in 1805, bequeathing his collection to the British Museum, and this collection was the largest in England of its type. Again Henry Blundell was most concerned that his collection should be known and have an effect upon taste, so he published two folios illustrating it through engravings.[24]

Sometimes one particular modern piece of sculpture formed the centrepiece of a room. The fourth Earl of Bristol, a famous eccentric and collector, commissioned the *Fury of Athamas*, inspired by the description in Ovid's *Metamorphoses*. This dramatic and powerful group, based on the Laocoön, showed the infuriated Athamas seizing the child Learchus from the arms of Ino, whilst Melicertes, a mere infant, clings to her, terror-stricken. This group was placed in the hall at Ickworth, Lord Bristol's Suffolk country house, and was lit from the apex of the dome. The sculptor John Flaxman was paid six hundred guineas for the work, yet eventually found himself out of pocket. However, writing to Sir William Hamilton, he made it clear that such a commission, 'reanimated the fainting body of Art in Rome'.[25] It is plain that Lord Bristol had every desire to stimulate the arts and, as we shall see, arrange works so that they might influence the development of painting and sculpture. His idea was, he wrote, that '. . . young geniuses who cannot afford to travel into Italy may come into my [Bristol's] house and there copy the best masters'.[26]

72] Ince Blundell Hall, Lancashire. The Pantheon, 1802–10

Sometimes at a country house it was not antiquity which was worshipped, but a modern hero. The fifth Duke of Bedford (1765–1802) was an admirer of Charles James Fox, who was at the centre of an 'aristocratic Jacobin' circle sympathetic to the ideas of the French republican, and was devoted to liberty.[27] At Woburn, therefore, a Temple of Liberty [73] was created for the Duke of Bedford in 1801, Ionic in style and based upon the Ilissus by Henry Holland. It was in fact situated in the east end of the existing greenhouse, itself remodelled as a sculpture gallery, and its cella projected slightly beyond the original walls to house a bust of Fox by Nollekens. The bust stood upon a pedestal inscribed with a eulogy composed

73] Woburn Abbey, Bedfordshire. The Sculpture Gallery, 1801–18, with the Temple of Liberty at the far (east) end. Architect Henry Holland, with the main gallery completed by Jeffrey Wyatt (later Wyattville)

by the Duchess of Devonshire. Fox, lit from above, looked, with his cropped hair, like a benign Roman senator.[28]

Six friends who supported Fox politically were also represented by Nollekens. These men included Lord Lauderdale, Lord Robert Spencer, a bon vivant and gambler at Brookes, and the second Earl Grey, later Prime Minister – a supercilious man of violent temper. Their busts were set upon console brackets of yellow and black marble,. Fox, 'whose patriot zeal, and uncorrupted mind/Dared to assert the freedom of mankind . . .'[29] was consistently defeated in the House of Commons over such issues as suspension of habeas corpus and the extension of the Law of Treason in 1797. His motion for peace with France was unsuccessful; he withdrew from Parliament, and was also, two years later, removed from the Privy Council. Bedford's temple and busts of his political allies was an act of support for a much admired liberal figure.[30]

There were many other worshippers of Fox, and another Temple of Liberty – by James Gibbs, in a Gothic style at Stowe (see [50]). Also at Stowe was a Temple of British Worthies whose presence embodied the principles of an earlier generation of Whigs. By the turn of the century the heroes venerated by aristocratic admirers tended to be living ones. Lord Leicester planned to have a statue of Napoleon by Chantrey at Holkham and the sixth Duke of Devonshire asked Henry Holland to convert his orangery into a gallery for antique and modern sculpture in 1818. The Duke was a great admirer of Canova and had acquired a large bust of Napoleon (and a seated figure of Napoleon's mother). He wrote that 'A place that was to receive three of Canova's works excited grand ideas'.[31] The setting for such 'grand ideas' was important: the notion of a temple based on the Ilissus, as at Woburn, came from James Stuart's *Antiquities of Athens* (1762), although the Duke of Bedford's version was only three-quarters the size of the ancient original. The tympanum of the temple was designed by Flaxman and contained the figures of Peace, Agriculture and Commerce, with Liberty seated in the centre wearing a cap of liberty. The interior cell was richly decorated. Walls were veneered in marble by Richard Westmacott the elder.[32]

Just as both the fifth and sixth Dukes of Bedford were interested in having sculptured portraits of their contemporaries, so the sixth Duke of Devonshire really preferred works by sculptors he knew, and of personalities who were often his contemporaries – hence his interest in the Bonaparte family.[33] However, both the fifth and sixth Dukes of Bedford and the sixth Duke of Devonshire were great admirers of one particular living sculptor – Antonio Canova. The sculpture gallery at Woburn was filled by the sixth Duke of Bedford with works by Thorvaldsen and Chantrey as well as Canova. In 1818 Sir Jeffrey Wyattville was commissioned to enlarge the sculpture gallery with small blocks at either end. Westmacott produced reliefs for the areas above the arched entrances to these extensions, the subjects of which were *Love with the Graces and Hours* and *The Progress of Man*. At the west end of the gallery a Temple of Graces was created by Wyattville which was reached through *verde antico* columns *in antis* acquired in Rome. Jove's eagle with a laurel wreath in its beak and a thunderbolt in it talons decorated the entablature and double doors opened to the rotunda, which formerly housed Canova's *Three Graces*.[34]

This taste for modern sculpture was therefore a characteristic of the early nineteenth century. There was some difficulty in finding important, rather than second-rate, antique pieces. As we have seen, greater importance was now placed on the individual item, rather than simply creating a pleasing combination of interior classical motifs and whatever antique sculpture might be acquired either in the original or in the form of a cast.[35] Whereas the Dukes of Bedford and Devonshire had generally preferred modern foreign sculpture, the third Lord Egremont (1750–1837), whose father had collected antique marbles, preferred English Neoclassical works by contemporary artists.

Lord Egremont chose works which had the theme of English country life or subjects from poetry. The importance of individual works and particular genius was a feature of the gallery at Petworth, with sculpture by John Flaxman such as *St Michael Overpowering Satan* (1826) – inspired perhaps by Milton's *Paradise Lost* – exhibited in a specially designed area of the gallery.[36]

Loosely connected with the idea of the sculpture gallery was a taste for monuments and mausolea. Sculpture galleries such as that at Newby had contained sarcophagi, and Adam's seats in the hall at Kedleston were in the shape of sarcophagi. French architects such as Blondel and le Camus de Mézières had stressed the importance of sadness as well as other emotions like gaiety or majesty in architecture. The Abbé Laugier had argued that great men should be celebrated through public mausolea rather than monuments hidden in churches. There was a general belief also that virtue, especially civic virtue, should be expressed through public monuments.[37] As death, temples and the melancholy of the ruined tomb or mausoleum had a fascination for eighteenth-century patrons, Soane, Reynolds and Flaxman saw the celebration of famous men as an opportunity for public art, sculpture and history painting.[38] Many architects became interested in drawing existing tombs and designing new ones. Vanbrugh and Hawksmoor were attracted by the idea, and in his *Prima Parte di Architetture*, Piranesi illustrated antique sepulchres. Robert Adam also drew a number of tombs when on his Grand Tour.[39]

James Wyatt produced one of the most famous of mausolea – that at Brocklesby in Lincolnshire [74], erected between 1786 and 1795. This commemorates the life of the young Sophie Aufrere, and is a crisp neoclassical version of the Temples of Vesta at Tivoli and Rome. Here again, family piety, a sense of dynasty and a taste for reviving the antique are brought together in the form of a chamfered Greek cross with parts of imitation porphyry, Corinthian columns at the angles which supported a coffered dome. The monument to Sophie Aufrere was by Joseph Nollekens, but the earlier monuments of the Pelham family,[40] which predate the mausoleum, were produced in Italy in the late 1760s, and brought to England rather as antique sculpture was being imported.

PORTRAITS OF MEN

Portraits of men must clearly have been an important aspect of the decoration of rooms in country houses. The portrait of a nobleman often embodied the political and territorial powers of the British aristocracy in the eighteenth century and created a dominant image in state rooms. Sir Anthony Van Dyck, Sir Peter Lely and Sir Godfrey Kneller had contributed much to this very grand and important art form. It was Sir Joshua Reynolds, however, who from about 1750 to 1790 created a type of male portraiture which seems to embody the political and social significance of eighteenth-century aristocrats, landowners, politicians, and senior naval and army officers. In doing so he frequently added one of the most important elements to the country house.

Reynolds and his contemporaries invented a new way of expressing the dignity and status of male aristocratic sitters. Kneller had cleverly developed a formula for expressing the tastes and aspirations of the well-bred Whig sitter, but this had become somewhat hackneyed through overuse by the middle classes who sought to emulate their social superiors. One writer complained that during the 'genteel mania' of the 1750s, 'all clerks, prentices, etc., are gentlemen every evening'.[41] Reynolds devised a way of using 'The Grand Manner' – the accumulated gravitas especially of Italian Old Master history paintings – as well as the grandeur of seventeenth-century portraits, to bestow an imposing presence upon his patrons. Gentlemen were not to be painted in fashionable clothes: he favoured robes of state, military uniforms and other traditional garments which lent dignity and established a connection between

74] Brocklesby Park, Lincolnshire. The Mausoleum,
1786–95, architect James Wyatt

history painting and portraiture, rich flourishing robes appearing in both. He wished to achieve such a significant image of his sitter that it could be viewed not just as a portrait but as a great work of art, and in the temple of arts which the British country house afforded there would almost certainly be great works of art, some important history paintings perhaps, in various parts of the house.

Reynolds was not the only portrait painter to borrow form the grand manner in his portraits. It was, after all, an aspect of eighteenth-century country houses that reference to great art and architecture of the past should be made wherever the viewer might look, and that the domestic and seemingly personal should be made public through recognisable and traditionally grand imagery. Thus the south front of Kedleston was a Roman triumphal arch and the staircase at Wardour Castle was a version of the Pantheon.

75] Allan Ramsay, *Norman MacLeod, 22nd Chief of MacLeod,*
c. 1747

So, in 1748, Allan Ramsay painted Norman, twenty-second Chief of Macleod [75], in a plaid which has become a toga, and in a pose commonly associated with ancient Roman magistrates. The chief is transformed into a Roman statesman, a man whose responsibility and civic virtue was likened to that of the ancients.[42] Ramsay painted George III's chief adviser and future minister, the third Earl of Bute [plate 8], with a cross-legged pose, again found in ancient statues and much admired in the eighteenth century. Bute's portrait, executed in 1758, shows him in the crimson velvet and ermine of an Earl, and displays his magnificence and political importance.[43] It is an extremely public image and it is interesting to note that Luton Park, the house designed by Adam for Bute in 1767, was similarly public. Its west front, having no apartments, was windowless, and instead had niches to punctuate its elevation. Adam remarked that its decoration 'resembles that of a publick work rather than of a private building, and gives an air of dignity and grandeur, of which few dwelling houses are susceptible'.[44] The portrait and the house were designed for a public man. Adam even used capitals on the screen of columns on the stairs, which he said Wyatt had imitated for the Pantheon in Oxford Street, a public building. Bute was princely in his magnificence: foreigners were astonished at this almost royal display of robes, which also appeared in other portraits by Reynolds.[45]

Reynolds had devised a style where history painting was alluded to with subtlety, just as the settings of such portraits hinted at temples and Roman baths, recognisable to those who had been observant on the Grand Tour. Reynolds, although he attached so much importance to history painting in his *Discourses*, did not intend his sitters to be specifically represented as men of action. The viewer was not required to regard these works as episodes in heroic events of ancient or modern times. By borrowing from Titian and Veronese he was able to use in his portraits something of their dignity and sumptuousness, such as might be found in great scenes of action.[46]

Pompeo Batoni (1708–87) painted his sitters in Rome on their Grand Tours and the portraits were then sent back, often to hang in a country house. He was 'esteemed the best portrait painter in the world' until the early 1780s when he began to fall out of favour. Earlier in Batoni's career Lord Bristol had even had the idea that his house at Ballyscullion should have a gallery largely devoted to Batoni's work.[47] His reputation as a portrait painter was high and he produced about one hundred and sixty portraits of English sitters and forty of Irish, Welsh and Scots ones.[48] Most of his works represented young male aristocrats, elegantly attired and nonchalantly posed, surrounded by antique sculpture and looking rather like highly coloured and polished sculptures themselves. The first Lord Leicester appeared in white Van Dyck Roman carnival costume in 1774, Lord Haddo, son of the third Earl of Aberdeen, who was painted a year later, might well have chosen the antiquities with which he was portrayed, since they were not amongst Batoni's usual props. Whereas a landowner painted at home might have his estate in the background, here a familiarity with Italy was suggested by the Roman Campagna. Often the statuary in Batoni's pictures does not signify ownership, as it might in other types of male portrait, but suggests being *au fait* with classical learning.[49] The extravagant pose of Batoni's *Thomas Dundas, first Baron Dundas* [plate 9], suggests self-confident participation in or enthusiastic engagement with the antique. He was a collector and a member of the Dilettante Society, surrounded by the most famous of ancient works: the Apollo Belvedere, the Laocoön, the Belvedere Antinous and the Vatican Ariadne, arranged in a temple-like setting.[50]

Batoni painted few merchants or financiers[51] and Lord Dundas is every inch a milord in his portrait, unlike Sir Laurence Dundas, his father. Sir Laurence was a rich and successful merchant and contractor. Commissioner General of the Army in Scotland, Flanders and Germany and a Governor of the Royal Bank of Scotland, his fortune amounted to about £900,000.[52] He was never liked by the old families in Scotland, who no doubt remembered that his father had kept a woollen-draper's shop in Edinburgh and regarded him as an upstart. Sir Laurence hankered after a peerage, but his ambitions were rewarded only by a baronetcy. Batoni's Dundas married Lord Rockingham's niece, was made a Baron and his son became Earl of Zetland in 1838. The Dundas family certainly did not want for fine houses. Sir Laurence owned Aske Hall in Yorkshire, Moor Park in Hertfordshire, 19 Arlington Street and Chambers's fine Dundas House in Edinburgh.[53]

PORTRAITS OF WOMEN

If men were painted in the robes or in the poses of Roman magistrates, and their public role was emphasised, how were women depicted? Their portraits, frequently commissioned by male patrons, and hung in public spaces in the country houses, were nevertheless different in character from those of their male counterparts: the display of rank could not be achieved through the same allusions, since women did not occupy the same political or public roles. Nevertheless, women were shown in roles which contributed to the iconography of the country house. The artist was faced with a different problem when representing them to the country house visitor. Allan Ramsay revelled in portraying clothes; although he used a painter who specialised in painting drapery, he himself was also much concerned with the different garments and textures which composed the fashionable image. By the late 1730s, when Ramsay was working in London, there was a great taste for intricate finery. His portraits of the 1750s have a French quality of naturalism about them reminiscent of pastellist Maurice Quentin de la Tour,[54] whose work Ramsay admired for its naturalism and the artist's attempts at capturing the particular. Some of his portraits painted in the mid-1750s, emphasised the fashionable image of women and a Rococo love of embroidery and lace, which makes their portrayal intimate and luxurious.[55] Their status is often suggested through the prodigality with which embroidery is employed: only rich aristocratic women could afford this. Although Ramsay had been trained in the Grand Manner he rejected much of it for a style which owed something to the French Rococo style not only of La Tour but of Drouais and Nattier as well.[56]

Sir Joshua Reynolds observed in his Fourth Discourse, 'If a portrait painter is desirous to raise and improve his subject, he has no other means than by approaching it to a general idea.'[57] This generalisation appeared especially in Reynolds' portraits of women. Wishing to exclude the fashionable and transitory from his portraits he transformed women into allegorical images. Whereas portraits of men hanging in country houses might suggest landownership, country pursuits or rank (in the peerage or naval and military), the role of women was differently interpreted. The country estate was often evoked,[58] and in particular the landscape garden.[59] Often the Poussinesque Arcadia of the improved estate is suggested: *Elizabeth Gunning, Duchess of Hamilton and Argyll*,[60] in a pose derived from Tintoretto [plate 10], rests against a plinth with Paris carved upon it. Paris, as a shepherd, was linked to natural landscape and could be found in some planned eighteenth-century gardens. Reynolds used Venus, who in the classical story was chosen by Paris as the most beautiful of three goddesses. Elizabeth Gunning was, with her sisters, one of the great beauties of the time, and was painted again in 1767 as Venus, by Francis Cotes. Reynolds's portrait dates from the 1750s, and it is interesting to see how the imagery of Venus was used in different cultures and in differing circumstances: the Duchess's portrait merely alludes to Venus, whereas, in François Boucher's *The Toilet of Venus* (1751), Madame de Pompadour was identified with the naked goddess. She commissioned the picture, as one of a pair, for a room with erotic associations, the Salle de Bain, in the retreat she had created for Louis XV and herself at the Château de Bellevue.[61] Reynolds did not use mythology in a playful or erotic way. He employed the diaphanous bedgown attire to give a sense of timelessness – women in the works of Poussin and Claude wear such soft flowing garb. The Duchess's rank is carelessly suggested by her peeress's robe with its four rows of ermine, but as an emblem of status it does not dominate the composition in the way that occurs in portraits of male aristorcrats.

Even betrothal is made rural: Anne Dashwood, about to marry Lord Garlies, MP for Morpeth, was portrayed – as was quite usual for women who were 'marriageable' – as a shepherdess guarding some Claudian flock which has been cut from the landscape.[62] Betrothal and marriage were the important events for women and, if they were marrying into a large family, a celebration of this idea in a landscape garden setting was not inappropriate.[63] As proprietors made all kinds of political and literary statements through the planning and sculpture of their gardens, as at Stowe or Stourhead, to do so in portraiture was perfectly logical. Indeed, even if the family did not possess extensive estates, the symbolism was still powerful, since the idea of extensive acres suggested status and wealth.

Reynolds sometimes showed his sitters in a dark, leafy background with grand, classical garden buildings or even on occasion a tomb.[64] Tomb images found in Poussin's paintings were, as we have seen, a motif inside the country house; at Kedleston, tombs form Adam's hall seat furniture, and at Newby, the sculpture gallery contains a notable Roman tomb, as well as having the aspect of a mausoleum itself. *Lady Sarah Bunbury Sacrificing to the Graces* (1763) does so in a garden building which, like so many built on the eighteenth-century estates, resembles an antique temple. Indeed Woburn was later to have a 'temple' to house Canova's *Three Graces*.

Some of these images of women in an idealised country setting are somewhat passive: *Mrs Hale as Euphrosyne* (see [plate 5]) was not. The engraved version of her portrait contained a quotation from Milton's *L'Allegro*, and it is clear that the dancing Mrs Hale with her streaming hair and child attendants was intended as a Bacchic figure, amorous and even licentious, but carefully contained within the proprieties of marriage.[65] She may have been portrayed by Reynolds as a figure of sensual disorder, but the Music Room at Harewood, where the portrait was hung, was an ordered public space, designed by Robert Adam.[66] If the image of the country house interior was planned, formal and architectural, so (we have noted) was the image projected by the male portraits hanging there. Edward Lascelles, who built Harewood and commissioned Mrs Hale's portrait was, in contrast to his kinswoman, portrayed purposefully striding across his estate, a solid, serious figure in plum-coloured velvet.

Women, in contrast to men, tended to take less active roles as proprietors. They were provided with an image which was peaceful, decorative and childbearing, indicating the continuation of the family line. Often they alluded in a rather indirect way, perhaps through classical mythology, to the part played in their dynasty to the dominant heroic male.[67] Reynolds's use of emblematic figures from Ripa's *Iconologia*[68] in the *Montgomery Sisters* or his references to Guido Reni in *Lady Sarah Bunbury* depended on the response of the educated spectator.[69] Although he made reference to classicism, to the art of the past generally in applying it to portraiture, Reynolds was breaking new ground in a way which, because of its newness, might not be fully convincing. Of Lady Sarah, Mrs Thrale wrote that she 'never *did* sacrifice to the Graces; her face was gloriously handsome, but she used to play cricket and eat beefsteaks on the Steyne at Brighton'.[70]

There was a problem with the use of classical mythology or other aspects of the artistic heritage when they were applied, not only to portraits but also to the country house itself, and especially its interior. Like the painter, the architect was using antique forms in an innovatory fashion to supply a vocabulary in which to express the power and status of landowners.

76] Houghton Hall, Norfolk. The Tapestry Dressing Room, Mortlake tapestries designed by Francis Poyntz,
showing the Stuart dynasty, 1672

In 1758 Lord de La Warr commented adversely on pioneering neoclassical schemes by James Stuart for Lord Nuneham: 'God damn my blood, my Lord, is this your Grecian architecture? What villainy! What absurdity! If this be Grecian, give me Chinese, give me Gothick! Anything is better than this!'[71] It would seem that it was the rather simple dogmatic new Greek revival taste, for which no one in England was prepared which gave offence.

Horace Walpole, seeing Robert Adam's daringly remodelled interiors for Osterley, described the State bed 'with eight columns, too theatric, and too like a modern headdress, for round the outside of the dome are festoons of artificial flowers. What would Vitruvius think of a dome decorated by a milliner?'[72] The Etruscan room was in a style 'unlike anything hitherto practised in Europe', and no one else had 'any idea of applying this taste to the decoration of a room',[73] Adam wrote of his first exercise in the style, for the Countess of Derby at Grosvenor Square. Walpole, on the other hand, wrote of it, 'the last chamber . . . chills you; it is called Etruscan and is painted all over like Wedgwood's ware . . . I never saw such a profound tumble into the Bathos. It is going out of a palace into a potter's field'.[74]

Political sympathies could still be expressed through collections of portraits and their arrangement. At Houghton a firm and continuing allegiance to the royal dynasties of Stuart and Hanover seemed to be affirmed through portraits of Charles I and Henrietta Maria, supported by Walpole family portraits in the drawing room. It might suggest, also, that although the Walpoles served a dynasty which was new, they had a history of loyal service to a ruling family. In the Tapestry Dressing Room [76] full-length tapestry portraits of James I, his queen Anne, and King Christian IV of Denmark, her brother, were displayed.[75] Evidence that it was the Protestant line of James I which was being celebrated was confirmed by *George I in Coronation Robes*,[76] the only portrait to hang in the library, a room which was apparently, the inner sanctum of the Prime Minister.

However, other allegiances might be made apparent through portraiture and Stuart imagery in particular. It has been suggested that the portraits first seen by an eighteenth-century visitor to Chiswick were the key to a whole programme of decoration which favoured the restoration of the Divine Right of Kings through the re-establishment of the Stuart Dynasty. It has therefore been implied that Lord Burlington was a crypto-Jacobite. The doorway into his new villa was surmounted by a bust of the Emperor Augustus. Near at hand was a portrait of Charles I and his family [77], framed in bunches of grapes, which were seen as a symbol of the blood of Christ and of the Divine Right of Kings. Across the octagonal saloon, facing the royal portrait, was a family group with the young third Earl of Burlington and his three sisters. A greyhound, symbol of loyalty, is at the children's side, and one sister holds a pug, a symbol of fidelity, courage and secrecy. A basket of spring flowers is held by another of Burlington's sisters, and a hyacinth which has fallen from it may possibly suggest rebirth, which is apparently a common theme at Chiswick. The display of the busts and portraits here has been interpreted by some writers as alluding to the restoration of Augustus and possibly the reintroduction of ancient values through the restored house of Stuart which would ensure the maintenance of the Divine Right of Kings.[77]

The notion of ancient virtue was not exclusively a Jacobite preserve and the Whig Temple family at Stowe built themselves a Temple of Ancient Virtue believing they, rather than the Stuart dynasty, could celebrate it through adorning a landscape and embellishing their acres.[78] However, the Tory Curzon family at Kedleston adorned their state apartments with portraits which may have indicated political sympathies. The apartments consisted of an Ante-room, Dressing Room, State Bedchamber and Wardrobe. They were more private in planning and decoration than the hall or Saloon and were hung with family portraits dating back to the sixteenth century, which make clear connections with the Stuart kings. These portraits were bought specially at Sir William Stanhope's sale in 1733 – they were not simply an inheritance. There was a copy of a portrait of Charles I by Van Dyck, a portrait of James, Duke of York (1674), and one of Mary of Modena. Again the portrait of Mary Curzon, Countess of Dorset, who was governess to Charles I's children, was copied by William Hamilton from the original at Knole in 1776. William Wissing's portrait of Prince Rupert's illegitimate daughter, who married a member of the Curzon family, established links with the former royal dynasty.[79]

Not only was the political allegiance hinted at through such a collection, but the ancient and illustrious nature of the family was emphasised. Ancestors were valued and at Arundel Castle and Audley End family portraits which had disappeared were replaced by copies. At Arundel, perhaps to fit in with these ancestral portraits, Gainsborough painted the twelfth Duke of Norfolk [78] in historical costume of the Van Dyck period. Gainsborough seems to have specialised in portraying members of the aristocracy whose ancestors had been painted by Van Dyck, in a version of seventeenth-century dress. Sometimes patrons might suggest ancient lineage where none existed, by having themselves painted in historic costume: thus the second Viscount Folkestone was painted in Van Dyck clothing by Thomas Hudson in 1747. Of course the aesthetic appeal of such imagery was also very strong, as the court of Charles I was the apogee of elegant taste to eighteenth-century country house owners.[80] If Inigo Jones inspired the Palladian architecture, might they not also aspire to the grandeur of a Caroline room, like the Double Cube Room at Wilton, in the Jonesian style, the glory of which was Van Dyck's art?

Many Grand Tourists had their portraits painted when in Italy: as we have seen, one influence on this type of portraiture was the existence of a Jacobite court in Rome during the eighteenth century and the portraits produced for it. One of the principal artists who painted both Prince Charles

Edward Stuart and his brother, Henry Benedict, Cardinal York, was Antonio David, who was virtually the court painter to the Old Pretender.[81] The silvery Rococo prettiness of his portraits is akin to that of Allan Ramsay, who himself painted Norman Macleod of Macleod during the period when the wearing of highland dress was proscribed.[82]

  An interest in the Jacobites was clearly not uncommon. Apart from providing interesting gossip they could be used for valuable introductions for the Grand Tourist. Robert Adam when in Rome dined with Dr Irvine, the Stuarts' physician, and was helped by the Abbé Peter Grant of Blairfindy, who was the Scottish Catholic agent in Rome.[83] Scottish country houses and some English ones contained many mementos of the Stuarts, some of which were flagrantly Jacobite: portraits on rings, wine glasses and medals abounded. A particularly interesting memento was the portrait of Prince Charles Edward on a fan surrounded by classical gods, the family of George II retreating in

77] Chiswick House, Middlesex, architect Lord Burlington, c. 1726. Octagon showing the portrait of *The Family of Charles I*

78] Thomas Gainsborough, *Bernard Howard, 12th Duke of Norfolk*, 1788 confusion in the background.[84] Such images and objects belonged to the realm of the cabinet or tribuna; they provided a deliciously covert art form which could be made to disappear instantly if necessary. They also stood in contrast to the large, bold declarations of allegiance which hung in state rooms in massive frames.

LANDSCAPES

Country houses contained substantial collections of landscape paintings. From the beginning of the century artists had described the country estate in various different ways. Leonard Knyff created an image of the trim estate in the form of a 'purspect', usually a bird's eye view.of one of the seats of the nobility and gentry, which appeared in his *Britannia Illustrata* of 1707.[85] Many artists showed landowners against a background of their possessions. Arthur Devis painted landed proprietors and those aspiring to the status of gentry, throughout his career.[86] There is a delicate restrained pride shown by the artist and taken by the sitter in these landscapes, where ancestral or recently acquired acres, angular self-conscious villas, and progeny spread out almost like a living family tree to confront the spectator. They seem to record a family and its possessions, yet there is an element of fantasy in them. When Devis painted Atherton Hall in Lancashire, the home of Robert Gwillym, he had to 'invent' the facade for the picture. Nor was it as trim and prosperous-looking as the artist described it: Dr Richard Pococke in 1745 noted that 'it was not kept in good order'.[87] The rural landscape of the Royds Hall estate, near Bradford, peopled by silken-clad women folk, was also largely the invention of Devis. In fact the estate was the site of the Low Moor Ironworks and was rich in coal and iron, so that in reality the prosperity of the scene derived as much perhaps from industrial as from landed wealth. Nor was its owner, Edward Rookes-Leeds, as substantially landed as he might wish to seem, as he was wildly extravagant and committed suicide because of his mounting financial problems.[88]

Gainsborough also painted a squire with his lands and animals around him in *Mr and Mrs Andrews* (1748–49) [plate 11]. Here we see that not only are the yellow corn and gnarled oaks part of his East Anglian possessions but that his proprietorial air extends to his reticent wife.[89] His country clothes and the ease of his pose suggest a blunt self-confidence in a world that is his own and into which his wife comes invited as a timid stranger who does not plant herself firmly in the landscape as he does.

In most of the landscapes only a little agricultural labour occurs. In the first half of the century the owners of country houses did not really wish to see much activity in the landscapes that hung on their walls. On the whole they preferred to be reminded of Italy rather than their own landscape. Even in 1750 one writer noted 'our painters draw rocks and precipices and castellated mountains because Virgil gasped for breath at Naples, and Salvator wandered amongst Alps and Apennines. Our ever verdant lawns, rich vales, fields of haycocks and hop-grounds are neglected as homely and familiar objects'.[90]

The landscapes admired were by old masters. The tranquil classicism of Claude Lorraine and Gaspard Dughet or the wild rashness of scale of Salvator Rosa were what Grand Tourists bought either abroad or in London salerooms. The landscape room at Holkham [79] is a wonderful example of such a collection. Here Italianate landscapes can be viewed upon the walls, and Kent's landscape inspired by the Roman Campagna can be seen through the windows. Lord Leicester collected the perfectly harmonious, carefully composed landscapes by Claude, with their dark *repoussoir* trees and reconstructed classical temples over a period of about twenty-five years. Matthew Brettingham bought some on his behalf, but Leicester also bought from the

79] Holkham Hall, Norfolk. The Landscape Room

Duke of Portland's collection. He filled his landscape room with works not only by Claude, but also by Domenichino, Locatelli (d. 1741), Orizonte (d. 1749) and Claude Joseph Vernet (1714–89). Apparently between 1714 and 1730 twenty-four Claudes, sixty-six Gaspard Dughets and twenty-two Salvators passed through the London salerooms. Vernet was also very popular with English and Irish collectors.[91] It may be that Lord Leicester was inspired by the collection of landscapes in the cabinet at Felbrigg, made by his neighbour, William Windham, in the 1740s. Windham certainly admired Italianate landscape art, but would not hang British attempts at it upon his walls: 'I would not give the worst Busiri watercolours for four of the best pictures I ever saw by him', he wrote, referring to paintings by John Wootton (see [plate 3]).[92]

Not all the rooms of country houses were hung with idealised landscapes of the Claudian kind. Antonio Canaletto, whose views of Venice were avidly collected by the milordi, visited England and produced some landscapes which combined Venetian and English characteristics. In one of his four views of *Warwick Castle* [plate 12] for Lord Brooke, he appeared to seek topographical accuracy rather than idealised perfection. Yet in drawings related to this picture, he experimented with making the towers of the castle lower, presumably for a more pleasing effect. This English view seems neither rural nor urban. The space in front of the castle has become a place for meeting, as in Canaletto's Venetian scenes, but without conveying the same sense of *imbroglio*: the open chatter of finely dressed people can almost be heard under a near-Mediterranean sky and their jewel-like elegance contrasts with the sobre, beige-clad servants and gardeners, singly going about their work.[93] He produced a Capriccio, *River Landscape with a Ruin and Reminiscences of England*, for Lord King, with rustic figures and rough trees in the foreground and the shining sunfilled elegance of Vicenza in the background.[94] Although he painted country seats such as Alnwick Castle for the first Duke of Northumberland, many of his patrons were pleased to hang his Venetian *vedute* on their walls. The fourth Duke of Bedford, when in Venice in 1731, commissioned twenty-four views of the city from Canaletto which were eventually hung at Woburn Abbey.[95]

There is no doubt, however, that some country house owners valued an idealised view of their own estate in the manner of Claude. John Wootton and George Lambert had introduced some elements of this into their estate pictures, but it was Richard Wilson who succeeded in instilling into his work the qualities which the aristocracy admired. It was important that landscape paintings should convey an awareness of classical mythology, of a visit to Italy, but also a sense of possession. The 'portrait' of the estate needed to be recorded because it was an image of the source of political power and social prestige. In such paintings as his five views of Wilton House, Wiltshire (*c*. 1758–50) [80]), Wilson was able to create a Claudian image of a landscape which was famed for its classical buildings including the house itself by Inigo Jones,

80] Richard Wilson, *Wilton House from the South East, c.* 1758–60

and a Palladian bridge by the ninth Earl of Pembroke himself. To build such a version of Palladian architecture seems to have been important both to patrons and painters, and emphasised the taste of landowners. Pembroke built such a bridge and Wilson depicted it. Other versions were built at Prior Park and Stowe. Canaletto, ever eager to please the English, smartened up the Rialto Bridge in a similar fashion in a Palladian caprice for Consul Smith.[96] At Croome Court (1758) Wilson portrayed Capability Brown's 'natural' landscape, including a church which was not actually completed until five years after the picture was finished, possibly because the patron, Lord Coventry, wished to record the whole of his estate and monuments.[97]

Wilson also showed ancient Britain in his works.[98] His patron Sir George Lyttelton toured Wales five times between 1752 and 1773 and thus may have been responsible for Wilson's interest in its history, at a time when many histories of Britain were being written. Gradually Wilson reduced the overtly Italianate element in his landscapes. Landowners needed a new kind of landscape, one which impressed on the viewer that some aspects of country life were far from idle.[99] For patrons such as the Duke of Chandos's son, Lord Caernarvon, he was able to combine, in his works, the modern world with the medieval one of Edward I's castles, set in a believable, habitable arcadia.[100] However, it was the peaceful and rural which were emphasised: the bustle of the eighteenth century was generally eliminated and commerce was not evoked. To many landed gentlemen Wales had liberty since the commercial character which produced, they believed, luxury and indulgence in English cities was not present in Wales. This liberty was of a very different kind from that put forward by Wilkes and others who resented the upsurgence of royal power. However, to men like Lord Caernarvon it was Wilson's somewhat backward-looking notion of an historic rural Wales, 'unspoilt', and uncommercial which was desirable.[101]

The idea of the rural environment as somewhere unspoilt was close to the hearts of mid-eighteenth-century Englishmen.[102] The landscape as a place of retreat affected many artists' work. Gainsborough's fancy pictures suggested escape from the city. Sir Henry Bate-Dudley, who devoted much time to country activities and to the improvement of his estate,[103] Bradwell in Essex, enjoyed paintings of country cottages. Writing of one such work he noted that the painting showed 'one of those sweet recesses, where the mind never fails to find a source of enjoyment. 'Tis reading *poetry*, and compressing all its enchantments to the glance of an eye'.[104] The Duke of Rutland and Lord Mulgrave owned cottage door paintings with children playing, simple domestic activities taking place upon the doorstep and dogs barking in a comfortable homely *mêlée*.[105] Gainsborough himself had a cottage on Bate-Dudley's Bradwell estate,[106] and the aristocrats' habit of building for themselves *cottages ornées*, such as the Duke of Bedford's Endsleigh in Devon, seems to be part of the spirit of retreat.[107]

The idea of leaving the hectic pleasures of the city for the purity of a country estate or even a villa on the Thames may well have reminded the aristocracy of Roman statesmen. Cicero retreated to his country estate to give himself strength to oppose the nascent imperial corruption which threatened the virtuous republic. Many English landed gentlemen were troubled by the upsurgence of royal power, and saw the landed interest as a bulwark against George III's ministers, as well as an essential prop of the constitution. Richard Wilson created an image of the estate as a power base and idyllic retreat from metropolitan corruption, and seems to have likened it to the untainted rural bliss of antiquity.[108]

SPORTING PICTURES

The sporting picture was a major feature of many country house collections. Since hunting and shooting as well as horse racing were the pursuits of country gentlemen, they represented an important aspect of aristocratic life. Many artists found work producing paintings of the pleasures of the countryside. John Wootton (1682–1764), James Seymour (1702–52), Peter Tillemans (d. 1734) and George Stubbs (1724–1806) are amongst the best known.

Wootton provided a very distinctive form of sporting picture in the 1730s and 1740s for a number of country houses, including Althorp in

203

81] Althorp, Northamptonshire. The Hall, with portraits of horses by John Wootton, painted for the Earl of Sunderland in 1733

Northamptonshire [81], Badminton in Gloucestershire and Longleat in Wiltshire. His work combined the new interest in the thoroughbred horse with an Italianate landscape background. Frequently the country house itself would be at the centre of a composition which made use, as did Claude's work, of the *repoussoir* device of perfect foliage to frame it. His horse paintings were often large, and, as was the case with human sitters, Baroque features were introduced to suggest lineage and presence. As Reynolds borrowed from the grand manner to stress rank, so earlier in the century Wootton used the art of the past to stress animal pedigree.[109]

204

At the beginning of the eighteenth century hunting and similar country pursuits embodied masculinity and a kind of 'voluntary labour'[110] for the country gentleman who was not obliged to earn his living. For the hunter a connection was made between the beauty of 'verdant woods . . . /and/ . . . flowery meadows' and 'his table . . . his health, and the solace of his mind'.[111] Wootton's work brought forth this sensation of a bounteous earth and it secured him the patronage of Robert Harley, second Earl of Oxford, part of whose 'court' of artists and writers he formed. He was also patronised by the political enemies of Robert Walpole, who were old-fashioned Tories: the third Duke of Beaufort, the fifth Earl of Sunderland and the second Viscount Weymouth.[112] To such Tory noblemen these country pursuits were an aspect of their power and they felt little sympathy with the metropolitan sophistication of those Whigs who endorsed notions of 'party'. Wootton's pictures frequently portrayed servants as well as the gentry, and as they often hung in halls, they were seen by the more humble visitors to country houses performing some errand, who might well never go beyond the entrance hall. At Althorp the paintings included one showing a black servant, a local earth stopper, and it has been suggested that this portrayal indicates a sympathy for the plight of rural workers during a period of extreme economic hardship.[113]

In the middle of the eighteenth century there was much conflict over country pursuits. The middling classes were keen to imitate aristocratic pleasures, but often critical of them, and the game laws which supported hunting and shooting were seen to be increasingly ferocious and a threat to English liberty, especially since after 1755 the sale of game was forbidden.[114] The kind of aristocrat who gambled, drank heavily and hunted to the extent of neglecting his duties in Parliament was even censured by his fellow noblemen. The Duke of Newcastle wrote to warn the Duke of Richmond about such matters in 1768: 'Lord Rockingham told Me that you were unwilling to leave your hunting to come to Town . . . For God's sake, my dear Lord, Don't let it be said that upon Points of . . . Infinite Consequence to this Nation, Your Grace has suffer'd Your Fox Hunting to deprive the Cause and Your Friends of the Advantage of your Assistance . . . for the sake of a Fox Chase . . .'[115]

There was a desire for refinement in society. The 'friends of civilisation' were forever exhorting the lower orders to abandon bear-baiting, bull-running, pugilism and cudgellery. Aristocrats must not be seen enjoying their rough pleasures excessively. Bankers and barristers made common cause with at least some members of the gentry and aristocracy in supporting artists like Hogarth, who were concerned to create a new image of refinement.[116] It was in the more remote areas of Britain that the portrait groups of drunken coarse country squires lingered, almost by way of protest at the new chic alliance of polite bourgeois and new aristocrat.[117]

George Stubbs (1724–1806) has been regarded by some writers as an artist who produced a new type of sporting painting to adorn country houses and depict the pleasures of the great estate. Many of Stubbs's pictures stressed the dignity of the hunting field. His painting of *The Third Duke of Richmond with the Charlton Hunt* (1760) [82] emphasises the dignity of ducal hunting scenes and the role played by faithful servants. Aristocrats are at the centre of the composition, and of country life in such works, but the activities of groom and stableboys are also described in such works and their role in furthering country pursuits is recognised in an even more deliberate fashion than in Wootton's works: as Richmond had some undefined sympathies for the lower classes this was appropriate.[118] Although Stubbs was adept at showing class differences in his paintings through composition and gestures, he also painted the racecourse, a place of freedom where men of different station rubbed shoulders. Stubbs did not show the raffish atmosphere of places like Newmarket. Few gentlemen would have wished to have paintings, let alone prints distributed, which showed them behaving in a discreditable manner. Stubbs painted instead racehorses and pensive jockeys in spacious clouded courses.[119]

It is possible to read into Stubbs's paintings a radical levelling approach – servants and masters working together in support of country pursuits. However, not all his patrons were politically progressive. Stubbs also painted Sir Richard Grosvenor who, as he was at Newmarket when he was elevated to the peerage, could not remember whether he had been made a baron or a viscount. He was portrayed in *The Grosvenor Hunt* (1762) [83] stag hunting,

82] George Stubbs, *The Third Duke of Richmond with the Charlton Hunt*, c. 1759

a suitable royal activity for a man who countered radical Whig ideas with a new Tory adherence to the monarch as protector of his people.[120] Through his paintings and prints Stubbs could supply many who aspired to the status of country gentleman. Country pursuits seemed even to the new city man to convey status, and in Stubbs's work there was a new realism and an apparent absence of references to the art of the past.[121]

The new dignity conveyed by Stubbs was also present in portraits, and he seems to suggest the different roles that his patrons might play socially and even politically. However, the rumbustious quality of the countryside was not entirely forgotten. By the 1790s social unrest and the beginnings of industrialisation threatened society, and there was a nostalgia for the supposedly unspoilt rural life of former times. Thomas Gainsborough and George Morland suggested rural harmony and simple pleasures; the idea of the early eighteenth-century sporting squire became popular again.[122] The hunting, shooting nobleman was, at the time of the French Revolution, seen as a man of patriotism, loyalty and hospitality, and many sporting journals made fun of the French and their inability to understand fox-hunting.

Francis Wheatley (1747–1801), with an eye for the details of rustic scenes, could depict gamekeepers and their employers' interest in their occupations.[123] He had an almost sentimental regard for English country traditions, and a romantic desire to create a rural heritage, the equivalent of the urban heritage to be found in his *Cries of London*.[124]

83] George Stubbs, *The Grosvenor Hunt*, 1762

HISTORY PAINTING

History painting played some part in the decoration of eighteenth-century country houses in Britain. Several artists spent a good deal of their careers promoting the idea that a native school of history painting should be established. William Hogarth, Sir Joshua Reynolds and James Barry all practised this genre, but found it difficult to persuade patrons to commission such works from them. 'You surely would not have me hang up a modern English picture in my house, unless it were a portrait', retorted one collector, who having praised Benjamin West's *Pylades and Orestes* was asked why he had not bought a work of which he strongly approved.[125]

Late seventeenth- and early eighteenth-century houses were decorated by foreign, mainly French and Italian, artists. Such men as Louis Laguerre and Antonio Verrio worked on ceilings and walls with a florid Baroque illusionism at Burghley in Northamptonshire and Chatsworth in Derbyshire. Diplomats brought artists to Britain when they returned from foreign postings: the first Duke of Manchester returned from Venice with Luca Carle Varijs, Giovanni Antonio Pellegrini and Marco Ricci. Such artists were extremely accomplished, often dividing their activities between figure painting and *quadratura* work, the latter being a skilful form of architectural painting. Halls and staircase were covered with mythological scenes, gods and goddesses disporting themselves in splendid *trompe l'oeil* architectural settings. Sir James Thornhill, the first important English painter to produce such work, created a wonderfully grand classical city, with a profusion of temples and palaces unknown in England, when he decorated the Sabine Room at Chatsworth.

The proprietors of country houses were likened to the heroes of mythology. Verrio painted the life of Julius Caesar at Chatsworth in flattering allusion to the Duke of Devonshire, or possibly to William of Orange, the Whigs' Caesar, whom the duke had supported in his claim to the English throne. It has been suggested that when Pellegrini painted Phaeton driving the chariot of the sun and falling from heaven (in the hall at Castle Howard), this was intended as an allegory of the fall of the absolute monarchy of Charles II and James II. Naturally a Whig family such as that of the Carlisles would approve of the demise of autocratic monarchy.[126] Certainly the idea of celebrating the Whigs, who had, so their supporters believed, ensured the Protestant succession and banished absolutism, was not uncommon. Owen MacSwinney, a former manager of the Opera in the Haymarket, proposed to commission major Bolognese and Venetian artists to paint a set of twenty-four imaginary monuments surrounded by caprices of ruins. These were completed by 1729 and a set of engravings was to be published in 1741, showing William III, Mary II, Anne, George I, the first Duke of Devonshire and other leading statesmen, lawyers, naval and military commanders, philosophers and men of letters. The second Duke of Richmond acquired some of

PLATE 10

Sir Joshua Reynolds, *Elizabeth Gunning, Duchess of Hamilton and Argyll, c. 1759–60*

Thomas Gainsborough, *Mr and Mrs Andrews*, 1748–49

Canaletto, *Warwick Castle, The East Front*, 1748–49

PLATE 13

Holkham, the Saloon, showing Andrea Procaccini's *Tarquin and Lucretia* over the fireplace (Biagio Rebecca)

PLATE 14

Kedleston, Derbyshire, the Saloon, 1761–62. The large painting over the door is by William Hamilton and the *grisaille* painting to the left shows a classical version of *Eleanor Sucking the Poison from her Husband Edward the I's Wound*

the 'British worthies who were bright and shining ornaments to their country' and hung them in the dining room at Goodwood.[127]

This idea of 'shining ornaments' was important throughout the eighteenth century. The Earl of Shaftesbury promoted the idea in his writings that history painting was important because it promoted public virtue. George Turnbull in his *Treatise on Ancient Painting* said that history painting was appropriate to the education of youth, because it could represent 'Great Actions' performed by public heroes.[128] James Harris, addressing 'Art' in general, said that it could 'exhibit to mankind the admired tribe of poet and orators; the sacred train of patriots and heroes; the god-like list of philosophers and legislators . . .'[129]

To Whig sympathisers the destruction of absolute monarchy was the precondition for the creation of a 'public' with a freer and more genuine appreciation of art in the grand manner than absolute monarchs like Louis XIV could inspire, since artistic production in such states as France was rigidly focused on the crown.[130] Shaftesbury believed that the leisured 'real fine gentlemen' with substantial means who had travelled in Europe were the true 'Lovers of *Art* and *Ingenuity*'. These men were presumably most likely, from his aristocratic viewpoint, to promote great public art.[131] Certainly these were the people who were active in architectural fields and who were building great classical palaces in the first quarter of the eighteenth century. The theory that they were ideal patrons was not confined to Shaftesbury's writings. Horace Walpole also believed, fifty years later, that civilised gentlemen rather than absolute monarchs were the ideal patrons. In *Anecdotes of Paintings* he wrote that 'private curiosity and good sense' and the 'taste of a polished nation' were more effective than 'the command of Louis Quartorze or the expense of a Cardinal nephew'.[132]

However, heroic history painting by British artists was not actually favoured by aristocratic patrons for their country houses. They preferred to lure foreign painters to England, especially during the first quarter of the century; to commission easel paintings when on the Grand Tour; or to import paintings by Italian artists of the past, on grand themes. The first Earl of Leicester (1697–1750) commissioned works from a number of Italian painters when he was on the Grand Tour in 1714. From Sebastiano Conca[133] he bought *The Vision of Aenaeas in the Elysian Fields*. In this painting Aeneas looks upon the fields and sees the happy residents, the poet Virgil surrounded by philosophers and shepherds who sing his poems. Apparently Lord Leicester himself appeared as either Orpheus or Virgil. Since the *Aeneid* was Virgil's glorification of Rome and the Emperor Augustus, this may well have been a suitable picture for Lord Leicester to have bought, as it seems to suggest a search for Augustan values in England. Scholars are divided in their views as to whether Lord Leicester's pictures really mean he believed that Augustan values might be revived by the Hanoverians or whether he looked to the restoration of the Stuarts and the Divine Right of Kings.[134]

Lord Leicester also commissioned from Andrea Procaccini *Tarquin and Lucretia* [plate 13] and *Perseus and Andromeda*, and *The Continence of Scipio* from Giuseppe Chiari. It has been suggested that these themes, which are all concerned with benevolent conquerors and captives, raped or unjustly detained, may indicate a resistance to royalist oppression. Apparently on his Grand Tour, Lord Leicester showed some scorn for George I, so it may be that his choice of historical and mythological subjects was governed by a secret disapproval of the house of Hanover. Certainly, from the evidence of Matthew Brettingham it seems that Leicester appeared as Allucius in the *Continence of Scipio* and as Senator Numa Pomphilias in the Procaccini.[135] Again, in commissioning *Deborah and Barak* from Francesco Solimena he chose another similar theme, for the prophetess Deborah was calling upon Barak to deliver the Israelites form the tyranny of Jabin, King of Canaan.[136]

One British history painter who succeeded in attracting some aristocratic patronage for his works was Gavin Hamilton (1723–98). Hamilton worked on six pictures illustrating Homers's *Iliad* from c. 1760 to the later 1770s, including *Andromache Mourning the Death of Hector* (1758–61), for the seventh Earl of Northampton.[137] Hamilton was a gentleman-scholar who was a member of the large Scots group in mid-eighteenth-century Rome: his work was probably influenced by writings such as Robert Wood's *Essay on the Original Genius of Homer* (1769) and by an earlier work, *An Inquiry into the Life, Times and Writings of Homer* (1735) by Thomas Blackwell of Aberdeen. Johann Joachim Winckelmann admired Hamilton's *Andromache Weeping Over the Body of Hector*, writing that 'the composition is good, the figures are intelligently thought out and conceived with taste' and the heads were 'very close to the Grecian forms'.[138] The picture also owed to something to Poussin's works such as *The Sacrament of Extreme Unction*, and certainly Poussin was highly regarded by English collectors: Reynolds was to write to the Duke of Rutland in 1785, when *The Seven Sacraments* had been secured for his collection, that 'the Poussins are a real national object'.[139]

Hamilton had more success as a dealer in antiquities than as a painter of histories. When *Achilles Mourning the Death of Patroclus*, painted for Sir James Grant of Grant [84] was shown at the exhibition of the Society of Artists in 1765, Horace Walpole described it as 'a large piece, very ill coloured, faulty both in drawing and expression'.[140] However, the sense of scale was an essential part of the eighteenth-century attitude to history painting amongst theorists: Northcote wrote 'it is only in large pictures that the indispensable necessity exists of making art with precision and distinctness of all the parts'.[141]

The most successful history painters in England were those whose pictures fitted in with the schemes of the architects in country houses. Angelica Kauffman – who had several aristocratic patrons including Lord and Lady Spencer,[142] and the ninth Earl of Exeter (who introduced her to Reynolds) – produced a series of history paintings for Saltram in Devon in

1768–69. John Parker of Saltram, a friend of Reynolds, acquired the four pictures from Kauffman, representing scenes from the Trojan War. She may have used as her guide the Comte de Caylus's *Tableuax fixés de l'Iliade de l'Odyssée, d'Homère et de l'Enéide de Vergile* (1757), which provided a useful book for history painters in its suggestions for compositions from the classical epics. One of the works Kauffman painted, for the saloon at Saltram was *Hector Taking Leave of Andromache* [85].[143] The conflict between War and Love experienced by men and women was the theme of Angelica Kauffman's work: judgement versus passion, and the feminine virtues of softness and compassion set against the patriotism and bravery of men. Although the works would originally have hung in the saloon they seem to have been moved, perhaps by the early nineteenth century, to the staircase.[144]

Angelica Kauffman's husband Antonio Zucchi (1726–95) was employed by Robert Adam as a decorative painter. In the Eating Room at Osterley he painted the classical *capricci* at either end of the room (see [96]), showing figures in a ruined classical Roman bath.[145] This type of caprice, which brought back fond memories of the Grand Tour, provided a reminder of what inspired the decoration of the room, and also echoed the more fantastical reconstruction of ancient buildings in the work of neoclassical designers. Zucchi himself had worked in Rome with James Adam and was a free agent, inspired by Adam's drawing tutor in Italy, Charles Louis Clérisseau. The type of *capriccio* seen at Osterley and other Adam houses shows something of Adam's own work in free designs and reconstructions from classical buildings, and it also reflects the work of Piranesi.[146]

84] Gavin Hamilton, *Achilles Mourning the Death of Patroclus*, 1760–63

85] Angelica Kauffman, *Hector Taking Leave of Andromache*, 1768–69,
painted for Saltram House, Devon

As a balance to the work of the antique it also introduced a Turkish
theme which constituted the opposite of the ordered classical idea. The Turkish
figure might also be seen as a 'noble savage', unspoilt by civilisation. Heroic
history paintings frequently contained such characters.[147] The first Lord
Grosvenor told Benjamin West that he intended to 'have a room furnished
with English pictures only'. He bought West's *The Golden Age* and three of
his large battle pictures, including *The Death of General Wolfe* (one of four
large versions).[148] Here, although the scene is contemporary, the pose of
Wolfe is classical or certainly inspired by high art, deriving from either the
Dying Gaul or Michelangelo's Sistine Chapel Adam, or some representation
of the dead Christ. Wolfe was a hero in a modern history painting, a figure of
public virtue contrasted with the seated Indian, who gazes at this classic
heroism but represents unspoilt and untainted nature.[149] It was unusual to
find an aristocrat buying a painting of a modern heroic event. Robert Adam
made designs for rebuilding Eaton Hall for Lord Grosvenor in about 1766,
which were not executed. It is interesting to speculate upon the likely appearance of the modern heroism of *The Death of General Wolfe* in a neo-antique
setting devised by Adam.[150]

Jonathan Richardson said that it was possible for 'the Ancient Great
and Beautiful Taste in Painting' to be revived in England because of the
'Haughty Courage . . . Elevation of thought, a Greatness of Taste, a Love of
Liberty . . . which we inherit from our Ancestors'. Shaftesbury too had believed that 'a united Britain would soon become the principal seat of arts'.[151]

The aristocracy sometimes commissioned history paintings which made links between the antique and early or medieval English history. In the Saloon at Kedleston [plate 14] four large decorative paintings of Roman ruins over the doors might suggest that the English aristocracy hoped to create a new Classical order from the ruins of the old. However, between them are grisaille paintings by Biagio Rebecca of scenes from English history: *The Dukes of Northumberland and Suffolk entreating Lady Jane Grey to Accept the Crown*, *Edward the Black Prince Serving the French King (then his prisoner) at Supper*, *Elizabeth, widow of Sir John Grey imploring Edward IV to restore her husband's lands*, and *Eleanor sucking the poison from her husband Edward I's wound*. It is difficult to be sure what, if any, linking theme these paintings might have. As at Saltram, the intervention of women in great historical events is suggested, and perhaps the role of women at the centre of this great house is implied. Certainly the stoicism, nobility and magnanimity of English monarchs is emphasised in a way that would also have been apparent in a traditional neoclassical work. There is a suggestion that the Curzons of Kedleston were an ancient family prominent in the stirring times depicted in the paintings, and that a link might be made between antiquity, the English past and the eighteenth century.[152]

Histories, whether antique or medieval, do seem to have found some enthusiasts, although commissions often came to nothing. It may be that this was because the works were often large or in a series, and perhaps patrons were daunted by the prospect of commissioning huge, fairly unfamiliar works. Gavin Hamilton had hoped to decorate the Great Room at Yester House in East Lothian with a history picture for the Marquess of Tweedale in 1755. He wrote: 'taken the liberty to introduce a history picture . . . representing some great and heroic subject so as to fix the attention of the spectator and employ his mind after his eye is satisfied with the proportion of the room and the propriety of its ornaments. I am entirely of the Italian way of thinking, viz, that there can be no true magnificence without the assistance of either paintings or sculpture'. This scheme was not executed, but the first Viscount Curzon commissioned *Paris and Helen* from Hamilton in 1756 for Kedleston.[153]

Some patrons would have preferred Hamilton to produce British historical themes. The second Lord Palmerston commissioned him for a scene from Macbeth in 1766. The painter tried to persuade him to choose a Homeric theme and a larger composition: he clearly hoped that the prints of his work would popularise his style: 'I should be glad to know what your Lordship thinks of my print of Andromache bewailing the death of Hector; it is the first of a set of six prints I intend to publish from Homer and I am consequently anxious about the success of it . . .'[154] In the event, Hamilton only rarely produced works of British history, such as *Mary Queen of Scots Resigning her Crown* (1765–75). Perhaps as an archaeologist and dealer in classical sculpture he preferred classically draped figures in his paintings, which were themselves reminiscent of relief sculpture.

For some artists British historical themes appear to have lent themselves to the expression of political sympathies. John Hamilton Mortimer was a leading figure in this field as were John and Paul Knapton and Robert Dodsley. The Knaptons were behind a project to illustrate the history of Britain in fifty prints from works by Francis Hayman and Nicholas Blakey.[155] Mortimer had great faith in the values of ancient Britain and felt that many traditional rights were being destroyed by the Tory government of George III, whose chief minister, Lord Bute, seemed to be increasing royal power and overturning the principles of the Glorious Revolution of 1688. Mortimer painted *King John delivering Magna Carta to the Barons* (*c.* 1776) which was clearly a theme associated with the attempts to check royal power. Robert Edge Pine painted *Earl Warren Making Reply to the Writ, Commonly called Quo Warranto, in the Reign of Edward I.* Again the theme represented the monarchy attempting to sweep away traditional rights. Edward I introduced a statute known as Quo Warranto which compelled all landowners to produce legal titles and deeds to their properties. Since many of these had disappeared over the years, Edward hoped to gain by dispossessing landowners. Earl Warren drew his sword before one of the king's judges, saying that he had gained his estate by the sword and intended to keep it. The king withdrew the statute.[156] Pine sympathised with the politics of John Wilkes, who supported the rights of the individual against the powers of the Crown or Parliament. This painting appears to have been commissioned by Sir George Warren of Poynton, who claimed the Earldom of Warren and Surrey in 1782.

One important aspect of this taste for British subject matter was the Celtic revival in literature driven by James Macpherson's writings,[157] in particular his *Ossian*, which J. H. Mortimer had declined to illustrate. While James Barry's most ambitious historical work *The Progress of Civilisation* was produced not for a country house but for the Royal Society of Arts, the Scottish painter Alexander Runciman produced a series of major history paintings at Penicuik House, Midlothian, on a similar scale. Here in 1772 he showed the life of St Margaret of Scotland on an oval staircase and a series of self-contained tales from Macpherson's *Ossian* in Ossian's Hall. The works included massive figures reminiscent of Michelangelo, representing the Scottish rivers Clyde, Tweed, Tay and Spey as gods. The scheme was commissioned by Sir James Clerk of Penicuik to decorate his vast classical house, which is now roofless, having been seriously damaged by fire in 1899.[158]

The taste for Italian art of the past may have prevented the development of a flourishing school of native history painting in the British Isles during the eighteenth century. Certainly country house owners appear to have possessed only a limited number of examples. Two important schemes of patronage, Alderman Boydell's Shakespeare Gallery begun in 1786 with the aim of helping to form a British school of history painting, and Robert Bowyers's Historic Gallery,[159] which housed scenes from British history, came rather late in the century to stimulate country house heroic art.

Perhaps because the rich went on the Grand Tour at a formative age, they felt more confident in acquiring Italian pictures. Just as casts of antique sculpture were common in country houses, there was no stigma attached to importing copies of famous paintings. Much of the art the Grand Tourist viewed in Italy was by Raphael or Guido Reni, or in their style.[160] To own copies of history paintings by these artists and others was not uncommon. At Saltram, in Robert Adam's saloon, there were copies of Titian's *The Andrians* (from the original in the Prado) and *Danae* (from a late eighteenth-century copy in the Naples Museum). There was a late eighteenth- or early nineteenth-century copy of Correggio's *Jupiter and Antiope* (from the original in the Louvre) and one of Raphael's *St John in the Wilderness* (from the original in the Uffizi).[161]

At Stourhead there were eight copies of works, made by Jeremiah Dawson; one each after Veronese, Guercino, Bourdon and Van Dyck, and four after Guido Reni, including *The Toilet of Venus*. Pompeo Batoni copied *Salome with the Head of John the Baptist* which at the time was in the Colonna Gallery in Rome.[162]

THE FRAMING AND HANGING OF PICTURES

The framing and hanging of pictures in late eighteenth- and early nineteenth-century houses was a matter of great concern to owners. Few collections are displayed in the way that they were in the eighteenth century, and there have, of course, been many dispersals.

There was a great shortage of large pictures in Britain in the eighteenth century.[163] However, by 1738 Gerard de Lairesse's work *The Art of Painting* had been translated into English and he had some firm advice which concerned picture hanging. Rooms for women must be suitably decorated with works of fruit, flowers or landscape paintings, 'and the most clothed and modest histories'. Studies may, he wrote, 'be adorned with Paintings . . . of learned Men, Philosophers . . .'. He even suggested suitable pictures for kitchens, including 'hunting of Deer, the Picture of some Maid, or other Servant or Dog or Cat . . .'[164] Where there was a real shortage of paintings it was difficult for the owner of the house to be so selective. In fact there was often, to modern eyes, a certain carelessness about the way in which pictures were hung in early eighteenth-century rooms; they might well override the pattern in panelling or mouldings.[165]

The Palladians brought organisation to the display of pictures, and often produced picture plans for rooms. Colen Campbell did so for Wanstead and William Windham's Cabinet at Felbrigg Hall, Norfolk [plate 3]), was designed to house most of the pictures he had acquired on the Grand Tour, notably the landscape gouaches of Giovannia Battista Busiri (1689–1757). The Cabinet is a good surviving example of Grand Tour taste, containing twenty-six gouaches and several larger oils by Busiri.[166] Here James Paine remodelled a room of the 1690s incorporating the originally crusty plasterwork of the ceiling, and lightening it with Rococo additions in the form of garlands in the cove. This room with its Rococo overmantel surmounted by Busiri's *The Cascade at Tivoli* and red wall hangings (renewed in the early nineteenth century) indicates the way in which pictures, plasterwork, wall coverings and frames were brought together to produce a satisfying composition.[167]

The long gallery had, in the sixteenth century, been a space for hanging portraits of family and sometimes royal sitters. One gallery of paintings survives more or less intact from the eighteenth century, although pictures have been added to the arrangement: Corsham Court, which was extended for Sir Paul Methuen by Capability Brown. This gallery [86] was seventy-two feet long and twenty-four feet wide, with a coved ceiling. Its five windows created a harmonious relationship between the gallery and the landscape.[168] The appearance of the gallery is important because it is probable that Sir Robert Walpole's collection at Houghton was hung in a similar way before it was sold to Catherine the Great. Four large pictures occupied the main position in the gallery: Van Dyck's equestrian portrait of Charles I was placed in the centre of the north wall; over the chimneypiece was a version of the *Wolf Hunt* by Rubens, richly framed to a design by Adam; and in the centre of the wall on

86] Corsham Court, Wiltshire. The Gallery designed by Lancelot Brown, 1762

either side of the Rubens still hang *The Betrayal of Christ* by Van Dyck and a *Baptism of Christ* by Guido Reni. Around these four large paintings smaller works are symmetrically arranged, including pendants by Bernardo Strozzi, Luca Giordano and Salvator Rosa. Part of Sir Paul Methuen's large collection was displayed in a smaller suite of state rooms leading off the gallery: this included smaller pictures, cabinets and other curios bought in Italy.

The items in the gallery at Corsham fit together, despite later additions, like pieces in a jigsaw puzzle. The coffer-compartments in the ceiling, the work of Thomas Stocking, are bold enough to balance the strong pattern of frames on walls which were, from the creation of the room, filled with pictures.[169] Thirty armchairs, four settees, two stools, eight window seats, pier glasses and marble topped tables between the windows complete the furnishings of the room. This simplicity of the sofa design, the 'close nailing' of brass nails on the seat furniture,[170] and the way in which pier glass frames match the picture frame of the Rubens *Wolf Hunt* are essential eye-catching elements in this rich scheme.

Other galleries were not necessarily so well stocked with pictures. There seem to have been few, if any, in the gallery at Harewood for some time. Richard Warner, visiting the house in 1802, wrote that 'Nothing within interests the mind; no production of the arts, unless the labours of the gilder and upholsterer may be considered as deserving that character'.[171] Perhaps because of the shortage of paintings and the reluctance of British aristocrats to collect native history paintings, Robert Adam supplied fixed paintings as part of his design, especially in large rooms. He did so for the Eating Room at Headfort, Co. Meath, in the saloon at Nostell Priory and in the Music Room at Harewood (see [plate 5]), providing a definite theme for works in these cases. At Kedleston, there were fewer decorative paintings by Adam's team and many of the pictures, collected on the Grand Tour by Sir Nathaniel Curzon, were fixed in plaster frames or have in the main been *in situ* since the eighteenth century.[172] The most important works were in the drawing room, which James Paine had designed before Adam was appointed as architect. There were six religious works including *Christ and Mary Magdalen in the House if Simon* by Benedetto Luti (1666–1724) and a *Cain and Abel* by the same artist, who was one of the last important painters in the Baroque manner in Rome. Despite the scale and importance of these paintings, it is possible that Athenian Stuart, who produced designs for this room, intended to trim them to fit his scheme.[173] Another work hanging here is a copy of Guido Reni's *The Flight into Egypt* by Guiseppe Bartolomeo Chiari, a pupil of Carlo Maratta. It was this taste for the Italian grand manner, displaced especially in the works of Maratta, Chiari and Reni, which was typical of country house taste, and considered suitable for saloons, drawing rooms and galleries, particularly in the middle of the century.

Dining rooms were often decorated with still life paintings or a theme associated with the cultivation of the vine and worship of the god Bacchus. At Kedleston the pictures in the dining room (see [28]) were fixed in uniform plaster frames, an idea which conveys a strong sense of their distinctive message. Still lifes of fruit and dead game are arranged at the upper level to suggest dining, whilst the landscape below echoed that seen through the windows. It was the estate itself which provided the food upon which the diner could gaze, so that he was confronted by the painted ideal landscape and by a landscaped estate, itself influenced by the kinds of pictures that were in the collection.[174] In the Eating Room at Osterley, the overmantel painting by Cipriani depicted Ceres as goddess of plenty accompanied by maidens praising her in song, to the music of a lyre. There were also small painted rectangular pictures showing satyrs and nymphs, who educated Bacchus, engaged in festive activities.[175]

Entrance halls sometimes contained sculpture as at Kedleston, Wentworth Woodhouse and Holkham. Often they were hung with sporting paintings as at Althorp, Ashridge, Badminton and Longleat; the hierarchical nature of country house planning was reflected in the type of picture displayed. The gentry experienced saloons and dining rooms with grand manner paintings and complicated mythological narratives, requiring of the spectator a classical education. Tradesmen and servants were kept in the hall: if it were furnished with casts from the antique and suggestions of Roman atria it can hardly have appealed to them. However, the hall with hunting scenes and horses might have seemed welcoming to the ordinary countryman. This 'common touch' might be felt also in Hunting Halls, like the one at Houghton, where the hunt could meet before it set off, or to dine afterwards in warm bleary satisfaction. The Houghton Hunting Hall was a masculine room, sober in appearance, with practical painted floorcloths and hung by 1743 with two paintings of importance: Wootton's *Hunting Piece* and Rubens's *Susannah and the Elders*.[176] At Ditchley in Oxfordshire there were sporting rooms for hunting pictures and it may be that, as the game laws and this type of sport came under criticism in the 1760s, the display of works of art associated with it became less acceptable.[177]

As we have seen, at any British country house one of the most important collections would be that of portraits. If these were of the family they provided a sense of history, of the importance of lineage and the continuity of blood. At Stowe, the Grenville Room contained forty-six portraits of a great political family dating from the sixteenth to the eighteenth century.[178] Dynastic splendour did not govern all arrangements, though, for Lord Leicester at Holkham hung a series of portraits of his intellectual friends near his library.[179]

The framing of pictures also played an important part in the decoration of the country house. Often designed under the supervision of Palladian architects, the frames were part of the interior effect of the room, as carefully considered as the picture hanging plan itself. Adam designed frames and Chippendale was happy to supply them, as he did for Sir Roland Winn's Cabinet at Nostell Priory in 1768. Here he charged £63 10s for forty-one frames. William Linnell also provided the Duke of Bedford with 'a large picture frame very neat . . . with an eagle at the top, festoons down the sides and mozaiks at the bottom all very richly ornamented' at £25 18s. Robert Adam and William Chambers employed Sefferin Alken as a specialist carver and for Chambers he carved a frame for Reynold's *Marlborough Family* at Blenheim.[180] Sometimes a frame would relate, through very elaborate decoration, to the history and circumstances of the family for which it was commissioned. Francis Cotes painted *The Honourable Lady Stanhope and the Countess of Effingham as Diana and her Companion* [87]. In this enormously imposing work the figures are life size, and the carved gilt frame bears an armillary sphere with trumpets at the top, plumed helmets, halberds and swords. British heroes and naval victories are celebrated, particularly in this design for Lady Effingham's ancestor had been Lord High Admiral in Elizabethan times.[181]

Royal portraits presented by the monarch on occasion for some service rendered had grand or ornate frames, and there were regulations governing their presentation which were promulgated by the Lord Chamberlain's office. The portraits presented to Lord Bantry, for repelling a French invasion of Ireland in 1796, of George III and Queen Charlotte had especially elaborate Rococo frames.[182]

Whilst large works suited to the rooms of country houses had not always been readily available at the beginning of the eighteenth century, the French Revolution and the Napoleonic Wars, and the dominant position of London auction houses, ensured that major collections could be formed a century later. Sir John Leicester, a member of the Prince Regent's set, was created Lord de Tabley in 1820. He collected paintings from the 1790s onwards, and was especially interested in commissioning works from English artists. He was an early admirer of Turner, who painted *Tabley Mere, A Calm Morning*, which depicted part of the Tabley Hall estate in Cheshire. Thomas Harrison of Chester created a tripartite gallery on the principal floor of the house in a space previously occupied by drawing room, library and two chambers.[183]

Even more ambitious was John Nash's gallery [88] for the collection of the second Lord Berwick at Attingham in Shropshire. In 1805–8 an earlier staircase was swept away at considerable expense, in excess of £15,000, and a Chinese red gallery with porphyry scagliola columns and *faux marbre* doorcases was created. This modish room had innovatory curved cast iron window frames made at Coalbrookdale, and white marble chimneypieces in the Egyptian taste, suggesting the influence of Thomas Hope and celebrating Nelson's victory at the Battle of the Nile.[184] Another gallery was added to an eighteenth-century house by Robert Reid in 1811, at Paxton House in Berwickshire for George Home.[185]

The approach to decorating a country house with paintings or sculpture could depend on a number of factors. Guidance on what to collect might come from books which were guides to taste. Many of these were published in the eighteenth century. Jonathan Richardson published two works: an *Essay on the Whole Art of Criticism as it relates to Painting* and in the same

87] Francis Cotes, *The Honourable Lady Stanhope and the Countess of Effingham as Diana and her Companion, c.* 1768

volume *Argument on behalf of the Science of the Connoisseur* in 1719, and in 1722 *An Account of Some of the Statues, Bas Reliefs, Drawings and Pictures in Italy etc., with Remarks by Mr Richardson Senior and Junior.* These works may well have been used by connoisseurs to assist them in choosing works well into the eighteenth century.[186] Rome, Paris and Venice were the cities in which to buy works, to acquire them from a dealer or through one's own agent. In Rome the collector could find instruction. 'A regular course with an Antiquarian generally takes about six weeks, employing three hours a day, you may, in that time, visit all the churches, palaces and villas and ruins worth seeing', observed Dr John Moore.[187]

To create, as part of one's 'court', a colony of artists, or indeed architects, musicians or poets, was the ambition of many owners of country houses. The early eighteenth-century decorators working here such as Giovanni Antonio Pellegrini (1675–1741) brought to England by the fourth Earl (and first Duke) of Manchester, ambassador extraordinary to Venice, must have been part of the household. In fact between 1707 and 1719 two distinguished architects worked on the house, Sir John Vanbrugh and Alessandro Galilei,

88] Attingham, Shropshire. The Gallery, architect John Nash, 1805–8

who was later to design the facade for St John Lateran in Rome. Pellegrini painted *The Triumph of Caesar* between 1711 and 1712. These artists were, however, not there at the same time benefiting from each other's presence, or forming a civilised little circle around the Duke.

Lord Burlington did have such a circle, though it functioned mostly in London at Burlington House and rather less in the country. Nevertheless, Burlington employed Gibbs, owed much to Colen Campbell in terms of building experience, and introduced the Italian musician Buononcini. Alexander Pope was of course a friend and wrote his *Epistle to Lord Burlington on Taste*. William Kent was promoted as a painter and architect, as was Henry Flitcroft. Sebastiano and Marco Ricci were also patronised by Lord Burlington.[188]

Edward Harley, second Earl of Oxford, established what been described as a 'British School of Artists' at his country house Wimpole Hall in Oxfordshire. Harley commissioned forty landscape paintings by Michael Dahl. Sir James Thornhill was employed to decorate the chapel at Wimpole in 1723 and also did some easel paintings. He patronised J. M. Rysbrack, whilst James Gibbs was his architect and George Vertue his engineer. Harley was interested in the idea of founding a British School of Music which might vie with the German and Italian circle at Cannons, the Duke of Chandos's house, presided over by George Frederick Handel. Lord Oxford was on friendly terms with Prior, Pope, Swift and Gay.[189]

The owners of country houses had very different relationships with artists working for them. George Stubbs's early patron the third Duke of Richmond seems to have encouraged him with a number of commissions in about 1759–60. However, there is not much evidence to suggest that friendship blossomed: Stubbs's commission 'obliged him to go and reside at Goodwood . . . at Goodwood he continued for nine months'.[190] Perhaps social background and the hierarchies of subject matter had some bearing on friendships. Like English animal painters and practitioners of lesser genres, foreign decorative artists seeking their fortunes here may not have blended easily into British society. Andien de Clermont was described as 'Pembroke's little French painter'.[191]

Portrait painting, on the other hand, seems to have been a branch of the arts which allowed friendships to develop, perhaps because the sitter was so frequently in the presence of the artist. Allan Ramsay (1713–84) was the son of a poet, travelled in Italy and met a distinguished circle of antiquaries, connoisseurs and scholars at Dr Mead's Dining Club by the time he was twenty-six. In 1784 he travelled from London to Scotland in the suite of the third Duke of Argyll, and was a guest at Inveraray Castle.[192] Sir Joshua Reynolds made portrait painting serious and dignified through his very public career. He also stayed frequently at various country houses, often being a guest at Saltram, where Lady Theresa Parker was a knowledgable hostess.[193] Reynolds painted Miss Chudleigh, later Duchess of Kingston, whilst at Saltram, and possibly other portraits.[194] In 1777 Reynolds stayed for a fortnight at Blenheim to complete his large family portrait of the fourth Duke of

89] Thomas Girtin, *Harewood House from the South East*, 1801

Marlborough. The well-known story of his dropping his snuff and sharply counter-manding the Duchess's order to a servant to sweep it up lest it fly into the wet paint shows that he was quite socially assured.[195] Indeed he counted many landed families amongst his friends, such as the second Earl of Upper Ossery.[196]

Thomas Gainsborough was also a frequent visitor to country houses. The Reverend Robert Hingeston noted that 'Many houses in Suffolk, as well as in the neighbouring county, were always open to him, and their owners thought it an honour to entertain him'.[197] He spent a week at Wilton seeing old masters, and was also familiar with Corsham, Bowood, Longford Castle, Shobdon and Stourhead, all of whose owners were painted by him or bought his pictures. During his Bath period he seems to have visited Ralph Allen at Prior Park. Once Gainsborough recorded having met Lord Shelburne on his way home from Exeter. The artist noted, 'he insisted on my making them a short visit and I don't regret going . . . tho' I generally do to all Lords' Houses'.[198]

Perhaps it was in the nature of J. M. W. Turner's work that he travelled and stayed at country houses whilst painting estates, landscapes, ruins and draw-ing rooms. He stayed at Tabley House in Cheshire with Sir John Leicester in 1800 and a year later made his first visit to Petworth in Sussex. From 1810 to 1824 he went nearly every year to stay at Farnley Hall with Walter Fawkes, where he recorded the interior of the house. He stayed with the architect John Nash at East Cowes Castle and with Sir Walter Scott at Abbotsford.[199] Turner was one of a circle of watercolourists who painted at Harewood in Yorkshire, along with Thomas Girtin and John Varley. Girtin [89] became a

223

favourite of the first Earl of Harewood and the artist apparently 'had a room kept for him at Harewood House, where he lived for long periods together, and made some of his most important drawings'.[200]

The paintings and sculpture in the great house were symbolic. They expressed ideas about status and the ownership and pleasure of land. Sculpture and portraits, as we have seen, might suggest a link with the ruling classes of ancient time or indicate a knowledge of the fashions of Rome or Paris.

NOTES

1 Gervase Jackson-Stops, *The Country House in Perspective*, Pavilion, London, 1990, p. 107.
2 Adrian Tinniswood, *A History of Country House Visiting*, Basil Blackwell, Oxford, 1989, p. 104.
3 John Cornforth, 'Newby Hall, North Yorkshire', *Country Life*, CLXV, 7 June 1979, pp. 1802–6.
4 Stephen Deuchar, *Sporting Art in Eighteenth Century England: A Social and Political History*, Yale University Press, London, 1988, p. 86. After his tour of the north of England in the 1760s, Young wrote derisively of the 'unpopular and affected dignity of uncooperative house owners . . . the necessity of gaining tickets – of being acquainted with the family'.
5 Marcia Pointon, *Hanging the Head*, Yale University Press, London, 1993, p. 21.
6 Brian Fothergill, *The Mitred Earl: An Eighteenth Century Eccentric*, Faber and Faber, London, 1974, p. 176.
7 Frank Herrmann, *The English as Collectors*, Chatto and Windus, London, 1972, p. 96.
8 John Cornforth, 'Conversations with Old Heroes', *Country Life*, CXLIV, 26 September 1968, pp. 748–51.
9 John Cornforth, 'A Virtuoso's Gallery', *Country Life*, CXLIV 3 October 1968, pp. 834–41.
10 Francis Haskell and Nicholas Penny, *Taste and the Antique*, Yale University Press, London, 1983, p. 84.
11 *Ibid.*, p. 85.
12 Hugh Honour, 'English Patrons and Italian Sculptors in the First Half of the Eighteenth Century', *The Connoisseur*, LXVII, June 1958, pp. 220–6.
13 John Cornforth, 'Chatsworth, Derbyshire VII', *Country Life*, CXLIV, 1 August 1968, pp. 280–4.
14 Honour, 'English Patrons and Italian Sculptors', p. 224. Lord Malton bought *Samson Slaying the Philistines* by Vincenzo Foggini, which combined, curiously, something of the style of Michelangelo with that of Giovanni Bologna. It was, perhaps, a strange English way of acquiring the flavour of Italian civilisation in one rich helping.
15 John Kenworthy-Browne, 'Designing Around the Statues', *Apollo*, CXXXVII, April 1993, pp. 248–53.
16 *Ibid.*, p. 252.
17 *Kedleston Hall*, Guide, 1997, p. 55. Here were also installed, over the chimneypieces, plaster roundels of King Ethelred and King Alfred, which suggested to eighteenth-century visitors that the early history of England was connected with classical antiquity. Classical civilisation, it was believed, was brought to this country by the Caesars, and the establishment of the rights of the individual, through wise law, was the legacy of the Saxon monarchs.
18 Haskell and Penny, *Taste and the Antique*, p. 55.

19 Joseph and Anne Rykwert, *The Brothers Adam*, Collins, London, 1985, p. 139.

20 Ruth Guilding, 'Robert Adam and Charles Townley', *Apollo*, CXLIII, March 1996, pp. 27–32. At Syon the cool architectural entrance hall, the rich anteroom and the dining room were all used to display a mixture of antique statuary, casts and copies.

21 Damie Stillmann, 'The Gallery at Landsdowne House: International Neoclassical Architecture in Microcosm', *Art Bulletin*, March 1976, pp. 75–80.

22 Guilding, *Adam and Townley*, p. 31.

23 *Ibid.*, p. 30.

24 Jane Fejfer and Edmund Southworth, 'Summer in England: Ince Blundell Hall Revisited', *Apollo*, CXXIX, March 1989, pp. 179–82.

25 Fothergill, *Mitred Earl*, p. 130.

26 *Ibid.*, p. 120.

27 John Kenworthy-Browne, 'The Temple of Liberty at Woburn Abbey', *Apollo*, Vol. CXXX, July 1989, pp. 27–32.

28 Dorothy Stroud, 'Woburn Abbey, Bedfordshire I', *Country Life*, CXXXVIII, 15 July 1965, pp. 158–61.

29 Kenworthy-Browne, 'Temple of Liberty', p. 30.

30 Nicholas Penny, 'The Whig Culture of Fox in Early Nineteenth Century Sculpture', *Past and Present*, February 1976, pp. 94–105.

31 Cornforth, 'Chatsworth VII', p. 283.

32 Kenworthy-Browne, 'Temple of Liberty', p. 29.

33 John Kenworthy-Browne, 'A Ducal Patron of Sculptors', *Apollo*, Vol. XCVI, October 1972, p. 322.

34 Stroud, 'Woburn I', p. 161.

35 Cornforth, 'Chatsworth VII', p. 283. In his sculpture gallery the Duke of Devonshire not only installed the Bonapartes, but also Canova's statue of *Hebe* and Endymion and his dog.

36 Michael Hall, 'Petworth House, Sussex', *Country Life*, CLXXXVII, 10 June 1993, pp. 128–33. By 1830 the gallery was entirely top-lit. The advice of the painter Thomas Phillips was sought.

37 Giles Waterfield, *Soane and Death*, Dulwich Gallery, London, 1996, pp. 11–12.

38 *Ibid.*, p. 24.

39 Damie Stillman, 'Death Defied and Honour Upheld: The Mausoleum in Neoclassical England', *The Art Quarterly*, Summer 1978, pp. 175–213. Adam designed the mausoleum at Bowood in Wiltshire for the first Earl of Shelburne in 1761–64. With its dome, urns and sculpture, one comes close to the idea expressed at Newby of a neoclassical temple of the arts. Adam designed stools, themselves based on what was believed to be the tomb of Agrippa in Rome, which were used both in the mausoleum and in the entrance hall at Shelburne House in London.

40 *Ibid.* See also Nikolaus Pevsner and John Harris, *The Buildings of England: Lincolnshire*, Penguin, London, 1989, p. 190.

41 David Solkin, 'Great Pictures or Great Men? Reynolds, Male Portraiture and the Power of Art', *Oxford Art Journal*, 9, 1986, pp. 42–9.

42 *Ibid.*

43 Alastair Smart, *Allan Ramsay 1730–1784*, Scottish National Portrait Gallery, Edinburgh, 1992, p. 190.

44 Robert Oresko (ed.), *The Works in Architecture of Robert and James Adam*, Academy Editions, London, 1975, p. 53.

45 Nicholas Penny (ed.), *Reynolds*, Royal Academy of Art, London, 1986: 'An Ambitious Man: The Career and Achievements of Sir Joshua Reynolds', p. 25. Reynolds painted Lord Middleton (1761) holding a coronet, and the third Earl of Bellomont (*c.* 1774), lavishly portrayed in the sumptuous robes of the Order of the Bath.

46 Solkin, 'Great Pictures', p. 46. This was the case with his portrait of Frederick, fifth Earl of Carlisle.

47 Anthony M. Clark, *Pompeo Batoni: Complete Catalogue*, Phaidon, Oxford, 1985, p. 42.

48 *Ibid.*, p. 43.

49 Andrew Wilton, *The Swagger Portrait*, Tate Gallery, London, 1992, pp. 120–2. Lord Haddo's pose, deriving from an ancient statue in the Uffizi in Florence – believed to represent Mercury – lets us feel that he is alone with his world of marble and fragments.

50 Andrew Wilton and Ilaria Bignamini, *Grand Tour: The Lure of Italy in the Eighteenth Century*, Tate Gallery, London, 1996, p. 59. See also Hugh Brigstocke, *Masterpieces from Yorkshire Houses*, York City Council, York, 1994, pp. 69–70.

51 Clark, *Batoni*, p. 45.

52 Mary Webster, *Johan Zoffany 1733–1810*, National Portrait Gallery, London, 1976, pp. 49–50.

53 Denys Sutton, 'The Nabob of the North', *Apollo*, LXXXVI, September 1967, pp. 168–9. It is interesting to compare Batoni's portrait with Zoffany's *Sir Lawrence Dundas with His Grandson* (1769–70). Zoffany makes Sir Lawrence a solemn, grandfatherly figure, surrounded by his fine collection of paintings and sculpture. His portrait makes him seem much more ordinary than his grander son. As the Dundas's rose socially their portraits became more imposing.

54 Smart, *Ramsay*, p. 26.

55 *Ibid.*, p. 116. For example, Lady Helen and Lady Walpole Wemyss, daughters of the fifth Earl of Wemyss.

56 *Ibid.*, p. 15.

57 *Ibid.*, p. 26.

58 Penny, *Reynolds*, p. 218. See his portrait of *Mrs Riddell of Swinburne Castle, Northumberland* (1776) seen walking through a landscape garden.

59 *Ibid.*, p. 268. See portrait of *Lady Charles Spencer in Riding Habit* (*c.* 1775) who has dismounted whilst walking through wooded country.

60 *Ibid.*, pp. 197–9.

61 Alistair Laing and Pierre Rosenberg, *François Boucher*, Metropolitan Museum of Art, New York, 1986, pp. 255–8.

62 Penny, *Reynolds*, p. 221.

63 *Ibid.*, p. 262. See *The Montgomery Sisters: Three Ladies Adorning a Term of Hymen* which Reynolds painted in 1773 to celebrate the marriage of Elizabeth Montgomery to Luke Gardiner. The three sisters might be seen to represent stages associated with the married state. Elizabeth (1751–83) is in the centre, handing a garland to her sister Anne, Lady Townsend (1752–1819) who, being already married has passed the term of the god of marriage, whilst Barbara (1757–88) on the left is not yet betrothed.

64 *Ibid.*, pp. 243–4. In Reynold's *Hon. Mrs Edward Bouverie of Delapre with her Child* (1770) there is the suggestion of a garden building of imposing proportions and rusticated grandeur. She was also painted with her friend, Mrs Crewe, contemplating a tomb marked 'Et in Arcadia Ego'.

65 Marcia Pointon, *Strategies for Showing Women: Possession and Representation in English Culture 1665–1800*, Oxford University Press, Oxford, 1997, p. 197.

66 *Ibid.*, p. 187.

67 *Ibid.*, pp. 170–2. See *Mrs Congreve and her Children* by Philip Reinagle and p. 36, Francis Cotes, *Lady Stanhope and the Countess of Effingham as Diana and Companion*.

68 *Ibid.*, p. 262.

69 *Ibid.*, p. 224.

70 *Ibid.*

71 John Fleming, *Robert Adam and His Circle*, Harvard University Press, Cambridge, Massachusetts, 1962, p. 260. See also J. M. Crook, *The Greek Revival*, John Murray, London, 1972, p. 75. It was, in fact, Robert Adam, professionally jealous perhaps, who reported these remarks made in the presence of his friend Paul Sandby. It was the claimed lack of symmetry, with one doorway being supplied with architecture and

another, which should have corresponded, having only a pediment and no actual doorway that was derogated.

72 John Hardy and Maurice Tomlin, *Osterley Park House*, Victoria and Albert Museum, London, 1985, p. 107.

73 Eileen Harris, *Osterley Park, Middlesex*, The National Trust, 1994, p. 73.

74 *Ibid.*

75 Pointon, *Hanging the Head*, p. 21.

76 *Ibid.*

77 Toby Barnard and Jane Clark, *Lord Burlington: Architecture, Art and Life*, Hambledon Press, London, 1995, p. 252.

78 See chapter on gardens and landscapes.

79 *Kedleston Hall*, Guide, 1997, pp. 36–42.

80 Deborah Cherry and Jennifer Harris, 'Eighteenth Century Portraiture and the Seventeenth Century Past: Gainsborough and Van Dyck', *Art History*, 5, September 1982, pp. 287–309.

81 Francis Russell, 'Notes on Grand Tour Portraiture', *The Burlington Magazine*, CXXXVI, July 1994, pp. 438–43.

82 John Telfer Dunbar, *The Costume of Scotland*, Batsford, London, 1989, p. 51. Ramsay also painted the *Fifth Earl of Wemyss and His Wife* in highland dress in 1745.

83 Fleming, *Adam*, p. 146.

84 Rosalind Marshall (ed.), *Dynasty: The Royal House of Stewart*, National Galleries of Scotland, Edinburgh, 1990, p. 111.

85 Boris Ford (ed.), *The Cambridge Guide to the Arts in Britain: The Augustan Age*, Cambridge University Press, Cambridge, 1991, pp. 19 and 142.

86 Desmond Shawe-Taylor, *The Georgians: Eighteenth Century Portraiture and Society*, Barrie and Jenkins, London, 1990, pp. 127–8. The author notes of Devis's *Robert Gwillym of Atherton and His Family* (*c.* 1745–46): 'As this country squire points out his domain, his expansive gesture covers in equal measure his trees, formal lawns and house, his steward hurrying over with a letter, and also his wife and children'.

87 John Hayes and Michael Cross, *Polite Society Portraits of the English Country Gentleman and His Family by Arthur Devis*, Harris Museum and Art Gallery, Preston, 1983, p. 45.

88 *Ibid.*, pp. 64–5. For a discussion see *Edward Rookes-Leeds and His Family*.

89 Shawe-Taylor, *The Georgians*, pp. 128–9.

90 John Hayes, 'British Patrons and Landscape Painting', *Apollo*, Vol. CLXXXV, April 1967, pp. 254–60. However, in *The Drake Brockman Family* at Beachborough House, Kent, painted probably by Edward Haytley in *c.* 1745, the family looks out from the elegant rotunda at a panorama of fields, thin trees and thinner fences, with men fishing in the foreground. This indicated that some work was taking place within the landscape.

91 John Cornforth, 'Subtle Sequence Reconstructed', *Country Life*, Vol. CLXXXV, 13 June 1991, pp. 168–71.

92 Francis Hawcroft, 'The Cabinet at Felbrigg', *The Connoisseur*, June 1958, pp. 216–19.

93 W. G. Constable, *Canaletto*, 2 vols, Oxford University Press, Oxford, II, p. 430. See also J. Glinks, *Canaletto*, Phaidon, Oxford, 1982, p. 157.

94 Bruce Redford, *Venice and the Grand Tour*, Yale University Press, London, 1996, p. 80 and Plate 28.

95 J. G. Links, *Canaletto and His Patrons*, New York University Press, 1977, p. 45. It is unlikely that all twenty-four Canalettos were bought at once. They were, perhaps, delivered over several years.

96 Redford, *Venice*, p. 76.

97 David Solkin, *The Landscape of Richard Wilson*, Tate Gallery, London, 1982, p. 197.

98 *Ibid.*, pp. 88–91.

99 *Ibid.*, pp. 24–5. See also Ford, *Cambridge Guide to the Arts in Britain*, pp. 142–3.

100 Solkin, *Wilson*, p. 95. Wilson painted a view of *Caernarvon* for Lord Caernarvon in *c*. 1765.

101 *Ibid*. Solkin quotes a passage from a 'Gentleman in Wales' (1767), who wrote: 'The greatest part of the principality of Wales, by its situation, and the great distance it is from the metropolis, is almost entirely excluded from the advantages of commerce . . . [The Welsh have been] Happy in finding an asylum among those impregnable fortresses, built by the hand of nature, which were formerly their security against the power, and since against the luxury of the English. Environed on all sides by these, they enjoy tranquillity without indolence, liberty that degenerated not into licentiousness, and plenty without luxury. Thus they enjoy a happiness unknown in better cultivated counties, which opulence cannot purchase'.

102 Marcia Pointon, 'Gainsborough and the Landscape of "Retirement"', *Art History*, December 1979, pp. 441–55.

103 John Hayes, *Thomas Gainsborough*, Tate Gallery, London, 1980, p. 134. The painting was *Peasant Smoking at a Cottage Door*.

104 *Ibid.*, p. 154.

105 *Ibid.*, pp. 148–9.

106 *Ibid.*, p. 134.

107 Bridget Cherry and Nikolaus Pevsner, *The Buildings of England: Devon*, Penguin, London, 1989, pp. 352–5. The picturesque cottage was designed by Sir Jeffry Wyatville in 1810 for the sixth Duke of Bedford. The grounds were laid out by Repton.

108 David Solkin, 'The Battle of the Ciceros: Richard Wilson and the Politics of Landscape in the Age of John Wilkes', *Art History*, 6, December 1983, pp. 406–22. In likening Cicero to modern politicians who attacked the power of king and court and retreated to the country, Solkin quotes John Shebeare, *Letters to the English Nation* (1756) on the love of comparison between antique purity and the modern Englishman: 'No compliment, however well turned in its expression or elegant in its conception, can impart a more flattering idea to an Englishman than that which compares him to an Old Roman, the valour, prudence, love of liberty and country, with those other eminent qualities of our illustrious predecessors, are the attributes which he receives with most delight'.

109 Arline Meyer, 'Wootton at Wimpole', *Apollo*, CXXII, September 1985, pp. 212–19.

110 Deuchar, *Sporting Art*, p. 48.

111 *Ibid.*, p. 44.

112 *Ibid.*, p. 89.

113 *Ibid*.

114 Roy Porter and Marie M. Roberts (eds), *Pleasure in the Eighteenth Century*, Macmillan, London, 1996, p. 21.

115 Deuchar, *Sporting Art*, p. 198.

116 Porter, *Pleasure in Eighteenth Century*, p. 32. Deuchar, *Sporting Art*, p. 100, also quotes Vicesimus Knox: 'In the lower ranks of mankind we must not expect refinement . . .' [but] 'everything that lowers the great in the eyes of the vulgar injures society by disturbing the settled climate of subordination'. D. Solkin, *Painting for Money*, Yale University Press, New Haven, 1992, pp. 967 observes 'refinement, by definition not really accessible to the vulgar, was the upwardly mobile virtue of the formerly vulgar bourgeoisie. The new class of the polite was more inclusive than the old aristocracy, comprising all those who could manage to describe themselves as ladies and gentlemen'. He continues: 'Though the buyers of Hogarth's conversation pieces covered the entire spectrum of this new social formation, they tended to cluster around its lower echelons'.

117 *Ibid.*, p. 100.

118 Deuchar, *Sporting Art*, p. 110. The hunt is named after the village of Charlton near Goodwood.

119 Judy Egerton, *George Stubbs: 1724–1806*, Tate Gallery, London, 1984, p. 16. Horse races were attended by 'the nobility and gentry etc., who usually honour our horse races with their presence . . .' [and] 'all persons of every Rank and Degree'. Deuchar, *Sporting Art*,

points out, p. 110, that 'Stubbs's race meetings have a quiet cleanliness', with no crowds, no gambling, no disruption, which can hardly have been a true picture. Stubbs did not show the disreputable side of the racecourse. However, he did paint racecourse pictures for the nobility. For the second Viscount Bolingbroke he depicted *Gimcrack at Newmarket, Horse with Trainer and Stable Lad* (*c.* 1765).

120 Egerton, *Stubbs*, p. 66; see also Deuchar, *Sporting Art*, p. 108. The author sees Grosvenor as having reactionary and socially pretentious leanings.

121 *Ibid.*, p. 110.

122 *Ibid.*, p. 155.

123 David Coombs, *Sport and the Countryside*, Phaidon, London, 1978, p. 97; see also Mary Webster, *Francis Wheatley*, Paul Mellon Foundation, London, 1980, p. 137. Wheatley painted *The Return from Shooting* (1788) which showed the second Duke of Newcastle with his keeper Mansell, his specially bred French spaniels, his under-keeper putting game into a sack, and Clumber, his country house, in the distance.

124 Coombs, *Sport and the Countryside*, pp. 84–5.

125 Ellis Waterhouse, *Painting in Britain 1530–1790*, Penguin, Harmondsworth, 1978, p. 214.

126 Charles Saumarez Smith, *The Building of Castle Howard*, Faber and Faber, London, 1990, pp. 105–6. The author discusses the ideas put forward by Kerry Downes in his book on Vanbrugh, but is sceptical of the interpretation.

127 Edward Croft-Murray, *Decorative Painting in England*, Country Life, London, 1971, vol. II, pp. 23–4.

128 John Barrell, *The Political Theory of Painting from Reynolds to Hazlitt*, Yale University Press, London, 1986, pp. 14–15.

129 *Ibid.*, p. 20.

130 *Ibid.*, p. 37.

131 *Ibid.*, p. 17.

132 Claire Pace, 'Gavin Hamilton's Wood and Dawkins Discovering Palmyra: The Dilettante as Hero', *Art History*, 4, September 1981, p. 280.

133 Timothy Clifford, 'Sebastiano Conca at Holkham: A Neapolitan Painter and a Norfolk Patron', *Connoisseur*, 96, October 1977, pp. 93–103.

134 Jane Clark, 'Palladianism and the Divine Right of Kings: Jacobite Iconography', *Apollo*, CXXV, April 1992, pp. 224–30.

135 Clifford, 'Conca at Holkham', p. 99. John Cornforth, 'Augustan Vision Restored', *Country Life*, CLXXXII, 4 August 1988, pp. 90–2 quotes John Hardy in suggesting that the pictures are concerned with Roman virtues, and Juno presides over the room.

136 Andrew Moore, *Norfolk and the Grand Tour*, Norfolk Museums Services, Norwich, 1985, p. 116.

137 Duncan Macmillan, *Painting in Scotland: The Golden Age*, Phaidon, Oxford, 1986, p. 33. The paintings were: *The Anger of Achilles for the Loss of Briseis* (1769) for Lord Palmerston, *Hector's Farewell to Andromache* (*c.* 1777) for the Duke of Hamilton, *Achilles Mourning Patroclus* (1760–62), *Achilles' Revenge upon the Body of Hector* (1766) for the Marquis of Tavistock, *Priam Pleading for the Body of Hector* for Lord Mornington, *Priam Pleading with Achilles for the Body of Hector* for Luke Gardner and *Andromache Mourning the Death of Hector* (1758–61) for the seventh Earl of Northampton. For Lord Hope, Hamilton painted *The Oath of Brutus* and for Earl Spencer, *Agrippina with the Ashes of Germanicus*.

138 Julia Lloyd Williams, *Gavin Hamilton 1723–1798*, National Gallery of Scotland, Edinburgh, 1994, p. 10.

139 Herrmann, *The English as Collectors*, p. 112. Extract from Thomas Martyn, *The English Connoisseur*, 1776.

140 Brian Connell, *Portrait of a Whig Peer*, André Deutsch, London, 1957, p. 58.

141 Barrell, *Political Theory of Painting*, p. 116.

142 Wendy Wassyng Roworth (ed.), *Angelica Kauffman: A Continental Artist in Georgian England*, Reaktion Books, London, 1992, p. 37.

143 *Ibid.*, p. 45. The four pictures were *The Interview of Hector and Andromache* (a scene from *The Iliad*); *Penelope Taking Down the Bow of Ulysses* (from *The Odyssey*); *Venus Showing Aeneas and Anchates the Way to Carthage* (from *The Aeneid*) and *Achilles Discovered by Ulysses amongst the Attendants of Deidamia* (from *The Achilleid*) added in 1769.

144 *Ibid.*, p. 48.

145 Hardy and Tomlin, *Osterley Park*, p. 30.

146 A. A. Tait, *Robert Adam: The Creative Mind From One Sketch to the Finished Drawing*, The Soane Gallery, London, 1996, p. 46.

147 Pace, 'Gavin Hamilton's Wood and Dawkins', p. 282.

148 Egerton, *Stubbs*, p. 67.

149 Solkin, *Painting for Money*, p. 212.

150 Tait, *Adam*, p. 46.

151 Barrell, *Political Theory of Painting*, p. 37.

152 *Kedleston Hall*, Guide, p. 36.

153 Williams, *Gavin Hamilton*, p. 7.

154 Connell, *Whig Peer*, p. 55.

155 Sam Smiles, 'J. H. Mortimer and Ancient Britain: An Unrecorded Project and a New Identification', *Apollo*, CXLII, November 1995, pp. 42–7.

156 John Sunderland, 'Mortimer, Pine and Some Political Aspects of English History Painting', *The Burlington Magazine*, CXVI, June 1974, pp. 317–26.

157 Smiles, 'Mortimer and Ancient Britain', p. 45.

158 Duncan Macmillan, 'Alexander Runciman', *The Burlington Magazine*, CXII, January 1970, pp. 23–30.

159 Roy Strong, *And When Did You Last See Your Father? The Victorian Painter and British History*, Thames and Hudson, London, 1978, p. 21.

160 Francis Russell, 'The Stourhead Batoni and Other Copies after Reni', *The National Trust Year Book*, London, 1975–76, pp. 109–11.

161 St John Gore, *The Saltram Collection*, The National Trust, London, 1977, p. 37.

162 Russell, 'Stourhead Batoni', pp. 110–11.

163 John Fowler and John Cornforth, *English Decoration in the Eighteenth Century*, Barrie and Jenkins, London, 1974, p. 234.

164 Quoted by Deuchar, *Sporting Art*, pp. 87–8.

165 Fowler and Cornforth, *English Decoration*, p. 232.

166 Moore, *Norfolk and Grand Tour*, p. 125.

167 Gervase Jackson-Stops and James Pipkin, *The English Country House: A Grand Tour*, National Trust/Weidenfeld and Nicolson, London, 1989, p. 191.

168 Frederick Ladd, *Architects at Corsham Court*, Moonraker Press, Bradford-on-Avon, 1978, p. 34.

169 Dorothy Stroud, *Capability Brown*, Faber and Faber, London, 1975, pp. 88–9.

170 John Kenworthy-Browne, *Chippendale and his Contemporaries*, Orbis, London, 1975, pp. 226–8 for photographs of gallery and its furnishings.

171 David Hill, *Harewood Masterpieces*, Harewood Estate Office, Harewood, 1995, p. 6.

172 *Kedleston Hall*, Guide, p. 23.

173 *Ibid.*, p. 29.

174 *Ibid.*, p. 50.

175 Hardy and Tomlin, *Osterley*, p. 30.

176 Andrew Moore (ed.), *Houghton Hall*, Philip Wilson, London, 1996, p. 90.

177 Deuchar, *Sporting Art*, p. 198.

178 Pointon, *Hanging the Head*, p. 21.

179 *Ibid.*, p. 23.

180 Jacob Simon, *The Art of the Picture Frame*, National Portrait Gallery, London, 1997, p. 129.

181 Pointon, *Hanging the Head*, p. 35; see also Wilton, *Swagger Portrait*, p. 126.

182 Jacqueline O'Brien and Desmond Guinness, *Great Irish Houses and Castles*, Weidenfeld and Nicolson, London, 1992, pp. 94–5.

183 Peter de Figueiredo and Julian Treuherz, *Cheshire Country Houses*, Phillimore, Chichester, 1988, pp. 164–5. The gallery was in the taste of Thomas Hope with Grecian embellishments. The pictures have Neo-Rococo frames and were hung on deep crimson flock wallpaper.

184 *Attingham*, National Trust Guide, p. 7.

185 Sebastian Pryke, 'Paxton House, Berwickshire II', *Country Life*, CLXXXVII, 6 May 1993, pp. 62–5.

186 Herrmann, *The English as Collectors*, p. 10.

187 *Ibid.*, p. 25.

188 James Lees-Milne, *Earls of Creation*, Century Hutchinson, London, 1986, p. 122.

189 John Harris, 'Harley the Portrait Collector', *Apollo*, September 1985, pp. 198–204.

190 Egerton, *Stubbs*, p. 52.

191 Lees-Milne, *Earls of Creation*, p. 85.

192 Smart, *Ramsay*, pp. 9–10.

193 Roworth, *Kauffman*, p. 57.

194 Penny, *Reynolds*, p. 60.

195 Marion Fowler, *Blenheim: Biography of a Palace*, Penguin, Harmondsworth, 1991, pp. 110–11.

196 Hayes, *Gainsborough*, 1980 catalogue, p. 21.

197 *Ibid.*

198 *Ibid.*, p. 25.

199 John Rothenstein and Martin Butlin, *Turner*, Heinemann, London, 1964, pp. 79–80.

200 Hill, *Harewood Masterpieces*, p. 29.

6

Furnishing the country house

The furnishing of the country house was a major undertaking. Architecturally the Palladian style was intended to be purifying after the excesses of the Baroque, but it offered little to inspire the furniture designer since Andrea Palladio himself had only been concerned with building. Gradually the imposing, architectural-looking state apartments of Palladian country houses were enlivened, first by the rich Italian Baroque furniture of William Kent and later by the lightness of French Rococo naturalism, through the influence of Thomas Chippendale, Thomas Johnson, and Ince and Mayhew amongst others. However, this effect was often achieved through a lavish use of incisively carved mahogany, which became a national characteristic and was hardly a French one. There was a national taste also for the Gothic furniture of Chippendale and his contemporaries: as with Chinese taste, it relieved the solemnity of Palladian interiors, and was frequently favoured as a way of making libraries, and, in the case of Chinoiserie, bedrooms and boudoirs, lighter and more fashionable.

The taste for antique architecture and the admiration for ancient Rome which had led to the development of Neoclassicism affected furniture as well as architecture. Robert Adam's own furniture, which owed something to Kent and much to Roman architectural decoration, was only to be found in the grandest of houses, and was essentially architectural in feeling. However, the vocabulary of this furniture was taken up by George Hepplewhite and Thomas Sheraton: they produced furniture catalogues of useful household items which filtered the aristocratic Adam style down to the middle classes. Sheraton's later manner ushered in a heavier, more archaeologically exact taste in the form of the Greek Revival, favoured, along with more romantic Gothic furniture and a more convincingly exotic Chinese style, as a way of giving variety to the country house. The early nineteenth century also witnessed the break-up of formal arrangements of furniture: a new picturesque wayward spirit led to furniture being left in the middle of the floor rather than being arranged against the walls, as in the previous century.

There were clearly differences of region and class to be taken into account. Great houses were, at least in part, richly furnished at enormous expense, and the status of the owner was expressed in some prestige pieces of furniture. Robert Walpole's saloon at Houghton had a table commemorating his Order of the Garter (see [27]) as part of the decorative theme.[1] Similarly Lord Dumfries's furniture in the early 1750s had decorations which celebrated his becoming a Knight of the Thistle.[2] The 'marine' sofas by John Linnell at Kedleston [plate 15] combined with Michael Spang's programme of decorations[3] to celebrate naval victories of the Seven Years' War, which brought the first British Empire to its widest extent and favoured West Indian sugar planters.[4] 'What I admire here is the total defiance of expense',[5] said Dr Johnson on seeing the Beauvais tapestries and Aubusson covered chairs at Inveraray. In 1732, the trimmings, supplied by Turner, Hill and Pitter, for Walpole's green velvet bed at Houghton alone cost £1,219 3s 11d.[6] After 1759 Lady Leicester was left £2,000 a year to finish several of the state rooms at Holkham. Chippendale's most valuable contract was for the finishing of Harewood, which exceeded £10,000.[7] The upper gentry might spend less. Sir Thomas Wentworth, who was neither rich nor fashionable at the beginning of the eighteenth century, had a gilt parlour with beds, tables, carpets, curtains and a looking-glass all valued at £48.[8]

In Scotland some lairds and richer landowners had wonderfully furnished country houses, although until the 1720s even lowland Scotland was not an area where the consumption of household goods was as well developed as in England. It is interesting that there were also variations between town and country: professional townspeople were more inclined to fine things than were some of the well-to-do lesser landowners.[9] In remoter regions there were fewer great patrons to stimulate the taste for splendour. Chippendale's *The Gentleman and Cabinet Maker's Director* had five dukes, a marquess, five earls, six barons and five baronets or knights as subscribers. This was a London publication, however; most prominent aristocrats had town houses in the capital and would be aware of events there. No one in Wales subscribed to the *Director* nor to Sheraton's *The Cabinet Maker and Upholsterer's Drawing Book* when it was published.[10] In Ireland, John Smith, a Dublin bookseller, was mentioned as a supplier of the *Director* but only one craftsman in Ireland and apparently few in Scotland subscribed. The Scottish gentry and aristocracy bought more copies than did craftsmen.[11]

With the union of the Scottish and English Parliaments in 1707, there were numerous Scottish peers established in London. Lords Bute and Mansfield[12] were patrons of Adam, and it was through two other Scots, Lord Charles Hay and Lady Lindores that Adam met Edwin Lascelles and Nathaniel Curzon of Kedleston, who were to be amongst his most important patrons.[13] Such Scottish patrons were not remote lairds: they formed a metropolitan society, ordering furniture and architectural schemes and portraits from fellow Scots such as Adam and Allan Ramsay. In Scotland itself, furniture makers found greater difficulty in promoting themselves, often re-lying on personal recommendations, although by the early 1750s Edinburgh newspapers were increasingly used to reach a wider section of the public.[14] In this they differed from fashionable London furniture makers, who tended not to use newspaper advertisements or even labels on the furniture to advance their trade.

Very fine furniture might be made on the estate of the landowners or alternatively they might buy it locally or in the capital. Many furniture makers were to be found in particular areas of London. The area around St Paul's Cathedral was a traditional centre, although it ceased to be the place where grander pieces might be bought. Until 1745 it was in the courts around Covent Garden and St Martin's Lane that the premises of leading cabinet makers could be found. Vile and Cobb, Chippendale, William Hallett and France and Beckwith were all situated there.[15] Later in the eighteenth century, Soho, Bond Street and Golden Square had the smart furniture makers, and by the 1780s Oxford Street and Tottenham Court Road had begun to take over.[16]

The fashionable London furniture maker could be confident of supply-ing the best houses. William Hallett, for example, became successful during George II's reign. He supplied furniture to Lord Folkestone between 1737 and 1740, and was paid large sums for it.[17] In 1732 he established himself in Great Newport Street, Longacre. He made furniture for Lord Pembroke, and for Holkham and Uppark, and also supplied furniture to the Duke of Chandos at Cannons. Hallett's success may have been due to a close liaison with other prominent cabinet makers who furnished country houses, includ-ing William Vile and John Cobb. Vile and Cobb certainly worked at Holkham, for Lord Folkestone at Longford Castle and also for Sir Matthew Feather-stonehaugh at Uppark. William Linnell and his son John also supplied furni-ture to country houses from their premises at 28 Berkeley Square, London. These consisted of a dwelling house, an office and an upholsterer's shop. The site was well chosen, for whilst the north and east sides were occupied by tradesmen, noblemen's houses filled the rest of the square. Thus rich influential customers, such as Lord Shelburne who lived in a town house designed by Adam, dwelt side by side with craftsmen producing the most luxurious objects.[18]

The world of rich patrons and talented craftsmen often seems to have involved close-knit relationships: the fourth Duke of Beaufort employed the Linnell firm to create the Chinese bedroom at Badminton for him, after about 1745. How did the Duke come to know the firm? Perhaps because he had been a member of the Board of Trustees of the Radcliffe Camera at Oxford, where William Linnell had executed all the woodwork.[19] Beaufort's reason for deciding on a room in the Chinese taste might be that his London house was in Grosvenor Street, only a short distance from Mrs Montague's where a Chinese bedroom was being installed. Like other craftsmen, the

Linnells were adept at developing a grand manner and carrying it with them from one commission to another. For Lord Scarsdale at Kedleston, William Linnell, as we have seen, produced magnificent marine sofas, with mermaids and mermen as their decoration, using his previous experience of work on George III's state coach, with its Tritons, as a model for the sofas.[20]

William Linnell worked for the sixth Earl of Coventry, who furnished both his London house at 20 Piccadilly, and Croome Court, with great lavishness, patronising many different craftsmen in the 1760s. He also had library bookcases and wardrobes by Vile and Cobb, as well as dining tables from Ince and Mayhew, and in 1764 Pierre Langlois supplied him with a commode. A box from Chippendale and a state bed from France and Bradburn were amongst his other English commissions, but he also bought furniture in Paris at Poirer's shop and ordered Gobelins tapestries there too. The opportunity afforded to a number of leading craftsmen to see each other's work and to experience the stylishness of Lord Coventry's interiors was clearly an education for them, and provided information that could be passed on to other clients.[21] The range of a furniture maker's activities might be very wide indeed, as is indicated by the valuation of William Linnell's household goods and stock in trade. His premises contained a cabinet shop, glass room, chair room, upholsterer's shop, store room, counting house, joiner's shop and sawpit. William Linnell seems to have begun his career as a carver,[22] but his premises, like those of Thomas Chippendale, show that he could cover every aspect of the upholstery trade and cabinet making. The Linnells, however, continued to specialise in carving and gilding, whereas Chippendale had no space set aside for these activities, but did have a veneering room.[23]

Visiting furniture makers was clearly an important activity for the well-to-do. In 1786 Sophie van la Roche went to George Seddon's whilst she was staying in London. There were very large furniture workshops covering a site of two acres in Aldersgate Street. She noted that he had premises with six wings in which he employed about six hundred tradesmen. There were departments for sofas, chairs and stools, and Seddon supplied his customers with materials for curtains and bedcovers such as silk, wool and chintz, as well as carpets and hangings.[24] Sophie was also impressed by the quality of the tools used, believing that they helped Seddon and Company to make good furniture. 'I handled some of them [the tools]', she wrote, 'and regarded them as most valuable and beneficent inventions.'[25]

During the eighteenth century the term 'warehouse' was often applied to businesses which were also involved in the display of retail goods for the house. Sometimes these places were most elegantly fitted out and apparently not involved in the making or wholesaling of furnishings. One anonymous writer declared them to be 'more like palaces'. By the 1780s however, retail-only premises were becoming important enough to threaten the existence of warehouses.[26]

Important London furniture makers were more than simple crafts-men. John Linnell probably attended drawing classes at the St Martin's Lane Academy. His drawings show a Rococo freedom in the 1750s and early 1760s, with fantastic dragons and sinuous scrolls.[27] Possibly he knew through engravings the work of Gilles-Marie Oppenord. By the late 1760s his work seems to show a new formal classicism, derived, perhaps, from the designs of J. C. Delafosse. That furniture designers regarded themselves as more than ordinary craftsmen is indicated by the way in which, like painters, they attempted to attract patrons by presenting a piece of carved furniture to the Foundling Hospital.[28] They always needed to be seen as conversant with fashionable and foreign styles. Sheraton noted, 'When our tradesmen are desirous to draw the best customers to their ware rooms, they hasten to Paris, or otherwise pretend to go there'.[29]

Thomas Chippendale seems to have made certain that the well-to-do sought his services, whether in London or the provinces. He made sure that he was known well in his native county of Yorkshire. York itself was an important centre of craftsmanship, and the *York Courant* was the only pro-vincial newspaper, it seems, to carry notices of the publication of *The Gentle-man and Cabinet Maker's Director* in 1754. Like other prominent cabinet makers, once Chippendale was established in London, he did not place advertisements in newspapers simply advertising his business alone, but he did make sure that all publication notices concerning the *Gentleman and Cabinet Maker's Director* also advertised the skills offered by his workshop. An entry in the *General Evening Post* in June 1754 pointed out that 'All sorts of Cabinet and Upholstery work made by the Author in the neatest and most fashionable Taste and at the most Reasonable Rates' were available.[30] Chippendale was also elected to the Society of Arts, being proposed by Sir Thomas Robinson of Rokeby in 1760. Although the society was not club-like or especially sociable, he must have met the other members, some of whom were peers, landed gentry or professional men.

Close proximity to a nobleman's town house seems to have been advantageous to Chippendale as well as to the Linnells. The former moved to Somerset Court, off the Strand, in 1752, premises which adjoined the Earl of Northumberland's ancestral palace. By 1753 he was established in St Martin's Lane, where, it has been noted, there were thirty-two other prominent cabinet makers including William Vile and John Cobb, and William Hallett.[31] It is possible that Chippendale already had links with the area since he may, like John Linnell, have attended the St Martin's Lane Academy, where the leading Rococo draughtsman Hubert Gravelot taught. Certainly this was an area where painters, architects and sculptors had also settled. They included Thornhill, Hogarth, Hayman, Fuseli, Pine, Reynolds and Paine. Mark Girouard has pointed to Slaughter's Coffee House, which was directly opposite Chippendale's shop, as a centre where artists, craftsmen and their patrons might meet.[32]

Work on site as well as in London was also extremely important, and it was time consuming. Thomas Chippendale sent Samuel James to Harewood in October 1769 and he remained there for 58½ days, working twelve hours a day, simply to organise the bedrooms. His successor, William Reid, was in residence for most of 1770–72, working a six-day, seventy-two hour week in the capacity of upholsterer.[33] However, provincial furniture makers were also important. Well established were Robinson Cook of Liverpool; Thomas Malton of Nottingham; Farrier, Barker and Reynolds of York; and Edward Elwick of Wakefield. Men from Leeds and York worked on the furnishings of Harewood.[34] Leeds was becoming renowned for its textiles, and these were available to upholsterers there, centred around Briggate. In this area the most successful upholsterers combined the activities of cabinet making, chair making, japanning and gilding, as well as upholstery itself, in order to produce a sufficiently wide range of articles with which to furnish houses. By the mid-1770s Armitage's Upholstery and Cabinet Factory was supplying the area not only with his own furniture, but with London-made household objects as well.[35]

Some provincial furniture makers were skilled in a variety of other activities. Jeremiah and Joseph Hargrave of Hull were architects, architectural carvers, restorers and book illustrators. They worked as furniture makers, supplying Burton Constable in Yorkshire, but also collaborated with architects such as James Wyatt. They appear to have had a considerable amount of freedom and their own distinctive style, whereas later craftsmen, those working for Robert Adam for example, were hampered by having to conform to his disciplined, full-sized drawings.[36]

One of the most important furnishers of country houses was the firm of Gillow. Robert Gillow the Elder (1704–67) founded the company in 1730, and in 1769 a London manufactory and shop were established. The family was Catholic, and being thus excluded from public life, concentrated on business interests. Many of Gillow's customers were Catholic aristocracy and gentry, including, at the Lancashire branch of the firm, Lord Arundell of Wardour and Lady Clifford of Chudleigh. The severe geometrical style of the Wyatts was replacing the gilded, carved furniture of the elder Chippendale and Robert Gillow's friendship with Samuel Wyatt led to important commissions at, for example, Heaton House and Tatton Park. The Egertons of Tatton employed various members of the Wyatt family and bought fine, elegant and restrained furniture from the Gillows between 1780 and 1830. It is possible that the employment of the Gillows and Samuel Wyatt on both Heaton and Tatton was due to Sir Thomas Egerton of Heaton recommending them to his kinsman William Egerton of Tatton.[37]

The country house owner in Scotland could either buy his furniture in London or have it made locally. It was quite common for Chippendale and other furniture makers to supply one magnificent piece of furniture which a local maker might be commissioned to copy rather less expensively.

There are numerous incidences of this. The Dowager Lady Lothian wrote to her daughter-in-law about redecorating Newbattle Abbey in Midlothian, in 1776: 'My humble thought is that it may be best to get your chairs for the Old Drawing (room) at London to your taste . . . as for other chairs may be wanted you had better send patterns which you like to Sam Elliot . . . and he will make them.'[38]

Sam Elliot was the estate wright at Newbattle, and such craftsmen frequently copied furniture. William Shiells, estate wright, submitted estimates for copying furniture at Lord Lauderdale's house, Halton, for his principal seat, Thirlstane, in Berwickshire.[39] Lord Hopetoun's enormous Adam house, Hopetoun in West Lothian, was furnished by his estate wright, Thomas Welsh, who copied furniture made by the Edinburgh Upholstery Company and was even able to employ an apprentice on the strength of this commission. Sometimes considerable savings were made in this manner so that extravagance could rule elsewhere. Peter and Douglas Traill of Edinburgh copied suites of gilt furniture for the Duke of Argyll at Inveraray Castle in the 1770s. However, the Duke bought ten sets of chairs whilst in Paris and also had other chairs gilded by a specialist French craftsman, Dupasquier, who had established himself in Edinburgh.[40]

Sometimes the metropolitan English models seemed temptingly superior and the economy of provincial copying of less weight. Lord Dumfries had intended to economise by having some Chippendale furniture copied by Alxander Peter of Edinburgh for Dumfries House, Ayrshire, in 1754.[41] But, having visited Chippendale's St Martin's Lane showroom, he seems to have been dazzled by the Rococo array there and to have ordered everything important from the master in London. Lord Dumfries then had to insure the furniture that Chippendale had made for him, before it made its arduous journey by sea from London to Scotland. Frequently such cargoes had to be repaired when they arrived at their destination.

With the defeat of the Young Pretender at Culloden in 1745 the furnishing of country houses was probably given a boost by the new political stability. Local men often worked side by side with London craftsmen. Alexander Peter and his apprentice William Mathie worked with Chippendale at Dumfries House and even copied one of the plates of a side table, from the first edition of the *Director*.[42] Sometimes, as in England, the architect recommended a furniture maker, although one has the impression that if the client was not thinking of buying in London, the range of good Edinburgh furniture makers was not large. Francis Brodie, who had a shop on the south side of Lawnmarket, obviously saw himself as a classicist, having a portrait of Palladio as his shop sign. William Adam recommended him to the Duke of Hamilton as 'the best man in town', but added, 'I doubt if anyone else would please'.[43]

The situation began to change in the 1750s. One successful, if devious, businessman, was James Cullen. He was a London upholsterer who, perhaps to get away from debt, opened a shop in Edinburgh and with Lord Hopetoun's patronage was able to supply furniture for Hopetoun over a twenty-year period.[44] He could not set up as a wright as it was necessary to have certain skills which would enable one to join either the Incorporation of Wrights of Canongate or the other body simply known as the Incorporation of Wrights. Cullen simply used other craftsmens' designs, sometimes – as with some gilt frame design filched from Mathias Lock – he did not acknowledge their source.[45] Cullen ignored traditional procedures. The opportunity for other firms to move away from old, more rigid methods seems to have come with the building of the New Town in Edinburgh. This provided new opportunities to supply the town houses of the aristocracy and the well-to-do middle classes with crisp, carefully made Neoclassical pieces, with perfect cross-banding and veneering. Hugo Arnot, an Edinburgh lawyer observed, 'Now a private gentleman of moderate fortune is accommodated with much more commodious and even rich furniture . . . than could have been enjoyed by a Lord of the sixteenth century.'[46] One firm above all others supplied rather austere Grecian elegance: Young, Trotter and Hamilton. This firm dominated the Scottish market from 1730 to 1830, having a shop at 5 Princes Street and workshops in Waverley Market. In 1797 William Trotter (1722–1833) become a member of the Merchant Company, rather than working as a humble wright. Ever conscious, it would seem, of the need for a prominent social role, he became master of the Merchant Company in 1809, and between 1825 and 1827 was Lord Provost of Edinburgh.[47]

The role of the architect in designing furniture, or overseeing its supply, was also significant. Architects had played a prominent role in design in foreign courts in the seventeenth century, especially in France. Daniel Marot (1663–1752), an ornamentalist, had led the way in designing complete splendid interiors. William Talman's advice was sought after, not only as an architect but as a collector and man of taste. William Kent (1685–1740) was perhaps the first English architect to turn to wider aspects of design: he was a painter, landscape gardener and furniture designer.[48] Throughout the century other architects provided designs for furniture. William Jones (d. 1757), although a minor architect, published some of the earliest drawings for furniture as an appendix to James Smith's *Specimens of Ancient Carpentry. The City and County Builder's and Workman's Treasury of Design* by Batty and Thomas Langley (1740), which had furniture designs in the manner of William Kent and Rococo designs based on the work of Nicolas Pineau. Robert Adam, William Chambers, William Halfpenny and John Crunden were all architects who produced some furniture designs.[49]

In the *Works*, Robert and James Adam aimed at the highest echelons of society, referring continually to 'the noble proprietors' and to 'persons of rank and fortune'.[50] Both as an architect and a furniture designer, Robert Adam saw himself as an innovator whom others of a more lowly status would follow. Of the furniture he designed for Lord Bute at Luton Park, he

239

wrote that his stove grate 'seems to have given the idea of those in this form which now prevail so much both in public and private buildings'. His cornices for window curtains 'were introduced as an attempt to banish the absurd French composition of this kind, heretofore so servilely imitated by the upholsterers of this country'.[51] Apart from publishing the *Works* and publicising his style, Robert Adam had many skills and services to offer potential clients. Adam only very occasionally provided a wide range of furniture for a house. He did so at Osterley and at Derby House in London (demolished in 1862). His method of proceeding was fairly complicated. Adam would send his designs to a client who, if he approved them, would return them to the architect to be executed according to his specifications. Sometimes the client would pass on the furniture schemes to a cabinet maker who was responsible for completing the house. When the execution of his drawings was included in the commission, Adam found a craftsman to carry out the work, and it was he whom the cabinet maker must satisfy – and he who paid the latter's account. Sometimes prominent cabinet makers would be at work at a house at the same time as Adam, and sometimes they would produce furniture which was not in the spirit of his own work. At Kedleston, John Linnell worked in a Rococo style when Adam was producing Neoclassical designs, and the latter's swags and husks and paterae sat side by side with naturalistic curves and swirls.[52] Some of Adam's furniture was inspired by that of a rival architect James Stuart (1713–88) who in 1757 produced furniture designs for Kedleston. There were many other Neoclassical architects who designed furniture, including Thomas Leverton, George Richardson and the Wyatt family. The latter in particular showed interest in furniture design for patrons or in publications.

Furniture designers and manufacturers themselves began to produce publications, which mimicked the *gravitas* found in architects' writings. Although aiming at the craftsman, Thomas Chippendale's *The Gentleman and Cabinet Maker's Director* of 1754 was also designed to appeal to gentlemen about how to furnish their houses, as its title implies. Its explanation of the five orders of architecture also had a gentleman-scholar appeal, and its list of aristocratic subscribers indicated that it had the support of the nobility. It was, as we have seen, dedicated to the Earl, later first Duke of Northumberland, just as some architectural works were dedicated to an aristocrat who offered support. James Gibbs's *A Book of Architecture* (1728) had been similarly envisaged as 'of use to such Gentlemen as might be concerned in building' and to 'any Workman who understands lines', and was dedicated to the second Duke of Argyll and Greenwich. *A Book of Architecture* was widely used throughout Britain and the colonies during the eighteenth century.[53] Chippendale's *Director*, with its 161 folio plates (and 200 in its third edition of 1762) was similarly influential both in the United States and in Britain.

Of course some publications such as George Hepplewhite's *The Cabinet Maker and Upholsterer's Guide*, first published in 1788, did not strike such an

Kedleston, the Drawing Room, with one of four 'marine' sofas designed by John Linnell, *c.* 1762

Houghton, Norfolk. Saloon chair, one of twelve
designed by William Kent, *c.* 1731. It was probably
made by James Richards

PLATE 17

Saltram, the Saloon. Architect Robert Adam, 1768–69. The furniture was probably supplied by Thomas Chippendale. Only part of the bronze *garniture de cheminée* is visible in this photograph

PLATE 18

Petworth House, Sussex. The State Bed made by Samuel Norman, *c.* 1760

Badminton, the Badminton Cabinet, 1728

The Dessert Course. The 1750s silver epergne at the centre is filled with sweetmeats and surrounded by pyramids of marzipan shapes and candied fruit

exclusive tone. Although he wished his book to be 'serviceable to the gentle-men' and to 'unite elegance with utility',[54] he was concerned to establish standards of good taste for a wider audience. Mahogany chairs, he observed, should have seats of plain stripes or chequered horsehair, or alternatively, if cane-bottomed, they required cushions which matched the curtains. Again japanned or painted chairs could be coloured to harmonise with the room. Such advice might well be lapped up by lord and city alderman alike, but neither Kent nor Adam would have bothered himself with such ordinary details of soft furnishing, since their furniture designs were of a monumental kind designed for a particular client.

The dissemination of these aristocratic styles can be seen in the work of Thomas Sheraton (1751–1806). His *Cabinet Maker and Upholsterer's Drawing Book* (1791, 1793, 1794 and 1802) made use of familiar late Adam shapes, with most decorative classical ornament of the Louis XVI style. Sheraton probably moved around the London cabinet makers selling his skills as a draughtsman or designer. As he drew what was being made throughout the city, he provided other craftsmen with a record of what was available, albeit centred on his own contributions. His drawings could not adequately instruct the workman in any technical sense, but they could bring contemporary designs to a wider audience of the court and the country house, and themes from his work were to be found in the United States, Spain, Scandinavia and Germany after 1790.[55]

If one were able to walk round the country house at different periods throughout the eighteenth century, how would it have been furnished? What would the contents of the rooms have been? By the last quarter of the eight-eenth century furniture makers seem to have been sufficiently confident to suggest to the uncertain customer what his house would require.

James Hamilton, working for Young and Trotter of Edinburgh, wrote in 1775 to Thomas Mowatt of Uyeasound in Shetland about how a gentleman's house should be furnished.[56] The dining room must have a mahogany table in three parts, consisting of one square table with leaves and two semi-circular end parts. It must also have a mahogany sideboard, the length of which must usually be equal to one third of that side of the room where it was to be placed. Underneath this must be a mahogany wine cooler, lined with lead and mounted with brass hoops. Hamilton also advised Mowatt to have split back or 'Cockpen' chairs,[57] and two elbow chairs or stuffed back armchairs with horsehair upholstery and brass nails. A dining room should also have a handsome carved chimneypiece on which must stand candlesticks of either silver or mahogany (but not lustres, which he said were unfashionable).

A drawing room should have one large or two small sofas, stuffed back and seat chairs or Chinese chairs, which should be covered, like the sofa, in damask, calico or moreen. There should be one or two looking-glasses with handsome frames between the windows. Opposite these should be a pair of girandoles with doubles branches for candles. The drawing room would require

241

a pair of card tables and a tea table (or one card table and a similarly shaped tea table which could be used for cards). There should be a Scots carpet and a carved chimneypiece with china and cut glass ornaments.

The principal bedroom would require a four-post bed six-feet six inches long, five feet broad and seven feet six inches high, which was apparently the common size, as well as a chest of drawers with sconce glass over it. There should also be one mahogany night table, containing a close-stool if there were no water closet in the bedrooms, and a number of stuffed chairs covered to match the bed hangings. A swing dressing-glass should hang above the chest of drawers in place of the sconce, should there be no dressing room. If there were a dressing room, it should contain a mahogany shaving stand, with glass and basin stand, a toilet table and durrant cover, a box toilet glass and two elbow chairs.

Young and Trotter supplied a number of country houses, including Hopetoun and Mount Stuart on the Isle of Bute, with furniture, as well as furnishing some public buildings in Edinburgh, including the Assembly Rooms and the university. The furniture they provided for Paxton House, Berwickshire, both in the library and the picture gallery shows that they designed pieces in an elegant, rather spare Grecian style, with incisive carving making use of rosewood particularly. Their furniture was useful and practical and for Paxton they provided, for example, a pair of 'Grecian Couches' costing £27 10s 0d, a pair of rosewood Grecian sofas with backs costing £30 15s 0d, a pair of rosewood tables with lava tops and a sofa table. It is interesting to note in a letter from William Trotter to Mrs Home of Paxton, the former suggests that the sofas 'will look handsome even if taken out and placed occasionally in the middle of [the] room'. Paintings of Regency rooms show similar furniture in informal settings with furniture moved around as required. The bill for furnishings at Paxton was £1,040 6s 11d.[58]

The first room the visitor to a country house saw was usually the hall, the main impact of which was derived from the architectural features rather than the furniture. Isaac Ware, in 1768,[59] pointed out that such a room should be large and noble, and serve a number of functions. The furniture was fairly sparsely arranged in the hall and consisted largely of hall benches and seats, often in mahogany. At Houghton, c. 1728, there were six mahogany benches, and a large pair of mahogany side tables carved with wood-spirit masks.[60] At Harewood, Chippendale probably supplied the eight beech-frame chairs in the hall [90], emblazoned with the Lascelles coat of arms.[61] These, in his late Neoclassical style, were fairly grand in design and echoed the plasterwork of the room. He produced a simpler set for the lower hall. Such chairs were decorative in purpose, and presumably neither intimate friend not esteemed stranger would be expected to sit on them. The decorative motifs were inspired by antique Roman fragments, and such hall chairs are very different from the mahogany of the dining room or the sumptuous curves of Rococo bedroom chairs at Harewood.

90] Harewood, a hall chair by Thomas Chippendale, one of eight, *c.* 1770

THE SALOON

The provision of a saloon was a matter of prestige, but also a necessity where large numbers of people were to be entertained. Saloons were often boldly magnificent rooms of assembly – perhaps some of the newly built public assembly rooms in Bath or Doncaster emulated their grandeur.

In such formal rooms the furniture was intended to remain clear of the centre of the floor, which was not always carpeted.[62] The saloon at Erddig [91] was from 1685 to 1770 two rooms, and was thus much smaller than at present. The inventory of 1726 indicates that it was furnished with '8 caffoy walnut tree chairs' and a settee which has now disappeared. These were covered in a bold crimson and yellow caffoy. There was also a pair of gilt gesso girandoles, with glass arms supplied by John Belcher in

243

91] Erddig, Clywd, the Saloon

August 1724 at a cost of £14 each. In the 1720s they hung between the three windows.[63]

Inventories of Houghton indicate that furniture and materials were graded in accordance with the importance of the rooms, and they emphasise the way in which differences in degree of elaboration were maintained. The saloon was one of the most magnificent of the rooms. It was completed in May 1731 in order to entertain the Duke of Lorraine. As in other houses of this period, there was a progression of pattern and material, and the boldest were to be found in the saloon. Genoa crimson cut velvet was used there, 164 yards of it, according to Thomas Roberts, the supplier, whose bill amounted to £118 18s 0d in about 1729.[64] The 1745 inventory makes it clear that there were three marble tables, two settees, twelve chairs, four stools and two tea tables with cups and saucers. Here Kent was designing in the most magnificent style for a setting which he himself had devised. His furniture, probably carved by James Richards, was designed to be architectural, and he had little interest in the nature of the wood, tending often to disregard it.[65] Amongst the most magnificent pieces in the saloon, are the twelve chairs. The motifs associated with Venus, such as double scallop shells and fishscales were used both in the decoration of the ceiling and in these chairs [plate 16].

The key pieces of furniture required to complete such Palladian rooms as this were not based upon anything which Palladio had himself designed, since the latter had not left any clues as to suitable furniture for his own villas. On the whole, Kent's furniture was Baroque in feeling, and especially so in great rooms such as this. His ideas for such interiors were spread via the publications of the architect John Vardy, who produced *Some Designs of Mr Inigo Jones and Mr William Kent* in 1744.[66]

In furnishing the interior at Holkham, not far from Houghton, Lord and Lady Leicester were anxious to avoid waste, and much furniture was made locally rather than in London. Virtually all the seat furniture was made at the house, with upholstery produced by three Norwich craftsmen. Goodison supplied a pattern sofa and chairs when the state rooms were being furnished, and it is possible that Mathias Lock worked with Goodison and provided him with a design for the side table in the saloon. The saloon chairs incorporated lionheads from the cornice of the room and shells from the pier glasses and tables.[67]

On the whole, the saloons designed by Robert Adam were perhaps less richly furnished than the Palladian ones discussed. Adam's saloons often depended on a feeling of antique architectural coolness, and this is certainly the case with that of Kedleston, where the requirements of a polite space or parade are overlaid with memories of Panini's painting of the interior of the Pantheon. Kedleston's saloon has also lost its original Axminster carpet which echoed the coffering of the dome.[68]

Saltram in Devon has an Adam saloon [plate 17] in which the original furnishings are intact. A watercolour drawing of 1768 preserved at the house shows, with some amendments, what we can see today. This saloon was a place for entertaining where once more the floor would be left uncluttered. Here the fine carpet, for which John Parker paid Thomas Whitly, founder of the Axminster carpet factory, £126, still survives. It is probable that Whitly's factory was one of the few places where such a wide carpet could have been made. Its bold design in blues, pinks and browns was clearly meant to be visible, since the floor was for parading upon.[69]

It is almost certain, despite lack of drawings, that the carved giltwood suite of eighteen chairs and two settees was made by Thomas Chippendale. With their dentilated seat frames they are close in design to the chairs Chippendale is known to have made for Adam's Green Drawing Room at Harewood. John Parker's accounts certainly show that he paid Chippendale £120 in May 1771. Adam and Chippendale probably also supplied some of the picture frames, especially the very elaborate one above the chimneypiece. They may have been responsible as well for the giltwood box pelmets and four giltwood torchères that stand in the corners of the rooms. The torchères were designed to carry a set of four six-branch candelabra by Matthew Boulton, made of Blue John and tortoisehell with ormolu mounts.[70]

Small-scale decoration is important too. The seven bronzes form an important *garniture de cheminée* and were designed by Giacomo and Giovanni Zoffoli in the antique manner. In their centre is an equestrian statue of Marcus Aurelius, after that in the Piazza del Campidoglio in Rome. On either side are seated figures of Agrippina and Menander and copies of the Borghese Vase and the Medici Vase. There are other bronzes of the Capitoline Flora and the Farnese Flora. Theses 'suites of chimney ornaments' as they were more often called in England, were also produced for lesser rooms, but there they would be made of plaster or even coal. Wedgwood supplied black basalt garnitures at under £2 in total, whereas Lord Boringdon had paid the Zoffoli £9 9s for the Farnese Flora alone.[71]

Whereas the saloon was furnished and decorated for entertaining large numbers of people on a grand scale, the drawing room was rather less bold and opulent in appearance. Drawing rooms such as those at Houghton and Holkham flanked the saloon and were smaller than the latter. Often the walls were hung with damask – crimson was a favourite colour, as it was considered a suitable background for Italian pictures. The pictures were balanced by the formal arrangement of sets of chairs and sofas, but the furniture tended to be less massive than in the saloon, which had to be a 'great room intended for state'. Drawing rooms were decorated as spaces in which women especially might congregate. Often there was a taste for introducing lightness and sparkle into such rooms. In 1757 Mrs Lybbe Powis contrasted 'our delicateness' with 'our ancestors' taste for substantialness'. She predicted that to her descendants 'the light French of George II' would seem 'quite Lilliputian', and a characteristic of eighteenth-century furniture.[72]

Furniture with ormolu mounts and floral marquetry was especially favoured in drawing rooms.[73] Brilliantly coloured floral needlework was also found on some English suites. It seemed to aim at lightheartedness, and was much less formal than French examples.[74] Musical instruments were also considered a suitable decorative motif for drawing rooms, although the most splendid example, by Thomas Chippendale, was probably the bookcase supplied to the library at Wilton: it has a magnificently carved violin, other musical instruments and sheet music as its centrepiece. It was produced for the tenth Earl of Pembroke in about 1760.[75]

The 1760s witnessed the creation of some of the most lavish interiors, such as those by Luke Lightfoot at Claydon [92] in Buckinghamshire. John Channon (1711–79), an Exeter cabinet maker, used exotic woods, engraved brass inlay and brass mounts to create extravagant Rococo furniture. He moved to London at a time when luxury goods such as silver and clocks were at their most highly prized. It seems likely that Channon scoured the print shops of Great Newport Street for continental designs, and was influenced by Gaetano Brunetti's *Sixty Different Sorts of Ornament*, which had been published in 1736.[76]

92] Claydon House, Buckinghamshire. The Chinese Room by
Luke Lightfoot, 1750s

The contents of drawing rooms have perhaps changed more than those of other rooms, and it is difficult to gain an impression of their original appearance. Sir Matthew Featherstonehaugh's Red Drawing Room at Uppark [93] gives an impression of mid-eighteenth-century taste. It retains its original flock wallpaper, festoon curtains and Rococo furniture. Some of the paintings were collected on the Grand Tour by Sir Matthew. His portrait painted in Rome by Pompeo Batoni in 1757 hung over the fireplace. Two of the six Luca Giordanos he bought hung in this room, and depicted scenes from the Parable of the Prodigal Son. There were other landscapes which provided memories of the continent, including Tomaso Ruiz's four Neapolitan views.

247

Uppark had excellent pier glasses and the Red Drawing Room contained a pair of Rococo ones with male and female busts supporting baskets of flowers on their heads. The cornices of these have foliate cartouches with unusual pierced trelliswork. The rare English commodes in the Louis XV manner, veneered with Chinese lacquer panels are dated from the 1760s. Elaborate furniture of this kind would have been appreciated at close quarters; it has greater intricacy and detail than the huge pieces made by Kent for saloons. Although the suppliers of these looking-glasses and commodes at Uppark are unknown, both Thomas Johnson and Pierre Langlois provided just such rich pieces.[77] Langlois provided furniture which could 'finish a room so well', as Lady Holland wrote in 1763. He made commodes and bureaus with floral bouquets and sprays with knotted ribbon ties. Clients often provided their own pieces of home-produced Japan work which he would make into commodes for them. There were many books on designs for lacquerwork, including William Halfpenny's *New Designs for Chinese Temples* of 1750. Those who wished to make their own pieces could consult Robert Sayer's *The Ladies' Amusement or the Whole Art of Japanning Made Easy* published in 1762. The daughters of the well-to-do sometimes occupied themselves with courses in lacquering.[78]

93] Uppark, Sussex. The Red Drawing Room, decorations dating from 1754

The four giltwood armchairs at Uppark are also in the French manner and covered in mulberry coloured velvet: they date from *c.* 1770. There are also, from about 1755, a pair of wing chairs and two ensuite stools, and mahogany Chippendale side chairs of *c.* 1760 with red damask seat covers. A small table with cabriole legs and a mahogany architect's table with rising top, of about 1770, complete the eighteenth-century furniture of the room. There is a handsome George III London cut glass chandelier and an Axminster carpet. There are several pieces of Sèvres porcelain about the room.[79]

Robert Adam was often of course called upon to design drawing rooms, and in a few of these the furniture is either by him or in a style similar to that of the decoration he created. The drawing room at Osterley (see [30]) is a good example of a room which although not entirely by Adam, contains furniture in the Adamesque style. In fact, the floral 'mosaic' carpet which Adam designed in 1774 (supplied by Thomas Moore of Moorfields) echoes a ceiling which was probably created by William Chambers in the late 1750s.[80] Adam certainly updated the room. In 1772 he hung the walls with pea-green damask and a year later he provided designs for a pair of pier glasses surmounted by sphinxes and vestal virgins.[81] Some of the decoration is extremely refined and designed for contemplation, it would appear. The commodes have friezes with acanthus scrolls and urns in marquetry, at the centre of which are fine ormolu tablets consisting of a portrait medallion flanked by griffons. This was repeated in the fireplace, but the portrait was replaced by an urn. Adam had probably seen the motif of a medallion flanked by griffons at the Villa Madama in Rome, and had certainly made sketches of details designed by Raphael and Giovanni da Udine, which they had adapted from Roman originals. The drawing room contains a set of gilded oak and beech chairs en suite with two settees. The pea-green silk damask upholstery is modern, but copies the original which is listed in the inventory of 1782. The main emphasis of this room is Neoclassical, but the chairs are in a rather restrained Rococo style. To have this type of Rococo chair in an otherwise Neoclassical room was considered to be in the best Parisian taste, and other houses where Adam worked, such as Shardloes and Alnwick Castle, had similar sets. It is extremely likely that these chairs and sofas, the mirrors and commodes, were made in the workshop of John Linnell.[82]

THE DINING ROOM

The idea of having a dining room seems to have begun in about 1630.[83] By 1710 Le Blond noted that it was not uncommon in French houses to use the second antechamber of a formal house as a dining room.[84] At the beginning of the eighteenth century in England, the saloon was often used for dining on grand occasions, whereas the tenantry might expect, during celebrations, to be entertained in the hall. This seems to have been the case at Blenheim.[85]

There seems to have been some doubt about the idea of having a separate dining room well into the eighteenth century, although by 1755 it must have become common as Johnson included the word in his *Dictionary*.[86] It is difficult to discover quite how some early eighteenth-century dining rooms were furnished. At Castle Howard the dining room was next to the saloon and according to an inventory of *c*. 1758 contained amongst other furniture ten mahogany chairs with red morocco leather stuffed seats fixed with brass nails, two foreign marble top tables on iron brackets, two gilt framed pier glasses and a Derbyshire spar (Blue John) sideboard table with a walnut frame. It also contained a mahogany barometer, a clock on a mahogany bracket, two small leaved canvass fire screens and a 'scallop'd Indian close table'. It was therefore far from bare.[87]

In Scotland at the beginning of the eighteenth century the dining room still had an appearance which made it distinct from English examples. Melville House in Fife seems, in *c*. 1703, to have had a large oval gate-legged table, carved chairs and a smaller subsidiary table. The habit of using two tables was also sometimes to be found in England, but in some Scottish examples the dining room seems to be designed deliberately in two halves. At Dalkeith in Midlothian it was in the form of a double cube and had two fireplaces, as though diners were automatically split into two groups.[88]

At Houghton, Sir Robert Walpole altered one of the main apartments, the Marble Parlour, which was probably only used on fairly formal occasions for dining.[89] This was the final room in his Grand Storey, and the 1745 inventory indicates that it was decorated with green silk damask (to impress visitors no doubt), rather than a hard-wearing fabric which might otherwise have been used on the twelve armchairs and the single settee. There was some contrast between the furnishing of the dining room and that of the drawing room. The dining room was increasingly solid and masculine in its style.

As we have noted, men on the Grand Tour often collected mosaics or marbles which were then converted into pieces of furniture rather than remaining artistic fragments. The pair of buffets [94] in the Marble Parlour in an arched screen was the most magnificent and showed the greatest delight in rich gleaming effects.[90] The second Lord Palmerston, when on the Grand Tour in 1763 bought a collection of antique marbles, but also 'Two granite tables for £30 and two tables of green porphyry with Alabaster Border for £37'. Lord Palmerston's taste for semi-precious stones and marbles was conventional amongst grand tourists, and at Broadlands, his house in Hampshire,[91] they became an important decorative feature. However, not all dining rooms were uniformly masculine: that at Inveraray Castle [95] had French decoration and rather feminine furniture ordered for it, as well as a solid pair of side tables in Ross of Mull granite in about 1760.[92]

For much of the eighteenth century people preferred a number of small tables: two or four were not uncommon. Large tables only really became popular around 1780, when entertaining larger numbers became

94] Houghton. The Marble Parlour. One of a pair of
plumbed-in buffets in variegated marble with silver taps.
Architect William Kent, 1728–32

more common. The dining chairs were then usually drawn up to the table, rather than being arranged around the walls, which had commonly been the practice throughout much of the eighteenth century. Dining chairs during this period had plain uncarved backs since these faced the wall and were not exposed.[93] The centre of the room was left bare except when dining, so that the architectural formality of the room, perhaps the pattern of carpet might be admired. Robert Walpole had a huge table in the Marble Parlour at Houghton, which was made in four sections and expanded to over sixteen feet, but this seems to have been unusual.[94] At Hamilton Palace in Lanarkshire there was an impressive concertina-flap table dating from the 1740s which suggested that there was a fondness for dining in Scotland and little interest in the rather more temporary trestle-table which had been common earlier.[95] At Cannons, the Duke of Chandos had four tables in the dining room, one for himself, one for the chaplain, one for the gentlemen of the household, and the other for the officers of the household.[96] Having his own private orchestra, he was perhaps like the Duke of Norfolk who still, like a royal personage, sat under a canopy even in the 1750s, the last of the grandees.[97]   251

95] Inveraray Castle, Argyll. The State Dining Room by Robert Mylne, 1780, with decoration by French craftsman Guinard, who did the *grisailles* and Girard, who did the floral work in 1784

The dining room might be decorated with paintings or sculpture to suggest some antique or mythological theme: at Holkham, for example, it was specially designed to hold antique busts. Fine paintings tended not to be hung in dining rooms,[98] but at Houghton the Marble Parlour originally contained some old masters. At Easton Neston hunting pictures were thought suitable. There were Snyder's *Stag* and *Boar Hunts* and a version of Titian's *Diana and Actaeon*.[99]

At Osterley Robert Adam used the traditional iconography of the banqueting room. William Chambers had already supplied a ceiling with a pattern of vines, and the theme of Bacchus and wine was to be found elsewhere in the decoration. The chairs were probably supplied by John Linnell of Berkeley Square in about 1767.[100] They were of mahogany, and the mythological allusions on this occasion were in the form of Apollo's lyre [96], which formed the open splat on the backs. In 1773 Horace Walpole noted that 'the chairs are taken from antique lyres, and make charming harmony'.[101] One subtlety of eighteenth-century interiors was the way in which care was often taken to design one piece of furniture in a way which reflected another. Thus the chair legs in the dining room at Osterley are designed to echo the style of the firegrate.

Adam and his followers introduced a very distinctive type of side-board in the 1760s. Its origins may lie in the work of James Stuart, who produced a design for Kedleston in 1757–58, for a dining room recess with sideboard table flanked by urns. Stuart also produced a design for a marble wine cooler, supplied eventually by Richard Hayward, the sculptor. He made a drawing for an ormolu perfume burner, supposedly derived from the tripod which crowned the Choragic Monument of Lysicrates in Athens.[102] Eventually it was Robert Adam who, rivalling Stuart's earlier design, produced a design for the dining room recess. This consisted of three carved tables and two pairs of pedestals. These were to hold the gilt bronze tripod designed by Stuart, eight knife boxes, silver bases and silver wine fountains. The wine was to flow from the fountains into cisterns on pedestals. The Duchess of Northumberland noted in 1766 that the alcove was 'adorn'd with a vast quantity of handsome plate judiciously dispos'd on Tables of beautiful Marble and of very pretty shapes in the midst is Mr Stewart's Tripod and the cut Decanters are all bound with silver which has mighty pretty effect'.[103]

At Osterley (see [96]) the sideboard took the form of a central table flanked by urns on pedestals. The pedestals are Doric, and support vases with satyr mask handles. The sideboard table which they flank has lotus

96] Osterley, the Eating Room with a sideboard designed by Adam and chairs with lyre-backs supplied by Linnell, *c.* 1767

supports, a Grecian key-fret frieze ornamented with paterae and rams' heads. One vase here is lead-lined to hold water, and this was piped to taps in the pedestal. The other urn was a sham with a false tap. The effect was richly classical, and the suggestion was of Roman pedestal altars. The sideboard was made of gilded and white painted pine with ormolu mounts, but the table top was of mahogany.[104] The dining room at Osterley also had oval pier glasses, and beneath them tables designed to correspond with the sideboard table. They have floral marble 'antique' mosaic tops which were probably imported. The original dining room table was kept in a corridor, and it was only in about 1800 that a dining table was placed permanently in the centre of the room.[105]

Adam and Chippendale creatively developed the sideboard after introducing it at Kedleston in the 1760s. Urns had been added and if one looks at furniture by other designers one sees how the urns gradually became more unified. Sheraton supplied a plate in the 1802 edition of his *Drawing Book* (plate XXI) which shows how the table part of the sideboard gradually became more 'useful', being fitted with drawers in the centre and on either side, and a central tambour cupboard. The pedestals have vase knife-cases, which could be made separately and then screwed to the sideboard. Sheraton supplied a brass support at the back of the sideboard for silver, and gave it branches for lights to increase the glittering effect of any illumination.

In Scotland the distinctive feature of the eighteenth-century dining room was the buffet. This was used for the service of drinks; by displaying plate upon it the owner was also able to express his rank and status. It consisted of a cupboard with shaped, shell-like shelves, the curved edges of which were painted in different colours, for instance light blue or green, or sometimes gold. Silver as well as china punch bowls and jugs would adorn these shelves, whilst a hanging shelf below was used during dinner as a sideboard.[106] It was let down again after dinner, and the whole thing shut up behind doors which went nearly to the ceiling. Some buffets were more architectural with flanking pilasters which matched those of the opposite fireplace, and a few were very grand indeed, especially that of Dalkeith Palace which was made of veined white marble. This may have been an assertion of status on the part of the Duchess of Buccleuch and Monmouth, wife of Charles II's illegitimate son, who lived regally at Dalkeith.[107]

Increasingly the style of Adam was to be found in Scotland as well as England in the second half of the eighteenth century. Paxton House in Berwickshire, designed in the Adam style, had a dining room [97] fitted up by Chippendale in his Neoclassical, somewhat Adamesque manner with a sideboard table flanked by pedestals, and a dining room table in sections.[108]

By the early nineteenth century the massive, coffered ceiling of the dining room at Belvoir Castle [98] displayed a variety of styles which symbolise the re-emerging self-confidence of the aristocracy after Waterloo. Gilded arched recesses decorated with vines contain monumentally grand sideboards, probably designed, like the rest of the room, with the advice of the Reverend Sir John Thoroton, and made by Gillows. The chairs, in their scrolly strength, look back to the *ancien régime* in France for inspiration, as of course does the neighbouring Elizabeth Saloon. Massiveness is also a characteristic of the marble side table, carved by Matthew Coates Wyatt to look as though it were covered with a linen cloth, and decorated in 1827 with *pietra dura* flowers and fruit panels. It holds an enormous silver 'punch bowl', and the whole needed extra support from beneath lest it should sink through the floor. Ducal gravitas in weighty furniture is underlined with two portraits by Sir Joshua Reynolds: the Marquis of Granby, painted in a breastplate on a tempestuous German battlefield, and the fourth Duke of Rutland in Garter robes.[109]

Sheraton had shown an interest in archaeological furniture in his last publication, *The Cabinet Maker, Upholsterer and General Artists' Encyclopedia* (1804–6). Furniture was sometimes designed to be Egyptian in feeling with sphinxes heads, and Egyptian capitals on the sideboards. From Sheraton and his contemporaries, too, comes the emphasis on mechanical furniture, which folded up or which could be extended for large parties.[110] The dining room at Belvoir was large enough to hold more than thirty people at the table. There were many examples of folding dining tables of an intricate pattern. William Pocock of 26 Southampton Street, patented in 1806 what was

97] Paxton House, Berwickshire. The Dining Room. Sideboard by Thomas Chippendale, 1774

255

described as a 'sympathetic' dining table, where the twin flap tops swivelled and opened to allow three more flaps to be inserted. These were supported on a system of extending brackets.[111] Richard Gillow took out a patent in 1800 for an Imperial extending dining table with a system of slides which supported the flaps, and thus reduced the number of pillars, legs and claws required formerly.[112]

There were many smaller items of furniture which gradually appeared in the eighteenth-century and early nineteenth-century country house dining room. Many of these seem to have been designed to ease the process of dining, and to encourage conviviality. Cellarets were divided with compartments for bottles and were intended for storing wine in the dining room. Wine coolers were lined with lead, and bottles were kept in them surrounded by ice during the meal. Adam made them oval in form to resemble antique sarcophagi.[113] Since prolonged drinking was a habit after dinner in polite

98] Belvoir, the Dining Room. Furniture supplied by Gillows of Lancaster

society, special wine or social tables were designed after about 1750. *The Cabinet Makers' London Book of Prices* for 1793 shows a kidney shaped table for diners combined with a smaller table in which the drum consists of a cylinder of tin or copper and a mahogany top fitted into the cylinder and cut to contain five tin bottle cases. A horseshoe shaped drinking table appeared in Gillow's costbooks for July 1801, described as a 'social table' and probably for men. It was fitted with japanned ice pails. In such examples bottles might be contained in two metal coasters hinged to a brass rod.[114]

The dumb waiter which had started out in the 1720s with circular tiers and a tripod base continued in use in the Regency, with rectangular tiers and pillar and claw supports. The supper 'Canterbury' was described by Sheraton as 'a supper tray made to stand by a table at supper, with a circular end and three partitions crosswise, to hold knives, forks and plates at that end, which is made circular on purpose'. This was another useful small piece of furniture, in keeping with the informality of social management at the beginning of the nineteenth century.[115]

STATE BEDROOM

A state bedroom was an impressive chamber usually on the *piano nobile* of the country house, until perhaps the last thirty years of the century. The bed itself was frequently the most expensive piece of furniture in the house, and even though bedrooms were moved upstairs and lost something of their earlier ceremonial significance, there seems to have been a certain reluctance to dispense with their vivid splendour. The Baroque state bedroom had been part of the magnificent ceremonies associated with the *lever* and *coucher* of royalty and aristocracy throughout Europe. Although somewhat simplified by the mid-1720s, they could still be extremely dramatic. The green velvet bed designed by William Kent for Houghton was strongly architectural, with a formal straight cornice. In contrast, echoing the amorous spirit of the room's decoration, the bed has a double shell turning the whole piece of furniture into Venus's chariot.[116] As we have seen, the trimmings alone cost Sir Robert Walpole well over one thousand pounds. A fantastic new Rococo state bed was provided for 'The King of Spain's Apartment' at Petworth [plate 18] by Samuel Norman and James Whittle in about 1756–57. Its creation necessitated scrapping the Baroque bed of the Duke of Somerset in 1756. This had had 'Indian green and white satin with broad and narrow silver lace and thirty four silver tassels'. Some of the features of the former splendour were retained in a rather mutilated form. A full-length portrait of the Emperor Charles VI by Kneller was cut down to an oval. So finally there was a mixture of fashionable Rococo objects, Baroque lacquer and blue and white porcelain.[117] The Baroque lingered on too, in Scotland at Dalkeith Palace. Here the 1756 inventory described a Green Velvet Room with a bed striped with needlework and green velvet, and hangings of green velvet with scarlet and white satin striping. The Red Needlework Room had 'chequered velvet, scarlet and white needlework . . . lined with white satin'.[118] Chippendale designed elegant Rococo beds for the fifth Earl of Dumfries at Dumfries House in Ayrshire (1759–66) and for the fourteenth Earl of Morton, probably for Dalmahoy House, Midlothian, in the 1750s.[119] His design appeared as plate XXXIX in the third edition of the *Director* in 1762.

Whilst state bedrooms were often left partly untouched, their appearance being too venerable or expensive to disturb, lesser bedrooms might be given a light fashionable air. At Newby the Weddells' private apartments were remodelled in 1780 by William Belwood. He installed Bramah water closets, and fitted into the apse of Mrs Weddell's bedroom 'a large circular sofa in two parts'. This sounds like something illustrated in Sheraton's *Drawing Book*. Indian or Chinese styles were regarded as suitably light for bedrooms, and at Newby Mrs Weddell's private room was decorated with 'Indian paper'. The visitors' suite was also modernised by Belwood. This consisted of a dressing room, bedchamber and alcove room. The walls were hung with Chinese papers, and the furnishings were of tortoiseshell, satinwood and japanned ware, with upholstery in a grey satin stripe.[120] In Scotland richness of effect was certainly confined to the minority. However, the early eighteenth-century bedroom already had far more pieces of furniture and objects in it than had been the case in the previous century. In 1722, Lady Frazer's room at Castle Frazer had, rather surprisingly, a bed hung in black and white striped fabric with black wall hangings and window curtains. There were a large looking glass, two tables, two cabinets with drawers, a press and a sleeping chair. In her closet there was another press, a privy box and pan, two chairs, a press cupboard, a picture, an escritoire, a table shelf and a clock.[121]

In the second half of the century more items of furniture were designed for the bedroom. Clothing was still often kept in coffer chests, which were cheaper to make than chests of drawers. Clothes were laid flat inside and sweet smelling herbs were used to keep them fresh. Even the well-to-do did not automatically use wardrobes and chests of drawers, and some continued to rely upon the traditional kists or chests.[122]

A rare furniture plan for the bedroom floor of Kinnaird House in Stirlingshire of about 1770 indicates that the rooms were named after the textiles used in their decoration: for example, 'White Chintz' and 'Yellow Chintz'. Printed linens were manufactured successfully in Scotland and were used in bedrooms such as these around toilet tables. At Kinnaird the night tables were not at the bedsides, as is the modern habit, but at some distance from it. On either side of the bed stood chairs, possibly to aid the 'journey' to such a tall piece of furniture.[123]

Dressing rooms were normally attached to bedrooms. As women guests, in particular, frequently spent the morning in them, they were furnished as sitting rooms and increasingly, towards the end of the century, were for their occupant's personal use. Sheraton, in his *Drawing Book*, gave some designs for useful pieces of bedroom and dressing room furniture. He provided drawings for elegant washstands with inset basins and a cupboard or drawer which could be lead-lined for the basin to be emptied. He was always anxious that such items should be designed to resemble other types of furniture, so that they could stand 'in a genteel room without giving offence to the eye' and that they should be 'in a style elevated above their use'. His pot cupboard was equipped with an upper cupboard where medicines could be kept; this maintained privacy, for it could 'hold other articles which servants were not permitted to overlook'.[124]

Sheraton's 'Lady's Cabinet Dressing Table' and 'Cylinder Wash Hand Table' were extremely sophisticated pieces. The former had washing drawers and small drawers to hold 'ornaments of dress, as rings, drops &c.' The latter, made of mahogany, would 'look neat in any genteel dressing room' and had basin, water drawer and bidet. The top could be folded down, and false drawers masked cisterns and pipes. The various ladies' writing tables which Sheraton designed might all have been intended for the comfort, ease and intimacy of their dressing room or boudoir. They came equipped with a screen which could slide out, so that the writer could sit near the fire without burning her face. They were made of satinwood or black rosewood, small and delicate in scale, with space for trinkets or small books.[125]

Regency bedroom furniture could be substantial, and provide for every need. Gillows made the furniture for the bedrooms at Tatton in 1811–12 [99].

99] Tatton Park, Cheshire. The Lemon Bedroom, furnished by Gillows in 1812

For each of seven bedrooms they appear to have made a four-poster bedstead, a pair of pot cupboards, a night table, a pair of bed-steps, six chairs, a low wardrobe, and a bidet: each dressing room contained a dressing table, a writing table, a Grecian couch, a curricle chair, a landscape dressing glass, not to mention a washstand and second bidet. To these may perhaps be added the clothes-horse, dressing stools, the trunk-stands, the chests of drawers and the extra washstands which were supplied for 'sundry rooms' in 1812.[126]

INTERESTS OF THE OWNER

The furnishing of the country house was designed to support and enhance the interests of its owner. Many landed proprietors had a wide range of indoor activities as well as sporting ones. Although many rooms were for parade and were of a formal and public nature, others were more private; these were regarded as family rooms, or rooms where perhaps a circle of close friends with scholarly or literary interests might meet. How were such rooms furnished?

The library

The library was first treated as an architectural space in the 1720s. At Chicheley Hall in Buckinghamshire, Sir John Chester created concealed shelving behind panels of feathered oak, which, along with their fluted pilasters, plinths and dados, were designed to pull or swing open and reveal the valuable collection of books.[127] At Houghton, Kent designed solid mahogany shelves sunk into the inner walls of the room in an architectural mode in 1729.[128] It was perhaps Robert Adam who was the first architect in Britain to think of grand library furniture rather than merely considering the space. At Osterley in Middlesex he designed a suite of marquetry furniture consisting of a desk, a pair of writing tables, and eight armchairs mounted with ormolu in the French *Goût Grec* style. This furniture may have been made in the workshops of John Linnell in about 1768. Apollo's lyre, symbol of lyric poetry, forms the splat of the armchairs. It also appears as part of the trophy of music inlaid on the pedestal desk, together with trophies of the other arts, architecture, painting and sculpture.[129]

A similar desk was designed for Harewood by Thomas Chippendale, who also devised furniture for the library at Nostell Priory. Gradually by the 1770s, the library became a family sitting room as well as a place for the literati.[130] However, much special furniture was designed for it. Thomas Sheraton's *The Cabinet Maker and Upholsterer's Drawing Book* (1793) contained numerous pieces of library furniture. Plate XXX showed a library table 'already executed for the Duke of York'. This was oval, with book rests which could slide out at either end.[131] From the same source comes a library table with secretary drawers which was 'intended either to sit or stand and write at' and also for drawing.

Other furniture makers and architects turned their attention to the library. Henry Holland remodelled the library at Woburn Abbey, Bedford-shire [100], in 1787 and created an 'inner library' also. He provided a set of chairs with pierced backs in a pattern of lozenges and circles, in the style of Georges Jacob, and possibly supplied through the *marchand mercier* Dominique Daguerre. It would have been through Daguerre that Holland could have sent designs or specifications for furniture to Paris. From *c*. 1785 it is possible to discern a new style – a 'style étrusque' which was very different from the highly decorated pieces ornamented with ormolu or Sèvres plaques and favoured comparatively plain mahogany pieces. Holland him-self seems to have designed a library bookcase with reading desk for Woburn's library in this manner in 1795.[132] However, much of the new furniture was practical and sensible: it was suited to libraries used as family rooms, as it was to some of the London clubs such as Brooks's, which Holland designed in 1776. Thomas Chippendale the Younger (1742–1822) designed the library furniture for Stourhead in Wiltshire between 1800 and 1804. The work was commissioned by Sir Richard Colt Hoare, who was a scholar, traveller and antiquarian. Appropriately Chippendale designed a mahogany desk with carved Egyptian and philosophers' heads in 1805. This cost £115 and was supplied with a writing table, eight armchairs and two single chairs which incorporate sphinxes' heads.[133]

Sheraton illustrated in his *Drawing Book* much library furniture of a mechanical kind. Plate V in his Appendix shows steps originally supplied by Mr Campbell, Upholsterer to the Prince of Wales. The whole thing can be assembled in half a minute, according to Sheraton, and when folded forms a library table. The Stourhead library has equally impressive but rather more architectural-looking steps.

In his *Repository* Rudolph Ackermann insisted on designs for furniture with symbols relevant to their function.[134] Thomas Hope had stressed the im-portance of 'appropriate meaning' and the *Repository* continued to put forward this idea. Thus Hermes, a god of many arts, appeared on a bookcase design (plate 45, December 1812), as Bacchus might appear on a sideboard. It was thus appropriate in the library of an antiquarian which contained Vivant Denon's *Voyage dans la Basse et la Haute Egypte* that Egyptian heads should appear.[135]

Specialised pieces of furniture

Special furniture for particular rooms, expressing interests which were some-times eccentric, deserves some consideration. William Constable of Burton Constable commissioned various objects for his house which were connected with his scholarly interests. He consulted 'Capability' Brown about how to make his gallery into a library and philosophical room. His cabinet was filled with natural history specimens from all over the world, and with gems and medals. He also had a herbarium. His estate joiner, Thomas Higham, made him a mineral cabinet which was veneered in burr elm and is still full

100] Woburn Abbey. The Library remodelled by Henry Holland in 1787

of mineral specimens.[136] Benjamin Cole and George Adams supplied William Constable with a glazed cabinet for an air pump and also various electrostatic machines. His deep interest in plants, trees, shells and geology had a particular effect on the decoration of his furniture. Domenico Bartoli, scagliologist, worked on furniture for Burton Constable between 1763 and 1766. William Constable would not import table tops in *pietra dura* which were purely decorative and, for him, without meaning. He preferred to employ Bartoli, who painted a table to resemble 165 colourful specimens of marbles, granites, porphyries and polished stones as well as Blue John and lapis lazuli [101].

The cabinet as a curiosity room could extend, as we see, to the cabinet as a piece of furniture designed to contain curiosities. In 1728 the third Duke of Beaufort had installed a seventeenth-century Florentine cabinet [plate 19] as the principal showpiece of the great drawing room at Badminton. George Sandeman (1724–1803) designed a coin cabinet for the Duke of Atholl at Blair Castle in the form of a Roman temple.[137] An inventory of Castle Ashby in Northamptonshire made *c.* 1774 before a sale of its contents, gives us an

101] Newbridge, Donabate, Co. Dublin. The Museum decorated with Chinese paper

insight into the scientific interests of the eighteenth-century aristocracy. Lord Northampton shared such interests with George III and Lord Exeter. His workshop was equipped with many kinds of tools for wood and ivory turning, engraving and bookbinding. Lord Northampton also owned apparatus to bow and polish glass, as well as a 'Magic Lanthorn with prints', dividers, callipers, compasses, pliers and pinchers.[138]

Servants' furniture

The furniture made for servants deserves examination, although household management and the life of servants became more complicated and elaborate in the nineteenth century during the Victorian period.[139]

The kitchen offices were clearly of great importance. The kitchen, besides having cooking apparatus, was furnished with a large, very strong, solidly formed centre table, probably having a row of deep drawers beneath the top. There would also be one or more deal dressers backed by shelves, and probably a side dresser placed before the window with either cupboards or a pot cupboard beneath. Usually there would be smaller tables, sometimes consisting of hinged flaps fixed to the wall for occasional use. Substantial chopping boards, a towel roller, a clock and some chairs with wooden bottoms, a marble mortar for grinding herbs and spices, a meat screen for roasting on the spot and possibly a 'haster' which kept dishes of meat warm, would also be present.

At Erddig [102], Dunham Massey and Raby Castle, some of these features can still be seen. Erddig has a towering painted dresser with working surfaces of whitewood. At Harewood there is a kitchen table made of sycamore with a five-inch thick top, the cracks filled in with lead and the framework painted. Pieces of furniture such as dressers, closets and shelving were made by a joiner when the house was being completed. 'Hasters' were common by the end of the eighteenth century. They were made as a shallow cupboard with no back and the inside was furnished with iron shelves and lined with tin. They had castors attached to them so that they could be moved when necessary in front of the fire or out of the way.

The scullery was designed for washing dishes, gutting fish, cutting up vegetables and plucking and drawing game. It stood next to the kitchen and was supplied with sinks, a copper for heating water, a solid table, plate racks and shelving. There might also be vegetable racks and a few odd chairs. The scullery at Appuldurcombe House contained in 1780 'a copper fix'd, divided into two . . . a lead sink, 2 dressers of shelves, a plate rack, two tubs for washing dishes, one pail, two wash hand bowls, a brass dinner bell, a copper fish kettle and an iron stand'.

The cook's pantry or day larder was used to keep cooked meats, and was fitted with a broad dresser without drawers around three walls, a centre table and marble shelving. There was also a wet larder for raw meat. It required bacon racks, hanging irons, a table, a salt trough, chopping block, meat safe and stone shelving. It was usual in large houses to provide in

102] Erddig, the kitchen, newly built in the 1770s. It was housed in a separate building in an attempt to reduce the risk of fire spreading. The range is Edwardian

addition larders for fish, vegetables and pastry. At Harewood the inventory in 1795 describes the pastry larder as having 'One paste board, with drawers and a marble slab, two dressers with drawers, one cupboard, six shelves, one dresser with hooks for hanging poultry'. Usually there was a dairy with stone shelves which might adjoin the kitchen, or be situated in an outbuilding. The stone shelves were designed to keep butter and milk cool and there might also be a large central stone table with a channelled rim to contain cold water during warm weather. A scullery with facilities for scalding milk vessels was to be found attached to the dairy. The dairy was provided with much equipment including milk pails, marble dishes for cream, hair sieves, churns, butter moulds, cheese presses, washing tubs and wooden skimmers. At Harewood there is an early nineteenth-century dairy fitted with veined marble slabs. A bakehouse such as the one at Erddig was to be found at various country houses.

A laundry was also an essential part of the domestic arrangements. The laundry at Erddig was constructed in the early 1770s, and now contains a box mangle which may be part of the original equipment. When the handle is turned a box full of stones trundles backwards and forwards over three revolving wooden rollers, thus pressing the moisture from clothes laid beneath

103] Erddig, the Housekeeper's Room

them. There were drying racks warmed by a small stove, and irons were heated on the cast iron shelf above the stove. The wet laundry's stove had a long vent in the ceiling which helped to release the steam from the coppers in which the clothes and bed linen were boiled.[140]

The upper servants had rooms of their own, conferring a strong sense of status. Their interiors were often plain but well furnished. The butler had his pantry near the dining room, and the bedroom and the plate scullery were close at hand, so that he could guard the silver. The furniture he needed for his duties included a dresser with lead-lined sink, which had folding covers, a glass closet, a table napkin press, drawers for linen and plate chests. The butler at Appuldurcombe in the 1780s had a pantry with a deal press bed between two cupboards, and another large press for plate storage. It also contained a tea-table, two beech chairs, a mahogany-framed looking-glass and an oak bureau: it seems to have been used as a bed-sitting room.[141] The butler's pantry at Erddig had a particularly full inventory made of it in 1726. It contained one closet with shelves and double doors, a dresser, a basket to carry up knives and salvers, a wooden tray for carrying glasses and a variety of equipment such as funnel and brushes for the butler's use.[142]

The housekeeper's room [103] was the place for the upper servants to congregate. It served both as sitting room and office, as well as being used to

266

store tea, coffee, special grocery items and china, glass and linen, all of which were kept in large presses. The Erddig's housekeeper's room was probably improved by James Wyatt in the 1770s. It seems to have been furnished with a handsome, if plain, bureau with cupboard above, and a gate-legged table. The housekeeper's room at Harewood housed mahogany chairs, and three mahogany china presses containing more than 600 articles in glazed lockable cupboards.[143]

The still room also contained a sink, dresser, table and storage furniture. The Erddig still room has fixed shelves and drawers with the names of groceries, spices and sweetmeats painted upon them. Here coffee, tea and pickles could be kept. The steward of the household would also have a room in which to carry out business. At Temple Newsam at the beginning of the nineteenth century this contained a large deal desk, two larger drawers on a frame, two deal tables, with drawers, a deal cupboard, with space for books, buff painted deal drawers, a low nest of further drawers, four old chairs, a country stool and four old tables on trestles.[144] The steward might well live in some style. At Osterley there was a 'nut tree table, sideboard table, and marble slab. A large mahogany two flap dining table, a large oval ditto, fourteen walnut tree . . . chairs, a Scotch carpet, a barometer, A large Marble Cistern and two Chairback Screens'. The Harewood steward's room had some particularly good furniture, including two oak sideboards, a mahogany card table, a plate warmer and an oval pier glass.[145]

The lower servants would use the servants' hall. At Erddig (see [48]) and houses such as Chirk Castle, Lyme and Dudmaston, there were portraits of the staff, many of them painted in the eighteenth or the early part of the nineteenth centuries. On the ceiling of the servants' hall at Erddig there were trophies of swords, of the troop of the Denbighshire Militia, raised by the Yorke family. There was a refectory table and an oak settle, and stick back chairs, all dating from the eighteenth century.[146]

Separate bedrooms were normally provided for the upper servants, the butler, the housekeeper, the cook and the ladies' maid. They were often furnished, during the eighteenth century, with stained beech bedsteads. Shared attic rooms were provided for maids and menservants. The furniture was usually of deal, elm, walnut or beech, and frequently in poor condition, according to inventories. Sometimes, as at Newby, the upper servants had unfashionable furniture taken from the family rooms. However, Sir Rowland Winn provided new furniture for his servants at Nostell, including rush bottom chairs, and substantial chests of drawers. At Harewood very plain furniture, lacking the stringing and corner colonettes on chests of drawers, for example, was made locally for the servants' rooms. By the early nineteenth century painted pine was common for servants' rooms.[147]

Country houses were furnished with great care and consideration. Pattern books were important in popularising styles and the role of architects unified furniture and room design. An increasingly sophisticated way of life, as we shall see in the following chapter, led to special furniture for different activities, for eating, for reading in libraries, or for drinking tea in galleries.

NOTES

1 Michael Wilson, *William Kent*, Routledge and Kegan Paul, London, 1984, p. 113. Walpole was the first commoner to receive the Garter.

2 Francis Bamford, 'A Dictionary of Edinburgh Wrights and Furniture Makers 1660–1840', *Furniture History*, XIX, 1983.

3 John Hardy, 'The Kedleston Sofa', *Furniture History*, XXV, 1990, pp. 90–2. The four sofas, upholstered in blue damask, have gadrooned frames which are supported by dolphins. They are carved with laurel-wreathed medallions of the gods, including Juno, Iris the mother of Eros, as well as Bacchus, god of festivities, and Mercury, the gods' messenger. The side sofas have mer-attendants resting in their arms 'while they listen to the music of the nereids'. One of the latter plays the lyre to celebrate the triumphs of Neptune. The nereids and tritons support the fireside sofas, and one of the latter blows his conch shell to 'still the waves at the god's command', Hardy suggests.

4 Kenneth Morgan, *Bristol and the Atlantic Trade in the Eighteenth century*, Cambridge University Press, Cambridge, 1993, pp. 21–2. Despite convoys protecting trading vessels, during the Seven Years' War, Spanish and French privateers captured sixty-eight ships sailing to colonies and fifty-five on the return journey. Apart from fortunes being made in the colonies, some woods were imported from them. Initially much mahogany came from Jamaica; in the 1760s satinwood came from the West Indies (although not exclusively). Some rosewood came, via the East India Company, from the Indian sub-continent: see Clive Edwards, *Eighteenth Century Furniture*, Manchester University Press, Manchester, 1996, pp. 76–80.

5 Quoted in Sheila Forman, *Scottish Country Houses and Castles*, Collins, London, 1967, p. 157.

6 Andrew Moore (ed.), *Houghton Hall: The Prime Minster, the Empress and the Heritage*, Philip Wilson, London, 1996, p. 37.

7 James Lees-Milne, *Earls of Creation*, Century Hutchinson, London, 1986, p. 263; see also Christopher Gilbert, *The Life and Work of Thomas Chippendale*, 2 vols, Studio Vista/ Christie's, London, 1978, vol. I, pp. 195–220. Chippendale supplied some of his most elaborate furniture for Harewood, furnishing many rooms. The Diana and Minerva commode 'curiously inlaid and engraved' with marquetry on a satinwood ground and brass antique ornaments cost £86. The dining room furniture, especially the sideboard, was enormously grand, and elaborately inlaid, as was the library table of rosewood, with much Neoclassical marquetry.

8 Lorna Weatherill, *Consumer Behaviour and Material Culture in Britain 1660–1760*, Routledge, 1988, p. 171. It is difficult to make distinctions between aristocracy and gentry in terms of patronage and expenditure. For example, Randle Wilbraham and his son altered Rode Hall in Cheshire between about 1752 and 1813. They ordered much furniture from the designer Oakley and from the firm of Gillow. Randle Wilbraham, who began the work, was a successful barrister; his son married into the Bootle family, later Earls of Lathom, whose Palladian house, Lathom House near Ormskirk, was a splendid aristocratic pile by Giacomo Leoni. There are portraits at Rode by Reynolds, Opie, Hoppner and Beechy, of the Baker family who married into the Wilbraham family in the nineteenth century. Here we find an upper middle-class family displaying somewhat aristocratic taste and marrying into the peerage: see Clive Aslett, 'Rode Hall, Cheshire', *Country Life*, CLXXVII, 2 May 1985, pp. 1186–91, and P. de Figueiredo and J. Treuherz, *Cheshire Country Houses*, Phillimore, Chichester, 1988, pp. 156–8.

9 Weatherill, *Consumer Behaviour*, p. 183.

10 Gilbert, *Thomas Chippendale*, I, p. 72.

11 *Ibid.*

12 Margaret Sanderson, *Robert Adam and Scotland*, HMSO, Edinburgh, 1992, p. 62.

13 *Ibid.*, p. 56.

14 Bamford, 'Dictionary of Edinburgh Wrights', p. 18; Gilbert, *Thomas Chippendale*, pp. 25–6, notes that Chippendale and Rannie promoted the *Director* and their various activities as cabinet makers and furnishers through notices in the *General Evening Post* a month after a new Parliament had met and owners of estates would be in the capital.

15 Edwards, *Eighteenth Century Furniture*, p. 30.

16 *Ibid.*, p. 31.

17 Anthony Coleridge, 'A Reappraisal of William Hallet', *Furniture History*, I, 1965, p. 11.

18 Patricia Kirkham, 'The Careers of William and John Linnell', *Furniture History*, III, 1967, p. 31.

19 Helena Hayward and Patricia Kirkham, *William and John Linnell*, (2 vols), Studio Vista/Christie's, London, 1980, I, pp. 106–7.

20 Leslie Harris, *Robert Adam and Kedleston*, The National Trust, London, 1987, p. 41.

21 Hayward and Kirkham, *Linnells*, p. 106.

22 Kirkham, 'Careers of William and John Linnell', p. 31.

23 *Ibid.*, p. 31.

24 Geoffrey Beard, *Upholsterers and Interior Furnishing in England 1530–1840*, Yale University Press, London, 1997, pp. 13–14.

25 Edwards, *Eighteenth Century Furniture*, p. 74.

26 *Ibid.*, p. 52.

27 Beard, *Upholsterers and Interior Furnishing*, pp. 212–13 discusses the Linnells' work and lists references.

28 Hayward and Kirkham, *Linnells*, p. 108.

29 Thomas Sheraton, *Cabinet Dictionary*, 1803, p. 116 quoted by Gilbert, *Thomas Chippendale*, I, p. 16.

30 Gilbert, *Thomas Chippendale*, p. 8.

31 *Ibid.*, p. 9.

32 Mark Girouard, 'Coffee at Slaughters: English Art and the Rococo I', *Country Life*, CXXXIX, 13 January 1966, pp. 58–61.

33 Mary Mauchline, *Harewood House*, David and Charles, London, 1974, pp. 96–7.

34 Gilbert, *Thomas Chippendale*, I, p. 72.

35 Anthea Mullins, 'Local Furniture Makers at Harewood House as Representatives of Provincial Craftsmanship', *Furniture History*, I, 1965, p. 33.

36 Ivan Hall, 'Jeremiah and Joseph Hargrave of Hull: Architects, Carvers, Furniture Makers', *Furniture History*, XII, 1976, pp. 52–5.

37 Lindsay Boynton, *Gillow Furniture Designs 1760–1800*, The Bloomfield Press, Royston, 1995, p. 20; see also Nicholas Goodison and John Hardy, 'Gillows at Tatton Park', *Furniture History*, VI, 1970, pp. 1–39.

38 Sebastian Pryke, 'Pattern Furniture and Estate Wrights in Eighteenth Century Scotland', *Furniture History*, XXX, 1994, p. 101.

39 *Ibid.*, pp. 100–2.

40 John Cornforth, 'Inveraray Castle, Argyll 1', *Country Life*, CLXIII, 18 June 1978, pp. 1619–22.

41 Bamford, 'Dictionary of Edinburgh Wrights', p. 14.

42 *Ibid.*, p. 12.

43 *Ibid.*, p. 16.

44 *Ibid.*, p. 19.

45 Anthony Coleridge, 'James Cullen Cabinet Maker at Hopetoun House 1', *Connoisseur*, 163, November 1966, pp. 154–9, and December 1966 pp. 231–4; see also Bamford, 'Dictionary of Edinburgh Wrights', p. 19.

46 *Ibid.*, p. 25, quoting Hugo Arnott, *History of Edinburgh*, 1779, p. 13.

47 Bamford, 'Dictionary of Edinburgh Wrights', p. 33.

48 Jill Lever, *Architects' Designs for Furniture*, Trefoil Books, London, 1982, p. 14.

49 *Ibid.*, p. 15.

50 Robert Oresko (ed.), *The Works in Architecture of Robert and James Adam*, Academy Editions, London, 1975, p. 59.

51 *Ibid.*, p. 54, plate VIII is described.

52 Eileen Harris, *The Furniture of Robert Adam*, Academy Editions, London, 1973, pp. 29–30.

53 Terry Friedman, *James Gibbs*, Yale University Press, London, 1984, p. 257.

54 George Hepplewhite, *The Cabinet Maker and Upholsterer's Guide*, London, 1794, quoted in Ralph Edwards, *Hepplewhite Furniture Designs*, A. Tiranti, London, 1955, pp. 5–6.

55 Thomas Sheraton, *The Cabinet Maker and Upholsterer's Drawing Book*, Dover Reprints, New York, 1972, Introduction by Joseph Aronson, pp. xii–xix.

56 Bamford, 'Dictionary of Edinburgh Wrights', pp. 30 and 118–25.

57 *Ibid.*, p. 31. These seem to have been 'Chinese' in appearance with a trellis back panel. They took their name from some formerly in Cockpen Church (Angus) and now at Brechin Castle.

58 *Ibid.*, pp. 118–21.

59 John Fowler and John Cornforth, *English Decoration in the Eighteenth Century*, Barrie and Jenkins, London, 1974, p. 66.

60 Moore, *Houghton Hall*, p. 117.

61 Gilbert, *Thomas Chippendale*, II, p. 97. At a smaller, more informal bourgeois house such as David Garrick's villa at Hampton in Middlesex, there was much painted furniture, some of which was in the hall. Chippendale supplied, in about 1770, birch hall chairs with a white ground and green painted swags, leaves and ribbons for decoration, rather than the coats of arms and coronets of aristocratic houses: see *ibid.*, I, p. 96 and Maurice Tomlin, *Catalogue of Adam Period Furniture*, Victoria and Albert Museum, London, 1972, p. 124.

62 Fowler and Cornforth, *English Decoration in the Eighteenth Century*, p. 71.

63 *Erdigg*, National Trust Guide, 1990, pp. 18–19.

64 John Cornforth, 'Houghton Hall, Norfolk 1', *Country Life*, CLXXXI, 30 April 1987, pp. 124–9.

65 Wilson, *Kent*, p. 108.

66 Peter Thornton, *Authentic Decor: The Domestic Interior 1620–1920*, Weidenfeld and Nicolson, London, 1984, p. 89.

67 John Cornforth and Leo Schmidt, 'Holkham Hall, Norfolk III', *Country Life*, CLXVIII, 7 February 1980, pp. 359–62.

68 Gervase Jackson-Stops and James Pipkin, *The English Country House: A Grand Tour*, Weidenfeld and Nicolson, London, 1984, p. 95.

69 Nigel Neatby, *The Saltram Collection*, The National Trust, London, 1977, pp. 32–8.

70 *Ibid.*, pp. 33–4. There is also a drawing of 1769 for five large pier glasses by Adam. The side tables between the windows may have been designed by Adam or by Joseph Perfetti, who made them at a cost of £41 1s 0d in 1771. The tops were inlaid with a chequer design of Florentine marble specimens. Such tables often formed part of the decoration of rooms of parade, and the saloon at Holkham also contained a pair. They must have provided evidence to visitors of the owner's antiquarian tastes. At Holkham younger Brettingham obtained during his seven-year Italian visit, beautiful mosaic hearthstones from Hadrian's Villa, which were mounted to form table tops by Michael Rysbrack: see *Holkham Hall*, Guide, Norwich, Jarrold, 1969, p. 10.

71 *Ibid.*, p. 34; see also Christopher Gilbert and Anthony Wells-Cole, *The Fashionable Fireplace*, Leeds City Art Galleries, Leeds, 1985, pp. 73–6. Sir Lawrence Dundas had antique bronzes in his library at 19 Arlington Street which appear in his portrait with his grandson by Zoffany of 1769. Perhaps in a room where the architect had played an important role, the garniture was conceived as part of the chimneypiece.

72 E. T. Joy, 'A Pair of English Rococo Armchairs', *The Connoisseur*, 161, April 1966, p. 245.

73 E. T. Joy, 'A Pair of Decorated Commodes by Pierre Langlois', *The Connoisseur*, 161, April 1966, p. 251. Pierre Langlois specialised in using floral bouquets, sprays and knots to give delicacy to rooms. He seems to have provided commodes decorated in this fashion for Woburn, and his trade card indicated that he specialised in using brass and tortoiseshell in the manner of André Charles Boulle as well.

74 Beard, *Upholsterers and Interior Furnishing*, p. 193. A suite of four settees, a daybed and twenty chairs in gilt beech and walnut were supplied by James Pascall of London for the seventh Viscount Irwin.

75 Roger Whitworth, 'Chippendale in his Setting', *Country Life*, CLXXXVII, 29 April 1993, pp. 68–73; see also Gilbert, *Thomas Chippendale*, I, pp. 148 and 42 (illustration). There was a pair of breakfront bookcases also, in a less elaborate style.

76 Christopher Gilbert and Tessa Murdoch, *John Channon and Brass Inlaid Furniture 1730–1760*, Yale University Press, London, 1993, pp. 10–13. Channon's most magnificent pieces were the fantastic paired bookcases he made for Lord Courtenay for an upstairs library at Powderham Castle in Devon.

77 Margaret Meade-Fetherstonhaugh, *Uppark*, The National Trust, London, 1981, pp. 26–9 (guide revised 1976); see also Helen Hayward, *Thomas Johnson and English Rococo*, Alec Tiranti, London, 1964, pp. 35–6. Johnson was engaged in publishing designs in 1760. His clients sought his elaborate carving and it was successful enough for him to move to larger premises in Tottenham Court Road, near other purveyors of such intricate decorations like Mathias Lock and Langlois himself. Clients would give direct orders for unusual items to the upholsterer or cabinet maker who was providing the general furnishings for their houses. The cabinet maker would then find the independent craftsmen who could produce the exceptional objects. The pier glasses at Uppark might be compared with those provided in 1763 by George Cole for Blair Castle in Perthshire. These three had the essential elements of Johnson's decoration, including a man in a ragged dress with a leaf hat and a long moustache. Here the carver was virtually a sculptor. This Rococo playfulness was continued well into the Neoclassical period and gave a sense of contrast within the house.

78 Edwards, *Eighteenth Century Furniture*, p. 105.

79 Meade-Fetherstonhaugh, *Uppark*, pp. 27–8.

80 John Hardy and Maurice Tomlin, *Osterley Park House*, Victoria and Albert Museum, London, 1985, p. 61.

81 *Ibid.*, pp. 61–5.

82 Tomlin, *Catalogue of Adam Period Furniture*, p. 51. Adam was aware no doubt that in Paris, Rococo chairs were to be found in otherwise Neoclassical interiors, and he was an admirer of French taste.

83 Fowler and Cornforth, *English Decoration in the Eighteenth Century*, p. 66.

84 Thornton, *Authentic Decor*, p. 51.

85 Mark Girouard, *Life in the Country House*, Yale University Press, London, 1978, p. 158.

86 Fowler and Cornforth, *English Decoration in the Eighteenth Century*, p. 66.

87 Charles Saumarez Smith, *The Building of Castle Howard*, Faber and Faber, London, 1990, p. 111.

88 Annette Carruthers, *The Scottish Home*, National Museum of Scotland, Edinburgh, 1996, p. 128.

89 Fowler and Cornforth, *English Decoration in the Eighteenth Century*, p. 67.

90 Moore, *Houghton Hall*, pp. 139–40.

91 Hugh Roberts, 'Furniture at Broadlands, Hampshire I', *Country Life*, CLXIX, 29 January 1981, pp. 288–90.

92 Anthony Coleridge, 'English Furniture in the Duke of Argyll's Collection at Inveraray Castle', *The Connoisseur*, 158, March 1965, pp. 154–61; see also John Cornforth,

'Inveraray Castle, Argyll I', *Country Life*, CLXIII, 8 June 1978, pp. 1619–22 and 15 June 1978, pp. 1734–7.

93 Fowler and Cornforth, *English Decoration in the Eighteenth Century*, p. 68.

94 *Ibid.*

95 Carruthers, *Scottish Home*, p. 129.

96 Fowler and Cornforth, *English Decoration in the Eighteenth Century*, p. 68.

97 Girouard, *Life in the English Country House*, p. 182. The Duke of Norfolk dined under a canopy in the 1750s.

98 Jackson-Stops, *The English Country House*, pp. 123–5.

99 *Ibid.*, p. 123.

100 Hardy and Tomlin, *Osterley*, p. 30; see also Tomlin, *Adam Period Furniture*, pp. 19–21.

101 *Ibid.*, p. 106.

102 Harris, *Robert Adam and Kedleston*, p. 27.

103 *Ibid.*, pp. 30–1.

104 Tomlin, *Adam Period Furniture*, pp. 23–5. The dining room at Harewood also had Neoclassical furniture almost certainly designed by Chippendale in 1771, although the bills for it do not survive. There was a splendid sideboard table with pedestals supporting lead-lined urns, one being fitted as a plate warmer and the other providing an arrangement for washing glasses during meals. One of the pedestals contained a pot cupboard. The sideboard table itself was one of a pair veneered in rosewood and satinwood with gilt bronze mounts. The cellaret beneath the sideboard is a grand piece of furniture, considered to be the most lavish commissioned by a patron in England. It has a lid radially fluted like a shell and is decorated in ormolu ribbons, swags of husks, and satyr masks; see Gilbert, *Thomas Chippendale*, I, p. 201 and II, p. 192.

105 Hardy and Tomlin, *Osterley*, p. 35.

106 Carruthers, *Scottish Home*, p. 129.

107 *Ibid.*

108 *Ibid.*, p. 135. This grand scheme by Chippendale was paid for with money accumulated by William Home who had a sugar plantation in the West Indies.

109 James Yorke, 'Belvoir Castle, Leicestershire I', *Country Life*, CLXXXVIII, 23 June 1994, pp. 89–93. The chairs may have come from John Swabey of Wardour Street.

110 Frances Collard, *Regency Furniture*, Antique Collectors Club, Woodbridge, 1985, p. 17, shows an example by William Pocock of London; see also Sheraton's *Drawing Book*, p. 363, for 'Universal Tables'.

111 *Belvoir Castle*, Guide, English Life Publications, London, 1985, p. 14.

112 Collard, *Regency Furniture*, p. 85.

113 *Ibid.*, pp. 13 and 218 for illustrations of cellarets.

114 Margaret Jourdain (revised R. Fastnedge), *Regency Furniture*, Country Life, London, 1965, p. 87.

115 Ralph Edwards and L. C. G. Ramsey, *The Connoisseur Period Guides: Regency Period*, The Connoisseur, London, 1958, p. 48.

116 Moore, *Houghton Hall*, p. 36.

117 Gervase Jackson-Stops, 'A Rococo Masterpiece Restored', *Country Life*, CLXXV, 14 June 1984, pp. 1698–1700. The bed was probably covered by James Whittle.

118 John Dunbar and John Cornforth, 'Dalkeith House, Lothian III', *Country Life*, CLXXV, 3 May 1984, pp. 1230–33.

119 Gilbert, *Thomas Chippendale*, I, p. 139. Plate XXXIX of the *Director* (third edition) was a bed supplied for the Earls of Dumfries and Morton. Lord Dumfries's bed survives and cost more than £100. It had an elaborate headboard and cornices, and fluted, branched footposts and was originally upholstered in green silk and worsted damask.

120 Jill Low, 'Newby Hall: Two Late Eighteenth Century Inventories', *Furniture History*, XXII, 1986, pp. 135–76.

121 Carruthers, *Scottish Home*, p. 188.

122 *Ibid.*, pp. 189–90.
123 Ian Gow, *The Scottish Interior*, Edinburgh University Press, Edinburgh, 1992, p. 21.
124 Sheraton, *Drawing Book*, pp. 393–4.
125 *Ibid.*, p. 405.
126 Goodison and Hardy, 'Gillows at Tatton Park', pp. 1–39.
127 James Lees-Milne, *English Country Houses: Baroque*, Country Life, London, 1970, p. 325.
128 Jackson-Stops, *English Country House*, p. 199.
129 Eileen Harris, *Osterley Park*, The National Trust, London, 1994, p. 43.
130 Jackson-Stops, *English Country House*, p. 204.
131 Sheraton, *Drawing Book*, p. 70.
132 Dorothy Stroud, *Henry Holland*, Country Life, London, 1966, p. 79.
133 Collard, *Regency Furniture*, p. 213.
134 Pauline Agins, *Ackermann's Regency Furniture and Designs*, The Crowood Press, Marlborough, 1984, p. 19.
135 Jackson-Stops, *English Country House*, p. 208.
136 Ivan Hall, 'Range of a Dilettante: William Constable and Burton Constable', *Country Life*, CLXXI, 22 April 1982, pp. 1114–17.
137 Simon Jarvis, 'Cabinets and Curiosities', *Country Life*, CLXXXVIII, 10 October 1985, pp. 1278–9. William Vile and John Cobb supplied an ivory inlaid cabinet to house Queen Charlotte's jewels in 1761. Sir William Chambers designed a metal cabinet for Lord Charlemont for his Dublin house, and in 1782 Mrs Childe of Osterley owned a 'very elegant Gilded Cabinet . . . Containing various India and other curiosities'. Old cabinets themselves became curiosities. The Yellow Drawing Room at William Beckford's Fonthill contained a cabinet designed, it was claimed, by Holbein for Henry VIII. It has been observed that the cabinet, once a miniature museum, had become a museum piece itself.
138 Gervase Jackson-Stops, 'Castle Ashby, Northamptonshire, III', *Country Life*, CLXXIX, 6 February 1986, pp. 310–15.
139 Christopher Gilbert, *English Vernacular Furniture 1750–1900*, Yale University Press, London, 1991, pp. 71–84.
140 *Erdigg*, Guide, The National Trust, London, 1990, p. 11.
141 Gilbert, *Vernacular Furniture*, p. 83.
142 Merlin Waterson, *The Servants' Hall*, The National Trust, London, 1990, p. 175.
143 *Ibid.*, p. 79.
144 Gilbert, *Vernacular Furniture*, p. 77.
145 *Ibid.*, p. 78.
146 *Erdigg*, Guide, p. 13.
147 Gilbert, *Vernacular Furniture*, p. 83.

7

Entertainment

Pleasure, it has been suggested, became less private in the eighteenth century and developed into something visible to one's friends. The creation of happiness was dependent upon social circulation, and it became competitive amongst the increasingly rich aristocracy and gentry.[1] The social round depended, amongst this class, on entertainment at country houses, both indoor and outdoor. At the beginning of the eighteenth century, noblemen like Exeter, Montagu, Manchester, Pembroke, Bingley, Strafford, Bathurst and Oxford surrounded themselves with small artistic courts.[2] Their splendour was metropolitan and continental in its magnificence. Despite his estate being over half the size of George I's had been when he was Elector of Hanover, Philip Duke of Wharton was not really interested in the country.[3] The francophile Lord Chesterfield wrote to his illegitimate son, 'I think that you are above any of these rustic ill-bred sports of guns, dogs and horses which characterise our English Bumpkin Country Gentleman'.[4] Entertaining in the country gradually became, in the eighteenth and early nineteenth centuries, a sophisticated and elegant activity. Regulations in all spheres, from the Pump Room at Bath to Surrey cricket matches meant that there was no longer such a gulf between boorish squire and the nobleman who sighed for the pleasures of the Grand Tour.

In visiting, admiring gardens, estates and houses – different social values came to the fore. The narrow stagnant rustic social circle where, as one writer observed, 'You have not made water five minutes before the whole town is acquainted with it'[5] was scorned and avoided.

The improved country estate gave refreshment to family and friends alike. An advertisement for the sale of Hayes Place in Kent in 1789 makes clear how covetable such an estate was and how it had been created for enjoyment. Rebuilt by the Elder Pitt in 1764, it was an elegant spacious villa with twenty-four bedrooms. Its pleasure grounds were 'disposed with taste, fringed with rich plantations maturely grown'. The paddock was improved 'with a sheet of water', and 'the grounds adorned with seats and alcoves'.[6] It seems important to consider Hayes, for it was not a major estate such as Stowe or Blenheim, but something much smaller, and yet it is clear that pleasure in every aspect of the estate was now regarded as an important pursuit. For Pitt his estate work was both a symbol of his importance as a leading statesman and a refuge from it.[7]

For some, the pleasure became their *raison d'être* and if beneficial activities were seen as emanating from the country estate to the countryside beyond they were praised. Lord Kinnoull who retired as Paymaster General to the Forces in Scotland to spend the rest of his life improving his country seat was visited by Mrs Montagu in 1770. She did not report, it would seem, on specific country activities, but praised Lord Kinnoull in a general, vaguely high-minded fashion, making it clear that his attitude to the countryside was far from self-indulgent. 'I was delighted to find an old friend enjoying the heartfelt happiness which attends a life of virtue. He is continually employed in encouraging agriculture and manufacture, protecting the weak from injury, assisting the distressed, and animating the young to whatever is fit and proper'.[8]

A national figure such as Pitt took pleasure in the facilities his country house provided. There he was on show, and many other politicians used their houses as stages upon which to entertain. The 'bad Lord Lonsdale',[9] although possessor in 1768 of an immense estate, lacked this sense of a public persona. He was rough and 'assumed the haughty demeanour of a feudal chieftain' at Lowther castle in Westmorland. It was said that he 'professed a thorough contempt for modern refinements ... Grass grew in the neglected approaches to his mansion. If he had occasion to go from Lowther to Penrith, it would be in a rusty old coach drawn by fine but untrimmed horses'.[10]

Outdoor activities were clearly of great importance to the landed aristocracy in the eighteenth and early nineteenth centuries. There was a passionate love of all field sports. Men rode to hounds, shot duck, fished for salmon, learned early how to snare and kill wild fowl, hares, rabbits and badgers. Some countrymen, like George Osbaldeston, Master of the Quorn, excelled at boxing, pigeon-shooting, steeple-chasing, billiards, cricket, rowing and tennis. He also kept harriers, gamecocks and fighting mastiffs.[11] The Duke of Wellington believed that 'the people of this country like to see their great men take part in their amusements. The aristocracy will commit', he said, 'a great error if they fail to mix freely with their neighbours'.[12]

Fox-hunting was the great sport of the privileged in the eighteenth century. Landed status was bound up with the right to hunt game from the late fourteenth century: the law restricted the hunting of deer, pheasants, hare, rabbits and partridge to those members of society with £40 per annum.[13] In 1671 the game laws were strengthened to prevent anyone from hunting hares, pheasants, partridge or moorfowl unless they held freeholds of £100 a year, or long leaseholds worth £150. Lords of Manors 'many under the degree of an esquire' were authorised to appoint gamekeepers who had the right to seize guns and dogs. This law of 1671 excluded those whose wealth came from non-landed sources from engaging in these sports. Those in trade were forbidden to course hares or shoot partridges, although is not entirely certain why the legislation was passed. Lesser freeholders and tenant farmers suffered hardship by this exclusion from hunting game. Perhaps the landowners of both houses of Parliament were strengthening their position and attempting to draw a clear distinction between themselves and the urban middle classes. It could be claimed that Parliament was preserving wild creatures, but this was harder to defend once breeding of partridge and pheasants had begun.[14] Efforts in 1772 and 1790 to repeal these laws were unsuccessful, as they had come to be regarded as part of the structure of the social order. It was only in 1831, not long before the Great Reform Act which dealt a blow to the political power of the landed classes, that these game laws were finally changed.[15]

Fox-hunting was not an ancient sport. It was hardly known until the end of the seventeenth century. The production of wool, especially in the West Riding of Yorkshire, Gloucestershire and Somerset, enriched the landowners of good grazing ground and they were able to spend some of their income on breeding better horses and both hunting and running hounds.[16] At first hunters did not breed hounds especially for fox-hunting, but began to chase the fox with whatever hounds they possessed, which were generally harriers. The fox depended upon speed. Early fox-hunters arose when it was still dark, hoping to catch a slow fox, tired after its night's hunting. This made fox-hunting with untrained dogs an unexciting activity and often the fox escaped in the dark of early evening. Things changed, however, when in 1753, the young Hugo Meynell rented Quorn or Quorndon Hall in North Leicestershire.[17] He saw that it was possible to breed very fast hounds which could easily keep pace with the fox and thus he revolutionised fox-hunting. The large areas of grassland in Leicestershire were suited to the very fast hounds. The new speed made fox-hunting far more exciting and sociable. It made it possible for the hounds to meet at 10.00 a.m. or 11.00 a.m. rather than at dawn. Fashionable young men, who were far too smart to rise early, began to see the attraction and dash of fox-hunting. Hugo Meynell himself had London friends who could bestow upon his hunt the necessary prestige.[18] Other sportsmen began to converge upon Leicestershire as Meynell's reputation grew. At first they were accommodated at Quorndon Hall: later as their numbers increased, they filled the local inns, and by 1780 were looking for houses to rent in towns such as Loughborough. They then were able to find sport with the Duke of Rutland's Belvoir Hounds and Sir William Lowther's Cottesmore Hounds, on days when Meynell was not hunting and the attractions of Loughborough seemed limited. By the 1790s hunting men were settling temporarily in Melton Mowbray. News of the Meltonians was spread through periodicals such as the *Sporting Magazine*.[19]

Hunting was no longer the activity of men such as Vanbrugh's fictional Sir Tunbelly Clumsy, but had considerable social prestige. Peter Beckford wrote in 1781: 'Fox-hunting is now become the amusement of gentlemen: nor need any gentleman be ashamed of it'.[20] Beckford regarded hunting as 'the soul of country life'. It was felt that gentlemen would stay in the countryside and not be tempted by the pleasures of London if hunting were well established. This would then be beneficial to rural society as the upper classes would then, it was generally believed, be of service to society. Fox-hunting made men hardy, and was excellent training for war; it 'prevents our young men', said one writer, 'from growing quite effeminate in Bond Street'.[21]

One family which banished any notion that fox-hunting and rusticity were necessarily companions was that of the Dukes of Beaufort. The third duke employed William Kent to design the inspired Worcester Lodge at Badminton in Gloucestershire at the entrance to the Park. Kent was also presumed to be responsible for ornamenting the facade and adding pavilions. The third duke still hunted the stag, but the fifth duke (1744–1803) was a fox-hunting pioneer; at the end of a disappointing day's stag hunting in the early 1760s he turned to the fox and then decided to enter his hounds for that species only. He took over from Lord Foley the Heythrop country in Oxfordshire and advised his nephew, the Duke of Rutland, on re-establishing the Belvoir kennels. When he died in 1803 Badminton was on a level with Quorndon and other leading hunts.[22]

Hunting, even in the early eighteenth century when it still had boorish and rustic overtones, was seen as a relief from high office. Sir Robert Walpole's 'progresses' to Norfolk in the 1720s and 1730s were never of long duration but included chasing, with his neighbours, across the heath after hare or fox. The gentlemen of Lynn were afterwards well entertained with haunches of venison as a present from Sir Robert.[23] William Pitt the Younger, who as Lord Warden of the Cinque Ports had an official residence at Walmer Castle in Kent, enjoyed as a respite from Parliament, riding, shooting, sailing and farming, and like Walpole built up huge debts for himself in pursuit of the ideal life of a country gentleman.[24] Such occasions for the politician at the height of his career were necessarily short. However, Walpole in retirement at Houghton as Earl of Orford seems to have allowed the coarse bucolic streak in his nature to dominate. It was said that even when he was the King's first minster a letter from his huntsman or gamekeeper took precedence over any political dispatch.[25]

Socially prominent artists, as well as politicians, hunted. Sir Joshua Reynolds hunted daily when he stayed at Saltram, or went partridge shooting.[26] Certainly by the 1790s there was much to be enjoyed, both in terms of the social arrangements for the meet and dressing up for it which had become fashionable.[27] It had become more visually elegant and was to remain socially exclusive. As the Reverend Benjamin Newton observed, 'Went hunting with Mr Bell's hounds, had tolerable sport, these hounds please me much as they are attended by gentlemen only, no farmers'.[28] As hunting became more fashionable and more formal there were also potential pitfalls for the socially ambitious. The second Lord Palmerston wrote as early as 1765 of his solicitor Mr Boehm who had been invited to join the hunt: 'Boehm à la chasse I think you may conceive to be an amazing phenomenon. He pulled off his coat some part of the chase because it was too hot and rode in a lapelled blue silk gold waistcoat without sleeves'.[29] Sometimes eccentricity was equally attributed to the landed gentry themselves in matters of sport. Sir Henry Harpur of Calke in Derbyshire was intensely shy with a taste for solitude. He withdrew from most of the social obligations of a landed gentleman. He did not hunt, but nevertheless in 1789 bought Lord Moria's pack. However, he accepted the killing of wild animals was at odds with his fondness for watching them, and he gave strict instructions to his keepers that hares and pheasants which were bred within the sight of his windows should be allowed to feed undisturbed.[30]

A sport which brought all classes together, it was claimed, was cricket. It was a village game originally, until it was 'organised' by the aristocracy. The first surviving code, *The Articles of Agreement*,[31] was drawn up in 1727, between the second Duke of Richmond and Gordon and Mr Alan Brodrick of Peper Harow in Surrey, for two twelve-a-side. The articles were mostly concerned with procedures and the conduct of players was not mentioned. There were other great aristocratic cricket lovers including Lord Tankerville and the Duke of Dorset who was addicted to it. The Earl of Winchelsea and Lord Charles Lennox were closely involved in the founding of MCC in 1787.[32] Judging by illustrations of the 1740s, one might assume that dress was not important in early matches, and there were some oddities.[33] There was no middle stump, the ball was hurled along the ground, the bats were curved and heavy and the umpires also had bats. There were certain eccentric variations upon the standard game. Sir Horatio Mann, who had estates at Bishopbourne,[34] preferred playing the game on horseback, with, of course, long bats. Cricket was stylish, women enjoyed watching it, and because of the general love of gambling throughout the eighteenth century, huge sums of money were wagered on the outcomes of matches. As with hunting, the politically prominent involved themselves in it.[35] Considerable organisation went into arranging matches and finding players. 'I could tell you of Lord Mountford's making cricket matches, and fetching up parsons by express from different parts of England to play matches on Richmond Green', claimed Horace Walpole (who disliked the game) in 1749.[36] In the 1760s Charles James Fox played cricket and tennis, although the hours before dinner were devoted to Greek. Of Fox it was observed that 'a relationship was sometimes claimed between the size of his stomach and the frequency of his runs out at cricket'.[37] Unlike the hunting fraternity the players came from widely differing social backgrounds. Lord Sackville played at Knole in a team captained by his gardener, and Tankerville – whose seat was Mount Felix, near

Walton-on-Thames – patronised Surrey cricket, where his butler and gardener played for the county.[38] The game was also played in Scotland. *The Cathcart Family* can be seen, resting with their bats and balls in front of an elegant tea-tent, painted by David Allan in 1785 [104].

There were clearly many other country activities which gave pleasure out of doors. Walking, riding and driving were prominent amongst them. In 1786 Lady Fetherstonhaugh of Uppark was visited by her niece Miss Iremonger, who wrote: 'This country has always peculiar charms. There is nothing like it and I am always sorry to quit it . . . My aunt and I Frequently drove in the Harvest-fields by moonlight, in an open carriage & supped at our return by the same light without candles. Perhaps you did not suspect I was such a Lunatick'.[39]

Jane Austen wrote in June 1800, 'Thursday . . . yesterday passed quite à la Godmersham . . . the gentlemen rode about Edward's farm and returned in time to saunter along with us; and after dinner we visited the Temple Plantation'.[40] Charles James Fox enjoyed the calm of the countryside after 'feaverd gambling at Almack's'. He spent much time at St Anne's Hill near Chertsey,[41] which stood in well-coppiced countryside and was favoured by nightingales. The house figured a good deal in his correspondence and he described it as 'a little piece of Arcadia', spending his evenings walking in the country around it.[42]

Walks could become more elaborate occasions in different ways. The first Duchess of Northumberland was attached to the medieval ruins and picturesque scenery of Hulne Priory near Alnwick Castle in Northumberland as a picnic site. Robert Adam was commissioned to design the Brislee Tower (1781) [105], and a Gothic cottage as a picnic house.[43] Oatlands Park in Surrey had a three-roomed grotto which provided a resting place for Beau Brummell on his elegantly indolent walks around the estate. Strolls here must have been full of exotic surprises. The grotto where Brummell's hosts, the Duke and Duchess of York, often breakfasted and dined was decorated with artificial stalactites. The Duchess kept ostriches and kangaroos in the paddock, monkeys on the lawn, and eagles and macaws in her flower garden.[44]

The captivating idea of a retreat from large, grand, formal spaces was always present in the mind of the upper classes. If it were not a cottage or grotto, then a boat might be a pleasant variation. The third Earl of Orford liked sailing and dubbed himself 'Admiral of the Fens'. He and Lord Sandwich ran regattas at Whittlesey Mere. Getting away from the 'big house' sometimes meant relaxing in the more louche society of the demi-monde, and Orford was accompanied on his yacht by his mistress Patty Turk.[45]

Walking, sketching and visiting other country houses was often reported. Jane Austen wrote in 1811, 'Mr Tilson took a sketch of the Great House before dinner, and after dinner we all three walked to Chawton Park, meaning to go in, but it was too dirty, and we were obliged to keep on the outside. Mr Tilson admired the trees very much, but agreed that they should not be turned into money . . .'[46] Jane Austen was describing a rather sedate occasion. However, the picturesque or even sublime qualities of nature were usually admired at the end of the eighteenth and the beginning of the nineteenth centuries, and sometimes even dramatised. William Beckford's coming of age party at Fonthill in Wiltshire, in September 1781, was such an event. Bonfires were lit on the surrounding downs to spread the news and form a glowing background. In front of the house there was an illuminated triumphal arch and the lake was arranged to look like a Venetian regatta; there were musicians hidden behind shrubs and a display of fireworks. Helping nature to become an exciting backdrop for extraordinary effects at Fonthill may have been the responsibility of Philip de Loutherbourg, who worked at David Garrick's theatre. It has been suggested that he used his eidophusikon to produce dramatic lighting effects, achieved by coloured glass gauzes moving in front of a lamp. Painted and cut out settings and backdrops moved as scenes changed.[47]

Many activities at country houses were pursued quietly indoors. This was nevertheless an opportunity to enjoy a wide variety of amusements. At Castletown, near Dublin, Lady Louisa Connolly wrote letters after breakfast, and the women and old people staying there spent their time reading

104] David Allan, *The Cathcart Family Group*, 1785

105] Alnwick Castle, Northumberland. The Brizele Tower, an ornamental buildin in the park, two miles north c the castle, built in 1781, probal to the designs of Robert Adar

novels, poetry, histories, sermons and books of travel.[48] Libraries were certainly much appreciated and enjoyed. Sometimes reading and study were essential. The third Earl of Bute lived in the country until he could afford a London house. 'Lord Bute', said Horace Walpole, 'having no estates of his own, had passed his youth in studying mathematics and medicines in his own little island' (of Bute).[49] *The Gentleman's Register*, in describing his 'palace' at Luton in Bedfordshire, noted that it had a library of three rooms.[50] At Kedleston too, there was an excellent architectural library, begun in the seventeenth century and continued in the eighteenth.[51] The library at Felbrigg, which was completed in 1753, had three hundred volumes, pamphlets, poems and plays. The books were bound in quarter calf with marbled borders. William Windham II was interested in bookbinding and subscribed for many books and volumes of prints.[52] On the other hand, William Whitbread's library at Southill in Bedfordshire was not so entertaining, consisting as it did of large collections of tracts on the war against Revolutionary France.[53]

Not all reading or other work was done earnestly or silently. When Jane Austen was staying at Godmersham Park in Kent in 1799 it was observed by her niece that she would sit 'quietly by the fire in the library saying nothing for a good while, and then would suddenly burst out laughing, jump up and run across the room to a table where pen and paper were lying, write something down and then come back to the fire and go on quietly working as before'.[54] 'Working' in this context would have meant needlework. Some light reading was done early. François de la Rochefoucauld noted that 'the morning papers are on the table and those who want to do so read them during breakfast'.[55] Even the way libraries were used could prove distracting to the serious reader. Creevey, staying at Cantley for the Doncaster races in September 1827, observed a variety of activities taking place in the library there. 'In the opposite corners of the same sofa sat Lady Appleby making a purse and Lady Malvern reading a novel...His Lordship of Appleby...fast asleep with a newspaper on his knee, Mrs Poole and Miss Tyrwhitt enlivened themselves with a noisy game of backgammon...Lacy was alternately occupied in taking, reading, drawing caricatures on the back of a letter he had just received, and watching the proceedings of Agnes, who was replacing some broken harp strings.'[56]

Women especially were involved in a variety of indoor activities. Frequently they were left alone whilst their male relations were at the hustings, at Westminster, at war or at the hunt. Lady Mary Wortley Montagu was stranded by her politically ambitious husband at Middlethorpe just outside York in August 1713. Sometimes, alone, she was taken up with domestic trivia. Should she hire pewter plates at half a crown a dozen for four months? Should she brew her own beer? When Queen Anne died a year later, rebellion was anticipated in the north. The City of York became a city of women, Lady Mary noted, when 'all the principal men of any figure took post for London' to participate in the problems of royal succession. She was invited

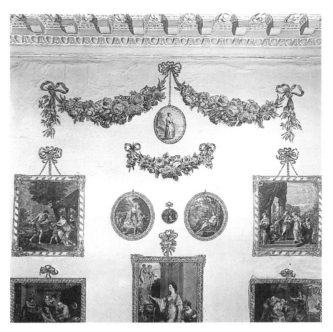

106] Castletown, Cellbridge, Co. Kildare. Detail of the wall of
the Print Room, made in the 1760s by Lady Louisa Connolly

to Castle Howard, where again there were no men, merely the frightened
daughters of Lord Carlisle. Lest her husband should be concerned about her
fidelity, she assured him, 'Tis the same thing as pensioning in a nunnery, for
no mortal man ever enters the doors'.[57]

In the 1770s at Castletown in Ireland, Lady Louisa Connolly was
spending her time indoors on a major decorative project. She turned the
gallery into an informal living room, so that the state rooms were hardly
used except for important occasions. The plain unadorned room was completed in a Pompeian manner by 1774, by a Mr Reily, who had worked at
Goodwood, for £100. Louisa and her sister chose the subjects from books of
engravings from the antique and from Renaissance paintings which were to
be found in most gentlemen's libraries. Montfaucon's *L'Antiquité expliquée*
provided the sisters with much of their inspiration.[58]

Louisa's love of informal space led her to create a cottage for herself
where she could relax without servants. She also took the antechamber to
the state bedrooms at Castletown, where rather baroque levées had formerly been held, and turned it into a print room [106]. She had, like most
aristocratic girls, been taught to draw, and this work of cutting out and
pasting occupied much of her time in the 1760s. Male relations making the
Grand Tour sent many of the prints to her from Rome.[59] Emily, Duchess of
Leinster also created a print room. Whereas men tended to have engravings
collected whilst on the Grand Tour, pasted in a dressing room perhaps,

women, it seems, chose more engravings of relations and friends as well as genre scenes. Lady Clanbrassil, who was a friend of the Duchess of Leinster, had the closet decorated with portraits of friends at her house at Tempelogue near Dublin.[60]

Like Louisa Connolly, Emily, Duchess of Leinster sought tranquillity in her *cottage orné* at Carton. Waterstone, as this cottage was named, had its roof removed and a dome with Gothic skylights was built in its place. Inside, Emily and Louisa created a private fantasy of shell and geometric patterns of stained bamboo. Although superficially similar to the shell grotto at Goodwood, it possessed greater order and regularity. However, it displayed some of the Rococo love of exuberant natural forms in its riot of oyster shells, conches and crystalline specimens.[61]

Aristocratic women certainly enjoyed the rustic freedom and romantic privacy of the remote cottage. Lady Louisa Stuart wrote in 1778 to Lady Portarlington of the Lodge at Wharncliffe in Yorkshire: 'This lodge is placed like an eagle's nest upon the summit of a very steep rock, which is entirely covered with wood . . . We each have a bedchamber, and there is a room entirely hung with old tapestry to dine and sit in. What can one desire more? To say truth it is an old farmhouse, and has little furniture, but yet the old housekeeper keeps it so nicely and neat and clean, that it puts me in mind of romance where you meet with cottages belonging to shepherds and shepherdesses . . . I would sooner lay my cap upon the floor than upon a chair at Luton.'[62]

If reading and various kinds of embroidery occupied women in country houses, there was also a real interest in painting.[63] Louisa Connolly took lessons from Mr Warren, a Dublin drawing master.[64] Sandby, Girtin and Gainsborough all taught women and, by 1800, hundreds of drawing masters were employed by the gentry. The cult of the Picturesque was forwarded by ladies of leisure doing watercolours, and the Claudian landscape glimpsed from a boudoir window might well have been inspired by an enthusiast like the Countess of Hertford, who bought paintings and prints in Europe which enabled her to devise garden schemes inspired by Claude.[65] Aristocratic women also produced pastel portraits. Prominent amongst the amateurs were the Countess of Buckinghamshire, Lady Diana Beauclerk, Lady Lyttleton and Lavinia, Countess Spencer.[66] Perhaps women artists were able to convey something of this comfortable and intimate world within their portraits. Certainly this would seem to be a quality found in the 1770s portraits of Angelica Kauffmann, with their gauzy draperies and pseudo-Turkish informality [107].[67]

The exotic qualities of Turkish costume had theatrical appeal and many country house owners enjoyed producing plays [108]. At Seaton Delaval, in Northumberland, Sir Francis Blake Delaval had the assistance of the playwright Samuel Foote. The dramatic Baroque house was transformed into an Italianate palace with lights in the grounds and music welling

107] Angelica Kauffman, *Mary, Duchess of Richmond*, 1775

108] James Gillray, *Dilettanti Theatricals; – or – A Peep at the Green Room.
Vide Pic-Nic Orgies*, 1803

up at appropriate times. These amateur performances took place throughout the 1750s, and Delaval and Foote undertook 'theatrical research' by visiting ridottos, green rooms and masquerades whilst in London. In the 1760s, the rakish Lord Sandwich organised theatricals at Hinchingbrook House in Huntingdonshire, having retired from a business career in politics and an exhausting one at the Hell Fire Club. The performances were so successful that they began to threaten the winter bookings at Bath. Other aristocrats enjoyed performing in these plays: the second Viscount Palmerston was Prospero in a 1760 production of *The Tempest*. The Prince of Wales stayed for three days during one season and saw Fielding's ballad opera *The Mock Doctor*. In the 1780s the Blenheim theatricals were established, with the Duke's children playing in *She Stoops to Conquer* in 1786 and the future Prime Minister Lord Liverpool in Burgoyne's *The Maid of the Oaks*.[68] More famous still were the plays produced at Wynnstay in Denbighshire by Sir Watkin Williams Wynn, fourth Baronet between 1770 and 1789 and by the fifth Sir Watkin between 1803 and 1810. In 1722 James Gandon, the Dublin architect, remodelled a kitchen built originally for a coming of age party, turning it into a grand theatre. In 1783 *The Clandestine Marriage* was performed and in the following year, *Macbeth*. Sir Watkin pressed his servants into acting and even persuaded David Garrick, who disliked amateur performances, to be a spectator in 1777.[69]

The Earl of Barrymore, a rake and friend of the Prince of Wales, like Lord Sandwich also had a theatre at Wargrave in Berkshire. This cost £60,000 to construct and scenes were painted for it by Mr Young of the Opera House in Covent Garden. Mrs Inchbald's *The Midnight Hour* was performed there in 1788 with an entire transparency, then a fashionable part of the set, forming a moonlit garden. The Earl, known as the 'Thespian Maecenas' suffered great financial reverses, and scenery and costumes were seized by the Sheriff of Berkshire in 1792.[70] Apart from performing well-known plays and musical pieces, enthusiasts searched for the plays of the past which might have fallen into obscurity. Queen Caroline, consort of George II, 'collected all the old pieces she could find' – both of the English and French theatre, according to Horace Walpole.[71]

Charades were also popular in eighteenth-century country houses. The word 'charade' for the speech or action of a clown, was used by Jane Austen to mean a verbal rather than acted riddle. In the 1830s the Duke of Buckingham's theatre at Stowe began producing pantomimic charades. By this time the word charade was generally used to cover a wide variety of country house plays. Rooms in country houses were adapted for such performances. Earl de Grey designed an alcove in his dining room at Wrest Park in Kent which would create a proscenium, moved on hinges, to make a more flexible stage. Apparently Lord de Grey painted some of the scenery himself.[72] The love of bizarre theatrical effects could sometimes be catered for on a small scale. Sarah Jennings, Duchess of Marlborough, had wax figures made for a puppet show impersonating the second Duchess, her grandson's wife, and some of her cousins.[73]

There were, of course, some very grand occasions at country houses. Some of these involved royalty. Despite a reputation for plain living George III and Queen Charlotte insisted on being entertained with the utmost formality by their aristocratic subjects. In 1788 the king and queen visited Audley End in Essex, Deene Park in Northamptonshire and Wilton in Wiltshire. When they visited Tottenham Park in Wiltshire in 1789 plates and beds had to be borrowed and dinner was served in six different places to fifty-eight people.[74]

A ball was clearly an opportunity for lavish display, but also for discomfort and disquiet. Jane Austen described a ball at Manydown, the Hampshire home of the Bigg-Wither family, in 1799: 'There was the same kind of supper as last year and the same want of chairs. There were more dancers than the room could conveniently hold, which is enough to constitute a good ball at any time.' She added, 'I do not think I was very much in request. People were rather apt not to ask me till they could not help it.'[75] More splendid perhaps than a ball was the private *fête champêtre* given to celebrate the betrothal of Lord Stanley, later twelfth Earl of Derby, to Lady Betty Hamilton at The Oaks, Carshalton, Surrey, in 1774. Robert Adam designed a vast aisled ballroom [109], which was his largest interior, and a supper room also. The masque was composed by Mr Barthelemon.[76] The young were dressed as swains and shepherdesses and peasants, and Lord Stanley and Lady Betty as Rubens and his wife, as though the spirit of Rubens' painting *The Garden of Love* (*c*. 1634) was brought to life. Antonio Zucchi painted the scene and showed the visitors to the ball wearing costumes like those in an eighteenth-century *fête galante* picture by Watteau or Pesne.[77]

109] Antonio Zucchi, *The Oaks Pavilion, Carshalton, Surrey,* 1774

Not all large-scale gatherings were quite as elegant as this, and it is clear that some country house owners wished for an entertainment which was 'blacker'. Lord Byron revelled in parties at Newstead where there was orgiastic drinking, masquerading as monks and romping with a tame bear.[78]

It has been observed that many quiet absorbing indoor pastimes occupied women. However, men also liked to entertain themselves in similar ways.[79] Lord Bute had his laboratories at Highcliffe and, having spent £100,000 on Luton,[80] forsook it for a more frugal lifestyle studying agriculture, botany and architecture. Lord Chesterfield, feeling that such interests led to loss of caste, believed Bute to have a mind which was industrious rather than elevated.[81] At Felbrigg, William Windham II could indulge his taste for the mechanical and inventive. He had a room filled with a turning shop and another for making fireworks: indeed he bought treatises on firework production.[82] At Erddig, Philip Yorke, who collected antiquarian books, set up his Tribes Room following the publication of his own *The Royal Tribes of Wales* (1799). He also formed a family museum with a picturesque array of antiquities including human skulls, Chinese figures, swordfish blades, a hornets' nest, old coins and primitive weapons. Such museums as this contained a strange mixture of scientific instruments and ethnographical, natural history specimens or archaeological relics (see also [101]).[83]

Music was also a popular activity in country houses during the eighteenth and nineteenth centuries [110]. The royal family gave encouragement to musicians, being fond of opera, and George II subscribed £1,000 to the Royal Academy of Music when it was founded in 1719. It was established by several noblemen, including the Dukes of Newcastle, Montagu and Chandos as well as Lord Burlington. Chandos himself had an orchestra of thirty at Cannons, his country house, directed by Dr Johann Pepusch who had a salary of £100 per annum. Musicians performed both in the house and chapel forming a small music academy. There were two organs and two harpsichords and in 1717 Handel became the resident composer at the house, although Pepusch remained director of music.[84]

It was hard for both composers and performers to find aristocratic patronage, on the scale existing in, for example the German states. Foreigners were sought and beautiful sopranos married into the aristocracy on occasion: Anastasia Robinson married Lord Peterborough, Lavinia Fenton, the Duke of Bolton, and Martha Ray the Earl of Sandwich. Some aristocrats performed at country houses. The first Earl of Egmont belonged to the Society of Gentlemen Performers of Music, and there were other aristocratic amateurs. Lord Brudenell of Boughton, son of the Duke of Montagu, was painted holding a copy of Corelli's Violin Sonata Opus 5, No. 6. Sir John Clerk of Penicuik House had even had lessons in Rome from Corelli at the beginning of the eighteenth century.

Attitudes changed to the idea of aristocrats actually playing instruments. Lord Chesterfield wrote to his son in 1749: 'If you love music, hear it, go to operas, concerts . . . but I insist upon your neither piping nor fiddling yourself. It puts a gentleman in a very frivolous contemptible light.' However, William Herschel wrote in 1761, 'A long stay [at Halnaby Country Durham] to accompany Lady Milbank who was an excellent performer on the harpsichord'.[85]

Country house libraries often contained large collections of music. From the 1780s onwards successive Duchesses of St Albans collected music and at Dalkeith Palace two of the Dukes of Buccleuch's daughters collected vocal music between 1780 and 1800. By the early nineteenth century the women of the family became the chief performers of music in drawing rooms. Mary Bennet in *Pride and Prejudice* had 'worked hard for knowledge and accomplishments [and] was always impatient for display'. On the whole men were not expected to play the piano in the drawing room.[86]

In Scotland there was considerable interest shown in music in great houses which took over court patronage when James VI went to London in 1603. It was expensive, however, to maintain professional musicians as part

110] Heaton Hall, Lancashire. The organ built by Samuel Green with a case designed by James (or Samuel) Wyatt, decorated by Biagio Rebecca for the Music Room. Robert Adam also designed a fine Neoclassical organ for Newby

of the household. In the Highlands some musicians were employed, and they were apparently working regularly at Dunvegan Castle on the Isle of Skye. Thunderton House in Elgin had musicians in 1710, and there was also a strong musical household at Kilvarock Castle near Nairn presided over by Hugh Rose, Lord Kilvarock. The sixth Earl of Kellie was, according to his obituary in the *Gentleman's Magazine* in 1787, 'one of the first musical composers of the age'. He wrote minuets for the *fête champêtre* at The Oaks in Surrey to celebrate the marriage of Lord Stanley to Lady Betty Hamilton.[87]

Sometimes music was treated in a perfunctory manner by visitors bored with rainy weather and confined to the house for too long. Creevey at Cantley commented on a certain restlessness: 'Music and billiards had their turn; some went to play at battledore and shuttlecock in the hall; others beguiled the hours in ransacking albums and portfolios. Mr Tyrwhitt, in despair, proposed écarté; and one of his sisters suggested that they should act charades . . . Some of the ladies worked a little and some of the gentlemen tried to be useful; one helped to unravel silk, and another delivered his opinion upon colours and patterns.'[88] Indoor games developed considerably during the eighteenth century and chess and billiards, both ancient games, became more formal and increasingly popular.[89]

Gambling was the great thrill of society, with men like Charles James Fox winning and losing vast sums. It filled in endless evenings for the Duke of Marlborough, who after his stroke could still roam the countryside on horseback during the day and in the evening looked forward to cards with members of his family. Edmund Burke, on the other hand, despite his admiration for the aristocracy, was bored by their pastimes, especially cardplay and horse racing.[90] Sometimes cardplaying would have been difficult to avoid. The second Viscount Palmerston, despairing of his eccentric solicitor Mr Boehm, wrote in 1765, 'He is now bound for Ireland . . . As he can neither drink nor play at cards I fear he may be disappointed.'[91] Occasionally gambling and cards were an emotional escape. Frances Pelham was a brilliant and fashionable woman. She was thwarted in her attempts to marry Lord March, the Duke of Richmond's heir, and consequently resorted to the gambling tables.[92]

In the 1790s Saltram in Devon was a centre for sport and gaming of all kinds. Georgiana, fifth Duchess of Devonshire, was a frequent visitor: though a great gambler she found the stakes high and favoured the game of whist.[93] Billiards, too, was an entertainment regarded as especially suited to men. Jane Austen wrote with some relief when at Godmersham in 1813, 'The comfort of the billiard table here is very great. It draws all the gentlemen to it whenever they are within, especially after dinner, so that my Br., Fanny and I have the library to ourselves in delightful quiet.'[94]

Sometimes the country house became a meeting place or refuge for artists and writers who provided a more serious form of entertainment for families and their visitors. Of course some aristocrats were deeply interested in the arts at a very advanced level, for instance, Lords Burlington, Pembroke, Bathurst and Leicester were all involved in architectural design. Enjoying various branches of the arts was a common pursuit in country houses.

The Duke of Newcastle owned lands in eleven counties and six country houses. Claremont in Surrey was his most luxurious seat. Added to by Vanbrugh with gardens by Kent, it was, Newcastle reported, 'The only place where I am really easy'. Here he could have 'happy and quiet days' despite its fame as a place for political entertaining, and here also he could exercise his taste for landscaping and building. The Duke built up an impressive library, he entertained Jacob Tonson, a friend from Kit-Cat days and, as has been observed, took an interest in music.[95] There was a real taste for perfecting some artistic activity, perhaps at a drawing master's in the capital, and sometimes as a 'mature student'. Henry Seymour Conway wrote to Horace Walpole in August 1749 from London, 'And, dear Horry, I have at least begun to draw: you will not be sorry to hear that I shall confine myself chiefly or entirely to perspective views of buildings, landscapes &c . . . I have a notion Lewis is dead, so I have taken a good old German who was recommended to me by my master of mathematics (for you must know I am in the midst of that and fortifications). He seems to be good at that kind of drawing and has done some views of London, which I really think pretty.'[96] Perhaps Conway, like the aristocratic boys at Carton, had had some early lessons in the kind of geometrical drawing considered suitable for well-to-do young men who might be taking up a military career or wishing to survey and alter their parklands.[97]

Artistic activity linked to some other country pursuits must have been quite a common occurrence. Animal painters attended race meetings and were on friendly terms with aristocratic patrons. John Wootton, with his 'pleasant engaging demeanour' was sent to Newmarket to paint the horses by the second Duke of Richmond, his patron, who also presented him with, on one occasion, at least a haunch of venison.[98] The hunting field, too, was the place where the artist could convey status, but combine it with rural informality. Robert Walpole was painted by Wootton, not as a grandee, but as a country squire, out hunting with only the Garter star discreetly indicating his rank.[99]

Lord Spencer in the 1760s had a circle of friends made up of aristocrats as well as painters and writers including Lord Nuneham,[100] a connoisseur and early patron of 'Athenian Stuart', Laurence Sterne, David Garrick and Angelica Kauffmann.[101] Sir George Beaumont entertained Wordsworth at Coleorton Hall in Leicestershire in the 1820s. Sir George was a demanding host and of Wordsworth it was said that 'no one could have done more to see Beaumont through the long winters when he ardently wished himself in Rome'. Coleridge and Mrs Siddons stayed at Coleorton and John Constable spent six weeks there in the autumn of 1823. Constable wrote, 'I am almost choked in this breakfast room. Here hang four Claudes, a Cousens and a

Swanfelt.' Apart from painting and sketching he breakfasted early with his host and visited neighbouring country houses, returning to dine with Sir George and Lady Beaumont, the latter reading aloud from the *Morning Herald*. They spent their evenings after dinner in the drawing room drinking tea, whilst Constable looked through portfolios and Sir George read plays aloud.[102]

Architects might well also be part of a country house circle. Robert Adam always regarded himself as a social equal of his patrons and mixed with them accordingly. He went on the Grand Tour with Charles Hope, son of the Earl of Hopetoun, and like his father, worked at Hopetoun House.[103] Sometimes the relationship seems more that of higher servant and employer. Sir William Chambers as tutor to the Prince of Wales was summoned to do likewise for the Duke of Richmond and noted, 'Attendance on his Grace to teach him Architecture – Five guineas'.[104] This tension between the grand, formal and socially elevated on the one hand and the informal and egalitarian – even disorganised – on the other, is difficult to analyse. We have already seen how grand and carefully organised was the splendid party at The Oaks. Lord Bute at Luton and the Duke of Newcastle at Claremont both held parties which were intended to rival and surpass each others. Sir Robert Walpole's splendid entertaining at Houghton made his brother-in-law Lord Townshend madly jealous.[105]

The formality of Luton was almost frightening: Lady Mary Coke describing it in 1774 remarked: 'The Apartment I lay in was done in white satin and I was so afraid that my maid's hands should not be clean, that I lay with one side of the bed curtains open'.[106] Much of the furniture was covered in light green and white satin, and Lady Mary claimed that she had never seen a house so fully furnished.[107] However, it did not appeal to Lord Bute's family. Lady Louisa Stuart complained of the 'intolerable yawnings' of the gatherings there. She preferred, she said, sitting in her little bow-windowed room overlooking the restless blue of the Channel writing to friends. Lord Bute's personality seemed split between the princely figure portrayed full-length by Allan Ramsay in ermine and velvet, and the bookish, parsimonious Scots laird who preferred the introspective seclusion of a study to the glitter of a ballroom. In July 1778 Lady Louisa wrote to her sister Lady Caroline, presenting a curious picture of life at Luton:

> For my part I am sufficiently accustomed to dumb people, for here are brothers Frederick and William who speak about six words a day and instead of being any company, only serve to give me the vapours by walking up and down the room without ceasing; don't think I mean my room, for I assure you they never deign to visit that, but after tea, as my Father and Mother always retire to the library, I have brought down my work and sat with these two gentle-men to try if any acquaintance could be made with them, and I tell you I am entertained with their eternally walking backwards and forwards, and now flinging themselves upon the couch, yawning and asking such questions as When do we go to London? When does Caroline come back?[108]

Country houses could be uncomfortable as well as formal or boring. At Felbrigg William Windham was executing James Paine's plan in the 1750s, which entailed removing the late seventeenth-century staircase and creating an 'eating parlour' with bedrooms above in its place. For long periods the house was almost uninhabitable. Windham would pay frequent visits, sleeping in whatever room happened to be available and dining on mutton roasted by a dairymaid.[109]

Panshanger, although not the scene of alterations, was uncomfortable enough in December 1828 for Harriet Granville to write to the Duke of Devonshire: 'I am at near Two, returned to my room, fire out, no housemaid having been near it, not a single morsel of writing paper in either of our rooms, one bad pen and a drop of ink'.[110] These were seen as serious discomforts for visitors retiring from the formal rooms of state. Harriet Granville at Saltram in 1815 seemed almost pleased to avoid Adam's elegant icy blue Saloon when she wrote: 'We live in two very comfortable rooms – a small library and a drawing room; keep early hours... Yesterday evening was after my own heart – work, reading, talking, and neither dancing acting, romping or joking'.[111]

The country house often seems as much at the mercy of its varied visitors as a modern hotel. It was almost as 'open'. Visitors to Kedleston in the 1760s were shown over the house by Mrs Garnett, the housekeeper. She provided visitors with a printed catalogue written in 1769 which went through four editions by 1800.[112] Apart from 'tourists', aristocratic friends could expect to stay at a country house even if the family was not itself in residence. These visitors brought their own personal servants but depended on the hosts' staff for meals, laundry services, heating and stabling.[113] The social status of guests might vary. The life of the Chute family at The Vyne in Hampshire was on a fairly modest scale in the 1780s. Mr Chute's brother came to stay for two or three months during the winter. The Chutes, although not egalitarian, were prepared to cover the costs of lodging less well-off friends and relations and to play hosts to anyone from a Scotch linen draper to a duke. In general they entertained friends from local rectories, although their entertaining became more ambitious socially when the Duke of Wellington moved to Stratfield Saye.[114]

At Downhill, his Irish property, Lord Bristol – the Earl-Bishop – enjoyed a rather raffish social life. There were many toasts at dinner, there was music and plenty of practical jokes. Young clergymen enjoyed Lord Bristol's hospitality, staying with him often enough for their accommodation to be referred to as the curates' corridor. In another corridor the rather worldly bishop discovered that a woman guest was conducting an affair by sprinkling flour outside certain bedroom doors.[115]

An important aspect of entertaining in the eighteenth and early nineteenth centuries was the consumption of elaborate and often enormous meals. Much research has recently been devoted to meals, their organisation and presentation. The day began with a fairly late breakfast at which ladies seldom appeared. This was often a simple meal of bread, butter and tea or chocolate.[116] At Castletown guests arose at about 8.00 a.m. and came down to breakfast at 9.30 a.m. or 10.00 a.m.[117] Some visitors objected to the length of time spent over breakfast. In 1781 the Countess of St Germans wrote to her aunt the Marchioness Grey, of her stay at Wimpole in Cambridgeshire: 'One thing here is disagreeable to me as I have never been used to it, that is the sitting up so long after breakfast and dinner. We breakfast at 10 and sit till 12 . . .' Indeed little seems to have been done between meals. Lady St Germans continued the description of her day: 'From half past two till four is spent dressing. From four till past six at dinner. Then coffee, afterwards working, looking at prints, talking till ten, when I go to bed and supper is announced. Before breakfast everyone goes to the library, which is a noble apartment, [but] I always take a walk in the garden.'[118]

Despite the fact that breakfast was simple, the gentry and aristocracy were discriminating tea buyers, sending to London for supplies of Imperial, Green and Bohea tea and sometimes obtaining coffee and chocolate from the capital as well.[119] Best Bohea tea cost thirty shillings a pound in 1710 and by 1780 the average price was still sixteen shillings a pound, at a time when the average labourer's wage was seven or eight shillings a week. Nevertheless tea drinking increased: at the beginning of the eighteenth century twenty thousand pounds of tea were imported and by the end, about twenty million.[120] The breads eaten at breakfast were sometimes spiced, and buns flavoured with caraway seeds were favoured, served hot and buttered, along with muffins which were especially popular in the north of England. At Saltram, muffins were eaten for breakfast and supper.[121] Breakfast seems to have remained informal, although the pattern varied somewhat and the meal became more substantial. Staying at Petworth in 1826,[122] Thomas Creevey was looked after by 'two gentlemen out of livery with coffee pots, tea pots, kettles, chafing dishes to keep rolls etc. hot and everything in the eatable way'.[123]

As hunting became more organised and more sociable so hunting breakfasts were established as distinctive meals. When the Prince of Wales and the Duc de Chartres went shooting at Uppark meat dishes were provided. Gradually the breakfast party became fashionable. By the 1770s serving cold and hot food and listening to music in the grounds of a country house was established.[124]

Luncheon or 'Nuncheon' was often only a snack taken at midday. Dr Johnson described it as 'whatever could be taken in the hand' – perhaps bread, cake, cold meats, although apparently not sandwiches. Cider, wine, a glass of buttermilk or sweetened whey from the dairy or coffee or chocolate might be drunk. Towards the end of the eighteenth century cold meats, pies, salads, cakes and brioches were sometimes served. As the dinner hour became later, so luncheon became more substantial.[125]

The principal meal was obviously dinner. At the beginning of the eighteenth century it was at midday, but gradually it moved to 3.00 p.m., by the 1780s it was at five o'clock, and during the Regency it was at 7.00 p.m. Fashionable people dined later, traditional country people sometimes adhered to midday throughout the eighteenth century. Dinner consisted of two or three courses. Five dishes per course might be served if only the family were present, but twenty-five per course for a 'Grand Table' or 'Capital Entertainment' for a large gathering was not uncommon.[126] English dinners lasted for much of the day if the occasion were an important one. La Rochefoucauld noted that it was customary to start at three o'clock and stay until ten. The meal itself he described as 'one of the most wearisome of English experiences, lasting as it does four or five hours'. Considerate hosts had dinner parties at the time of the full moon, so that visitors could make the difficult journey home over rough country roads with greater ease.[127]

Dinner was an immensely formal occasion. La Rochefoucauld observed, 'at four o'clock precisely you must present yourself in the drawing room with a great deal more ceremony than we are accustomed to in France. This sudden change in social manners is quite astonishing and I was deeply struck by it'.[128] In the morning, he had learned, it was possible to appear in riding boots and a shabby coat. In the evening one was obliged to be well washed and well groomed and the 'standard of politeness', he noted, 'is uncomfortably high'. When dinner was announced the mistress of the house requested the lady first in rank to show the way to the rest, and the hostess brought up the rear. The master of the house proceeded in the same way with the male guests.[129] Men and women did not sit next to each other for most of the eighteenth century, although by the later 1780s it had become acceptable.

The table itself was covered with a floor-length white cloth which protected it and hid the joins in the table. The table itself might be made up of several leaves which were kept outside the dining room. Once the cloth had been removed, earnest drinking began. The decanters for the table were breathtaking in their splendour and intricacy; silver candelabra and baskets of either fruit or flowers alternated down the long stretch of the white cloth. Food was arranged down the length of the table on either side. Classical temples, artificial gardens, shepherds, shepherdesses and urns made of sugar paste were replaced later in the century by the same kind of object manufactured in porcelain.[130]

The different courses consisted of a variety of savoury and sweet dishes followed by a dessert. The first course would be composed of soups, boiled meats and fish, small roasts and pies, with dishes of vegetables and sometimes a sweet pudding. When the first course was all but consumed, the 'remove' dish was introduced. This was an impressive joint or fowl which was intended to produce delight and exclamation amongst the diners and distract attention from the servants' task of removing the remains of the first course. The second course usually concentrated on roasted meats, with various dishes such as fricassees, ragouts, fish, fruit pies and custards in addition. If there were to be a third course there would be a second remove dish of a more ornate and dazzling appearance than the first. If no third course was served, then the dessert would be brought into the dining room.[131]

Sir Robert Walpole's dinners at Houghton were an important example of the eighteenth-century taste for visual display. Since it was the habit throughout this period to present all the dishes for a single course on the table at once, rather than as at present to serve them *à la russe*, that is in sequence, at a large party the effect of so much food must have been stupendous. Walpole wrote on 21 July 1731: 'Our company at Houghton swelled at last into so numerous a body that we used to sit down to dinner a little snug party of about thirty odd, up to the chin in beef, venison, goose, turkeys etc. and generally over the chin in claret, strong beer and punch.'[132] Despite this overwhelming hospitality, Walpole was able to use such occasions to discuss personalities and politics with men such as Townshend, Henry Pelham and Newcastle.[133]

Even a smaller dinner was often sumptuous by modern standards. The Duchess of Devonshire's daughter described a dinner for two laid on, apparently at short notice, by Lord Stafford at Trentham in 1810:[134] 'The dinner for us two was soup, fish, fricassee of chicken, cutlets, venison, veal, hare, vegetables of all kinds, tart, melon, pineapple, grapes, peaches, nectarines with wine in proportion . . . Before this sumptuous repast was well digested about four hours later, the doors opened and in was pushed a supper in the same proportions, in itself enough to have fed me for a week.'

Sometimes these bouts of entertaining went on for several days. When the Prince of Wales stayed at Uppark in 1772, members of the family had to vacate their rooms for the royal visitors. The party regularly consisted of eighty during that summer three-day extravaganza, but other neighbours joined the household temporarily swelling its numbers further, and the Prince alone brought twelve intimates.[135] Huge quantities of food and drink were provided by Sir Harry Fetherstonhaugh. This included '2 bucks, a Welsh sheep, a dozen ducks, four hares, dozens of pigeons and rabbits, flitches of bacon, lobsters and prawns, a turtle weighing 120lbs, 116lbs of butter, 370 eggs, 67 chickens, 23 pints of cream, 30lbs of coffee, 10lbs of fine tea'. The number of bottles of wine was equally vast. Forty-one bottles of port and seven of brandy were consumed, and the butcher's bill for ham and tongues amounted to £10 4s 9d.[136] This, then, was for perhaps one hundred people over approximately three days. Entertaining aristocratic visitors entailed providing for their servants as well. In the 1780s the Duke of Devonshire hosted parties at Chatsworth which might last about a fortnight. On one occasion there were 180 visitors and their servants who consumed sixteen sheep a week and five bullocks in the fortnight.[137] Providing such dinners was seen as one of the social obligations of a landowner. Edmund Burke, writing of the Earl of

Egremont (1751–1837) spoke of his 'delighting to reign in the dispensation of happiness': 'His greatest pleasure', wrote Benjamin Robert Haydon, 'was sharing with highest and humblest the luxuries of his vast income.'[138]

Although visitors were expected to select dishes from each course of a splendid dinner, rather than attempt to eat some of everything that was available, being entertained must sometimes have been rather daunting. Yet there is little indication of abstemiousness. The Younger Pitt, whose health deteriorated after 1797, dieted carefully from time to time, missing luncheon, but having a good dinner and contenting himself with two glasses of madeira with the meal and restricting himself to a mere pint of port after it.[139] The second Viscount Palmerston noted in 1798 that 'the abstaining much from meat and fermented liquors, which I was obliged to do to keep myself down in bulk, disagreed with my stomach'.[140] Occasionally the prospect of yet another festive dinner is contemplated with anxiety. The second Lord Egremont wrote in 1761, 'Well, I have but three turtle dinners to come and if I survive them I shall be immortal'.[141]

Not all dinners were planned in advance, and the country house diner was sometimes more like an unexpected guest in a modern hotel. Anne Parker of Saltram wrote in 1781, 'I do assure you we came away in a tricky moment, for on Friday at two o'clock the Duke of Rutland came in, eat some dinner and set out again for Exeter to meet the Duchess . . .'[142]

Drinking toasts was an important part of dinner and it was regarded as correct to 'raise your glass and look fixedly at the one with whom you were drinking, bow your head and take your wine with gravity'.[143] Port was drunk throughout the meal: Dr Johnson once drank thirty-six glasses with a sugar lump in each. Claret was regarded by many as an unpatriotic Frenchified drink for adolescent boys.[144] Much drinking took place during the dessert, and sometimes this would be served with as much ostentation as possible in a dessert room adjoining the dining room. Southey recorded as late as 1800 that the habit survived of leaving the dining room to eat this course and reported that the drawing room had become 'the common place for eating the dessert'.[145] Generally, by the Regency, the dessert had become the continuation of dinner and was a splendid finale to the meal. A foreign observer pointed out: 'At the dessert the scene changed; cloth, napkin, everything disappeared. The mahogany dining table shone in all the lustre that wood is capable of receiving from art. It was quickly covered with brilliant crystal decanters filled with exquisite wines, comfits in fine crystal vases, dried fruits of different kinds piled up in porcelain fruit baskets and china dishes.' Josiah Spode and other Staffordshire potters enriched the dining tables of the rich with dessert services in striking contrasting colours, such as canary yellow, rose or soft lilac set against brilliant vermilion, glowing claret, burnished gold and gleaming white.[146]

The dessert course would be the most expensive part of the meal [plate 20]. Pyramids of glass *tazze* piled one upon another were replaced during the 1790s by glass or silver épergnes for holding fruit, flowers or sweetmeats. Much prized were Sèvres dessert services, sometimes of one hundred pieces including fruit stands, compotes for stewed fruits, ice pails, ice cups for serving ice-creams and wine coolers and monteiths. Three decanters containing claret, port, sherry or madeira were placed in little silver stands or in a silver-wheeled waggon in front of the host. The ladies would leave after the dessert and a glass of wine or two. They returned to the drawing room for coffee or tea. The men would either join them later or possibly not at all, having drunk themselves into a stupor. La Rochefoucauld was shocked by the grossness and freedom of the conversation of men, and by the use of chamber pots necessitated by the endless circulation of bottles around the table.[147]

Traditional annual festivities and local events of importance were celebrated at country houses during the eighteenth and nineteenth centuries. There was, however, some resistance on the part of landowners to entertaining all comers with the lavishness of earlier times.[148] Christmas was still an important festival, although the hospitality accorded to neighbours and visitors for fourteen days from Christmas Eve until Epiphany did not always flow as it had in past times.[149] The elegant world and polite society of Bath or Tunbridge Wells found popular recreation socially disruptive, although in the north of England the 'Twelve Days' of Christmas were still often celebrated amongst the 'generality of the vulgar till Candlemas' (2 February).[150] Perhaps this was part of the polarisation of polite and popular culture. The elite disengaged itself from traditional pastimes, inhabiting elegant, controlled, orderly often classical spaces far from the rough and tumble of the popular event.[151] Henry Bourne in *Antiquities* (1725) even disapproved of Christmas carols which he noted were 'customary among the common people'. They were accompanied by 'rioting and chambering'; they were 'no glory but an affront to that holy season, a scandal to religion and a sin against Christ'.[152]

Where the aristocracy intervened in popular activities, it was to introduce rules, as in cricket. In 1757, at Belton in Lincolnshire, it was only the younger members of the gentry who took part in the ceremony which traditionally replaced the head of the family with a servant as Lord of Misrule. Adults were now less willing to join their households and servants in revels which diminished their dignity.[153] Nevertheless some aspects of tradition, even feudal festivity remained. Jesters and pipers and other musicians survived to a certain extent in Scotland and the north of England, although even by the seventeenth century many such entertainers were paid to come in only when there were festivals. 'Fools' disappeared in the eighteenth century with the death of Lord Suffolk's fool in 1728. In 1758 the Duke of Argyll still had a jester who stood at the sideboard among the servants. Sir Watkin Williams-Wynn had a harpist in the person of John Parry (1710–82), the Blind Harpist of Ruabon, and Edward Jones lived in St James's Palace in 1805 as 'Bard to His Majesty the Prince of Wales'.[154] By 1815 'Gothic rowdiness' was being revived and in the Baron's Hall at Arundel Castle the Duke of Norfolk gave a medieval banquet.[155]

Some eighteenth-century aristocrats expressed a dislike of traditional festivities. Horace Walpole wrote: 'Here I am down to what you call keep my Christmas. Indeed it is not in all its forms: I have stuck no laurel and holly in my windows, I eat no turkey and chine. I have no tenants to invite, I have not brought a single soul with me'.[156] Lord Byron even fled temporarily from home to escape from the traditional celebrations for his coming of age, in 1807. He claimed not to be able to bear ale and punch and tenants: 'an ox and two sheep to tear in pieces, with the ale and uproar of the "rabble"'.[157] Certainly celebrating an event with tenantry was a massive undertaking. At the coming of age of Sir Watkin Williams-Wynn in 1770, 15,000 tenants were entertained on 30 bullocks, 300 chickens, 421 pounds of salmon, 18,000 eggs and vast amounts of wine.[158]

These were occasions for revelry amongst ordinary country people. Christmas Day itself was the highlight of the winter for agricultural and estate workers, and their only paid holiday of the year.[159] In Scotland greater attention was paid to New Year rather than to Christmas itself. In Wales, Christmas lasted three weeks and Christmas Eve was celebrated especially by boys and young men in Carmarthenshire: they rushed about madly waving blazing torches from midnight to dawn.[160] Throughout the British Isles there was ceremonial dancing, processions around the village demanding a contribution from every household to be spent on eating and drinking at the end of the day. Easter was often marked by football, cricket, bell-ringing and cock-fighting. From many of these activities the aristocracy remained aloof.[161]

Clearly they did not withdraw completely and were active where it was possible for them to take a social lead. According to Macky, writing in 1724, 'here in England during the twelve days of Christmas the nobility and gentry retire to their respective seats in the country, and there with their Relations, Neighbours and Tennants, keep Carnivals, in their own houses, Hospitality, Musick, Balls: and play as much during this season all over England as in any kingdom whatever'.[162]

Perhaps participation in festivities depended on the extent to which the landowner was attached to a particular county, or whether he migrated from his lands in one county to properties in another. Sir John Verney, Viscount Fermanagh of Claydon in Buckinghamshire, certainly fulfilled his social obligations on festive occasions. His daughter Lady Cave of Stamford Park in Leicestershire sent him a swan for Christmas which he shared with some of his neighbours. Fermanagh was Lord of the Manor and Knight of the Shire. He therefore felt it his duty to entertain the farmers of the neighbourhood: handbell ringers, mummers and wassailers arrived at all hours of the night to be feasted on beef and plum pudding. The mummers acted their Christmas play of St George and the Dragon, with Beelzebub and the Prince of Paradise as principal characters, in the big barns of the Home Farm, and the Wassail bowl was filled again and again with spices, ale and gifts of money. Lord Fermanagh did not entirely enjoy these events: 'our home is very full of country people, like an election time', he wrote. 'Every day with the noise of Drums, Trumpets, Hautboys, Pipes or Fiddles; some days 400 guests, very few under a hundred, so that besides the vast expense, it has been very tiresome.' The Whitsun Ales was another county festival which fell heavily on the Fermanaghs. The house was full of morris men who had to be given money, and 'substantial freeholders' who, as Lady Fermanagh pointed out, 'can't be denyed eating or drinking'.[163]

Some Christmas holidays at country houses were far less raucous. Thomas Dampier, a guest at Felbrigg, wrote to William Windham to thank him for being entertained in 1756. It was 'the elegance and convenience', the *utile dulci*, the 'freedom and ease' that he praised.[164] There was 'just enough civility without ceremony'. Clearly this was very different from Lord Fermanagh's experiences. Indeed houses were gradually becoming more suited to elegance and convenience than to huge rowdy events. The old medieval idea of a first-floor great chamber was still to be found in some eighteenth-century country houses. Beningborough in Yorkshire, completed in 1716, has one. However, these great rooms were used only on special occasions when family silver and gold plate decorated them, and were otherwise sparsely furnished. James Wyatt remodelled the great Chamber at Belton in Lincolnshire in 1778, turning it into a fashionable dining room.[165]

Food at Christmas was especially rich and splendid. Yorkshire pie was often served for supper on Christmas Eve and for breakfast on Christmas Day, aristocratic families sent each other presents of food, sometimes from their estates. Mrs Delany was presented in 1772 with venison, pork and turkey, fowls and hares from Sandford and a 'perigot pie' – a Yorkshire pie with truffles in it – by the Duchess of Portland.[166] Gilling Castle where the Fairfax family lived, some twenty miles from York, had a 20,000-acre estate. Matthew Robinson, the 'odd man' for the house made frequent journeys to York throughout the winter with a 'basket' carrying carp from the Gilling ponds, pigeons, pheasants, venison, geese and peacocks.[167]

Country houses were, of course, decorated for Christmas. Garlands, swags and wreaths were made using holly, laurel, ivy, box, yew, bay and rosemary. Mistletoe was not considered suitable, as it was associated with love and the pagan world and might only appear in the kitchen. For table decorations the aristocracy preferred artificial flowers and elaborate parterres and figurines.[168] Yule logs were sometimes dragged into the kitchen. This log was the wood of a large tree or part of its trunk and was placed in the kitchen hearth and lit. It had to burn for twelve hours to avert ill luck.[169] It was Queen Charlotte, consort of George III, who introduced the Christmas tree when the court was spending the festive season at either Windsor or Kew. She had lived at the Castle of Mirow in the Duchy of Mecklenburg-Strelitz where the practice of decorating a dark green bough with lighted tapers was common. By 1800 Dr John Watkins reported seeing at Windsor an immense tub with a yew tree placed in it from the boughs of which hung sweetmeats, raisins, almonds in papers as well as fruits and small lighted candles.[170]

Royalty, aristocracy and gentry fed the poor and entertained them at Christmas. Queen Charlotte gave a substantial dinner and entertainment for sixty poor families at Windsor in 1800. Parson Woodforde usually entertained about fifteen elderly people for dinner on Christmas Day, often giving them beef, and sending dinner out to those who were unable to attend.[171] In 1788 he decked his parlour and kitchen windows with Halver boughs,[172] and at New Year in 1780 his niece Nancy and a friend, full of wine, stayed up until midnight, locking Woodforde in a closet and pulling his wig to pieces.[173] Woodforde's Christmas festivities were times when food was even more lavish than was the normal practice throughout the year, but his entertainment involved humble people. He entertained his clerk, and gave 6d each to the fifty-two poor of the parish in 1795.[174] However, the tireless Nancy, when not ruining his wig or making him up 'an apple pye bed' was not content to stay at home. On Christmas Day 1788, she and a female companion went off in the Norwich chaise at 7.00 a.m. to dine at the King's Head, but were back in time for tea in the afternoon.[175]

It was in the nineteenth century that the 'traditional Christmas', reviving past revelry and borrowing foreign festivity began to affect the country house. Washington Irving invented an old-fashioned Christmas at the imaginary Bracebridge Hall in 1817.[176] There was laughter in the servants' hall, where Hoodman blind, shoe-the-wild-mare, hot cockles, bob apple and other traditional games were being played. The Yule log was lit in the great fireplace of the hall. Outside the village gathered to sing carols by moonlight. On Christmas morning there were cold meats and ale for breakfast, church, and then an invitation from the squire to the parishioners, to go to the hall, 'to take something to keep out the cold weather'. Before dinner, country lads gathered to perform a dance, with beribboned shirts and hats decorated with greenery. At the Christmas dinner there was a harpist, yule candles on the sideboard and a pig's head decorated with rosemary and lemon. There was a wassail bowl of ale with nutmegs and apples bobbing on its surface, and after dinner the children performed a Christmas masque.[177]

In 1822, in the United States, Dr Clement Clark Moore wrote 'T'was the night before Christmas' and invented Father Christmas, who was of course secular and replaced the Lord of Misrule, part of the rowdy medieval Christmas that country house owners felt beneath their dignity and tiresomely time-consuming.[178] In the 1820s, too, it was becoming possible, if not comfortable, to visit family and friends with greater ease. The fast stage and mail coach which travelled all through the night took sixty hours to drive from London to Edinburgh.[179] A famous snowstorm in 1835 produced pictures of such coaches, loaded with turkeys, geese and hampers, dashing through the snow: an image which has become traditional on Christmas cards.[180] With the reduction of duties on imported foodstuffs in the early 1840s, poultry from France and Germany competed for the Christmas table with beef from Scotland, geese from Yorkshire and turkeys from Norfolk.[181]

The attractions of the country houses were numerous. Sir Robert Walpole's, dependent upon the slaughter and consumption of vast quantities of game, were coarsely convivial, whilst Jane Austen's in the library at Godmersham were contemplative and Girtin's watercolours of Harewood suggest the pleasure of solitude in a tranquil landscape.

NOTES

1 J. H. Plumb, *Georgian Delights: The Pursuit of Happiness*, Weidenfeld and Nicolson, London, 1980, p. 8.

2 Judith Hook, *The Baroque Age in England*, Thames and Hudson, London, 1976, p. 75.

3 Mark Blackett-Ord, *Hell Fire Duke*, Kensal Press, Windsor, 1982, pp. 39 and 88–9. Philip Wharton was a courtier. He sold Rathfarnham Castle, one of the family seats near Dublin. Other properties were let except for Wharton Hall which nobody wanted to take on.

4 Quotation by Stella Margetson, *Leisure and Pleasure in the Eighteenth Century*, Cassell, London, 1970, p. 118.

5 Earl of Albermarle, *Memoirs of the Marquis of Rockingham and His Contemporaries*, 2 vols, Richard Bentley, London, 1852, I, p. 393. Letter from Field Marshal Henry Seymour Conway to Horace Walpole, 25 October 1743.

6 Stanley Ayling, *The Elder Pitt*, Collins, London, 1976, p. 325.

7 *Ibid.*, p. 327.

8 Albermarle, *Memoirs of the Marquis of Rockingham*, I, p. 146, footnote.

9 *Ibid.*, II, p. 70.

10 *Ibid.*

11 Arthur Bryant, *The Age of Elegance 1812–22*, The Reprint Society, London, 1954, p. 262.

12 *Ibid.*, p. 289.

13 J. V. Becket, *The Aristocracy in England 1660–1914*, Basil Blackwell, Oxford, 1986, p. 342.

14 *Ibid.*, p. 343.

15 *Ibid.*

16 Roger Longrigg, *The History of Fox-Hunting*, Macmillan, London, 1975, p. 57.

17 David Itzkowitz, *Peculiar Privilege: A Social History of English Fox-Hunting 1753–1885*, Hassocks, Sussex, 1977, pp. 6–7.

18 *Ibid.*

19 *Ibid.*, p. 9.

20 Peter Beckford, *Thoughts on Hunting*, 1781, quoted by Itzkowitz, *Peculiar Privilege*, p. 12.

21 *Ibid.*, p. 20. Letter from James Yorke to Countess de Grey, 1802.

22 J. N. P. Watson, 'Badminton Blue and Buff: The Duke of Beaufort's Hunt', *Country Life*, CLXVI, 20 December 1979, pp. 2368–70.

23 J. H. Plumb, *Sir Robert Walpole: The Making of a Statesman*, Cresset Press, London, 1956, p. 88.

24 John W. Derry, *William Pitt*, Batsford, London, 1962, p. 138.

25 William Speck, 'Britain's First Prime Minister', in Andrew Moore (ed.), *Houghton Hall*, Philip Wilson, London, 1996, p. 12.

26 Ronald Fletcher, *The Parkers at Saltram 1769–1789*, BBC Publications, London, 1970.

27 John Armitage, *Man at Play: Nine Centuries of Pleasure Making*, Frederick Warne, London, 1977, p. 96.

28 *Ibid.*

29 Brian Connell, *Portrait of a Whig Peer*, compiled from papers of the Second Viscount Palmerston 1739–1802, André Deutsch, London, 1957, p. 63.

30 Howard Colvin *et al.*, *Calke Abbey*, The National Trust, London, 1989, p. 14.

31 David Allen, *Cricket: An Illustrated History*, Phaidon, Oxford, 1990, p. 18. See also Robin Simon and Alastair Smart, *The Art of Cricket*, Secker and Warburg, London, 1983, p. 2. Royalty and the aristocracy patronised the game of cricket from the Restoration onwards and teams were composed of members of differing strata of society.

32 Allen, *Cricket*, p. 22 and Simon and Smart, *Art of Cricket*, p. 22 discuss Lord Winchelsea. Simon and Smart also describe the contribution of the second and third Dukes of Dorset, pp. 2–6. The second duke was Master of the Horse to Frederick Prince of Wales, and arranged cricket matches at Hampton Court in 1723. The third Duke, with the Dukes of Richmond and Devonshire was a most enthusiastic patron of cricket. Dorset was also a patron of Reynolds, Hoppner, Opie and Romney. He kept a stable of cricketers, almost as he might have supported racehorses, at a cost of £1,000 per annum. Only the outbreak of the French Revolution prevented the Duke, who was British ambassador, from arranging for his team to play in France.

33 Armitage, *Man at Play*, p. 98.

34 Allen, *Cricket*, p. 22.

35 Armitage, *Man at Play*, p. 99.

36 *Ibid.*

37 Stanley Ayling, *Fox: The Life of Charles James Fox*, John Murray, London, 1991, pp. 51 and 206.

38 Allen, *Cricket*, p. 22.

39 Margaret Meade-Fetherstonhaugh and Oliver Warner, *Uppark and Its People*, Century, London, 1988, p. 59.

40 Penelope Hughes-Hallett, *Jane Austen: 'My Dear Cassandra'*, Collins and Brown, London, 1990, p. 65.

41 Ayling, *Fox*, p. 224.

42 *Ibid.*, p. 206, quoting J. B. Trotter, *Memoirs of the Latter Years of Charles James Fox*, George Sidrey, London, 1811.

43 Duff Hart-Davies, 'Heroic Panorama', *Country Life*, CLXXXIV, 22 February 1990, pp. 84–7.

44 Hubert Cole, *Beau Brummel*, Mason Charter, New York, 1973, p. 56.

45 Plumb, *Georgian Delights*, p. 118.

46 Hughes-Hallett, *Jane Austen*, p. 90.

47 Derrick Knight, *Gentlemen of Fortune*, Frederick Miller, London, 1978, p. 115. Correspondence suggests that de Loutherbourg brought with him his new eidophusikon, although there is no detailed account of Beckford's party.

48 Stella Tillyard, *Aristocrats: Caroline, Emily, Louisa and Sarah Lennox, 1740–1832*, Vintage, London, 1994, p. 17.

49 Jonathan Curling, *Edward Wortley Montague 1713–1776*, Andrew Melrose, London, 1954, p. 53.

50 E. Stuart-Wortley, *A Prime Minister and His Son. From The Correspondence of the Third Earl of Bute and Lt. General the Hon. Sir Charles Stuart*, John Murray, London, 1925, p. 211.

51 Leslie Harris, *Robert Adam and Kedleston: The Making of a Neoclassical Masterpiece*, The National Trust, London, 1987, p. 10.

52 R. W. Ketton-Cremer, *Felbrigg: The Story of a House*, Boydell Press, London, 1976, p. 142.

53 Roger Fulford, *Samuel Whitbread 1769–1815: A Study in Opposition*, Macmillan, London, 1967, p. 227.

54 Hughes-Hallett, *Jane Austen*, pp. 81–2.
55 Michael Branden, *The Georgian Gentleman*, Saxon House, Farnborough, 1973, p. 62.
56 Alison Adburgham, *Silver Fork Society: Fashionable Life and Literature 1814–48*, Constable, London, 1983, p. 138.
57 Curling, Wortley *Montagu*, pp. 19–20.
58 Tillyard, *Aristocrats*, p. 206.
59 *Ibid.*, pp. 202–3.
60 *Ibid.*, p. 204.
61 *Ibid.*, p. 196.
62 Stuart-Wortley, *Prime Minister and His Son*, p. 212.
63 L. W. Cowie, *Hanoverian England*, G. Bell and Sons, London, 1967, p. 35. The daughters of rich and noble families were usually brought up at home, but the boarding schools which became more common at the end of the eighteenth century taught arithmetic, literature, music, dancing and deportment. Women were discouraged, by education, from having learned pastimes.
64 Tillyard, *Aristocrats*, p. 203.
65 Germaine Greer, *The Obstacle Race*, Secker and Warburg, London, 1979, p. 286.
66 *Ibid.*, p. 283.
67 Wendy Wassyng Roworth (ed.), *Angelica Kauffman: A Continental Artist in Georgian England*, Reaktion Books, London, 1992, p. 60.
68 Sybil Rosenfeld, *Temples of Thespis: Some Private Theatres in England and Wales 1700–1820*, Society for Theatre Research, London, 1978, pp. 95–110 *passim*.
69 *Ibid.*, pp. 76–81.
70 *Ibid.*, pp. 16–32.
71 Paget Toynbee (ed.), *Reminiscences Written By Mr Horace Walpole in 1788 For the Amusement of Miss Mary and Miss Agnes Berry*, Clarendon Press, Oxford, 1924, p. 121.
72 Simon Houfe, 'Playing with Words', *Country Life*, CLXXXIII, 31 August 1989, pp. 86–8.
73 Toynbee, *Reminiscences of Walpole*, p. 90.
74 John Cornforth, 'Fit for a King', *Country Life*, CLXXXVI, 21 May, 1992, pp. 54–7.
75 Hughes-Hallett, *Jane Austen*, p. 31.
76 R. Brimley Johnson, *Mrs. Delaney at Court and Among Wits*, Stanley Paul and Co., London, 1925, p. 238.
77 David King, *The Complete Works of Robert and James Adam*, Butterworth, London, 1991, pp. 375–9.
78 Elizabeth Longford, *Byron*, Weidenfeld and Nicolson, London, 1976, p. 18.
79 Stuart-Wortley, *Prime Minister and His Son*, p. 217.
80 Connell, *Whig Peer*, p. 170.
81 Curling, *Wortley Montagu*, p. 53.
82 Ketton-Cremer, *Felbrigg*, p. 144.
83 M. Waterson, G. Jackson-Stops, *Erddig*, The National Trust, London, 1977, p. 35. See also Ivan Hall, 'Range of a Dilettante: William Constable and Burton Constable I', *Country Life*, CLXXI, 22 April 1982, pp. 1114–17. Constable collected specimens and had a mineral cabinet full of scientific instruments, an air pump and electrostatic machines.
84 Michael Foss, *The Age of Patronage: The Arts in Society*, Hamish Hamilton, London, 1971, pp. 122–30.
85 H. Diack Johnstone and R. Fiske (eds), *The Blackwell History of Music in the Eighteenth Century*, Basil Blackwell, Oxford, 1989, pp. 11 and 316–17. See also Robin Langley, 'The Music', in Tessa Murdoch (ed.), *Boughton House*, Faber and Faber, London, 1992, pp. 175–7.
86 Nicholas Temperley, *The Athlone History of Music in Britain: The Romantic Age 1800–1914*, The Athlone Press, London, 1981, pp. 118–19.
87 David Johnson, *Music and Society in Lowland Scotland in the Eighteenth Century*, Oxford University Press, Oxford, 1972, pp. 26–72 *passim*.

88 Adburgham, *Silver Fork Society*, p. 138.

89 J. A. R. Pimlott, *Recreations*, Studio Vista, London, 1968, pp. 22 and 33.

90 John W. Derry, *Charles James Fox*, B. T. Batsford, London, 1972, p. 126.

91 Connell, *Whig Peer*, p. 63.

92 Nicholas Penny (ed.), *Reynolds*, Royal Academy of Arts, London, 1986, p. 188.

93 Trevor Lummis and Jan Marsh, *The Woman's Domain: Women in the English Country House*, Viking, London, 1990, p. 68.

94 Hughes-Hallett, *Jane Austen*, p. 104.

95 Reed Browning, *The Duke of Newcastle*, Yale University Press, London, 1975, p. 42.

96 Albermarle, *Rockingham Memoirs*, p. 374.

97 Tillyard, *Aristocrats*, p. 203.

98 W. T. Whitley, *Artists and Their Friends in England*, 2 vols, Benjamin Bloom, London, 1968, I, pp. 77–8.

99 Elizabeth Einberg (ed.), *Manners and Morals: Hogarth and British Painting 1700–1760*, Tate Gallery, London, 1987, pp. 14–15.

100 Whitley, *Artists and Their Friends in England*, I, p. 73. Nuneham (later Earl Harcourt) was a practising artist, entering etchings in the Society of Arts exhibitions: see vol. II, p. 269. Nuneham attended the first Royal Academy dinner in 1770.

101 Joseph Friedman, *Spencer House: Chronicle of a Great London Mansion*, Zwemmer, London, 1993, p. 201.

102 Felicity Owen and David Blayney Brown, *Collector of Genius: A Life of Sir George Beaumont*, Yale University Press, London, 1980, pp. 217–19.

103 John Fleming, *Robert Adam and His Circle*, Harvard University Press, Cambridge, Massachusetts, 1962, p. 9.

104 John Harris, *Sir William Chambers*, Zwemmer, London, 1970, p. 42.

105 Browning, *Newcastle*, p. 201.

106 Stuart-Wortley, *Prime Minister and His Son*, p. 211.

107 *Ibid.*

108 *Ibid.*, p. 215.

109 Ketton-Cremer, *Felbrigg*, p. 132.

110 Virginia Surtees (ed.), *A Second Self: The Letters of Harriet Granville 1810–1845*, Michael Russell, Salisbury, 1990, p. 232.

111 *Ibid.*, p. 82.

112 Harris, *Robert Adam and Kedleston*, p. 7.

113 Lummis and Marsh, *Woman's Domain*, p. 77.

114 *Ibid.*, p. 102.

115 Brian Fothergill, *The Mitred Earl: An Eighteenth Century Eccentric*, Faber and Faber, London, 1974, p. 44.

116 Rosemary Joeckes, 'Capital Entertainment', *Country Life*, CLXXXI, 3 December 1987, pp. 146–9.

117 Tillyard, *Aristocrats*, p. 117.

118 *Wimpole Hall*, The National Trust Guide, London, 1984, p. 58.

119 Joan Johnson, *The Gloucestershire Gentry*, Alan Sutton, Gloucester, 1989, p. 186.

120 Fletcher, *Parkers at Saltram*, p. 166.

121 Sara Paston Williams, *The Art of Dining*, The National Trust, London, 1993, p. 204.

122 *Ibid.*, p. 241.

123 Elizabeth Burton, *The Georgians at Home*, Arrow Books, London, 1967, p. 200. The author quotes Thomas Love Peacock, *Headlong Hall*. In 1816 when the Rev. Dr Gaster and friends stopped for breakfast at a coaching inn, they were given 'not only the ordinary comforts of tea and toast, but . . . a delicious supply of new laid eggs and a magnificent round of beef'.

124 Paston Williams, *Dining*, p. 243.

125 Joeckes, 'Capital Entertainment'.

126 *Ibid.*

127 Paston Williams, *Dining*, p. 245.

128 Branden, *Georgian Gentlemen*, p. 62.

129 Paston Williams, *Dining*, p. 248.

130 *Ibid.*, p. 250.

131 *Ibid.*, p. 253.

132 Plumb, *The Making of a Statesman*, p. 87.

133 J. H. Plumb, *Sir Robert Walpole: The King's Minister*, Cresset Press, London, 1960, p. 90.

134 Cole, *Brummel*, p. 56.

135 Meade-Fetherstonhaugh, *Uppark*, p. 56.

136 *Ibid.*

137 Cole, *Brummel*, p. 52.

138 G. Jackson-Stops, *Petworth*, The National Trust, 1981, p. 45.

139 Louis Kroenberger, *The Extraordinary Mr Wilkes*, New English Library, London, 1974, p. 139.

140 Connell, *Whig Peer*, p. 408.

141 Jackson-Stops, *Petworth*, p. 44.

142 Lummis and Marsh, *Woman's Domain*, p. 77.

143 Paston Williams, *Dining*, p. 257.

144 Kroenberger, *Wilkes*, p. 222.

145 G. Bernard Hughes, 'The Lavishness of the Georgian Dessert', *Country Life*, CXLVI, 4 December 1969, pp. 1464–8.

146 *Ibid.*

147 Paston Williams, *Dining*, p. 262.

148 Peter Brown, *The Keeping of Christmas: England's Festive Tradition 1760–1840*, York Civic Trust, York, 1992, p. 6.

149 *Ibid.*

150 Peter Clark (ed.), *The Transformation of English Provincial Towns*, Hutchinson, London, 1985, p. 253.

151 *Ibid.*, p. 249.

152 Brown, *Keeping of Christmas*, p. 31.

153 Lummis and Marsh, *Woman's Domain*, p. 60.

154 Clive Wainwright, *The Romantic Interior*, Paul Mellon, London, 1989, pp. 21–5.

155 *Ibid.*

156 *Ibid.*, p. 19.

157 Longford, *Byron*, p. 18.

158 David Solkin, *The Landscape of Richard Wilson*, Tate Gallery, London, 1982, p. 130 and footnote 31, p. 141.

159 Joeckes, 'Capital Entertainment', p. 146.

160 Mary Corbett Harris, 'The Welsh in Festive Spirit', *Country Life*, CLVI, 5 December 1974, p. 1778.

161 Michael Reed, *The Georgian Triumph*, Paladin, London, 1984, p. 252.

162 Johnson, *Gloucestershire Gentry*, p. 189.

163 Stella Margetson, *Leisure and Pleasure in the Eighteenth Century*, Cassell, London, 1970, pp. 121–3.

164 Ketton-Cremer, *Felbrigg*, p. 144.

165 G. Jackson-Stops, *The Country House in Perspective*, Pavilion Books, London, 1990, p. 66.

166 Brown, *Keeping of Christmas*, p. 24.

167 *Ibid.*, p. 28.

168 *Ibid.*, p. 11.

169 *Ibid.*, p. 6.

170 Bea Howe, 'Queen Charlotte's Christmas Tree', *Country Life*, CL, 2 December 1971, p. 1521.

171 James Woodforde, *The Diary of a Country Parson 1758–1802*, ed. John Beresford, Oxford University Press, Oxford, 1987, p. 28.

172 *Ibid.*, p. 340.

173 *Ibid.*, p. 167.

174 *Ibid.*, p. 515.

175 *Ibid.*, p. 341.

176 J. E. B. Munson, 'Geoffrey Crayon Gent: His Christmas', *Country Life*, CLXXIV, 1 December 1983, pp. 1649–51.

177 *Ibid.*

178 Reginald Nettel, 'The Man Who Invented Father Christmas', *Country Life*, CLXVI, 29 November 1979, pp. 2056–8.

179 Stella Margetson, 'Going Home for Christmas', *Country Life*, CLX, 2 December 1976, pp. 1652–4.

180 Charles Lane, 'Too White a Christmas: The Snowstorm of 1836', *Country Life*, CLXVI, 29 November 1979, pp. 2053–5.

181 John Golby and William Purdue, 'The Goose is Getting Fat', *Country Life*, CLXXX, 4 December 1986, p. 1780.

Conclusion

The eighteenth-century British country house has been examined in different ways. The wealth which supported it has been investigated as has its architecture, landscape, domestic arrangements, pictures, furniture and entertainments. The period covered by this book, 1700 to 1830, is generally recognised as one in which many impressive country houses were built and filled with fine objects. Indeed many of the houses visited by the public, belonging to the National Trust, or appearing increasingly in televised Jane Austen, belong to these one hundred and thirty years. However, it is necessary to ask if this period was really a distinct one in the development of such houses.

Nationally these decades were important, for this was the age in which Great Britain became a nation. It was a time when not only Englishmen, but Scots, Welsh and Irish began to share a common visual culture, supported by wealth derived from commercial success and imperial expansion. The country house of any size was, clearly, an aspect of grand culture, which few could hope to share. Nevertheless, fashion, or luxury, whether they be in the form of Classical polish, Rococo charm or Gothic gloom, were increasingly available for consumption by a growing middle class.

At the beginning of this period the aristocracy gained immense political power. Great houses like Houghton, Woburn and Wentworth Woodhouse were the seats and meeting places of that power. The signing of the Treaty of Utrecht in 1713, the peaceful age of Robert Walpole, produced the right conditions for major developments in building.[1] A concern with architecture. collecting and patronage helped men like Lord Burlington to establish aesthetic dominance as well as political control.

Stylistically the Classicism of Palladio gave way to a more archaeologically inspired Neoclassicism, supported as it was by numerous scholarly works on the ruins of antiquities and by quantities of pattern books. Patrons, educated by the experience of the Grand Tour to enjoy the Antique could, by about 1760, relish the elaborate neoclassical intricacies of Adam's style, the popularity of which coincided with another period of peace and prosperity after the Treaty of Paris in 1763.

The American War of Independence, beginning in 1776, ended the building boom.[2] In part, at least, from economic necessity, a new taste for a less expensive, plainer, 'more chaste' style developed. The Louis XVI manner now established by Henry Holland and Greek Revival severity and solidity often turned the country house into an unadorned, manageable villa.

The Regency period, when enthusiasm for Greece was at its height, was also the time of increasing taste for Picturesque variety, in Gothic, cottage, or occasional oriental form. If the eighteenth century had witnessed the rise of the nobleman-architect, the early nineteenth century was the period of the rich aesthete-scholar, such as Uvedale Price, William Beckford, Payne Knight, Charles Monck and Thomas Hope. Their sensibility led them to publish books about taste, architecture and landscape. Their houses were illustrated in lavish folios for like-minded gentlemen to admire.[3]

By the 1830s, however, both society and therefore the country houses were beginning to change. The Great Reform Bill of 1832 swept away the rotten borough associated with aristocratic power in the previous century and established a wider franchise. A further victory for the middle classes, clearly beyond the scope of this book, may be seen in the repeal of the Corn Laws in 1846.[4] The great house with rooms of state had begun to seem inappropriate even at the end of the eighteenth century.[5] Within a few years the Neoclassical style itself, was criticised for its coldness and austerity. In 1833 John Claudius Loudon attacked the 'Greek style' and included in his criticisms classical architecture from Inigo Jones to the nineteenth century.[6]

Country houses became more private,[7] their owners less concerned with displaying the trophies and symbols of a gentlemanly international Neoclassicism. The substantial Gothic or Elizabethan style and a pride in an imagined Old England,[8] replaced taste and sensibility. The antiquarians with their love of English medieval history began to outnumber the virtuosi and connoisseurs who had collected Roman statues and Claudian *cappricios*.[9]

NOTES

1 Giles Worsley, *Classical Architecture in Britain: The Heroic Age*, Yale University Press, London, 1995, p. 85.

2 *Ibid.*, p. 289.

3 Mark Girouard, *The Victorian Country House*, Yale University Press, London, 1990, p. 15. The author lists lavish monographs on Sezincote (1818), Fonthill (1823), Ashridge (1823), Eaton Hall (1826) and Deepdene (1826) amongst others.

4 Roger Dixon and Stefan Muthesius, *Victorian Architecture*, Thames and Hudson, London, 1978, p. 8.

5 John Cornforth, *English Interiors 1790–1848: The Quest for Comfort*, Barrie and Jenkins, London, 1978, p. 14.

6 Girouard, *Victorian Country House*, p. 52.

7 *Ibid.*, p. 16.

8 R. W. Symonds and B. B. Whineray, *Victorian Furniture*, Studio Editions, London, 1987, p. 20. Books such as Joseph Nash's *Mansions of England in the Olden Time* (first vol. 1838) led many people to an interest in a picturesque past.

9 Clive Wainwright, *The Romantic Interior*, Paul Mellon, London, 1989, p. 5.

Select bibliography

BOOKS

Abbott, Mary, *Family Ties: English Families 1540–1920*, Routledge, London, 1993

Adburgham, Alison, *Silver Fork Society: Fashionable Life and Literature 1814–48*, Constable, London, 1983

Agius, Pauline, *Ackermann's Regency Furniture and Designs*, The Crowood Press, Marlborough, 1984

Albermarle, Earl of, *Memoirs of the Marquis of Rockingham and His Contemporaries*, 2 vols, Richard Bentley, London, 1852

Allen, David, *Cricket: An Illustrated History*, Phaidon, Oxford, 1990

Amussen, Susan Dwyer, *An Ordered Society: Gender and Class in Early Modern England*, Columbia University Press, Oxford, 1988

Anon, *Memoirs of the Life, Family and Characters of Charles Seymour, Duke of Somerset*, n.d.

Armitage, John, *Man at Play: Nine Centuries of Pleasure Making*, Frederick Warne, London, 1977

Arnold, Dana (ed.), *The Georgian Villa*, Allan Sutton, Stroud, 1996

Ayling, Stanley, *The Elder Pitt*, Collins, London, 1976

Ayling, Stanley, *Fox: The Life of Charles James Fox*, John Murray, London, 1991

Barker, Hannah and Chalus, Elaine, *Gender in Eighteenth Century England*, Longmans, London, 1997

Barker Benfield, G. J., *The Culture of Sensibility*, University of Chicago Press, London, 1992

Barnard, Toby and Clark, Jane (eds), *Lord Burlington: Architecture, Art and Life*, The Hambledon Press, London, 1995

Barrell, John, *The Political Theory of Painting from Reynolds to Hazlitt*, Yale University Press, London, 1986

Bayne-Powell, Rosamund, *The English Child in the Eighteenth Century*, John Murray, London, 1939

Beard, Geoffrey, *Decorative Plasterwork*, Phaidon, London, 1975

Beard, Geoffrey, *Craftsmen and Interior Decoration in England 1660–1820*, Bloomsbury Books, London, 1981

Beard, Geoffrey, *Upholsterers and Interior Furnishing in England 1530–1840*, Yale University Press, London, 1997

Bearstall, T. W., *A North Country Estate*, Phillimore, London, 1975

Becket, J. V., *The Aristocracy in England 1660–1914*, Basil Blackwell Ltd, Oxford, 1986

Bence-Jones, Mark, *Clive of India*, Constable, London, 1974

Bettye, J. H., *Estates and the English Countryside*, B. T. Batsford Ltd, London, 1993

Biddulph, Violet, *The Three Ladies Waldegrave*, Peter Davies, London, 1938

Binney, Marcus, *Sir Robert Taylor*, George Allen and Unwin, London, 1984

Blackett-Ord, Mark, *Hell Fire Duke*, Kensal Press, Windsor, 1982

Blunt, Reginald, *Mrs Montague 'Queen of the Blues'*, 2 vols, Constable, London, 1923

Boyce, Benjamin, *The Benevolent Man: A Life of Ralph Allen of Bath*, Harvard University Press, Cambridge, Massachusetts, 1967

Boynton, Lindsay (ed.), *Gillow Furniture Designs 1760–1800*, The Bloomfield Press, Royston, 1995

Braham, Alan, *The Architecture of the French Enlightenment*, Thames and Hudson, London, 1980

Branden, Michael, *The Georgian Gentleman*, Saxon House, Farnborough, 1973

Brauer, George, *The Education of a Gentleman: Theories of Gentlemanly Education 1660–1775*, Bookman Associates, New York, 1959

de Breffny, Brian and Ffolliott, Rosemary, *The Houses of Ireland*, Thames and Hudson, London, 1975

Brennan, Gerald, *A History of the House of Percy*, 2 vols, Fremantle and Co., London, 1902

Brewer, John, *The Pleasures of the Imagination: English Culture in the Eighteenth Century*, HarperCollins, London, 1997

Brewer, John and Porter, Roy (eds), *Consumption and The World of Goods*, Routledge, London, 1994

Brimley Johnson, R., *Mrs Delaney at Court and Among Wits*, Stanley Paul and Co., London, 1925

Bristow, Ian, *Architectural Colour in British Interiors 1615–1840*, Yale University Press, London, 1996

Brockman, H. A. N., *The Caliph of Fonthill*, Werner Laurie, London, 1956

Brown, Peter, *The Keeping of Christmas: England's Festive Tradition 1760–1840*, Civic Trust, York, 1992

Browning, Reed, *The Duke of Newcastle*, Yale University Press, London, 1975

Bryant, Arthur, *The Age of Elegance 1812–22*, The Reprint Society, London, 1954

Bryant, Julius, *Finest Prospects, Three Historic Houses: A Study in London Topography*, English Heritage Exhibition Catalogue, 1986

Burton, Elizabeth, *The Georgians at Home*, Arrow Books, London, 1967

Butler, E. M. (ed.), *The Letters of Prince Pucklow-Muskau*, Collins, London, 1957

Buxbaum, Tim, *Scottish Garden Building: From Food to Folly*, Mainstream Publishing Ltd, Edinburgh, 1989

Calder-Marshall, Arthur, *The Two Duchesses*, Hutchinson, London, 1978

Cannon, John, *Aristocratic Century*, Cambridge University Press, Cambridge, 1984

Carruthers, Annette (ed.), *The Scottish Home*, National Museum of Scotland, Edinburgh, 1996

Carswell, John, *The South Sea Bubble*, Cressett Press, London, 1960

Chalkin, C. W. and Wordie, J. R., *Town and Countryside: The English Landowner in the National Economy 1660–1860*, Unwin Hyman, London, 1989

Chambers, Douglas D. C., *The Planters of the English Landscape Garden: Botany, Trees and the Georgics*, Yale University Press, New Haven and London, 1993

Chambers, J. D. and Mingay, G. E., *The Agricultural Revolution 1750–1880*, B. T. Batsford Ltd, London, 1984

Cherry, Bridget and Pevsner, Nikolaus, *The Buildings of England: Devon*, Penguin Books, London, 1989

Clark, Anthony M., *Pompeo Batoni: Complete Catalogue*, Phaidon, Oxford, 1985

Clark, Peter (ed.), *The Transformation of English Provincial Towns*, Hutchinson, London, 1985

Cole, Hubert, *Beau Brummell*, Mason Charter, New York, 1973

Collard, Frances, *Regency Furniture*, Antique Collectors Club, Woodbridge, 1985

Colley, Linda, *Britons: Forging the Nation 1707–1837*, Vintage, London, 1994

Collins Baker, C. H. and Baker, Muriel, *The Life and Circumstances of James Brydges, First Duke of Chandos*, Clarendon Press, Oxford, 1949

Colvin, Howard, *A Biographical Dictionary of Architects*, John Murray, London, 1954

Colvin, Howard (ed.), *The Country Seat: Studies in the History of the British Country House*, Allen Lane, The Penguin Press, London, 1970

Connell, Brian, *Portrait of a Whig Peer*, André Deutsch, London, 1957

Coombs, David, *Sport and the Countryside*, Phaidon, Oxford, 1978

Cornforth, John, *English Interiors 1790–1848: The Quest for Comfort*, Barrie and Jenkins, London, 1978

Cornforth, John, *The Inspiration of the Past: Country House Taste in the Twentieth Century*, Viking, Harmondsworth, 1985

Cornforth, John, *The Search for a Style*, André Deutsch, London, 1988

Cowie, L. W., *Hanoverian England*, G. Bell and Sons, London, 1967

Croft-Murray, Edward, *Decorative Painting in England*, Country Life, London, 1971

Crook, J. M., *The Greek Revival*, John Murray, London, 1972

Curling, Jonathan, *Edward Wortley Montagu 1713–1776*, Andrew Melrose, London, 1954

Daiches, David, *The Paradox of Scottish Culture: The Eighteenth Century Experience*, Oxford University Press, London, 1964

Davidoff, Leonore and Hall, Catherine, *Family Fortunes: Men and Women of the English Middle Class 1780–1850*, Hutchinson, London, 1987

Davies, John, *A History of Wales*, Penguin, Harmondsworth, 1994

Davis, Terence, *John Nash*, David and Charles, Newton Abbot, 1973

Defoe, Daniel, *The Complete English Gentleman* (introduction by Karl Bulbring), David Nutt, London, 1890

Derry, John W., *William Pitt*, Batsford, London, 1962

Derry, John W., *Charles James Fox*, Batsford, London, 1972

Deuchar, Stephen, *Sporting Art in Eighteenth Century England: A Social and Political History*, Yale University Press, London, 1988

Dickinson, Frances, *The Reluctant Rebel: A Northumbrian Legacy of Jacobite Times*, Cressett Books, Newcastle, 1996

Dixon Hunt, John, *William Kent, Landscape Garden Designer: An Assessment and Catalogue of his Designs*, A. Zwemmer Ltd, London and New York, 1987

Dixon Hunt, John, *The Figure in the Landscape: Poetry, Painting and Gardening during the Eighteenth Century*, The Johns Hopkins University Press, Baltimore and London, 1976 (hardback), 1989 (paperback)

Dixon Hunt, John and Willis, Peter (eds), *The Genius of the Place: The English Landscape Garden 1620–1820*, Paul Elek, London, 1975

Doubleday, W. H. and de Walden, Lord Howard, *The Complete Peerage*, 13 vols, St Catherine's Press, London, 1936

Downes, Kerry, *Vanbrugh*, Zwemmer, London, 1977

Dunbar, John Telfer, *The Costume of Scotland*, B. T. Batsford, London, 1989

Edgeworth, Maria, *Essays on Practical Education*, 2 vols, J. Johnson and Co., London, 1811

Edwards, Clive, *Eighteenth Century Furniture*, Manchester University Press, Manchester, 1996

Edwards, Michael, *Warren Hastings: King of the Nabobs*, Hart Davis, MacGibbon, London, 1976

Edwards, Ralph, *Hepplewhite Furniture Designs*, A. Tiranti, London, 1955

Edwards, Ralph and Ramsay, L. C. G., *The Connoisseur Period Guides: Regency Period*, The Connoisseur, London, 1958

Egerton, Judy, *George Stubbs: 1724–1806*, Tate Gallery, London, 1984

Egerton, Judy, and Snelgrove, Dudley, *British Sporting and Animal Drawings 1500–1850: The Paul Mellon Collection*, Tate Galley for the Yale Center for British Art, London and New Haven, 1978

Ehrman, John, *The Younger Pitt: The Years of Acclaim*, Constable, London, 1969

Einberg, Elizabeth (ed.), *Manners and Morals: Hogarth and British Painting 1700–1760*, Tate Gallery, London, 1987

Elwyn Jones, Gareth, *Modern Wales: A Concise History*, Cambridge University Press, Cambridge, 1995

Evans, E. D., *A History of Wales: 1660–1815*, University of Wales Press, Cardiff, 1993

Everett, Nigel, *The Tory View of the Landscape*, Yale University Press, New Haven and London, 1994

Falk, Bernard, *The Berkeleys of Berkeley Square*, Hutchinson and Co., London, 1944

Figueiredo, Peter de and Treuherz, Julian, *Cheshire Country Houses*, Phillimore, Chichester, 1988

Fleming, John, *Robert Adam and His Circle*, Harvard University Press, Cambridge, Massachusetts, 1962

Fleming, Lawrence and Gore, Alan, *The English Garden*, Michael Joseph Ltd, London, 1979

Fletcher, Ronald, *The Parkers at Saltram 1769–1784*, BBC Publications, London, 1970

Floud, Roderick and McCloskey, Donald (eds), *An Economic History of Britain Since 1700*, Cambridge University Press, Cambridge, 1994

Ford, Boris (ed.), *The Cambridge Guide to the Arts in Britain: The Augustan Age*, Cambridge University Press, Cambridge, 1991

Forman, Sheila, *Scottish Country Houses and Castles*, Collins, London, 1967

Foss, Michael, *The Age of Patronage: The Arts in Society*, Hamish Hamilton, London, 1971

Foster, R. F., *Oxford History of Ireland: Ascendancy and Union*, Oxford University Press, Oxford, 1989

Fothergill, Brian, *The Mitred Earl: An Eighteenth Century Eccentric*, Faber and Faber, London, 1974

Fowler, John and Cornforth, John, *English Decoration in the Eighteenth Century*, Barrie and Jenkins, London, 1974

Friedman, Joseph, *Spencer House: Chronicle of a Great London Mansion*, Zwemmer, London, 1993

Friedman, Terry, *James Gibbs*, Yale University Press, London, 1984

Fry, Michael, *The Dundas Despotism*, Edinburgh University Press, Edinburgh, 1992

Fulford, Roger, *Samuel Whitbread 1769–1815: A Study in Opposition*, Macmillan, London, 1967

Gérin, Winifred, *Horatio Nelson*, Clarendon Press, Oxford, 1970

Gerzina, Gretchen, *Black England: Life Before Emancipation*, John Murray, London, 1995

Gifford, John, *William Adam*, Mainstream Publishing, Edinburgh, 1989

Gilbert, Christopher, *The Life and Work of Thomas Chippendale*, 2 vols, Studio Vista/Christie's, London, 1978

Gilbert, Christopher, *English Vernacular Furniture 1750–1900*, Yale University Press, London, 1991

Gilbert, Christopher and Murdoch, Tessa, *John Channon and Brass Inlaid Furniture 1730–1760*, Yale University Press, London, 1993

Gilbert, Christopher and Wells-Cole, Anthony, *The Fashionable Fireplace*, Leeds City Art Galleries, Leeds, 1985

Girling, Richard, *The Making of the English Garden*, Macmillan, London, 1988

Girouard Mark, *Life in the English Country House*, Yale University Press, New Haven and London, 1978

Glin, The Knight of, Griffin, David and Robinson, Nicholas, *Vanishing Country Houses of Ireland*, The Irish Architectural Archive and The Irish Georgian Society, Dublin, 1988

Goodwin, Albert. (ed.), *The European Nobility in the Eighteenth Century*, Harper torchbooks, London, 1967

Gore, John (ed.), *Creevey's Life and Times*, John Murray, London, 1934

Gow, Ian, *The Scottish Interior: Georgian and Victorian Decor*, Edinburgh University Press, Edinburgh, 1992

Gow, Ian, and Rowan, Alistair, *Scottish Country Houses 1600–1914*, Edinburgh University Press, Edinburgh, 1995

Green, David, *Sarah, Duchess of Marlborough*, Collins, London, 1967

Greer, Germaine, *The Obstacle Race*, Secker and Warburg, London, 1979

Greig, James (ed.), *The Diaries of a Duchess: Extracts from the Diaries of the First Duchess of Northumberland 1716–1776*, Hodder and Stoughton, London, 1926

Harbison, Peter, Potterton, Homan and Sheehy, Jeanne, *Irish Art and Architecture from Prehistory to the Present*, Thames and Hudson, London, 1978

Hardyment, Christina, *Behind the Scenes: Domestic Arrangements in Historic Houses*, The National Trust, London, 1997

Harris, Eileen, *The Furniture of Robert Adam*, Academy Editions, London, 1973

Harris, Eileen and Savage, Nicholas, *British Architectural Books and Writers 1556–1785*, Cambridge University Press, Cambridge, 1990

Harris, John, *Sir William Chambers*, Zwemmer, London, 1970

Harris, John, *Headford House and Robert Adam*, RIBA, London, 1973

Harris, John, *The Palladians*, Trefoil Books, London, 1981

Harris, John, *The Design of the English Country House 1620–1920*, Trefoil Books, London, 1985

Harris, John, *The Palladian Revival: Lord Burlington, His Villa and Gardens at Chiswick*, Yale University Press, London, 1994

Harris, John, *No Voice from the Hall*, John Murray, London, 1998

Harris, Leslie, *Robert Adam and Kedleston: The Making of a Neoclassical Masterpiece*, The National Trust, London, 1987

Haskell, Francis and Penny, Nicholas, *Taste and the Antique*, Yale University Press, London, 1983

Haslam, Richard, *The Buildings of Wales: Powys*, Penguin/University of Wales Press, Harmondsworth, 1979

Hayes, John, *Thomas Gainsborough*, Tate Gallery, London, 1980

Hayes, John and Cross, Michael, *Polite Society: Portraits of the English Country Gentleman and His Family by Arthur Devis*, Harris Museum and Art Gallery, Preston, 1983

Hayward, Helena and Kirkham, Patricia, *William and John Linnell*, 2 vols, Studio Vista/Christie's, London, 1980

Hepplewhite, George, *The Cabinet Maker and Upholsterers Guide*, Harewood, 1794

Herrmann, Frank, *The English as Collectors*, Chatto and Windus, London, 1972

Hill, Bridget, *Women, Work and Sexual Politics in Eighteenth Century England*, UCL Press, London, 1994

Hill, Bridget, *Servants: English Domestics in the Eighteenth Century*, Clarendon Press, Oxford, 1996

Hill, David, *Harewood Masterpieces*, Harewood Estate Office, Harewood, 1995

Hind, Charles (ed.), *New Light on English Palladianism*, The Georgian Group, London, 1988

Hook, Judith, *The Baroque Age in England*, Thames and Hudson, London, 1976

Hubbard, Edward, *The Buildings of Wales: Clwyd*, Penguin, Harmondsworth, 1986

Hughes-Hallett, Penelope, *Jane Austen: 'My Dear Cassandra'*, Collins and Brown, London, 1990

Hunter, James, *The Making of the Crofting Community*, John Donald Publishers Ltd, Edinburgh, 1982

Hussey, Christopher, *English Gardens and Landscapes 1700–1750*, Country Life Ltd, London, 1967

Hussey, Christopher, *English Country Houses: Early Georgian 1715–1760*, Antique Collectors Club, London, 1986

Hussey, Christopher, *English Country Houses: Mid-Georgian 1760–1800*, Antique Collectors Club, London, 1986

Hussey, Christopher, *English Country Houses: Late Georgian*, Antique Collectors Club, London, 1986

Hutton, W. H., *The Marquess Wellesley KG*, Clarendon Press, Oxford, 1893

Hyams, Edward, *Capability Brown and Humphry Repton*, J. M. Dent Ltd, London, 1971

Itzkowitz, David, *Peculiar Privilege: A Social History of English Fox-hunting 1753–1885*, Hassocks, Sussex, 1977

Jackson-Stops, Gervase (ed.), *The Fashioning and Functioning of the British Country House*, National Gallery of Art, Washington, 1989

Jackson-Stops, Gervase, *The Country House in Perspective*, Pavilion Books, London, 1990

Jackson-Stops, Gervase, *An English Arcadia 1600–1990*, The National Trust, London, 1992

Jackson-Stops, Gervase and Pipkin, James, *The English Country House: A Grand Tour*, Weidenfeld and Nicolson, London, 1984

Jackson-Stops, Gervase, and Pipkin, James, *The Country House Garden: A Grand Tour*, National Trust, published by Pavilion Books Ltd, London, 1987 (hardback), 1995 (paperback)

Jacques, David, *Georgian Gardens: The Reign of Nature*, Batsford Ltd, London, 1983

Jenkins, Frank, *Architect and Patron*, Oxford University Press, London, 1961

Jewitt, Llewellyn, *The Wedgwoods*, Virtue Bros, London, 1865

Johnson, David, *Music and Society in Lowland Scotland in the Eighteenth Century*, Oxford University Press, Oxford, 1972

Johnson, Edith, *Ireland in the Eighteenth Century*, Gill and Macmillan, Dublin, 1974

Johnson, Joan, *The Gloucestershire Gentry*, Alan Sutton, Gloucester, 1989

Johnstone, Diack, H. and Fiske, R. (eds), *The Blackwell History of Music in the Eighteenth Century*, Basil Blackwell, Oxford, 1989

Jones, J. R., *Marlborough*, Cambridge University Press, Cambridge, 1993

Jones, Vivien (ed.), *Women in the Eighteenth Century*, Routledge, London, 1994

Joy, Edward, *English Furniture 1800–1851*, Sotheby Park Bernet, London, 1977

Kelch, Ray, *Newcastle: A Duke Without Money*, Routledge and Kegan Paul, London, 1974

Kerr, John, *Elizabeth Fry*, B. T. Batsford, London, 1962

Ketton-Cremer, R. W., *Felbrigg: The Story of a House*, Boydell Press, London, 1976

King, David, *The Complete Works of Robert and James Adam*, Butterworth, London, 1991

Knight, Derrick, *Gentlemen of Fortune*, Frederick Miller Ltd, London, 1978

Knyff and Kip, *Britannia Illustrata*, ed. John Harris and Gervase Jackson-Stops for the National Trust, Paradigm Press, Bungay, Suffolk, 1984

Kronenberger, Louis, *The Extraordinary Mr Wilkes*, New English Library, London, 1974

Ladd, Frederick, *Architects at Corsham Court: A Study in Revival Style Architecture and Landscaping 1749–1849*, Moonraker Press, Bradford-on-Avon, 1978

Langford, Paul, *A Polite and Commercial People: England 1723–1783*, Oxford University Press, Oxford, 1990

Larmon, Paul, *Belfast: An Illustrated Architectural Guide*, Friar's Bush Press, Belfast, 1987

Lasdun, Susan, *The English Park: Royal, Private and Public*, André Deutsch Ltd, London, 1991

Leach, Peter, *James Paine*, Zwemmer, London, 1988

Lees-Milne, James, *English Country Houses: Baroque*, Country Life, London, 1970

Lees-Milne, James, *The Country House*, Oxford University Press, Oxford, 1982

Lees-Milne, James, *Earls of Creation*, Century Hutchinson, London, 1986

Lenman, Bruce, *Integration and Enlightenment: Scotland 1746–1832*, Edinburgh University Press, Edinburgh, 1981

Lever, Jill, *Architects' Designs for Furniture*, Trefoil Books, London, 1982

Lewis, W. S. (ed.), *The Yale Edition of Horace Walpole's Correspondence*, Oxford University Press, London, 1965

Lindsay, Ian and Cosh, Mary, *Inveraray and the Dukes of Argyll*, Edinburgh University Press, Edinburgh, 1973

Links, J. G., *Canaletto and His Patrons*, New York University Press, New York, 1977

Longford, Elizabeth, *Wellington: Pillar of State*, Weidenfeld and Nicolson, London, 1972

Longford, Elizabeth, *Byron*, Weidenfeld and Nicholson, London, 1976

Longrigg, Roger, *The History of Fox-hunting*, Macmillan, London, 1975

Lubbock, Jules, *The Tyranny of Taste: The Politics of Architecture and Design in Britain 1550–1960*, Yale University Press, London, 1995

Lugar, Robert, *The Country Gentleman's Architect*, J. Taylor Architectural Library, London, 1815

Lummis, Trevor and Morris, Jan, *The Woman's Domain: Women and the English Country House*, Viking, London, 1990

Macaulay, James, *The Gothic Revival 1745–1845*, Blackie, London, 1975

Macaulay, James, *The Classical Country House in Scotland 1600–1800*, Faber and Faber, London, 1987

Macmillan, Duncan, *Painting in Scotland: The Golden Age*, Phaidon, Oxford, 1986

McParland, E., Rowan, A. and Rowan, A. M. (eds), *The Architecture of Richard Morrison and William Vitruvius Morrison*, Irish Architectural Archive, Dublin, 1989

McWilliam, Colin, *The Buildings of Scotland: Lothian*, Penguin, Harmondsworth, 1978

Maguire, W. A., *Living Like a Lord: The Second Marquis of Donegal*, Appletree Press, 1984

Malet, Hugh, *The Canal Duke*, Phoenix House, London, 1961

Malins, Edward, *English Landscaping and Literature 1660–1840*, Oxford University Press, Oxford, New York and Toronto, 1966

Malins, Edward and Glin, the Knight of, *Lost Desmesnes: Irish Landscape Gardening 1660–1845*, Barrie and Jenkins Ltd, London, 1976

Mandler, Peter, *The Fall and Rise of the Stately Home*, Yale University Press, London, 1997

Margetson, Stella, *Leisure and Pleasure in the Eighteenth Century*, Cassell, London, 1970

Marshall, Rosalind (ed.), *Dynasty: The Royal House of Stewart*, National Galleries of Scotland, Edinburgh, 1990

Mauchline, Mary, *Harewood House*, David and Charles, London, 1974

Mavor, Elizabeth, *The Grand Tour of William Beckford*, Penguin, Harmondsworth, 1986

Meade-Fetherstonhaugh, Margaret and Warner, Oliver, *Uppark and Its People*, Century, London, 1988

Mingay, G. E., *Enclosure and the Small Farmer in the Age of the Industrial Revolution*, Macmillan Press Ltd, London, 1979

Mingay, G. E., *A Social History of the English Counryside*, Routledge, London, 1992

Mitchison, Rosalind, *Lordship to Patronage: Scotland 1603–1745*, Edinburgh University Press, Edinburgh, 1983

Montgomery-Massingberd, Hugh, *Great Houses of Scotland*, Lawrence King, London, 1997

Moore, Andrew, *Norfolk and the Grand Tour*, Norfolk Museums Service, Norwich, 1985

Moore, Andrew (ed.), *Houghton Hall: The Prime Minister, the Empress and the Heritage*, Philip Wilson, London, 1996

Morgan, Kenneth, *Bristol and the Atlantic Trade in the Eighteenth Century*, Cambridge University Press, Cambridge, 1993

Morris, Christopher (ed.), *The Illustrated Journeys of Celia Fiennes 1685–1712*, Macdonald and Co., London, 1982

Morris, Richard and Howard, Ken, *The Buildings of Bath*, Alan Sutton, Stroud, 1993

Mowl, Tim and Earnshaw, Brian, *Trumpet at a Distant Gate: the Lodge as Prelude to the Country House*, Waterstone, London, 1985

Mowl, Tim and Earnshaw, Brian, *John Wood: Architect of Obsession*, Millstream Books, Bath, 1988

Naish, George (ed.), *Nelson's Letters to His Wife and Other Documents*, Navy Records Society, London, 1958

O'Brien, Jacqueline and Guinness, Desmond, *Great Irish Houses and Castles*, Weidenfeld and Nicholson, London, 1992

Oresko, Robert (ed.), *The Works in Architecture of Robert and James Adam*, Academy Editions, London, 1975

Orme's Graphic History of the Life, Exploits and Death of Horatio Nelson, Orme, London, n.d.

Owen, Felicity and Blayney-Brown, David, *Collector of Genius: A Life of Sir George Beaumont*, Yale University Press, London, 1980

Pares, Richard, *A West Indies Fortune*, Longmans, London, 1950

Parry, J. H., *A Short History of the West Indies*, Macmillan Education, London, 1987

Paston Williams, Sarah, *The Art of Dining*, The National Trust, London, 1993

Penny, Nicholas (ed.), *Reynolds*, Royal Academy of Art, London, 1986

Perry, Gill and Rossington, Michael (eds), *Femininity and Masculinity in Eighteenth-Century Art and Culture*, Manchester University Press, Manchester, 1994

Pevsner, Nikolaus, *The Buildings of England: Shropshire*, Penguin, Harmondsworth, 1974

Pevsner, Nikolaus, and Harris, John, *The Buildings of England: Lincolnshire*, Penguin, London, 1989

Pevsner, Nikolaus and Radcliffe, Enid, *The Buildings of England: Yorkshire and the West Riding*, Penguin, Harmondsworth, 1974

Pevsner, Nikolaus and Verey, David, *The Buildings of England: Gloucestershire*, Penguin, Harmondsworth, 1978

Phillipson, N. T. and Mitchison, Rosalind (eds), *Scotland in the Age of Improvement*, Edinburgh University Press, Edinburgh, 1970

Pimlott, J. A. R., *Recreations*, Studio Vista, London, 1968

Plumb, J. H., *Sir Robert Walpole: The King's Minister*, Cresset Press, London, 1956

Plumb, J. H., *Sir Robert Walpole: The Making of a Statesman*, Cresset Press, London, 1956

Plumb, J. H., *Georgian Delights: The Pursuit of Happiness*, Weidenfeld and Nicholson, London, 1980

Pointon, Marcia, *Hanging the Head*, Yale University Press, London, 1993

Pointon, Marcia, *Strategies for Showing: Women, Possession and Representation in English Culture 1665–1800*, Oxford University Press, Oxford, 1997

Porter, Roy, *Coke of Norfolk: A Financial and Agricultural Study*, Clarendon Press, Oxford, 1975

Porter, Roy, *English Society in the Eighteenth Century*, Penguin, London, 1990

Porter, Roy and Roberts, Marie M. (eds), *Pleasure in the Eighteenth Century*, Macmillan, London, 1996

Quennell, Peter (ed.), *The Private Letters of Princess Lieven to Prince Metternich 1820–1826*, John Murray, London, 1937

Redford, Bruce, *Venice and the Grand Canal*, Yale University Press, London, 1996

Reed, Michael, *The Georgian Triumph*, Paladin Books, London, 1984

Reid, Loren, *Charles James Fox: A Man for the People*, Longmans, London, 1969

Richardson, George, *New Vitruvius Brittanicus*, 2 vols, J. Taylor, London, 1802–8, 1808–10

Riddell, Richard, 'The Palladian Portico', in Charles Hind (ed.), *New Light on English Palladianism*, The Georgian Group, London, 1988

Robinson, John Martin, *The Wyatts: An Architectural Dynasty*, Oxford University Press, Oxford, 1979

Robinson, John Martin, *The Dukes of Norfolk*, Oxford University Press, Oxford, 1982

Robinson, John Martin, *Georgian Model Farms: A Study of Decorative and Model Farm Buildings in the Age of Improvement 1700–1846*, Oxford University Press, Oxford and New York, 1983

Robinson, John Martin, *The English Country Estate*, Century/National Trust, London, 1988

Robinson, John Martin, *Temples of Delight: Stowe Landscape Gardens*, George Philip Ltd (for The National Trust), London, 1990

Robinson, John Martin, *A Guide to the Country Houses of the North West*, Constable, London, 1991

Rococo Art and Design in Hogarth's England, Victoria and Albert Museum, London, 1984

Rogers, Katherine, *Feminism in Eighteenth Century England*, Harvester Press, Brighton, 1982

Rosenfeld, Sybil, *Temples of Thespis: Some Private Theatres in England and Wales 1700–1820*, Society for Theatre Research, London, 1978

Rowan, Alistair, *Designs for Castles and Country Villas by Robert and James Adam*, Phaidon, Oxford, 1985

Roworth, Wendy Wassyng (ed.), *Angelica Kauffmann: A Continental Artist in Georgian England*, Reaktion Books, London, 1992

Rule, John, *The Vital Century: England's Developing Economy 1714–1815*, Longmans, London, 1992

Rykwert, Joseph and Anne, *The Brothers Adam*, Collins, London, 1985

Sanderson, Margaret, *Robert Adam and Scotland*, HMSO, Edinburgh, 1992

Saumarez Smith, Charles, *The Building of Castle Howard*, Faber and Faber, London, 1990

Saumarez Smith, Charles, *Eighteenth-Century Decoration, Design and the Domestic Interior in England*, Weidenfeld and Nicolson, London, 1993

Schweizer, Karl and Osborne, John, *Cobbett in His Times*, Leicester University Press, Leicester, 1990

Sekora, John, *Luxury: The Concept in Western Thought: Eden to Smollett*, The Johns Hopkins University Press, London, 1977

Shawe-Taylor, Desmond, *The Georgians: Eighteenth Century Portraiture and Society*, Barrie and Jenkins, London, 1990

Sheraton, Thomas, *The Cabinet Maker and Upholsterers Drawing Book*, introduction by Joseph Aronson, Dover Reprints, New York, 1972

Sheridan, Richard Brinsley, *The Rivals* (1775), ed. Elizabeth Duthie, A. and C. Black, London, 1914

Sidgwick, Frank, *The Complete Marjory Fleming*, Sidgwick and Jackson, London, 1934

Simon, Jacob, *The Art of the Picture Frame*, National Portait Gallery, London, 1997

Smart, Alastair, *Allan Ramsay 1713–1784*, Scottish National Portrait Gallery, Edinburgh, 1992

Smiles, Samuel, *Josiah Wedgwood: His Personal History*, Plutarch Press, Ann Arbor, 1971

Smith, Adam, *The Wealth of Nations*, introduction by Andrew Skinner, Penguin, Harmondsworth, 1978; 1st pub. 1776

Solkin, David, *The Landscape of Richard Wilson*, Tate Gallery, London, 1982

Somerville-Large, Peter, *The Irish Country House: A Social History*, Sinclair Stevenson, London, 1995

Spencer, Alfred (ed.), *Memoirs of William Hickey*, 4 vols, Hurst and Blackett, London, 1913

Stewart, J. D., *Sir Godfrey Kneller*, G. Bell and Sons, London, 1971

Stillman, Damie, *The Decorative Work of Robert Adam*, Academy Editions, London, 1973

Stirling, A. M. W., *Coke of Norfolk and His Friends*, The Bodley Head, London, 1908

Stone, Lawrence, *The Family, Sex and Marriage in England 1500–1800*, Weidenfeld and Nicolson, London, 1977

Strong, Roy, *And When Did You Last See Your Father? The Victorian Painter and British History*, Thames and Hudson, London, 1978

Strong, Roy, Binney, Marcus and Harris, John, *The Destruction of the Country House 1875–1975*, Thames and Hudson, London, 1974

Stroud, Dorothy, *Henry Holland*, Country Life, London, 1966

Stroud, Dorothy, *Capability Brown*, Faber and Faber, London, 1975

Stuart-Wortley, E., *A Prime Minster and His Son: From the Correspondence of the Third Earl of Bute and Lt. General the Hon. Sir Charles Stuart*, John Murray, London, 1925

Stutchbury, Howard, *The Architecture of Colen Campbell*, Manchester University Press, Manchester, 1967

Summerson, John, *Architecture in Britain 1530–1830*, Penguin, Harmondsworth, 1977

Summerson, John, *The Classical Country House in Eighteenth Century England*, Thames and Hudson, London, 1990

Surtees, Virginia (ed.), *A Second Self: The Letters of Harriet Granville 1810–1845*, Michael Russell, Salisbury, 1990

Tait, A. A., *The Landscape Garden in Scotland 1735–1835*, Edinburgh University Press, Edinburgh, 1979

Tait, A. A., *Robert Adam: The Creative Mind*, The Soane Gallery, London, 1996

Tate, W. E., *The English Village Community and the Enclosure Movement*, Victor Gollancz, London, 1967

Taylor, George (ed.), *Plays of Samuel Foote and Arthur Murphy*, Cambridge University Press, Cambridge, 1989

Temperley, Nicholas, *The Athlone History of Music in Britain: The Romantic Age 1800–1914*, The Athlone Press, London, 1981

Thacker, Christopher, *The Genius of Gardening: The History of Gardens in Britain and Ireland*, Weidenfeld and Nicolson, London, 1994

Thomas, Keith, *Man and the Natural World: Changing Attitudes in England 1500–1800*, Allen Lane, London, 1983

Thomson, Duncan, *Raeburn*, Scottish National Portrait Gallery, Edinburgh, 1997

Thompson, Neville, *Wellington After Waterloo*, Routledge and Kegan Paul, London, 1986

Thornton, Peter, *Seventeenth Century Interior Decoration in England, France and Holland*, Yale University Press, London, 1981

Thornton, Peter, *Authentic Decor in the Domestic Interior 1620–1920*, Weidenfeld and Nicolson, London, 1984

Tillyard, Stella, *Aristocrats: Caroline, Emily, Louisa and Sarah Lennox 1740–1832*, Vintage, London, 1994

Tinniswood, Adrian, *History of Country House Visiting*, Basil Blackwell, Oxford, 1989

Tomlin, Maurice, *Catalogue of Adam Period Furniture*, Victoria and Albert Museum, London, 1972

Toynbee, Paget (ed.), *Reminiscences Written by Mr Horace Walpole in 1788 for the Amusement of Miss Mary and Miss Agnes Berry*, Clarendon Press, Oxford, 1924

Toynbee, Paget (ed.), *Horace Walpole's Journals of Visits to Country Seats*, vol. 16, Walpole Society, Oxford, 1927–28

Trumbach, Randolph, *The Rise of the Egalitarian Family: Aristocratic Kinship and Domestic Relations in Eighteenth Century England*, Academic Press, London, 1978

Turner, Michael, *Enclosures in Britain 1750–1830*, Economic History Society, Macmillan Press Ltd, London, 1984

Turner, Roger, *Capability Brown and the Eighteenth Century English Landscape*, Weidenfeld and Nicolson, 1985

Tyart, Geoffrey, *Warwickshire Country Houses*, Phillimore, Chichester, 1994

Victoria and Albert Museum, *The Garden: A Celebration of One Thousand Years of British Gardening*, Exhibition Catalogue, London, 1979

Wainwright, Clive, *The Romantic Interior*, Paul Mellon, London, 1989

Ward, J. T. and Wilson, R. G., *Land and Industry: The Landed Estate and The Industrial Revolution*, David and Charles, Newton Abbot, 1971

Waterfield, Giles, *Soane and Death*, Dulwich Gallery, London, 1996

Waterhouse, Ellis, *Painting in Britain 1530–1790*, Penguin, Harmondsworth, 1978

Waterson, Merlin, *The Servants' Hall*, The National Trust, London, 1990

Waterson, M. and Jackson-Stops, G., *Erdigg*, The National Trust, London, 1977

Watkin, David, *Thomas Hope and the Neoclassical Idea*, John Murray, London, 1968

Watkin, David, *The Life and Work of C. R. Cockerell*, Zwemmer, London, 1974

Watts, W., *The Seats of Nobility and Country from a Collection of the Most Interesting and Picturesque Views*, 1779

Weatherill, Lorna, *Consumer Behaviour and Material Culture in Britain 1660–1760*, Routledge, London, 1988

Webster, Mary, *Johan Zoffany 1733–1810*, National Portrait Gallery, London, 1976

Weir, Hugh, *Houses of Clare*, Ballinkella Press, Whitegate, 1986

White, Geoffrey, *The Complete Peerage*, St Catherine's Press, London, 1953

Whitley, W. T., *Artists and Their Friends in England*, 2 vols, Benjamin Bloom, London, 1968

Wilkes, Lyall, *John Dobson*, Oriel Press, Stocksfield, 1980

Williams, Julia Lloyd, *Gavin Hamilton 1723–1790*, National Gallery of Scotland, Edinburgh, 1994

Williamson, Tom, *Polite Landscapes: Gardens and Society in Eighteenth Century England*, The Johns Hopkins University Press, Baltimore, 1995

Wilson, Michael, *William Kent*, Routledge and Kegan Paul, London, 1984

Wilton, Andrew and Bignamini, Ilaria, *Grand Tour: The Lure of Italy in the Eighteenth Century*, Tate Gallery, London, 1996

Winch, Donald, *Riches and Poverty: An Intellectual History of Political Economy in Britain 1750–1834*, University of Cambridge Press, Cambridge, 1996

Winkley, George, *The Country Houses of Norfolk*, Tyndale and Panda Publishing, Lowestoft, 1986

Woodforde, James, *The Diary of a Country Parson 1752–1802*, ed. John Beresford, Oxford University Press, Oxford, 1987

Worsley, Giles, *Architectural Drawings of the Regency Period*, André Deutsch, London, 1991

Worsley, Giles, *Classical Architecture in Britain: The Heroic Age*, Yale University Press, London, 1995

Yelling, J. A., *Common Field and Enclosure in England 1450–1850*, Macmillan Ltd, London, 1977

Yorke, Philip, *The Life and Times of Philip Yorke, Earl of Hardwicke*, 3 vols, Cambridge University Press, Cambridge, 1913

Youngson, A. J., *The Making of Classical Edinburgh*, Edinburgh University Press, Edinburgh, 1966

ARTICLES

Bamford, Francis, 'A Dictionary of Edinburgh Wrights and Furniture Makers 1660–1840', *Furniture History*, XIX, 1983

Beard, Geoffrey and Hayward, Helena, 'Interior Design and Furnishings at Woburn Abbey', *Apollo*, June 1988, pp. 393–400

Binney, Marcus, 'Worksop Manor, Nottinghamshire I', *Country Life*, CLIII, 15 March 1973, pp. 678–82

Blutman, Sandra, 'Books of Design for Country Houses 1780–1815', *Architectural History*, II, 1968

Boynton, Lindsay, 'Sir Richard Worsley's Furniture at Appuldurcombe Park', *Furniture History*, I, 1965, pp. 39–58

Boynton, Lindsay, 'The Furniture of Warren Hastings', *The Burlington Magazine*, CXII, August 1970, pp. 508–20

Cherry, Deborah and Harris, Jennifer, 'Eighteenth Century Portraiture and the Seventeenth Century Past: Gainsborough and Van Dyck', *Art History*, 5, September 1982

Clifford, Timothy, 'Sebastian Conca at Holkham: A Neopolitan Painter and a Norfolk Patron', *Connoisseur*, 96, October 1977, pp. 224–30

Coleridge, Anthony, 'A Reappraisal of William Hallett', *Furniture History*, I, 1965, p. 11

Corbett Harris, Mary, 'The Welsh in Festive Spirit', *Country Life*, CLVI, 5 December 1974, p. 1778

Cornforth, John, 'Chatsworth, Derbyshire VII', *Country Life*, CXLIV, 1 August 1960, pp. 280–4

Cornforth, John, 'James Cullen Cabinet Maker at Hopetoun House', *Connoisseur*, 163, November 1966 and December 1966

Cornforth, John, 'Conversations with Old Heroes', *Country Life*, CXLIV, 26 September 1968

Cornforth, John, 'A Virtuoso's Gallery', *Country Life*, CXLIV, 3 October 1968, pp. 834–41

Cornforth, John, 'Inveraray Castle, Argyll I', *Country Life*, CLXIII, 8 June 1978, pp. 1619–22

Cornforth, John, 'Inveraray Castle, Argyll II', *Country Life*, CLXIII, 15 June 1978, pp. 1734–7

Cornforth, John, 'Houghton Hall, Norfolk I', *Country Life*, CLXXXI, 30 April 1987, pp. 124–9

Cornforth, John, 'Hagley Hall, Worcestershire I', *Country Life*, CLXXXIII, 4 May 1989, pp. 136–9

Cornforth, John, 'Subtle Sequence Reconstructed', *Country Life*, CLXXXV, 13 June 1991, pp. 168–71

Cornforth, John, 'Fit for a King', *Country Life*, CLXXXVI, 21 May 1992, pp. 54–7

Cornforth, John and Schmidt, Leo, 'Holkham Hall, Norfolk III', *Country Life*, CLXVIII, 7 February 1980, pp. 359–63

Crook, J. M., 'Strawberry Hill Revisited I', *Country Life*, CLIV, 7 June 1973

Draper, Marie, 'Houses of the Russell Family', *Apollo*, June 1988, pp. 387–92

Dunbar, John and Cornforth, John, 'Dalkeith House, Lothian III', *Country Life*, CLXXV, 3 May 1984, pp. 1230–3

Edward, Joy, 'A Pair of Documented Commodes by Pierre Langlois', *The Connoisseur*, 161, April 1966, p. 251

Edward, Joy, 'A Pair of English Rococo Armchairs', *The Connoisseur*, 161, April 1966, p. 243

Fejfer, Jane and Southworth, Edmund, 'Summer in England: Ince Blundell Hall, Revisted', *Apollo*, CXXIX, March 1989, pp. 179–82

Girouard, Mark, 'Coffee at Slaughters: English Art and the Rococo I', *Country Life*, CXXXIX, 13 January 1966, pp. 58–61

Girouard, Mark, 'Hogarth and His Friends: English Art and the Rococo II', *Country Life*, CXXXIX, 27 January 1966, pp. 189–90

Girouard, Mark, 'The Two Worlds of St Martin's Lane: English Art and the Rococo III', *Country Life*, CXXXIX, 3 February 1966, pp. 224–7

Golby, John and Purdue, William, 'The Goose is Getting Fat', *Country Life*, CLXXX, 4 December 1986, p. 1780

Goodison, Nicholas and Hardy, John, 'Gillows at Tatton Park', *Furniture History*, VI, 1970, pp. 1–39

Guilding, Ruth, 'Robert Adam and Charles Townley', *Apollo*, CXLIII, March 1996, pp. 27–37

Hall, Ivan, 'Jeremiah and Joseph Hargrave of Hull: Architects, Carriers, Furniture Makers', *Furniture History*, XII, 1976, pp. 52–5

Hall, Ivan, 'Range of a Dilettante: William Constable and Burton Constable I', *Country Life*, CLXXI, 22 April 1982, pp. 1114–17

Hardy, John, 'Newby Hall, North Yorkshire', *Country Life*, CLXV, 7 June 1979, pp. 1802–6

Hart-Davies, Duff, 'Heroic Panorama', *Country Life*, CLXXXIV, 22 February 1990, pp. 84–7

Hawcroft, Francis, 'The Cabinet at Felbrigg', *The Connoisseur*, June 1958, pp. 216–19

Hayes, John, 'British Patrons and Landscape Painting', *Apollo*, CLXXXV, April 1967, pp. 254–60

Honour, Hugh, 'English Patrons and Italian Sculptors in the First Half of the Eighteenth Century', *The Connoisseur*, LXVII, June 1958, pp. 220–6

Houfe, Simon, 'Playing with Words', *Country Life*, CLXXXIII, 31 August 1989, pp. 86–8

Howe, Bea, 'Queen Charlotte's Christmas Tree', *Country Life*, CL, 2 December 1971, p. 1521

Hughes, G. Bernard, 'The Lavishness of the Georgian Dessert', *Country Life*, CXLVI, 4 December 1969

Hussey, Christopher, 'Callaly Castle, Northumberland, II', *Country Life*, CXXV, 9 February 1959, pp. 358–61

Ingram, I. L., 'John, Fourth Duke of Bedford 1710–1771', *Apollo*, CXXVII, June 1988, pp. 382–6

Jackson-Stops, Gervase, 'A Rococo Masterpiece Restored', *Country Life*, CLXXV, 14 June 1984, pp. 169–70

Jackson-Stops, Gervase, 'Castle Ashby, Northamptonshire, III', *Country Life*, CLXXIX, 6 February 1986, pp. 310–15

Jackson-Stops, Gervase, 'Badminton House, Gloucestershire II', *Country Life*, CLXXXI, 16 April 1987, pp. 136–9

Jackson-Stops, Gervase, 'A Ducal Shopping Spree', *Country Life*, CLVXXVI, 13 February 1992, pp. 34–7

Jackson-Stops, Gervase, 'Living with the Louis', *Country Life*, CLXXXVI, 1 October 1992, pp. 68–9

Jarvis, Simon, 'Cabinets and Curiosities', *Country Life*, CLXXXVIII, 10 October 1985, pp. 1278–9

Joeckes, Rosemary, 'Capital Entertainment', *Country Life*, CLXXXI, 3 December 1987, pp. 141–6

Kennedy, I. G., 'Claude and Architecture', *Journal of the Warburg and Courtauld Institute*, 35, 1972, pp. 260–83

Kenworthy-Browne, John, 'A Ducal Patron of Sculptors', *Apollo*, XCVI, October 1972, pp. 322–31

Kenworthy-Browne, John, 'The Temple of Liberty at Woburn Abbey', *Apollo*, CXXX, July 1989, pp. 27–32

Kenworthy-Browne, John, 'Designing Around the Statues', *Apollo*, CXXXVII, April 1993, pp. 248–53

Kirkham, Patricia, 'The Careers of William and John Linnell', *Furniture History*, III, 1967, pp. 29–44

Lane, Charles, 'Too White a Christmas: The Snowstorm of 1836', *Country Life*, CLXVI, 29 November 1979, pp. 2053–5

Leach, Peter, 'James Paine's Designs for the South Front of Kedleston Hall: Dating and Sources', *Architectural History*, 40, 1997, pp. 159–70

Lomax, James, 'Heaton House', *Transactions of the Lancashire and Cheshire Antiquarian Society*, 82, 1983

Lord, John, 'Sir John Vanbrugh and the 1st Duke of Ancaster: Newly-Discovered Documents', *Architectural History*, 34, 1991, pp. 136–44

Low, Jill, 'Newby Hall: Two Late Eighteenth Century Inventories', *Furniture History*, XXII, 1986, pp. 135–76

Macmillan, Duncan, 'Alexander Runciman', *The Burlington Magazine*, CXII, January 1970, p. 23

Mullins, Anthea, 'Local Furniture Makers at Harewood House as Representatives of Provincial Craftsmanship', *Furniture History*, I, 1965, p. 33

Munson, J. E. B., 'Geoffrey Crayon, Gent: His Christmas', *Country Life*, CLXXIV, 1 December 1983, pp. 1649–51

Nettel, Reginald, 'The Man Who Invented Father Christmas', *Country Life*, CLXVI, 29 November 1979, pp. 2056–8

Pace, Claire, 'Gavin Hamilton's Wood and Dawkins Discovering Palmyra: The Dilettante as Hero', *Art History*, 4, September 1981, pp. 271–90

Penny, Nicholas, 'The Whig Culture of Fox in Early Ninetenth Century Sculpture', *Past and Present*, Feburary 1976, pp. 94–105

Pointon, Marcia, 'Gainsborough and the Landscape of "Retirement"', *Art History*, 6 December 1979, pp. 441–55

Pryke, Sebastian, 'Paxton House, Berwickshire II', *Country Life*, CLXXXVII, 6 May 1993, pp. 62–5

Pryke, Sebastian, 'Pattern Furniture and Estate Wrights in Eighteenth Century Scotland', *Furniture History*, XXX, 1994, pp. 100–4

Rosoman, T. S., 'The Decoration and Use of the Principal Apartments at Chiswick House 1727–1770', *The Burlington Magazine*, CXXVII, October 1985, pp. 663–70

Rowan, Alistair, 'Wedderburn Castle, Berwickshire', *Country Life*, CLVI, 8 August 1974, pp. 354–7

Rowan, Alistair, 'Robert Adam's Last Castles (1718–1792)', *Country Life*, CLVI, 22 August 1974, pp. 494–7

Russell, Francis, 'The Stourhead Batoni and Other Copies after Reni', *The National Trust Year Book*, London, 1975–76, pp. 109–11

Russell, Francis, 'Luton House, Bedfordshire I', *Country Life*, CLXXXVI, 16 June 1992, pp. 44–7

Russell, Francis, 'Notes on Grand Tour Portraiture', *The Burlington Magazine*, CXXXVI, July 1994, pp. 438–43

Smiles, Sam, 'J. H. Mortimer and Ancient Britain: An Unrecorded Project and a New Identification', *Apollo*, CXLII, November 1995, pp. 42–7

Solkin, David, 'The Battle of the Ciceros: Richard Wilson and the Politics of Landscape in the Age of John Wilkes', *Art History*, 6, December 1983, pp. 406–22

Solkin, David, 'Great Pictures or Great Men?: Reynolds, Male Portraiture and the Power of Art', *Oxford Art Journal*, 9, 1986, pp. 42–9

Standen, Edith, 'Tapestries in Use Indoors', *Apollo*, CXIII, July 1981, pp. 6–15

Stillman, Damie, 'The Gallery at Landsdowne House: International Neoclassical Architecture in Microcosm', *Art Bulletin*, March 1976, pp. 75–80

Stillman, Damie, 'Death Defied and Honour Upheld: The Mausoleum in Neoclassical England', *The Art Quarterly*, Summer 1978, pp. 175–213

Stroud, Dorothy, 'Woburn Abbey, Bedfordshire, I', *Country Life*, CXXXVIII, 15 July 1965, pp. 158–61

Sunderland, John, 'Mortimer Pine and Some Political Aspects of English History Painting', *The Burlington Magazine*, CXVI, June 1974, pp. 317–26

Sutton, Denys, 'The Nabob of the North', *Apollo*, LXXXVI, September 1967, pp. 168–9

Watson, J. N. P., 'Badminton Blue and Buff: The Duke of Beaufort's Hunt', *Country Life*, CLXVI, 20 December 1979, pp. 2368–70

'Wentworth Woodhouse, Yorkshire', *Country Life*, XIX, 31 March 1906, pp. 450–61

Wordie, R., 'The Chronology of English Enclosure 1500–1914', *Economic History Review*, 36, 1983

Worsley, Giles, 'Wicked Woman of Marl', *Country Life*, CLXXV, 14 March 1991

Worsley, Giles, 'Jewels in a Rich Coronet', *Country Life*, CLXXXXVII, 14 October 1993, pp. 68–71

GUIDES TO PROPERTIES

Attingham, National Trust Guide, London, 1997
Colvin, Howard *et al.*, *Calke Abbey*, The National Trust, London, 1989
Erdigg, National Trust Guide, 1990
Harris, Eileen, *Osterley Park, Middlesex*, National Trust, 1994
Hartley, Christopher and Kay, William, *House of Dun*, National Trust for Scotland
Holkham Hall, National Trust Guide
Kedleston Hall, National Trust
Meade-Fetherstonhaugh, *Uppark*
Osterley Park House, Victoria and Albert Msueum, 1985
Petworth House, National Trust
St John Gore, *The Saltram Collection*, National Trust, London, 1977
Wimpole Hall, The National Trust, London, 1984

Index

Note: 'n.' after a page reference indicates the number of a note on that page.